Lecture Notes in Computer Scien

T0238078

Commenced Publication in 1973
Founding and Former Series Editors:
Gerhard Goos, Juris Hartmanis, and Jan van Leeuwen

Matteo Cesana   Luigi Fratta (Eds.)

Wireless Systems and Network Architectures in Next Generation Internet

Second International Workshop
of the EURO-NGI Network of Excellence
Villa Vigoni, Italy, July 13-15, 2005
Revised Selected Papers

 Springer

Volume Editors

Matteo Cesana
Luigi Fratta
Politecnico di Milano - DEI
Via Golgi 34/5, 20133 Milano, Italy
E-mail: {cesana, fratta}@elet.polimi.it

Library of Congress Control Number: 2006925115

CR Subject Classification (1998): C.2, H.4, H.3

LNCS Sublibrary: SL 5 – Computer Communication Networks and Telecommunications

ISSN   0302-9743
ISBN-10   3-540-34025-4 Springer Berlin Heidelberg New York
ISBN-13   978-3-540-34025-6 Springer Berlin Heidelberg New York

Springer is a part of Springer Science+Business Media

springer.com

© Springer-Verlag Berlin Heidelberg 2006
Printed in Germany

Typesetting: Camera-ready by author, data conversion by Scientific Publishing Services, Chennai, India
Printed on acid-free paper   SPIN: 11750673   06/3142   5 4 3 2 1 0

Preface

The Network of Excellence on Next Generation Internet (EuroNGI) is a European project funded by the European Union within the IST programme. The target of the EuroNGI Network is to put together European centers of excellence in the field of networking and engineering with the specific purpose of promoting the development of effective technological solutions for the support of the future-generation Internet. Besides the Research Activities (RAs), the Network is composed of Integration Activities (IAs), whose purpose is to foster collaborations among different research groups, and Spreading of Excellence Activities (SEAs), whose focus is on the technological transfer of the Network research.

The joint workshops on "Wireless and Mobility" and on "New Trends of Network Services and Architecture" were organized as an integration activity with the precise target of fostering collaboration among research centers spread all over Europe and of animating the discussion on the networking topics addressed by the EuroNGI Network. The workshops were held in parallel in July 2005 in the stimulating environment of Villa Vigoni on Lake Como, Italy.

The present volume contains a revised selection of 19 papers presented at the workshops on cutting-edge research issues in the field of wireless technologies and network services definition. Furthermore, the editors solicited an invited contribution by the Georgia Institute of Technology in the specific field of wireless sensor networks.

Thanks to the utmost importance of the topics addressed and the high level of all 20 contributions, this volume provides an advanced summary of the main research efforts in the field of wireless communication and network services evolution.

February 2006

Matteo Cesana
Luigi Fratta

Table of Contents

Wireless Connectivity Solutions: From Wireless LANs to Ad Hoc and Sensor Networks

Cellular Systems: Models and Algorithms

QoS Support in Next Generation Networks

Peer to Peer Architectures and Services

Introduction

Matteo Cesana and Luigi Fratta

Dipartimento di Elettronica e Informazione, Politecnico di Milano,
Piazza L. da Vinci, 32 - Milan, 20133 - Italy
{cesana, fratta}@elet.polimi.t

1 The Evolution of Telecommunication Networks

We are nowadays spectators of a deep and rapid change in the world of communications which is mainly driven by two factors: the evolution of wireless technology and the amazing success of IP based applications.

The offer of wireless technology is vast and always increasing both with different standards and proprietary solutions. In this scenario, the end user equipment is often geared with multiple wireless network interface and consequently one has the choice on which technology to use as a gateway for connectivity.

Such freedom from cables and classical networking infrastructures is pushing the end user demand for connectivity anywhere at anytime and with the very same services required in a wired infrastructure.

As the technology diversity and complexity explode, the management of such a heterogeneous environment becomes crucial for the network designers, who have to cope with problems like users mobility, technology convergence and interoperation, Quality- of-Service (QoS) provisioning, etc...

This new environment makes obsolete the methods and tools currently available and forces the scientific community to develop new design, planning, dimensioning, and management principles and tools. These require to investigate new multi-technology architectures for providing a seamless end-to-end connectivity and environment diversity to service developers and users.

2 The EuroNGI Project

The mission of the Euro NGI Network of Excellence is to put together the the most prominent European research centers in engineering with the specific target of supporting the European Information Society in the design of the Next Generation Internet.

In this field, the two main issues addressed by the NoE are:

- mastering the technology diversity (vertical and horizontal integration) for the design of efficient and flexible NGI architectures
- providing required innovative traffic engineering architectures adapted to the new requirements and developing the corresponding appropriate quantitative methods

M. Cesana, L. Fratta (Eds.): Wireless Syst./Network Architect. 2005, LNCS 3883, pp. 1–3, 2006.

Besides the research activities on specific technical topics, at the EoroNGI Networks endorses also integration and spreading of excellence activities, the former with the purpose of fostering cooperation among centers of excellence, the latter devoted to the technological transfer of the research products.

3 About This Book

The present book collects twenty papers out of those presented the second EuroNGI workshops on "Wireless and Mobility" and on "New Trends in Network Services and Architectures" organized by the EuroNGI Community as an integration activity at Villa Vigoni, Italy in July 2005.

The two workshops were organized in parallel with the specific purpose of putting together different networking expertise, thus fostering collaborations among different European research groups even working in different fields of networking. The joint workshops covered three days of scientific program including 26 talks and brainstorming sessions on the topics addressed during the talks.

The twenty accepted papers of this volume have been organized in four subsections:

- Wireless Solutions: from from Wireless LANs to Ad Hoc and Sensor Networks
- Cellular Systems: Models and Algorithms
- QoS Support in Next Generation Networks
- Peer To Peer Architectures and Algorithms

The section on *Wireless Connectivity Solutions* comprises the first six contributions. In their paper *Optimizing routing schemes for fast moving users in MST-based networks* De Greve et al. gives models and algorithm to determine minimal sets of spanning trees in Multiple Spanning Trees based networks, for optimizing routing in the case of fast moving wireless users like trains. The paper *Receiver Oriented Trajectory Based Forwarding* by Capone et al. proposes a packet forwarding method for ad hoc networks based on the definition of spatial trajectories towards the final destination. In the following paper *Power-Controlled Directional Medium Access Control for Wireless Mesh Network* Capone at al. propose effective access algorithms for wireless mesh networks adopting directional antennas. Garoppo et al. present an enhancement to the IEEE 802.11 DCF access scheme in the peper *Achieving flow isolation in 802.11 networks with the DTT scheduler*, while Lopez et al. in *Subnet Formation and Address Allocation Approach for a Routing with Subnets Scheme in MANETs* discuss the issue of IP addresses organization in ad hoc networks. The last paper of the section is an invited contribution by Melodia et al. which completes the technology scenario by addressing the issued of sensors networks.

The following section on *Cellular Systems* is devoted to the analysis of effective algorithms for call admission control and channel estimation in cellular systems. Iversen proposes effective models to describe cellular systems with restricted accessibility in the paper *Modelling restricted accessibility for multi-service traffic*. The paper *A Low Computation Cost Algorithm to Solve Cellular Systems with Retrials Accurately* by Domenech-Benlloch et al. provides an approximated method to solve cellular systems with retrials, whilst the following two papers by Gimenez-Guzman et al. address the issue of designing effective admission control strategies (*An Afterstates Reinforcement Learning Approach to Optimize Admission Control in Mobile Cellular Networks* and *Hierarchical Admission Control in Mobile Cellular Networks Using Adaptive Bandwidth Reservation*). Finally, Maeder et al. aims at optimizing the HSDPA service of the UMTS by estimating the perceived interference in *Interference Estimation for the HSDPA Service in Heterogeneous UMTS Networks*.

In the section on "QoS Support in Next Generation Networks" the focus is on the design and optimization of QoS provisioning. Pereira gives a framework to negotiate service level agreement in future generation networks based on differentiated services. The paper *MIPv6 Binding Authentication for B3G Networks* by Celentano et al. proposes an authentication solution for next generation networks based on mobile IP version 6. Capone et al. propose in *Distributed Dynamic Resource Management in Quality of Service Networks* a novel routing solution with QoS support.

The last section of this volume is on *Peer To Peer Architectures and Algorithms*. The first two papers within this section *A P2P-based framework for distributed network management* by A. Binzenhofer et al. and *Time-Discrete Analysis of the Crawling Strategy in an Optimized Mobile P2P Architecture* by Hossfeld propose effective network architectures for the support of peer to peer services. Hoyou et al. focuses on the problem of supporting peer to peer services in heterogeneous wireless scenarios where multiple wireless networks may cooperate. The following two contributions by Fiedler et al. *The Throughput Utility Function: Assessing Network Impact on Mobile Services* and Chevul et al. *Measurement of Application-Perceived Throughput of an E2E VPN Connection Using a GPRS Network* address the delicate issue of finding consistent figures to measure the performances of given services. Finally, the last paper *A Seamless Mobile Community Support System* by Klein et al. discusses the design of a completely integrated system to support mobile services.

Optimizing Routing Schemes for Fast Moving Users in MST-Based Networks

Filip De Greve, Frederic Van Quickenborne, Filip De Turck,
Ingrid Moerman, and Piet Demeester

Ghent University - IBBT - IMEC - Department of Information Technology,
Gaston Crommenlaan 8, 9050 Gent, Belgium
{Filip.DeGreve, Frederic.VanQuickenborne}@intec.ugent.be

Abstract. With the currently emerging trials for best-effort internet solutions on trains, solutions are required for delivering multimedia services
to fast moving users. Research has already been devoted to dimensioning Ethernet aggregation networks, taking user movement into account
while neglecting the experienced network performance. This paper extends this design for resilient networks and aims at minimizing packet
loss and packet reordering in the dimensioning and routing process. For
deployment in an Ethernet network which supports Multiple Spanning
Trees (MSTs), effective path aggregation methods are proposed for finding a minimal set of spanning trees and these are thoroughly evaluated
for different scenarios. Moreover the spanning tree assignment problem
with predefined backup conditions is studied.

Keywords: Ethernet, user mobility, spanning trees.

1 Introduction

1.1 Motivation

The challenge telecom operators are facing is to examine how multimedia applications can be provided to users in fast moving vehicles. While satellite systems
were the first best-effort solutions on the market, on-roof antenna architectures
with WiFi/WiMax base stations located near the railroad track are recently
gaining interest. We proposed such a WiMax-based architecture in [1] but more
research is required for combining the performance that mobile hosts experience
along their journey with a cost-effective design. The network must deliver packets to the correct point of attachment while minimizing the effects of packet
loss (PL) and packet reordering (PR) that are caused when switching paths between access gateways. A lot of research has been performed in order to achieve
seamless connectivity. At network layer methods have been proposed in order
to improve performance degradation in case of packet reordering due to path
delay variations or packet loss due to motion across wireless cell boundaries: e.g.
triangular routing or bi-casting [2]. However to the authors' knowledge no work
intends to relate the fast moving aspect of users with the cost-effective design of

M. Cesana, L. Fratta (Eds.): Wireless Syst./Network Architect. 2005, LNCS 3883, pp. 4–20, 2006.

the network infrastructure. If this work is combined with the above mentioned techniques, it will lead to lower buffer capacities, less forwarding overhead or improved real-time behavior.

1.2   Contribution

We present a design technique for resilient Ethernet networks which tries to minimize PL and PR in the dimensioning and routing process. Because the flow routing is optimized, we still have to find a way of enforcing these paths in a multiple spanning tree (MST) environment [3]. In a MST network the available paths must be placed on one of the active Spanning Tree Instances (STIs). Classic spanning tree problems try to find optimal routes within a single spanning tree: e.g. resource-efficient transport of multi-cast traffic [4] [5] but the problem of finding multiple STs is rarely studied. Heuristic techniques are presented which aim to find a minimal set of trees covering the set of paths calculated in the design phase. In [6] we presented a similar approach (see Fig. 1) without taking network reliability into account. In this paper we will extend this study: design of networks that are resilient against single network failures requires more resources and the path assignment problem on a minimal set of STIs is more difficult because recovery is based on ST and not on a path-per-path basis.

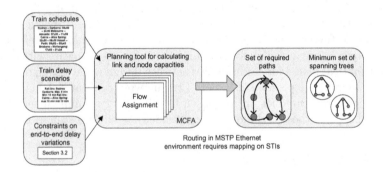

Fig. 1. Design approach of Ethernet environment for fast moving users

1.3   The System Architecture

Our FAMOUS (= FAst MOving USers) network architecture is illustrated in Fig. 2. There is a single Service Gateway (SGW) and a number of Access Gateways (AGWs) which are placed along the railroad tracks. Service guarantees can be assured by making on-time resource reservations. Data connections of fast moving users will be mapped on VLAN tunnels that are responsible for the delivery to the correct AGW in the aggregation network. The VLANs are fixed end-to-end tunnels, automatically installed with GVRP (GARP VLAN Registration Protocol). At their due time, tunnel reservations are registered for the aggregated flow, but only shortly before the flow will be effectively using the

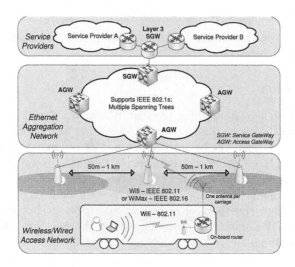

Fig. 2. Schematic representation of the network architecture - specifically designed to cope with requirements of train passengers

VLAN tunnel. When reservations are no longer required, they are immediately released. In this way the system will guarantee that the current and the next hop tunnel are able to maintain the service level and that capacity bottlenecks are prevented. For further details on the system architecture we kindly refer to [1].

This paper is organized as follows: first the influence of path switching and the mathematical model for cost-effective network design while taking user movement into account are presented. In Sec. 4 the network costs are evaluated. Next path aggregation techniques are proposed for obtaining a minimal set of trees. In the final section these techniques are extended for backup scenarios.

2 Path Switching

2.1 Influence on TCP Performance

First we studied the PL and PR which occurred at aggregation network level when switching between paths with different end-to-end delays on a Click/Linux test bed [7]. For CBR flows, the PL curves can be approximated as follows:

$$PL = \Delta \cdot BW/S. \tag{1}$$

with BW = the flow bandwidth and S = the packet size and Δ = decrease in e2e delay. Note that no pause in communication is assumed at aggregation network level: the losses represent theoretical minima that can be achieved depending on the performance of the implemented handover mechanism. Still, the only parameter in (1) that can be tuned at network design level, is the delay variation Δ. For non-reliable real-time applications, it are indeed the variations in e2e delays

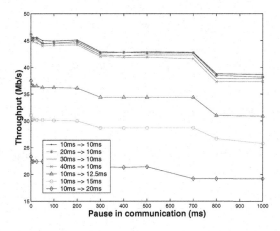

Fig. 3. Influence of end-to-end delay variations on TCP throughput

that are perceived as critical for human interaction. However, this assumption is not true for all application types. On Fig. 3 the influence of delay variations and connectivity disruptions during path switching on the TCP performance is evaluated. We assume that the handover period when the train's connection is moving from one AGW to another AGW, is short compared to the connection time to a single AGW. It shows that TCP throughput will not degrade severely due to delay variations in a train scenario environment but that absolute end-to-end delays are more important. Delay variations of several tens of milliseconds are not considered harmful for TCP sessions. The time-averaged end-to-end delays during the connection are more important for the TCP throughput performance. Due to the fact that we assume a low congested network operation by making resource reservations, absolute end-to-end delays will not form a bottleneck on the TCP performance. For the remainder of the paper we will further assume applications which are sensitive to e2e variations such as real-time traffic.

2.2 Motivation of Routing Schemes for Reducing PL and PR

In this section we will motive that PL and PR can be reduced in the design phase. When the source-destination path is altered, packets that are on their way on the old path, run the risk to be reordered or lost. It is clear that packets might be lost in the *down* direction (from SGW to AGW) while packets might be reordered in the *up* direction (from AGW to SGW), not vice versa. The amount of affected packets depends on the implemented trigger mechanism that correlates the train positioning with the tunnel switching. For the topologies of Fig. 4 we measured the PL and PR when switching tunnels from node 3 to node 4 for a 10 Mb/s flow with a packet size of 128 bytes. We illustrated the principle for a 5ms delay per link. In a second phase we activated the impairment node 2 (=20ms additional delay). Tunnel switching was always triggered 3ms after the successful delivery of all packets destined for node 3. The results are depicted

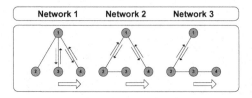

Fig. 4. Three example network topologies

Table 1. Packet loss (PL) and packet reordering (PR) due to path switching for the topologies of Fig. 4

	Network 1	Network 2	Network 3
PL ↓	2	2	0
PR ↑	0	53	0
With impairment node 2			
PL ↓	12	12	0
PR ↑	208	265	0

in Table 1. The first network has equal e2e path delays but due to the fact that tunnel switching cannot occur at both ends of the tunnel at the exact moment, PL is to be expected. The second network does not have equal e2e path delays but still has similar results for PL; PR however is worse. The third network has increasing e2e path delays, therefore the tunnel switching mechanism has a bigger margin for making a lossless swap decision. However, a network design with ever increasing path delays remains not preferable and unscalable. This fact reveals that PL or PR can of course never fully be eliminated in the design phase but that intelligent techniques are required in order moderate the e2e path variations at the moment of tunnel switching. Now, which schemes were used to design the network of Fig. 4 ? Network 1 can be designed by applying shortest path routing: this network has a good delay performance but is typically not the cheapest solution. Network 2 is a more cost-effective solution which has similar characteristics. It has only limited delay variations and was designed with limited hop count variations (see Sec. 3.2). Network 3 was designed with the shared routing constraints (see Sec. 3.2). Routing schemes which promote shared routing, have the main advantage that impairment nodes or congested nodes (typically situated closer to the aggregation point) in the shared part have less impact on the applications' performance.

3   Motion-Aware Capacity and Flow Assignment Problem

3.1   Theoretical Model

In previous work we proposed a theoretical model for calculating the dynamic tunnels that meet the traffic demands and for optimizing the utilization of the network resources: a Motion-aware Capacity and Flow Assignment (MCFA) problem. In this paper we add reliability constraints to the ILP formulation.

Decision Variables. The following variables give information about the number of fibres and the usage of every link l and the number of line cards available in each node:

$$u_l = \begin{cases} 1, & \text{if link } l \text{ is used} \\ 0, & \text{otherwise} \end{cases} \tag{2}$$

$$x_l^v = \# \text{ of fibres with link speed } C_v \text{ on link } l. \tag{3}$$

$$z_n^{vw} = \# \text{ of Ethernet cards with } O_{vw} \text{ interfaces} \tag{4}$$
$$\text{of speed } C_v \text{ on node } n.$$

Each card has a specific cost, c_{vw}: v indicates the speed type and defines the speed C_v of the interfaces while w indicates the interface type of the card and defines the number of interfaces O_{vw} available on the card.

Next we define a set of possible paths $P_{ik} = \{p_{ikq}\}$ in which index q is used to indicate the different considered paths between AGW i and SGW k. They are calculated by taking M candidate paths between the two end nodes. We define a variable to indicate which path $p \in \bigcup_{i,k} P_{ik}$ is used:

$$y_{pijk} = \begin{cases} 1 \text{ if path } p \text{ is used between AGW } i \\ \quad \text{and SGW } k \text{ for flow } j \\ 0, \text{ otherwise} \end{cases} \tag{5}$$

Node Capacity Constraints. Every node needs enough interfaces with appropriate link speeds to provide the links that are connected to it:

$$\forall n, \forall v : \sum_{w=1}^{|w_{max}|} z_n^{vw} \cdot O_{vw} \geq \sum_{l \text{ incident to node } n} x_l^v \tag{6}$$

Link Capacity Constraints. This constraint sets the capacity of each link and imposes that the traffic that is transported over a link does not exceed the capacity of that particular link at any time. Traffic demands are defined as $d_{ijk}(t)$: the demand at time t between AGW i and SGW k for flow j.

$$\forall l : \sum_k \sum_i \sum_j \sum_p y_{pijk} \cdot \delta_{pl}^{ik} \cdot d_{ijk}(t) \leq \sum_v x_l^v \cdot C_v \tag{7}$$

$$\delta_{pl}^{ik} = \begin{cases} 1, & \text{if path } p \text{ uses link } l \text{ to get to} \\ & \text{destination k from source } i \\ 0, & \text{otherwise} \end{cases} \tag{8}$$

Path Activation Constraints. This constraint takes care of the fact that we only need a single path for a specific flow j for every SGW-AGW pair:

$$\forall i, \forall j, \forall k : \sum_p y_{pijk} = 1 \tag{9}$$

Reliability Constraints. Reliability is taken into account by providing a second dedicated backup path, disjunct from the working path. Assume you have N_T trains running on the railroad track, redundancy can then be modelled by taking two flows per train: a *working* flow (2j') and a *backup* flow (2j'+1) with the condition that flows (2j') and (2j'+1) use disjunct paths. Assume that between every AGW i and every SGW k M possible paths are available. Suppose that for every path p_{ikq}, element of P_{ik}, n paths ($0 \leq n \leq M$) of P_{ik} are not fully node and link disjoint. The collection of these paths is denoted as $P_{P_{ik}}^{ND}$. Working flows and backup flows for the same train must be routed on disjunct paths. To assure a correct dimensioning in case of single failures, the following constraints must be added to the problem formulation:

$$\begin{aligned}
&\forall j' : 0...N_T \\
&\forall i, \forall k, \forall p_{ikq} \in P_{ik} : p_{ik1}, p_{ik2}, ..., p_{ikn} \in P_{P_{ik}}^{ND} : \\
&y_{p_{ikq}i2j'k} + y_{p_{ik1}i(2j'+1)k} \leq 1 \\
&y_{p_{ikq}i2j'k} + y_{p_{ik2}i(2j'+1)k} \leq 1 \\
&... \\
&y_{p_{ikq}i2j'k} + y_{p_{ikn}i(2j'+1)k} \leq 1
\end{aligned} \tag{10}$$

Objective Function o

$$o = \alpha \sum_l u_l \cdot c_l + \beta \sum_n \sum_v \sum_{w=1}^{|w_{max}|} z_n^{vw} \cdot c_{vw} \tag{11}$$
$$+ \gamma \sum_k \sum_i \sum_j \sum_p y_{pijk} \cdot HopCount_p$$

The first term represents the cost to install fibers, the second represents the cost to install network equipment with sufficient interface cards and the final term represent the sum of hop counts of all required SGW-AGW tunnels (= tiebreaker term).

3.2   Routing Schemes

In this section routing schemes are proposed which improve the performance of fast moving users. These schemes will lead to extra constraints that have to be added to the MCFA (Motion-aware Capacity Flow Assignment) problem as previously presented.

Limited Hop Count Variations Routing (LHCV): The experienced hop count variation along the trajectory is limited: less than or equal to HC_{diff}. The following constraints are added for the path hop counts HC_p:

$$\forall i, \forall j, \forall k, \forall p \in P_{ik}, \forall q \in P_{i_{next}k} :$$

$$\sum_p y_{pijk} \cdot HC_{pijk}$$

$$- \sum_q y_{qi_{next}jk} \cdot HC_{qi_{next}jk} \leq HC_{diff} \tag{12}$$

Shared Routing: Previous routing schemes still have the disadvantage that different physical routes are chosen with inherent different congestion levels. Therefore an approach is developed which favors route sharing in the design. One of the following constraints is added for every connection:

- (i) The current path of the connection must share at least the first $HC_{previous} - K$ nodes with the previous path of the connection
- (ii) The previous path of the connection must share at least the first $HC_{current} - K$ nodes with the current path of the connection.

with HC_{path} as the path hop count used for a connection and the parameter K for tuning the routing's strictness.

Incremental Routing: This is a special case of the previous routing scheme with non-decreasing path lengths. It has the advantage that PR is unlikely to occur.

4   Reliability Constraints vs. Routing Schemes

In this subsection the network cost of single rail line networks will be optimized in terms of required networks cost with respect to PL and PR constraints and reliability constraints. We considered several scenarios with up to 4 trains, varying traffic loads per train ranging from 500 Mb/s up to 1.5 Gb/s, time schedule variations and low installation cost of fibers - or dominant routing cost - in order to focus on the moving user aspect ($\beta \gg \alpha$, $\beta \gg \gamma$ in equation 11). The results with M (= number of parallel candidate paths between every 2 nodes) high enough to find optimal solutions are presented in Fig. 5. Figure 5 shows up to 60% additional costs for making the network resilient (35% on the average). As can be expected incremental routing turns out to be very resource consuming which makes it not suitable for large-scale telecom networks. Surprisingly in most cases addition of the constraints for LHCV and shared routing do not further increase the cost of the network solution. This can be explained by the effect that the network is ideally provisioned with knowledge of the moving trains trajectory: examination of the network solutions for ideal routing, reveal that the hop count variations between two consecutive working tunnels (connecting to two adjacent AGWs) for a specific tunnel are often already small. And similar: in case of LHCV routing in many cases two consecutive tunnels of a working flow will already share parts of their route. However while the network costs are equal, different paths are selected to satisfy the additional constraints for the working flows as is represented in Table 2. Obviously adding resilience constraints increases the required amount of tunnels. The most tunnels are required

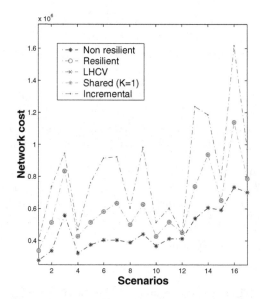

Fig. 5. Influence of routing schemes on the network cost and the set of required paths for single rail line scenarios, ordered from left to right for increasing number of AGWs

Table 2. Averaged amount of required tunnels for the scenarios of Fig. 5

	Without resilience	Resilient	LHCV	Shared (K=1)	Incremental
Number of tunnels	10.67	15.5	14.4	10.3	8.5

for resilient networks without additional constraints. Adding more routing constraints leads automatically to a more limited set of available paths which is shown by the decreasing amount of required tunnels if the routing scheme becomes more severe: therefore the most severe routing scheme (i.e. incremental routing) uses the least paths.

Routing constraints ensure that hop count variations are confined during the entire journey of the users. Of course non-ideally designed networks will experience a lower throughput with such routing schemes. We can conclude that by adding simple constraints - according to one of the presented routing schemes - to the MCFA problem, lower delay variations can be attained during path switching. In case of dominant routing cost this can be achieved without increasing the network cost significantly.

5   Path Aggregation Technique for Calculating a Minimal Set of Spanning Tree Instances (STIs)

Deployment of routing schemes in Ethernet networks requires mapping of the required routes as calculated for the MCFA problem on VLANs and STIs. The

IEEE 802.1s standard does not specify details of mapping VLANs on one or more STIs. The amount of VLANs that need to be configured is determined by the number of AGWs (Access Gateways) and the number of parallel paths to each AGW. Within aggregation network scope, the amount of required VLANs will clearly remain under the 4096 upper limit. For the ST assignment we present a path aggregation (PA) algorithm that forms a minimal set of STIs. We compare our heuristic with a *Random Assignment* (RA) which aggregates paths randomly in loop-free sets of trees and with a PA heuristic that tries to merge paths which share a common feature e.g. pair of edges. This heuristic was introduced in [8] and we will refer to this method as the *Shared Assignment* (SA).

Algorithm 5.1. SUB-PATH ASSIGNMENT($STIs$)

Set of all paths : $\Phi \leftarrow (p_0, ..., p_m)$
$\Phi \leftarrow order(\Phi)$
comment: in descending order of path length

Set of all path pairs : $PP \leftarrow \{(p_0, p_1), ..., (p_{m-1}, p_m)\}$
Set of path pairs taking part of same STI : $PP_{same} = \emptyset$
Set of all spanning trees : $T = \emptyset$
while $(\exists \{p_k, p_l\} \in PP)$ **true**

do $\begin{cases} \textbf{comment: } \text{Sub-path substitution step} \\ \text{Remove}\{p_k, p_l\}\text{fromPP.} \\ \textbf{if } p_k \subseteq p_l \begin{cases} \text{Add } \{p_l, p_k\} \text{ to } PP_{same}. \\ \text{Remove } p_k \text{ from } \Phi. \end{cases} \\ \textbf{if } p_l \subseteq p_k \begin{cases} \text{Add } \{p_k, p_l\} \text{ to } PP_{same}. \\ \text{Remove } p_l \text{ from } \Phi. \end{cases} \end{cases}$

while $(\exists p \in \Phi)$ **true**

do $\begin{cases} \text{Remove } p \text{ from } \Phi \\ \textbf{if } (\exists t \in T : \text{checkloop}(p, t) == \textbf{ true }) \\ \quad \textbf{then } \text{Merge } p \text{ with } t \text{ and} \\ \forall q \text{ with } (p, q) \in PP_{same} : \text{Merge } q \text{ with } t. \\ \quad \textbf{else } \text{Add } p \text{ to new tree in } T \text{ and} \\ \forall q \text{ with } (p, q) \in PP_{same} : \text{Merge } q \text{ with new tree.} \end{cases}$

Joining paths with shared features is a good idea but provides no absolute guarantee to obtain a minimal set. For an aggregation network that supports fast moving users, typically a lot of the paths will be sub-paths of other paths. With this knowledge, the idea is to aggregate those paths on the same STI - *Sub-path Assignment* (SpA) - and this is in fact a more relevant condition for obtaining a minimal set. The pseudo-code of the SpA algorithm is presented in Algorithm 5.1.

The remainder of this section is dedicated to the evaluation of the heuristic's performance in large test sets. In [6] we already presented performance tests but we allowed the same path to be selected more than once. This clearly favored

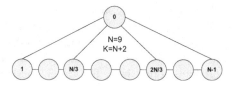

Fig. 6. Aggregation test network with amount of AGW-SGW links limited to 4

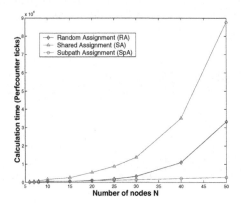

For k=1		
SpA	**SA**	**RA**
1	1	1

For k=2		
SpA	**SA**	**RA**
2	3	4

For k=3		
SpA	**SA**	**RA**
3	3	5

For k=4		
SpA	**SA**	**RA**
4	4	6

Fig. 7. Calculation times for the PA problem for aggregation networks such as depicted in Fig. 6.

Fig. 8. Number of STIs for aggregation networks (depicted in Fig. 6) and with k-shortest paths active to every AGW

SpA because SpA specifically makes sure that these paths are assigned to the same tree. In all the tests of this paper we didn't allow the same path to be selected twice for tree assignment. It will be shown that under these conditions SpA remains the most favorable heuristic method. First we examine the calculation times[1] for aggregation networks with various rail lengths and the amount of SGW-AGW links limited to four (as illustrated in Fig. 6). The calculation times and the minimal number of STIs are presented in Fig. 7 and Fig. 8. For this simple topology and for k parallel paths ($1 \leq k \leq 4$) to every AGW, SA and SpA find similar solutions but the SpA takes less time, even for larger problems it takes less time than RA due to the fact that less loop checks are required. However RA itself doesn't succeed in finding the optimal solution. This result confirms the assumption that SpA finds the best non-optimal solution in the shortest time for aggregation network scenarios. The loop check calculations are performed every time paths from the ordered set Φ are incrementally assigned to a specific tree. Paths are expressed as an ordered vector of nodes. A tree is represented as a subset of loop-free paths from Φ which are part of the tree. We call this the Path Composition representation. This is actually quite similar as the Predecessor representation [9]. Additionally the set of nodes is maintained

---

[1] In the simulation a single perfcounter tick equals 0.3μ sec.

which form disconnected subtrees, part of the actual tree. This enables loop avoidance to be verified easily if paths are added incrementally. Intermediate tree solutions are not necessarily STs (i.e. covering all nodes) or are not necessarily fully connected (during the process a tree may consist of two disconnected subtrees). Before every assignment to a tree it is verified that the path and subtree it will be connected to, do not share a pair of nodes unless all nodes on the path between this pair of nodes are also shared. This loop check is $O(N^2)$. Checking loops will remain to be effortsome unless alternative tree notations such as Prüfer numbers [9] are used. However these representations lack locality and heritability. In other words very alike tree representations do not consist of similar substructures. This would require a lot of transformations between trees and Prüfer numbers (typically O(NlogN)) because it is crucial to verify that all paths of set Φ are covered by the set of STIs.

Characteristic Vector representations of trees which can be used in ILP-based formulations lack the probability of representing an actual tree. If the network contains N nodes and K edges, a tree T can be presented as a vector $E = e_k$, k=1 ... K and e_k is one if edge k is part of T and zero otherwise. In a fully meshed network $2^{N(N-1)/2}$ possible values exist for E. In [10] it is shown that a complete graph of N nodes contains N^{N-2} spanning trees. This means that the chance of having an E value which represents a tree is $\frac{2^{\frac{N(N-1)}{2}}}{N^{N-2}} = 2^{-N(N/2-log_2N+2(log_2N)/N-0.5)}$. For N=10 this chance equals 2.84E-06. Standard predecessor tree notations represent a tree with a probability 1/N. Moreover we have to represent a multiple tree structure (containing up to $| \Phi |$ trees). The chance of representing $|\Phi|$ valid trees is $2^{-|\Phi|N(N/2-log_2N+2*(log_2N)/N-0.5)}$ for the characteristic vector notation. For $|\Phi|$=5 and N=10 this equals 7.35E-10. It is clear that there are too many representations which are not trees. In our representation only $|\Phi|^{|\Phi|}$ representations are possible. For $|\Phi|$=10 and N=10 there are 5.5E+308 times more Characteristic Vector representations than Path Composition representations. This clearly shows the inefficiency of Characteristic Vector representations.

What about the algorithm's performance in other scenarios? In Tables 3 and 4 the comparison is made for grid networks (4x4, 5x5, 6x6 dimensions) and for mesh networks with a randomly assigned route pattern. The route pattern is chosen from a set of shortest paths between the node pairs. This makes it able to define a path density λ which indicates how many paths are selected. λ=1 means that all paths between the node pairs are selected for the PA problem: for 4x4, 5x5 and 6x6 grids this corresponds respectively to 120, 300 and 630 paths. As can be derived, SpA performs better for mesh networks: up to 14.7% less trees for λ=1 compared to SA. For low λ values SpA and SA are quite similar because the chance of finding paths with similar features starts to decrease. RA doesn't succeed in finding good solutions. For the symmetric full mesh networks, SpA and SA find the same solution and RA solutions remain competitive because under these conditions SpA and SA don't succeed in finding paths with similar features at all: all paths are direct links and no links are selected twice. While both heuristics are not designed to operate properly in these conditions, the calculated

Table 3. Grid networks: amount of STIs and calculation times for different path aggregation techniques

Grid		SpA		SA		RA	
Size	λ	STIs	t	STIs	t	STIs	t
(4x4)	0.04	1.6	1193	1.6	19920	1.66	966
	0.08	2.14	2681	2.2	32381	2.48	1077
	0.25	4.06	12624	4.1	76791	5.06	3922
	0.42	5.3	27522	5.4	139788	7.36	8827
	0.83	7.36	85733	7.94	3.1e5	11.88	27270
	1	7.78	1.1e5	9	3.8e5	13.22	36513
(5x5)	0.03	2.16	3132	2.2	78905	2.3	1411
	0.17	5.4	31892	5.52	3.7e5	7.08	12928
	0.33	7.84	99998	8.24	7.6e5	11.62	40264
	0.67	11.08	3.6e5	12.4	1.7e6	18.84	140757
	1	13.02	7.1e5	15.18	2.8e6	24.68	2.9e5
(6x6)	0.02	2.36	2922	2.26	1.8e5	2.42	1723
	0.06	4.94	27349	5.08	6.5e5	6.02	16843
	0.16	8.44	1.2e5	8.76	1.7e6	11.82	61576
	0.32	12.36	4.0e5	12.9	3.6e6	18.76	2.0e5
	0.63	17.06	1.4e6	18.68	8.7e6	30.36	7.1e5
	1	20.23	3.4e6	23.73	1.7e7	40.86	1.6e6

Table 4. Mesh networks (λ=1): amount of STIs and calculation times for different path aggregation techniques

Mesh	SpA		SA		RA		Exact
N	STIs	t	STIs	t	STIs	t	STIs
3	2	1333	2	1796	2	1187	2
4	2.16	1380	2.16	3110	2.2	916	2
5	3	3085	3	6496	3.02	549	3
6	3.6	3677	3.6	17633	3.66	1063	3
7	4.04	5714	4.04	37898	4.06	1153	4
8	4.68	9363	4.68	76424	4.8	1949	4
10	5.92	21449	5.92	3e5	5.92	2970	5
15	8.28	90940	8.28	3.5e6	8.28	10852	8
20	10.92	2.8e5	10.92	2.11E7	11	31489	10

solutions approximate the optimal solution. The optimal solution was derived by experimental validation. For a full mesh topology and λ=1 the following formula for the minimal amount of STs can be derived:

$$Number\ of\ trees = \begin{cases} \frac{N}{2}, & \text{if N even.} \\ \frac{N+1}{2}, & \text{if N uneven.} \end{cases} \qquad (13)$$

Due to the fact that SpA can't profit from the amount of shared paths that are typically found in the case of aggregation networks, SpA is no longer faster than RA in these scenarios. We can conclude that the rather simple SpA heuristic manages well to tackle the essence of the path aggregation problem.

6   Path Aggregation Technique for Calculating a Minimal Set of STIs with Predefined Backup Conditions

Classic PA techniques which aim to identify the most efficient spanning tree often do not take into account that this trees can reconfigure after network failures. Therefore we try to solve the more difficult PA problem for ST-based recovery with predefined backup routes. We will compare the amount of STIs with a centralized backup system (which doesn't rely on ST-based recovery such as [8]): the paths Φ are the working paths and if failures are detected by the central management system, the affected working paths are switched to predefined backup paths. This will be referred to as *Centralized Backup PA*. We will compare both techniques on their STI usage. The additional STIs that are required to fulfill the backup constraints are also examined: intuitively it is clear that backup conditions might double the amount of required trees in worst-case scenarios (or even more). We will verify this assumption for randomly generated traffic patterns and various network topologies. In Algorithm 6.1 an heuristic is presented for finding a set of STIs which aggregate paths with predefined backup paths for ST-based recovery. It is based on the SA algorithm instead of SpA because the sub-path substitution step of SpA can no longer be applied under backup conditions. Therefore the heuristic is referred to as *Backup Shared Assignment* (Backup SA).

Algorithm 6.1. BACKUP SHARED ASSIGNMENT($STIs$)

Set of all paths : $\Phi \leftarrow (p_0, ..., p_m)$
Set of all backup paths : $\Gamma \leftarrow (b_0, ..., b_m)$
$\Phi \leftarrow order(\Phi)$
comment: in descending order of path length

Set of all edge pairs : EP $\leftarrow \{(e_0, e_1), ..., (e_{K-1}, e_K)\}$
$EP \leftarrow orderfrequency(EP, \Phi)$
comment: in descending order of their frequency of appearance in members of Φ.

Set of all spanning trees : T $= \emptyset$
while $(\exists\{e_k, e_l\} \in EP)$ **true**
do $\left\{ \begin{array}{l} \textbf{while } (\exists p \in \Phi \text{ and } \{e_k, e_l\} \subset p) \textbf{ true} \\ \textbf{do} \left\{ \begin{array}{l} \text{Remove p from } \Phi \\ \textbf{if } (\exists t \in T : ((\text{checkloop}(p, t) == \textbf{ true }) \\ \textbf{and } (checkloop(p, b, t) == \textbf{ true} \text{ for all failures scenarios.}))) \\ \textbf{then } \text{Merge p with t.} \\ \textbf{else } \text{Add p to T.} \end{array} \right. \end{array} \right.$

In Fig. 9 the calculation times for aggregation networks are depicted. As shown in Sec. 5 the problem is quite easy to solve for the shortest paths, therefore

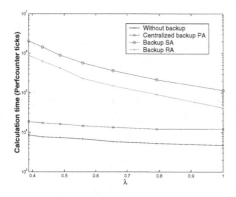
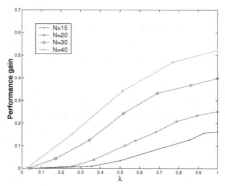

Fig. 9. PA calculation times for the aggregation networks with predefined backup paths and fixed amount of paths

Fig. 10. The reduction of the required amount of STIs of Backup SA compared to Backup RA for aggregation networks

this time the shortest or second shortest path are randomly selected as working path. The path density λ is varied by changing the network size and keeping the number of paths equal. For larger network sizes (or smaller λ) the calculation time of all heuristics will rise. However it is clear that backup PA techniques increase more because in every step the PA problem has to be solved for all possible link or node failures. This means $\text{Max}(O(N);O(K))$ PA problems more have to be calculated compared to non-resilient PA techniques at every step. Figure 10 shows clearly that in aggregation networks the Backup SA heuristic outperforms the Backup RA: for increasing network size and λ the gain increases. Compared to the centralized backup PA up to 20% more trees are required in aggregation networks. Compared to non-resilient PA the amount of supplementary trees increases with the network size: from 44% to 76% for λ=1. This would indicate that centralized backup PA requires less trees than Backup SA. However the calculations for mesh and grid topologies don't confirm this finding.

Calculations for a mesh network with N=10 and a 5x5 grid network are presented in Fig. 11 and Fig. 12. Similar as in aggregation networks the performance gain of Backup SA compared to Backup RA increases for increasing λ and increasing network size. In comparison to previous results the Centralized Backup PA requires more STIs compared to Backup SA for both mesh and grid networks: 100% to 61% additional STIs for the mesh network and 100% to 6% additional STIs for the grid network. This means that Centralized Backup PA doesn't necessarily require less STIs than ST-based recovery mechanisms. Therefore we repeated the tests for uncut aggregation networks with N-1 AGW-SGW links. Wether we selected the shortest paths, the 2nd, the 3rd shortest paths or combinations as working paths, in all cases the Centralized Backup PA method required up to 38% more STIs compared to Backup SA. Therefore we can conclude that in most cases ST-based recovery will require less trees because Centralized Backup requires separately configured trees for working and backup paths. The number of supplementary trees which are necessary to fulfill the

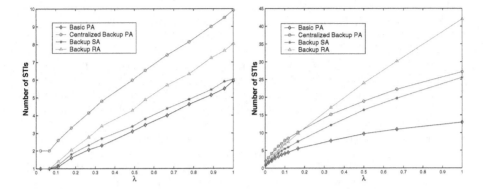

Fig. 11. Path aggregation for mesh networks with predefined backup routes

Fig. 12. Path aggregation for grid networks with predefined backup routes

backup conditions can also be derived: for the mesh network barely up to 10% extra STIs are required and for the grid the amount of trees is almost doubled. This strengthens the assumption that backup conditions can double the amount of required trees in worst-case scenarios but our calculations prove that in many cases far less additional trees are required.

7 Conclusions

We presented a cost-effective design technique for resilient aggregation networks which minimizes packet loss and packet reordering in the dimensioning process. It is shown that the additional resource usage of the presented routing schemes remains limited for aggregation networks. We presented efficient techniques for mapping the required paths on a minimal set of STIs. Evaluation of these methods in different scenarios proved that SpA performed well for aggregating working paths. Evaluations on path aggregation techniques with predefined backup conditions proved that ST-based recovery is truly a flexible way of providing efficient network recovery and that expensive and vulnerable centralized backup systems require rather more STIs for similar backup routes because they require separately configured trees for working and backup paths.

References

1. De Greve F., Van Quickenborne F., et al., *FAMOUS: A Network Architecture for Delivering Multimedia Services to FAstMOving USers*, Special Issue of the Wireless Personal Communications Journal Vol. 33, Numbers 3-4, pp. 281 - 304, 2005.
2. Campbell A.T., Gomez J. and Valko A., *An overview of cellular IP*, IEEE Wireless Communications and Networking Conference, pp. 606-611, 1996.
3. IEEE, *IEEE Standard for Local and Metropolitan Area Networks: Multiple Spanning Trees*, 2002.

4. Li Y., Ooi W.T., *Distributed construction of resource-efficient overlay tree by approximating MST*, The proceedings of ICME 2004, pp. 1507-1510, June 2004.
5. Dziong Z., Jia M., Mason L.G., *ATM Workshop Proceedings, 1998 IEEE*, pp. 186-194, 1998.
6. De Greve F., Van Quickenborne F., et al., *Cost-effective Ethernet routing schemes for dynamic environments*, IEEE Globecom, Dec 2005.
7. Kohler E. , Morris R., Chen B., Jannotti J. and Kaashoek M. F., *"The Click modular router"*, *ACM Transactions on computer systems*, Volume 18 number 3, pp. 236-297, 2000.
8. Sharma S., Gopalan K., et al., *Viking: A multi-spanning tree Ethernet architecture for metropolitan area and cluster networks*, IEEE Infocom 2004, Mar 2004.
9. Palmer, C., *Handbook of Evolutionary Computation*, Oxford University Press, 1997.
10. A. Gibbons, *Algorithmic Graph Theory*, Cambridge University Press, 1985.

Receiver Oriented Trajectory Based Forwarding

Antonio Capone, Ilario Filippini, Luigi Fratta, and Luca Pizziniaco

Dipartimento di Elettronica e Informazione, Politecnico di Milano,
Via Ponzio 34/5, Milano - Italy

Abstract. Trajectory Based Forwarding (TBF) is a new approach to routing in ad hoc wireless networks. It exploits node position information and, similarly to source routing, requires the source node to encode a trajectory into the packet header. The routing process does not require to specify forwarding nodes. As a matter of fact, forwarding nodes are dynamically selected while packets cross the network according to their position with respect to the trajectory. Therefore, this new approach is particularly suitable for application scenarios where network topology is fast varying, due to node mobility (e.g. inter-vehicular networks) or to energy management schemes (e.g. sensor networks), whereas the stability of the trajectories is guaranteed by the physical characteristics of the service area (roads, building aisles, etc.).

This paper describes a new TBF scheme that shifts forwarding decision from transmitter to receiver exploiting broadcast transmissions. We thoroughly analyze the behavior and the properties of the proposed scheme considering the impact of the medium access control mechanism and the effect of limited transmission ranges. We consider piecewise lines connecting source node to destination area and we extend the approach to the multicast case by defining trajectory-trees. Moreover, we propose a forwarding mechanism able to walk around obstacles along the trajectory.

1 Introduction

Wireless ad hoc networks have attracted the attention of the networking research community in the last years. Once explored general solutions for ad hoc networking, current research activities are focusing on specific application scenarios whose characteristics can be exploited to improve efficiency and reliability. The most promising applications include pervasive networks and vehicular networks.

Pervasive networks have the goal to provide computing and communication services all the time, everywhere, transparently to the users, using many low-cost small devices embedded in the surrounding physical environment. Networks nodes are battery operated and have limited computation and memory capabilities. Therefore, energy management schemes must be considered to extend network lifetime. Such schemes allow nodes to switch to low-activity states during which they do not receive/forward packets. As a result, even if most of the nodes have fixed positions the network topology changes frequently. In this scenario packet routing is not an easy task [1, 2], even if location systems can be exploited and location-based routing schemes can be adopted [3, 4].

M. Cesana, L. Fratta (Eds.): Wireless Syst./Network Architect. 2005, LNCS 3883, pp. 21–33, 2006.

Vehicular networks is another interesting scenario of ad hoc networking that allow intelligent devices on cars and along the road to exchange information. Vehicular networks are specially devised for road safety applications, even if they can provide traffic management tools, as well as applications for the mobile office and passengers entertainment. In this case, even if network nodes have no energy constraint, the network topology chances frequently due to nodes mobility. Moreover, information provided by positioning systems, such as GPS or GALILEO [5], can be exploited for routing.

In both pervasive and vehicular networks cases, routing paths, defined as sequence of forwarding nodes, are unstable due to topology changes, while geographical routes, defined as lines, are quite stable due to the physical characteristics of the service area.

Trajectory Based Forwarding (TBF) [6] exploits this basic observation proposing a routing scheme that, similarly to source routing, requires the source node to encode a geographical trajectory, into the packet header. Since the sequence of forwarding nodes is not specified, packets are routed hop-by-hop according to nodes positions with respect to the trajectory. There are two fundamental issues of TBF that must be considered: trajectory design and forwarding mechanism. In this paper we focus on the latter.

The forwarding schemes proposed in [6, 7, 8] are based on point-to-point transmissions. Each forwarding node, upon packet reception, sends the packet to the neighbor node in the best position with respect to the trajectory. The information on neighbor positions is essential for the forwarding algorithm, and it must be kept updated together with the information on neighbors' status (active, nonactive). The existing forwarding schemes adopt different neighbor selection algorithm and trajectory representations.

In this paper we describe SiFT (Simple Forwarding over Trajectory) [9], a novel TBF scheme that is based on broadcast transmissions and does not require neighbor positions and states, since the forwarding decision is shifted from the transmitter to the receiver.

In Section 2 we revise related work in the literature. In Section 3 we describe SiFT and address the critical issues related to the limited transmission range and medium access control. In Section 4 we describe the forwarding mechanism to overcome obstacles along the trajectory. In Section 5 we present simulation results, and in Section 6 we give some concluding remarks.

2   Related Work

Several routing protocols based on position information have been proposed in the literature. GPSR [10] is a routing protocol that takes forwarding decisions aiming at minimizing the number of hops to destination according to a simple greedy algorithm: the node closer to the destination is chosen for the next hop. Similar approaches are considered by GEAR [3], LAR [11], and DREAM [12]. We can consider these schemes special cases of TBF where the trajectory is a straight line from source to destination. Obviously, more complex trajectories provide more flexibility to the forwarding mechanism when the network topology and propagation conditions would prevent to go straight to destination.

GeRaF [13, 14] is a location-based forwarding scheme that does not make use of the information on neighbors' position. The selection of the next forwarding node is based on a receiver-oriented contention resolution mechanism. In addition GeRaF uses a busy tone transmitted on another channel that allows to avoid the hidden terminal problem and it is strongly integrated with the MAC layer. Similarly to previous schemes, packets ideally follow a straight line to destination.

As previously mentioned, TBF schemes proposed in [6], [7] and [8] are based on point-to-point transmissions.

Recently, another approach to TBF, named TEDD, has been proposed in [15]. The network is described by an energy map that represents the energy available at each node, and the dissemination of information from the sink node to the entire network is performed by designing trajectories which try to avoid low-energy areas. Its forwarding scheme is based on timers and aims at using the highest number of nodes in a sector of the energy map.

3   Simple Forwarding over Trajectory

Differently from previously proposed TBF schemes, SiFT uses broadcast instead of point-to-point transmissions. Wireless transmissions are broadcast in nature and allow to reach all active neighbors at the same time. Each node that receives a packet takes the decision whether forwarding it or not based on its own position, the transmitter position and the trajectory. Such an approach greatly reduces the control overhead and the energy consumption.

3.1   Single Stream Trajectory

Let us first consider the simple case where the packet has to be forwarded along a single stream trajectory that is defined as an ordered sequence of straight segments. Each node, upon a packet reception, sets a timer according to its position with respect to the trajectory and the transmitter:

$$T_{out} = \tau \frac{D_t}{D_l} \tag{1}$$

where D_t is the distance between the node and the closest trajectory segment, D_l is the distance from the last node that transmitted the packet, and τ is a constant representing the time unit. If a node receives another copy of the packet before the timer expires, the timer is stopped and the packet is deleted from the forwarding queue. Otherwise, when the timer expires, the packet is processed by the Medium Access Control (MAC) layer for transmission. As a result of this procedure, the packet is forwarded by the node with the minimum T_{out}, i.e. the node in the best position: far from the last the node and close to the trajectory.

The information needed by SiFT and carried in the packets header includes: the trajectory, the coordinates of the last node visited, the packet source identifier, the packet sequence number, and the hops count. To avoid cycles, each node must maintain a list of recently received packets (source ID and sequence number).

SiFT can be implemented over any MAC scheme, but its performance depends on the characteristics of the MAC scheme used. Note that this forwarding approach is quite robust against transmission error and collisions since, for its correct operation, it is sufficient that one of the neighbor nodes receives the packet. Moreover, in the unlucky case that no node successfully receive the packet, the transmitting node can detect the problem and retransmit the packet.

Similarly to source routing, the overhead to code the trajectory depends on the number of segments. Before forwarding a packet, the node modifies the trajectory information by keeping only the segments not yet travelled.

3.2   Forwarding Strip

Due to limited transmission ranges, the above procedure may enable more than one node to forward a packet. As shown in Fig. 1 a packet transmitted by A is first forwarded by C (the node in the best position). Its transmission prevents node B and D to forward the same packet, but not nodes E and F that are out of reach from C.

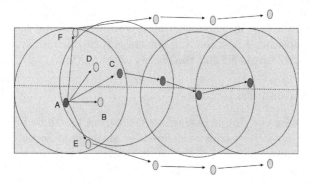

Fig. 1. Forwarding strip

This situation may lead to duplicated packets travelling in the network along "parallel" trajectories at a distance from the original trajectory at least equal to the transmission range. The trajectories, however, soon or later will merge again thus limiting the waste of network resources due to duplicated packet transmissions. We observed such a behavior in our simulation experiments in all network topologies.

To further limit packet duplication, a distance threshold (forwarding strip) can be introduced: if the distance from the trajectory is larger than the threshold, e.g. the transmission range, the node refrains from forwarding process.

3.3   Tree Trajectory

We now consider SiFT scheme operation when the trajectory is represented by a tree of segments. In this case, multiple forwarding is needed when the packet reaches a tree splitting point (tree branching). A copy of the packet must follow each branch to reach all intended destinations. According to the SiFT scheme, a node, upon reception of a packet carrying a tree trajectory information, computes a timer for each branch in its transmission range. Similarly to the single-stream trajectory case, the node modifies the trajectory information in the packet header including the segments belonging to the corresponding branch. In the example shown in Fig. 2, where the segments of the tree trajectory (dotted lines) are numbered from 1 to 7, a packet transmitted by A is received by B and C. Both nodes identify the two branches α and β. Node B is within transmission range with both branches and then computes timer T_α^B and T_β^B. The packet to be forwarded when T_α^B expires will identify in its header segments 2, 4 and 5, while the packet to be forwarded when T_β^B expires will identify segments 3, 6 and 7. Similarly, node C computes T_β^C and modifies packet header including segments 3, 6 and 7. At T_α^B, B transmits the packet that will follow branch α. Two copies of the packet to follow branch β are ready for transmission, but only the one with the smaller timer, will be forwarded. This procedure allows packet copies to complete the tree trajectory following all different branches.

Figure 3 shows a snapshot obtained by simulation with a simple trajectory-tree with two branches. Forwarding nodes are indicated with a darker circle in the picture.

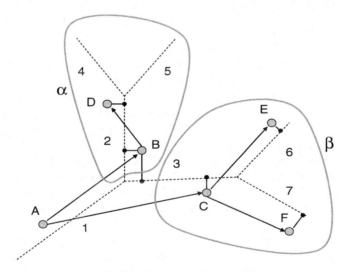

Fig. 2. Tree-based Forwarding

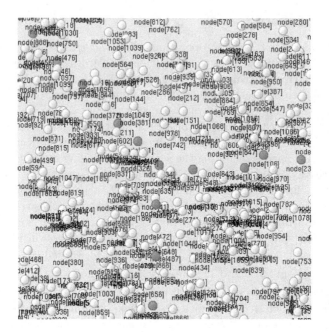

Fig. 3. SiFT: snapshot of multicast forwarding

3.4 Multiple Access

As previously mentioned, SiFT can be implemented over any MAC scheme. However, its performance improves when the MAC, such as AD-HOC MAC protocol [16], provides a reliable broadcast service. In order to show that SiFT is effective also with MAC layers with no guaranteed quality, we consider in the following a simple MAC scheme based on CSMA (Carrier Sense Multiple Access).

The simplest way of implementing SiFT on CSMA is to keep the two protocols separated at network and MAC layers respectively, without any interaction other than the 'send' and 'receive' service primitives. This can be easily achieved by implementing SiFT on top of the broadcast transmission mode of IEEE 802.11 [17] or the CSMA mode of ZigBee [18].

When a timer expires, SiFT forwards the packet to the MAC layer to be transmitted according to CSMA scheme. No feedback from neighbors is adopted and due to limited transmission range, collisions can occur (hidden terminal problem). However, as we observed above, SiFT still works properly since it is quite robust to collisions.

When the activity on the channel is high, several timers of potential forwarding nodes may expire while the channel is busy, leading to collisions as soon as the channel becomes available, as shown for the case of two nodes in Fig. 4 a). Another undesired effect, shown in Fig. 4 b), occurs when the timer expires during the packet transmission by another node. In this case multiple forwarding will occur at a rate that increases if timers are small compared to timer transmissions.

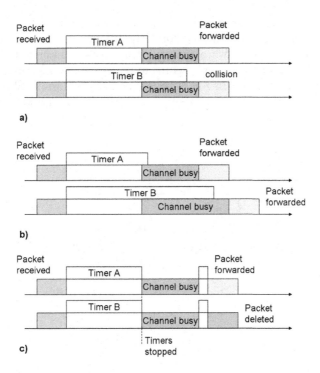

Fig. 4. SiFT operation without carrier sense, case a) – collision – and case b) – double forwarding –, and with carrier sense, case c)

The collision probability and the packet multiple forwarding can be drastically reduced by enforcing SiFT to stop timers when channel is busy (Fig. 4 c). To implement this feature the carrier sense information must be available at the network layer.

4   Obstacle Overcoming

The SiFT protocol, so far presented, successfully delivers the packet to its destination only if the trajectory is not interrupted. This unlucky situation, even unusual in most common environments, may occur because of a signal propagation obstacle or lack of active nodes along the trajectory. GPSR [10] overcomes the problem through graph local planarization which permits the application of the well-known right-hand rule. This technique is also considered in [6] as a possible obstacle overcoming algorithm. In SiFT, however, it cannot be used, since nodes do not know neighbors' positions. In the following we present a new method that can be implemented in SiFT even with the limited information available.

Since radio links are bi-directional and transmissions are broadcast, when a node forwards a packet its transmission is also received by the previous forwarding node. This information is interpreted as an acknowledgement that the packet forwarding is proceeding correctly. If such a transmission is not received, the node becomes aware that the trajectory is interrupted and some action has to be taken to further attempt to reach the destination. An example of such a situation is shown in Fig. 5, where a packet transmitted by node S is received by no nodes in the forwarding strip in the trajectory direction.

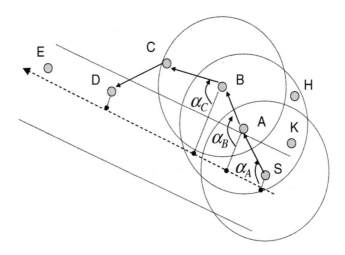

Fig. 5. Scenario with an interrupted trajectory

To overcome such a condition we propose the following mechanism called Blind Face Walking (BFW) that enables nodes out of the forwarding strip to contribute to the forwarding process. The basic idea is that a forwarding node that detects a trajectory interruption starts the BFW mechanism by setting the BFW flag in the packet header. A node on the right side of the trajectory when receives a BFW packet (a packet with the BFW flag on) sets the transmission timer, T_{out}, given by:

$$T_{out} = a\alpha, \tag{2}$$

where a is a constant [seconds/degrees], and α [degrees], $0 \leq \alpha < 360$, is the angle (clockwise) between the segment passing by the previous forwarding node and orthogonal to the trajectory and the segment between the previous and present forwarding nodes. The BFW phase ends when the forwarding node is inside the forwarding strip.

Similarly to regular SiFT forwarding scheme, the node with the smallest α forwards the packet when the timer expires. In the example in Fig. 5, node S, that has recognized the failure of SiFT forwarding scheme, sets the flag and forwards the BFW packet. Nodes A and K receive the packet and set their timers. Since $\alpha_A < \alpha_K$, A will first transmit the packet and will force node K to stop its timer and erase the packet. Similarly, the packet is then forwarded by nodes B, and C. Node D, inside the forwarding strip, ends the BFW phase and forwards the packet with the BFW flag off.

Due to the limited transmission range, multiple packet transmissions may occur as described in Section 3.2. In the example in Fig. 5, when node A transmits the packet, both nodes B and H receive it and set timers. Node B timer expires first and the packet is forwarded. However, node H, being out of the range of B, will not receive the packet and will forward again the same packet when its timer expires. To reduce packet duplication we can enable to transmission only nodes within a sector of size ϑ. The full area (360 degrees) around the node is explored sector by sector and only the nodes within $(i-1)\vartheta \le \alpha < i\vartheta$ can transmit. The index i is the number of transmissions of the same packet by the same node. The procedure is iterated until either the packet is forwarded or all sectors are explored. Note that in an environment with uniform propagation, in order to guarantee no packet duplication ϑ must be set less or equal to 60 degrees.

We have described the BFW procedure referring to nodes on the right side of the trajectory. Considering counterclockwise angles instead of clockwise, the procedure applies to nodes on the left side of the trajectory. To improve the effectiveness in overcoming obstacles, both alternatives can be implemented at the same time. The drawback is an increase of the probability of duplicating packet forwarding that stops when the forwarding node is back in the forwarding strip.

5   Performance Evaluation

To investigate the correctness and to evaluate the performance we implemented SiFT within Omnet++ simulation engine with the Mobility Framework [19]. We considered a square area $1000mx1000m$ with 100 active nodes uniformly random distributed. Each node has a transmitting range of 263 m. In the square area we consider 4 horizontal and 5 vertical straight trajectories, and one diagonal trajectory from the right-top corner to the left-bottom one. Packet sources are located on top of the vertical trajectories and on the left of the horizontal ones. Destinations are located at the opposite sides. All data have been collected on the diagonal trajectory, while Poisson-distributed interfering traffic has been generated on the others. The admissibility-strip width has been set equal to the transmission range.

The packets generated have all the same length equal to 192 bit. The channel bit-rate is equal to 100 $Kbit/s$, and timers are set according to:

$$T_{out} = 0.1\frac{D_t}{D_l} + 0.002 \quad [\text{s}] \tag{3}$$

where 0.002 is the packet transmission time.

In Figure 6 we show the delivery time measured on the diagonal trajectory versus the interfering traffic. Surprisingly, SiFT exploiting carrier sense information as explained in Section 3.3, performs worst, especially when traffic increases and channel is often busy. The increase in delay due to counter stopping is much longer than the delay caused by collisions and multiple forwarding.

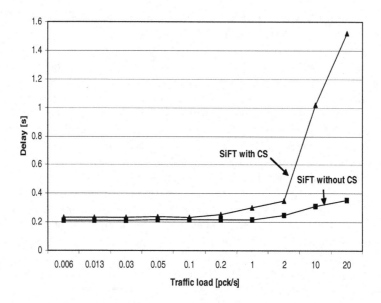

Fig. 6. Average delivery time versus traffic load

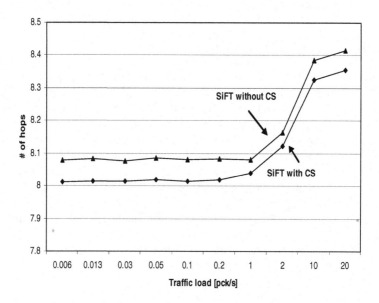

Fig. 7. Average number of hops versus traffic load

To closer investigate the effect of collisions we measured the average number of hops per delivered packet versus interfering traffic (Fig. 7). In case of SiFT without carrier sense information, we observed a slight larger number of hops because collisions may prevent the node in the best position to forward the packet.

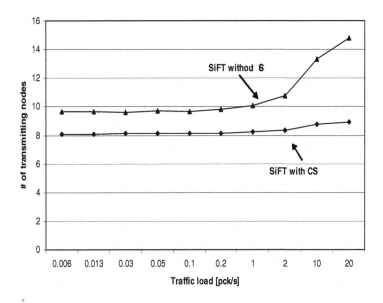

Fig. 8. Average number of forwarding nodes versus traffic load

The number of forwarding nodes per packet is larger than the number of hops per packet due to multiple forwarding. This undesired behavior is practically avoided by using carrier sense information in SiFT as it has been observed in our simulations (Fig. 8). On the contrary, if carrier sense information is not used, when the traffic load increases the multiple forwarding has a significant impact.

6   Conclusions

Trajectory-based forwarding is a promising new approach for routing in wireless ad hoc networks where topology is highly variable but constrained by the geographical positions of nodes and the physical characteristics of the environment. Interesting applications include pervasive networks and vehicular networks.

In this paper we have proposed SiFT, a new trajectory-based forwarding scheme that shifts the forwarding decision from the transmitter to the receiver. This allows a more effective and efficient operation since, differently from previously proposed schemes, nodes do not need to maintain a list of active neighbors and their geographical coordinates.

We have shown that SiFT is able to work even on top of very simple medium access schemes like CSMA. We evaluated and compared the performance of simple SiFT protocol and an enhanced version that exploits the carrier sense information provided by the MAC layer. Even if the enhanced scheme achieves a more effective operation by reducing the number of collisions and packet duplications, the simpler scheme is better as far as the packet delay is concerned.

This suggests that, because of its easy implementation, SiFT could be adopted with standard MAC protocols like IEEE 802.11 and ZigBee.

Acknowledgement

This work has been partially supported by the European Network of Excellence EURO-NGI (http://www.eurongi.org/) under the Specific Research Project VNET (Vehicular NETworks).

References

1. I.F. Akyildiz, W. Su, Y. Sankarasubramaniam, E. Cayirci, *A survey on sensor networks*, IEEE Communications Magazine, vol.40, no.8, Aug 2002,
2. D. Niculescu, *Communication paradigms for sensor networks* in IEEE Communications Magazine, vol. 43, no. 3, March 2005, pp. 116-122.
3. Y. Yu, D. Estrin, R. Govindan, *Geograohical and Energy-Aware Routing: A Recoursive Data Dissemination Protocol for Wireless Sensor Networks* in UCLA Comp. Sci. Dept. tech. rep., UCLA-CSD TR-010023, 2001.
4. Y. Xu, J. Heidemann, D. Estrin, *Geography informed Energy Conservation for Ad-Hoc Routing*, in proc. of ACM Mobicom '01, 2001
5. A. Rao, S.Ratmasamy, C.Papadimitriou, S.Shenker, I. Stoica, *Geographic Routing without Location Information*, in proc. of ACM MobiHoc '03, 2003.
6. D. Niculescu, B. Nath, *Trajectory Based and Its Application*, in proc. of ACM Mobicom '03, 2003.
7. B.Nath, D. Niculescu. *Routing on a curve* in ACM SIGCOMM Computer Communication Review, vol. 33, no. 1, January 2003.
8. M. Yuksel, R. Pradhan, S. Kalyanaraman, *An Implementation Framework for Trajectory-Based Forwarding in Ad-Hoc Networks*, in proc. of IEEE ICC '04, June 2004.
9. A. Capone, I. Filippini, M.A. Garcia and L. Pizziniaco. *SiFT: An efficient method for Trajectory Based Forwarding*. 2nd International Symposium on Wireless Communication Systems 2005 (ISWCS '05).
10. B. Karp and H. T. Kung. *GPSR: Greedy Perimeter Stateless Routing for wireless networks*, in Mobile Computing and Networking, pages 243-254, 2000.
11. W. Heinzelman, J. Kulik and H. Balakrishnan. *Adaptive protocols for information dissemination in wireless sensor networks*, in the Proceedings of the 5th Annual ACM/IEEE International Conference on Mobile Computing and Networking (MobiCom'99), Seattle, 1999.
12. S. Basagni, I. Chlamtac, V.R. Syrotiuk and B.A. Woodward. *A Distance Routing Effect Algorithm for Mobility (DREAM)*, in the Proceedings of the 4th Annual ACM/IEEE International Conference on Mobile Computing and Networking (MobiCom'98), Dallas, 1998.
13. M. Zorzi, R. R. Rao, *Geographic Random Forwarding (GeRaF) for Ad Hoc and Sensor Networks: Multihop Performance*, IEEE Transactions on Mobile Computing, vol. 2, no. 4, pp 337-348, Oct-Dec 2003.
14. M. Zorzi, R. R. Rao, *Geographic Random Forwarding (GeRaF) for Ad Hoc and Sensor Networks: Energy and Latency Performance*, IEEE Transactions on Mobile Computing, vol. 2, no. 4, pp 349-365, Oct-Dec 2003.

15. O. Goussevskaia, M.D.V. Machado, R.A.F. Mini, A.A.F. Loureiro, G.R. Mateus, J.M. Nogieira, *Data dissemination based on the energy map*, IEEE Communications Magazine, vol. 43, no. 7, July 2005, pp. 134–143.
16. F. Borgonovo, A. Capone, M. Cesana, L. Fratta, *ADHOC MAC: a new MAC architecture for ad hoc networks providing efficient and reliable point-to-point and broadcast services*, Wireless Networks, vol. 10, no. 4, pp. 359-366, July 2004.
17. IEEE 802.11 Working Group - http://grouper.ieee.org/groups/802/11/
18. E. Callaway, P. Gorday, L. Hester, J.A. Gutierrez, M. Naeve, B. Heile, V. Bahl, *Home networking with IEEE 802.15.4: a developing standard for low-rate wireless personal area networks*, IEEE Communications Magazine, vol. 40, no. 8, pp. 70-77, Aug. 2002.
19. OMNET++ Community Site - http://www.omnetpp.org/

Power-Controlled Directional Medium Access Control for Wireless Mesh Networks

Antonio Capone[1] and Fabio Martignon[2]

[1] Department of Electronics and Information, Politecnico di Milano,
Piazza L. da Vinci 32, 20133 Milan, Italy
capone@elet.polimi.it
[2] Department of Management and Information Technology, University of Bergamo,
Dalmine (BG) 24044, Italy
fabio.martignon@unibg.it

Abstract. Wireless Mesh Networks have emerged recently as a technology for next-generation wireless networking. To increase the performance of wireless nodes in such networks many approaches have been proposed, including directional and adaptive antennas. However, while adaptive antennas can improve the utilization of the wireless medium by reducing radio interference and the impact of the exposed nodes problem, they can also exacerbate the hidden nodes problem. Thus, MAC protocols for adaptive antennas need to be carefully designed to cope with this issue.

In this regard we propose a novel MAC protocol that exploits the potentials offered by adaptive antennas in Wireless Mesh Networks to improve system performance. As key innovative feature of the proposed MAC protocol with respect to existing solutions, the information about wireless medium reservation is spread to the maximum possible extent without interfering with the connections already established in the network. This is achieved by transmitting RTS/CTS frames in all antenna sectors at the maximum allowed power that does not cause interference with ongoing transmissions. The DATA/ACK exchange then takes place directionally and at the minimum necessary power.

We measure the performance of the proposed MAC protocol by simulation in several realistic network scenarios, and we compare it with the most notable solutions proposed in the literature. The results show that our proposed scheme allows to increase considerably both the total traffic accepted by the network and fairness between competing connections.

Index Terms: Wireless Mesh Networks, Adaptive Antennas, Medium Access Control, Power Control.

1 Introduction

Wireless Mesh Networks have emerged recently as a technology for next-generation wireless networking [1, 2, 3]. To increase the performance of wireless nodes in such networks many approaches have been proposed in the literature, including directional and adaptive antennas.

M. Cesana, L. Fratta (Eds.): Wireless Syst./Network Architect. 2005, LNCS 3883, pp. 34–46, 2006.

Adaptive antennas can be efficiently used in Wireless Mesh Networks. However, suitable Medium Access Control (MAC) algorithms must be designed, since the IEEE 802.11 standard MAC [4] has been optimized for omnidirectional antennas.

The problem of designing efficient MAC protocols that can exploit the potential of adaptive antennas has been deeply investigated in the research area of wireless mesh networks [5, 6, 7, 8, 9, 10, 11, 12]. Some solutions [13, 14, 15] envisage the utilization of power control techniques to further enhance spatial reuse and reserve the wireless medium as more efficiently as possible. We revise these solutions and related work in Section 2.

In this paper we propose *Power-Controlled Directional MAC* (PCD-MAC), a novel MAC protocol suitable for wireless mesh networks where nodes use adaptive antennas and power control. The key innovative feature of our proposition is that nodes spread information about wireless medium reservation to the maximum possible extent without interfering with the connections already established in the network. This is achieved by sending RTS/CTS frames in all antenna sectors at the maximum allowed power that does not cause interference with ongoing transmissions. The DATA/ACK exchange then takes place only directionally arid at the minimum necessary power.

We perform an extensive evaluation based on simulation of PCD-MAC, comparing its performance with the most notable solutions proposed in the literature. Numeric results measured in several realistic network scenarios show that PCD-MAC outperforms previously proposed MAC schemes both in terms of total load accepted in the network and fairness between competing connections.

This paper is organized as follows: Section 2 discusses related work; Section 3 describes our proposed Power-Controlled Directional MAC; Section 4 analyzes and discusses numeric results; finally, Section 5 concludes the paper and outlines future research issues.

2   Related Work

Several solutions have been proposed in the literature to enhance the standard 802.11 MAC to exploit the potential offered by directional and adaptive antennas. The common goal of all propositions is the exploitation of spatial reuse to increase network utilization. Some solutions use also power control techniques to limit the interference generated towards already established connections while, at the same time, save nodes' energy.

The Network Allocation Vector (NAV) definition is extended in [7, 8] using a direction field, indicating that the NAV applies only for that direction. The direction of arrival of each received transmission is estimated and the NAV is set only in such direction. Evidently, multipath phenomena can affect the accuracy of this information; however, since in Wireless Mesh Networks nodes positions are fixed, our proposed MAC is not affected by this problem.

In [8] the authors also propose a MAC protocol that transmits all frames directionally, i.e. in one sector. Directional transmissions have a larger range than omnidirectional ones. Each node listens omnidirectionally when in idle state, while in all other cases it listens only directionally with its antenna steered in the direction of the intended transmitter. This scheme presents some drawbacks due to the deafness [16] problem: whenever a node is occupied to transmit a frame directionally, it may not hear RTS/CTS exchanges between newly established transmissions, and consequently it can interfere with them once its transmission is completed.

In [5] the authors assume that each node knows its own position and that of neighbor nodes. Directional and omnidirectional transmissions have the same range, and two different schemes are proposed: in the first one, referred to as Directional RTS MAC (DRTS-MAC), the RTS frame is transmitted only directionally in the sector corresponding to the destination node; in the second scheme, referred to as Omnidirectional RTS MAC (ORTS-MAC), the NAV is checked and the RTS is sent omnidirectionally if all directions are free, otherwise it is sent only directionally as in the first scheme. In both schemes the CTS is transmitted omnidirectionally, while the DATA/ACK exchange takes place directionally. Note that if any of the antenna sectors of the node that receives the RTS frame is not free, the node cannot transmit the CTS frame and it simply drops the RTS frame.

Both schemes proposed in [5] allow to increase the performance with respect to the standard 802.11 MAC; however, the choice of transmitting the CTS frames always omnidirectionally represents a limitation for these schemes as such transmission is possible only if all antenna sectors are free in the surroundings of the receiving node.

The algorithm proposed in [9] assumes that each sector has associated a directional antenna; the 802.11 CSMA/CA protocol is replicated for each antenna, implementing a *Directional CSMA/CA*. Each node transmits every frame in all sectors that are free at the moment of the transmission according to the D-NAV information, regardless such frame is RTS, CTS, DATA or ACK. However, the choice of transmitting also DATA and ACK frames in multiple sectors increases the interference generated on neighbor nodes, thus preventing the contemporary transmission of parallel connections. In our proposed solution we transmit such frames only in the direction of the intended receiver and at the minimum necessary power to increase spatial reuse.

A scheme called *circular directional RTS* is proposed in [6], where the RTS frame is transmitted directionally and consecutively, in a circular way, scanning all the area around the transmitter. The CTS frame, on the contrary, is sent only in the direction of the RTS transmitter, and DATA/ACK frames are transmitted directionally. After the transmission of the RTS frame, the transmitting node waits for the reception of the corresponding CTS listening omnidirectionally. This choice can lead to an increased number of collisions experienced by the transmitter; to limit this effect, in our proposed solution, during the reception of the CTS, DATA and ACK frames the antenna is steered only in the sector that contains the transmitter of such frames.

In [10] the authors propose several solutions to limit the impact of the hidden terminal problem caused by directional antennas; three novel directional NAV indicators (*High Gain CTS*, *Backward RTS* and *Relayed CTS*) are introduced to indicate ongoing communications to a hidden terminal. However, even if effective, these solutions need several changes to the standard MAC protocol.

A MAC protocol that uses directional antennas is proposed in [11]; a receiver-centric approach for location tracking is proposed, so that nodes become aware of their neighborhood and also of the direction of the nodes for communicating directionally. A node develops its location-awareness from these neighborhood-awareness and direction-awareness. However, such awareness is achieved using periodical transmissions of beacon frames that can represent a consistent traffic overhead for the network.

Many schemes proposed in the literature combine the utilization of adaptive antennas to power control techniques [12, 13].

In [12] the authors propose to use a *short NAV* to exploit the increased opportunity for spatial reuse. Various power control techniques are proposed in this work; however, in all the proposed schemes power control is adopted only for the transmission of DATA frames, while we propose to extend its use also to RTS/CTS frames.

The solution proposed in [13] has some features in common with our proposition. Two novelties are introduced: the first is the use of a backoff procedure where both the interval boundaries and the method of backoff depends upon the event (e.g., no CTS, no ACK, channel busy) that caused the backoff; the second is the tight integration of power control with direction control.

To extend the D-NAV definition, the authors introduce a new field in the D-NAV table. This field is used to specify the power above which interference will occur; each antenna can transmit when the intended transmission is deemed sufficiently low power to not bother the busy nodes.

All frames are transmitted directionally. As we noted before, this choice can worsen the deafness problem and lead to severe unfairness and performance degradation [16]. For this reason, in our proposed MAC protocol RTS and CTS frames are transmitted in all sectors at the maximum allowed power to spread the information about wireless medium reservation as wider as possible.

3   Power-Controlled Directional MAC

Without loss of generality we describe our proposed Power-Controlled Directional MAC protocol (PCD-MAC) by considering steerable antenna systems [13] where a phased array antenna and a beamforming matrix are used to generate the desired beams. The transceiver can then choose between one or more beams for transmitting or receiving.

We assume for simplicity that an antenna can direct its transmissions into N sectors, each having an angle of $\frac{360}{N}$ degrees. Moreover, each antenna has M transmission power levels [14] that can be chosen to set different transmission ranges. Figures 1 and 2 illustrate an example scenario with the settings used in this paper, i.e. $N = 8$ sectors and $M = 8$ power levels.

Since nodes are usually fixed in Wireless Mesh Networks, we assume that each node knows its own location and that of neighbor nodes.

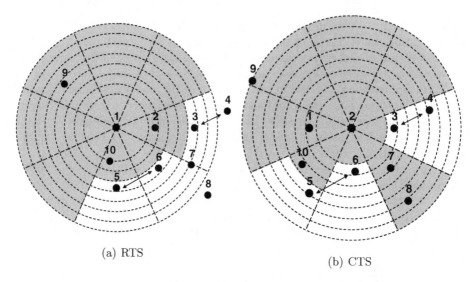

(a) RTS

(b) CTS

Fig. 1. PCD-MAC: antenna pattern (a) used by node 1 to send the RTS frame (b) used by node 2 to send the CTS frame; two connections are already established, between nodes (3-4) and (5-6)

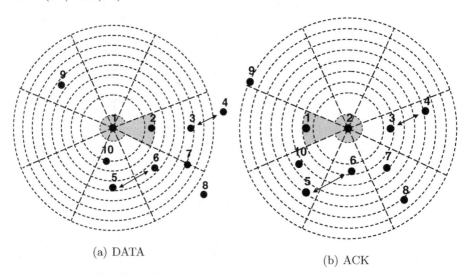

(a) DATA

(b) ACK

Fig. 2. PCD-MAC: antenna pattern (a) used by node 1 to send the DATA frame (b) used by node 2 to send the ACK frame; two connections are already established, between nodes (3-4) and (5-6)

We assume that nodes perform directional virtual carrier sensing, as proposed in [5, 6], where the NAV is augmented using a direction field, indicating that the NAV applies only for that direction (D-NAV). We further extend this idea, following the guidelines of [13], including power control as an integral part of the D-NAV: the D-NAV table therefore contains, in addition to the duration field, the sector number and the maximum allowed transmission power. This field indicates the maximum power allowed for transmissions in such sector, above which interference with ongoing transmissions occurs.

The D-NAV setting is performed as follows: whenever node n receives a RTS or DATA frame transmitted from node s to node t, with $t \neq n$, it determines the distance between itself and both s (d_{ns}) and t (d_{nt}). If both nodes are in the transmission range of n, the D-NAV is set for the antenna sectors that contain s and t for the period indicated in the *duration* field of the RTS frame, and all transmissions of n having a range larger than d_{ns} and d_{nt}, respectively, are forbidden in such sectors; otherwise, if t is outside the transmission range of n, the D-NAV setting is performed only for the sector containing node s. The same procedure is followed when node n receives a CTS or ACK frame, with the only difference that such frames contain only the indication of the destination node and not of its source.

Whenever a node s has a frame to transmit to node t, it first checks if such transmission is possible according to the D-NAV indication concerning the sector that contains t. If the transmission is not possible, then s performs the standard backoff procedure. Otherwise, as a key innovative feature, to allow information about wireless medium reservation be spread as much as possible, both s and t transmit RTS and CTS frames, respectively, in each sector at the maximum allowed transmission power. Then, s and t perform the DATA/ACK exchange at the minimum necessary power, maintaining their antennas steered in the direction of the ongoing transmission. The reception of CTS, DATA and ACK frames takes place directionally, i.e. with nodes having their antennas steered in the sector containing the node transmitting such frames, to limit to the maximum extent the interference.

To illustrate the functioning of PCD-MAC let us refer to the network scenario shown in Figures 1 and 2, where two connections are active between nodes 3-4 and 5-6, respectively. Node 1 wants to transmit a packet to node 2, and we further assume that these two nodes heard the RTS/CTS exchange of the two active connections, so that the information contained in their D-NAVs reflects correctly the current situation. The Figures report the antenna sectors and the transmission ranges corresponding to the different power levels that can be set in each node involved in the frame exchange.

The antenna pattern used for the transmission of the RTS and CTS frames sent by nodes 1 and 2, respectively, is illustrated in gray in Figures 1(a) and 1(b). The DATA/ACK exchange then takes place at the minimum necessary power, as illustrated in Figures 2(a) and 2(b). The realization of the antenna patterns resulting from the application of PCD-MAC can be obtained with adaptive array antennas [17].

In this sample scenario, the power control feature of our proposed MAC protocol allows to establish a connection between nodes 1 and 2, even if the D-NAV of node 1 is set in the sector that contains node 2. Moreover, the transmission of DATA/ACK frames at the minimum necessary power reduces remarkably the interference produced on all other nodes, thus potentially leading to an overall increase of total goodput as we will show in the next Section.

4   Numeric Results

In this Section we evaluate and compare by simulation, using the Network Simulator *ns* ver.2 [18], the performance of the following MAC protocols:

- The proposed PCD-MAC;
- The standard 802.11 MAC with omnidirectional antennas [4];
- The directional MAC scheme DRTS-MAC proposed in [5] and reviewed in Section 2;
- A variation of PCD-MAC, named *Directional MAC (D-MAC)*, where no power control is used; the behavior of D-MAC is the same as detailed in the previous Section, with a single transmission power level available in each node, P, that corresponds to the maximum level available for PCD-MAC. Hence, RTS/CTS frames are transmitted with power level P in all sectors that are free according to the D-NAV indication, and DATA/ACK frames are transmitted directionally with the same transmission power. The analysis of D-MAC allows us to gauge the performance gain achieved by the power control feature embedded in PCD-MAC.

The performance is measured by the total goodput, defined as the total load accepted in the network without considering packet retransmissions, and by the level of fairness achieved between competing connections, expressed using Jain's fairness index [19].

In all simulated scenarios the capacity of the radio interface was set to 11 Mbit/s, the transmission range of the nodes to 215 m and we implemented a realistic antenna model at the radio layer [20].

We consider both UDP and TCP traffic. More specifically, UDP traffic is modeled using Poisson packet arrivals at each sender, with a rate sufficiently high to saturate the capacity of the wireless link and packet size equal to 1000 bytes; we then consider bulk FTP transfers performed between the sender and the receiver using the TCP protocol, with full-sized segments (i.e. 1500 bytes).

We first evaluate the MAC protocols in simple network scenarios that allow us to underline the features of our proposed MAC, and then we consider grid and random topologies with a larger number of competing connections.

4.1   Validation Scenarios

We first consider the network scenario illustrated in Fig. 3, where 4 nodes are placed to form a square with edges of 100 meters.

The network is fully meshed and every node can reach directly in one hop every other node. On this network two connections are established: one between nodes 1 and 4 (C1) and the other between nodes 2 and 3 (C2). This scenario is critical for the 802.11 standard MAC with nodes equipped with omnidirectional antennas, as only one connection can be active at a time. On the other hand, the use of directional transmissions performed by PCD-MAC allows the two connections to be active simultaneously, thus increasing network performance.

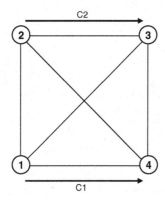

Fig. 3. Square topology scenario with two connections; lines represent wireless links and arrows represent connections

Table 1. Simulation results in the network scenario of Fig. 3: average goodput [Mbit/s] and Jain's fairness index for various MAC versions

MAC	Poisson Traffic		FTP Traffic	
	Goodput	Fairness	Goodput	Fairness
802.11 Standard	4.35	1	4.33	0.99
DRTS-MAC	5.44	1	4.69	0.99
D-MAC	8	1	8.13	1
PCD-MAC	**8**	**1**	**8.15**	**1**

Table 1 shows the average total load accepted in the network and the fairness index in this network scenario for all the considered MAC versions and for both the traffic types considered.

The directional DRTS-MAC proposed in [5] performs slightly better than the standard 802.11 omnidirectional MAC, but the choice to transmit CTS frames omnidirectionally greatly limits its performance.

Note that PCD-MAC allows to achieve improvements up to 85% with respect to omnidirectional MAC while maintaining, at the same time, perfect fairness between the two competing flows.

We then considered the network scenario illustrated in Fig. 4, where 3 connections are active, respectively, between nodes 1 and 2 (C1), between nodes 5 and 4 (C2) and between nodes 6 and 3 (C3); the traffic offered to the network by such connections has the same features as in the previous scenario.

Table 2 shows the performance achieved by the various MAC versions in this network scenario. The standard 802.11 MAC with omnidirectional antennas performs poorly also in this scenario since only one connection can be active at a time. Directional MAC schemes without power control features (like DRTS-MAC and D-MAC) allow connections C1 and C2 to be active simultaneously, while connection C3 is still penalized since node 3 is exposed to the directional

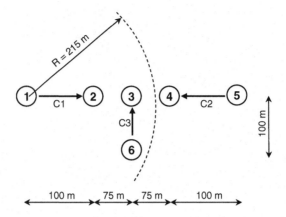

Fig. 4. Network Scenario with 3 connections

Table 2. Simulation results in the network scenario of Fig. 4: average goodput [Mbit/s] and Jain's fairness index for various MAC versions

	Poisson Traffic		FTP Traffic	
MAC	Goodput	Fairness	Goodput	Fairness
802.11 Standard	4.3	0.95	4.31	0.85
DRTS-MAC	6.02	0.71	7.31	0.67
D-MAC	6.84	0.71	7.8	0.67
PCD-MAC	**8.65**	**0.98**	**9.64**	**0.99**

transmissions of RTS and DATA frames of nodes 1 and 5. PCD-MAC allows all 3 connections to be active at the same time due to its power control features in the transmission of all frames, reaching a goodput gain of almost 100% with respect to omnidirectional MAC. Moreover, PCD-MAC achieves a higher fairness than all other MAC versions, since it makes competing connections share network resources fairly.

4.2   Grid and Random Scenarios

We first considered three different scenarios consisting of a 5×5 grid where nodes are, respectively, 70, 90 and 140 meters apart horizontally and vertically. We picked at random 10 couples of nodes. In each couple, one node acts like sender, the other like receiver, and all the flows are routed on the shortest path between the sender and the receiver.

We measured in all the scenarios the total load accepted by the network (goodput) and the Jain's fairness index, averaged on 5 random extractions. Results are shown in Table 3 for Poisson traffic and in Table 4 for FTP traffic, in all grid scenarios. These results confirm that PCD-MAC allows to improve the total accepted load and fairness between competing connections for both types

Table 3. Average goodput [Mbit/s] and Jain's fairness index for various MAC versions in the 5×5 grid network scenarios with inter-node spacing of 70, 90 and 140 m; 10 connections offer to the network a Poisson traffic

MAC	Grid 70 m		Grid 90 m		Grid 140 m	
	Goodput	Fairness	Goodput	Fairness	Goodput	Fairness
802.11 Standard	5.67	0.62	8.69	0.44	6.13	0.35
DRTS-MAC	8.98	0.69	11.98	0.68	12.47	0.57
D-MAC	9.27	0.71	11.71	0.68	15.23	0.66
PCD-MAC	**10.27**	**0.76**	**13.89**	**0.74**	**15.55**	**0.67**

Table 4. Average goodput [Mbit/s] and Jain's fairness index for various MAC versions in the 5×5 grid network scenarios with inter-node spacing of 70, 90 and 140 m; 10 connections offer to the network FTP traffic

MAC	Grid 70 m		Grid 90 m		Grid 140 m	
	Goodput	Fairness	Goodput	Fairness	Goodput	Fairness
802.11 Standard	6.17	0.42	9.93	0.34	8.83	0.31
DRTS-MAC	9.22	0.38	12.48	0.36	14.09	0.46
D-MAC	11.28	0.46	15.08	0.52	16.65	0.62
PCD-MAC	**12.72**	**0.58**	**15.53**	**0.62**	**16.8**	**0.63**

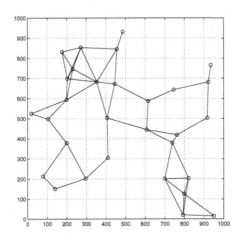

Fig. 5. Instance of a generated random topology with 30 nodes uniformly distributed on a 1000 m × 1000 m area

of traffic even in these scenarios. A great gain is obtained for dense grids where the power control feature of PCD-MAC allows more connections to be active simultaneously in the network.

We then considered a mesh network scenario in which multiple users are interconnected through a multi-hop wireless network. We considered a 1000 m×1000 m square area, where 30 nodes are distributed uniformly at random. Ten connections are randomly extracted with the same features as in the grid scenario. Fig. 5 illustrates an example of the resulting topology, assuming that all transmission ranges are equal to 215 m.

Table 5 shows the results for all the considered MAC protocols. PCD-MAC achieves higher goodput and fairness in all the considered network scenarios, and outperforms the other MAC schemes. The goodput gain is remarkable and reaches, in some situations, 65% with respect to the 802.11 standard MAC. Finally, fairness between competing connections is greatly increased with respect to both 802.11 omnidirectional MAC and previously proposed directional MAC schemes.

Finally, we considered a mesh network scenario in which multiple users are interconnected and access the Internet through a multi-hop wireless network. We considered, as in the previous scenario, a 1000 m × 1000 m square area, where 30 nodes are distributed uniformly at random. The area has been divided into 4 equal 500 m × 500 m square sectors. The 4 nodes that are located closest to the center of each of these sectors act as concentrators and collect the traffic of the neighbor nodes. All the other 21 nodes send their traffic to the closest

Table 5. Average total goodput [Mbit/s] and Jain's fairness index achieved by the various MAC schemes in the random network scenarios illustrated in Fig. 5 with 30 nodes and 10 connections

MAC	Poisson Traffic		FTP Traffic	
	Goodput	Fairness	Goodput	Fairness
802.11 Standard	10.18	0.46	12.4	0.44
DRTS-MAC	14.55	0.58	15.84	0.48
D-MAC	15.92	0.67	16.09	0.55
PCD-MAC	**17.02**	**0.68**	**17.84**	**0.59**

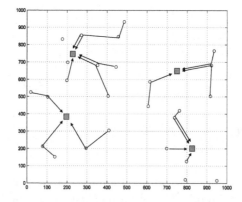

Fig. 6. Random topology with 4 concentrators. Connections' paths are indicated with arrows.

concentrator. Fig. 6 shows a sample scenario resulting from the random topology of Fig. 5, where concentrator nodes are indicated with squares and connections' paths with arrows.

Table 6 shows the performance, averaged over 5 random extractions, for all the MAC protocols considered with both Poisson and FTP traffic. Since in this network scenario the traffic is directed towards few nodes (the concentrators), the spatial reuse is allowed to a lower extent with respect to previous scenarios. However, the performance of PCD-MAC is in line with that of other MAC protocols for both types of traffic, and a remarkable gain with respect to the 802.11 standard MAC is observed.

Table 6. Average total goodput [Mbit/s] and Jain's fairness index achieved by the various MAC schemes in the random network scenarios illustrated in Fig. 6 with 30 nodes, 4 concentrators and 10 connections

	Poisson Traffic		FTP Traffic	
MAC	Goodput	Fairness	Goodput	Fairness
802.11 Standard	10.25	0.4	12.99	0.4
DRTS-MAC	12.49	0.65	15.75	0.36
D-MAC	13.83	0.61	15.66	0.43
PCD-MAC	**13.81**	**0.63**	**15.59**	**0.44**

5   Conclusion and Future Issues

In this paper we proposed a novel directional power-controlled MAC designed for wireless mesh networks where nodes are equipped with adaptive antennas. We compared the performance of the proposed MAC protocol with the most notable algorithms proposed in the literature in several realistic network scenarios, showing that our scheme allows to increase both the total load accepted in the network and fairness in network resources utilization among competing connections.

We are currently extending this work by developing an innovative routing scheme that exploits the features of our proposed MAC protocol to further increase the performance of wireless mesh networks in the presence of adaptive antennas.

References

1. I.F. Akyildiz, X. Wang, and W. Wang. Wireless mesh networks: a survey. *Computer Networks*, pages 445–487, vol. 47(4), 2005.
2. I.F. Akyildiz and X. Wang. A survey on wireless mesh networks. *IEEE Communications Magazine*, September 2005.
3. R. Bruno, M. Conti, and E. Gregori. Mesh networks: Commodity multihop ad hoc networks. *IEEE Communications Magazine*, pages 123–131, March 2005.

4. Wireless LAN Medium Access Control (MAC) and Physical Layer (PHY) specifications. *IEEE Standard for Information technology.* 1999.
5. Y.B. Ko and N.H. Vaidya. Medium Access Control Protocols Using Directional Antennas in Ad Hoc Networks. *Proceeding of IEEE INFOCOM*, Tel-Aviv, Israel, March 2000.
6. T. Korakis, G. Jakllari, and L. Tassiulas. A MAC Protocol for full exploitation of Directional Antennas in Ad Hoc Wireless Networks. *Proceeding of MobiHoc 2003*, pages 98–107, June 1-3, Annapolis, Maryland, USA 2003.
7. M. Takai, J. Martin, A. Ren, and R. Bagrodia. Directional Virtual Carrier Sensing for Directional Antennas in Mobile Ad Hoc Networks. In *ACM MOBIHOC*, Lausanne, Switzerland, June 2002.
8. R.R. Choudhury, R. Ramanathan, and N.H. Vaidya. Using Directional Antennas for Medium Access Control in Ad Hoc Networks. *Proceeding of ACM MobiCom*, Atlanta, Georgia, U.S.A, September 23-28 2002.
9. K. Kobayashi and M. Nakagawa. Spatially Divided Channel Scheme using Sectored Antennas for CSMA/CA - "Directional CSMA/CA". *Proceeding of IEEE PIMRC*, London, September 2000.
10. M. Sekido, M. Takata, M. Bandai, and T. Watomabe. Directional NAV Indicators and Orthogonal Routing for Smart Antenna Based Ad Hoc Networks. *Proceeding of IEEE ICDCSW*, Columbus, U.S.A., June 6-10 2005.
11. T. Ueda, S. Tanaka, D. Saha, S. Roy, and S. Bandyopadhyay. Location-Aware Power-Efficient Directional MAC in Ad Hoc Networks using Directional Antenna. *IEICE Transactions on Communications*, pages 1169–1181, 2005.
12. N.S. Fahmy, T.D. Todd, and V. Kezys. Ad Hoc Networks With Smart Antennas Using IEEE 802.11 - Based Protocols. *Proceeding of IEEE ICC*, April 2002.
13. R. Ramanathan, J. Redi, C. Santivanez, D. Wiggins, and S. Polit. Ad hoc networking with directional antennas: A complete system solution. *IEEE Journal on Selected Areas in Communications*, pages 496–506, vol. 23(3), March 2005.
14. Alaa Muqattash and Marwan M. Krunz. A Distributed Transmission Power Control Protocol for Mobile Ad Hoc Networks. In *IEEE Transactions on Mobile Computing*, pages 113–128, vol.3(2), April-June 2004.
15. Eun-Sun Jung and Nitin H. Vaidya. A Power Control MAC Protocol for Ad Hoc Networks. In *MobiCom'02*, september 23-28, 2002, Atlanta, Georgia.
16. R.R. Choudhury and N.H. Vaidya. Deafness: A MAC Problem in Ad Hoc Networks when using Directional Antennas. *Proceeding of the 2th IEEE International Conference on Network Protocols (ICNP)*, 2004.
17. H. Lebret and S. Boyd. Antenna array pattern synthesis via convex optimization. *IEEE Transactions on Signal Processing*, pages 526–532, vol. 45(3), March 1997.
18. ns-2 network simulator (ver.2).LBL. URL: http://www.isi.edu/nsnam.
19. R. Jain. *The Art of Computer Systems Performance Analysis: Techniques for Experimental Design, Measurement, Simulation and Modeling.* Wiley, New York, 1991.
20. U. Spagnolini. A Simplified Model to Evaluate the Probability of Error in DS-CDMA Systems With Adaptive Antenna Arrays. In *IEEE Transactions on Wireless Communications*, pages 578–587 vol. 3(2), March 2004.

Achieving Flow Isolation in 802.11 Networks with the DTT Scheduler

Rosario G. Garroppo, Stefano Giordano, Stefano Lucetti, and Luca Tavanti

Dipartimento di Ingegneria dell'Informazione, Università di Pisa,
Via Caruso, 16 - Pisa, 56122 - Italy
{r.garroppo, s.giordano, s.lucetti, luca.tavanti}@iet.unipi.it

Abstract. Though the IEEE 802.11 standard has reached wide acceptance, its main access function, the Distributed Coordination Function
(DCF), still suffers from some relevant problems coming from the specific
features of the wireless channel. By means of simulation, we analyse the
performance anomaly and the "inter-flow blocking" problems, highlight-
ing the mechanisms that generate them. Starting from these insights, we
propose a simple centralized channel aware scheduling algorithm, named
Deficit Transmission Time (DTT). The basic principle under the DTT
is measuring the channel quality in terms of frame transmission times.
This measurement is then used to take scheduling decisions that guarantee each downlink flow an equal time share of the channel. The proposed
scheduler has been developed and deployed in a Linux-based prototype
AP to experimentally evaluate its performance. The results clearly show
the improvements introduced by the DTT in terms of flow isolation and
reduction of the effects of the performance anomaly.

1 Introduction

The IEEE 802.11 standard [1] has by now become the most popular technology
for broadband wireless local area networking. As a corollary, we have seen a steep
rise in the efforts to increase system capacity and, more lately, a growing interest
in supporting service differentiation. Nevertheless, one of the most critical factors
driving the efficiency of 802.11 networks is still the ability to overcome the hurdles
imposed by the wireless channel. The capacity of the links is highly variable
in both time and space, thus leading to unpredictable frame delivery ratio and
times. The same 802.11 DCF mode of operation, coupled with the simple "First-
In First-Out" (FIFO) strategy employed at the access point (AP), does not deal
effectively with this problem. In fact, the multi rate capability and the induced
uplink/downlink unbalancing [2] are two aspects that contribute in hindering
network performance.

The 802.11 Distributed Coordination Function (DCF) has been designed to
offer the same long term channel access probability to all stations. In ideal conditions, this translates into an equal portion of the overall effective bandwidth
for each user [3]. On the other hand, as soon as some frame is not correctly received, 802.11 provides for the retransmission of the frame, with the possibility

M. Cesana, L. Fratta (Eds.): Wireless Syst./Network Architect. 2005, LNCS 3883, pp. 47–61, 2006.

of applying a rate fall-back algorithm. This kind of algorithms are freely designed by the manufacturer of each device, that defines the rules for employing more robust but less efficient modulations for the successive transmissions (e.g. the 1 Mbps DBPSK). Such retransmission attempts occupy the channel at the expenses of all other stations. Consequently these stations experiment a sensible reduction in their available bandwidth, regardless of the state of their own links. The performance of the network is thus driven by the station under the worst channel condition. This phenomenon, known as the "performance anomaly" of 802.11 [4], is more general, and also occurs if two (or more) stations simply uses two different transmission rates (e.g. 2 and 11 Mbps, or 11 and 54 Mbps in a mixed 802.11b/g network).

The space-time variation of link quality also has another consequence. Most commercially available APs use a single FIFO queue: all the frames stored after the currently served one must wait for it to be dequeued. This event occurs after either a transmission has been completed successfully or the retransmission limit has been reached. In both cases, these periods are influenced by the state of the channel, or, more precisely, of the link toward the destination station. Thus, the transmission delay experienced by each frame does not depend solely on the number of frames enqueued in front of it, but also on which station those frames are addressed to and in what condition those links are. This issue, which we refer to as "inter-flow blocking", becomes a noteworthy problem especially when there are large or bursty transfers of data, e.g. FTP. These packets, addressed to the same station, might build a continuous bulk in the queue of the AP, hence monopolizing the medium for a long time.

Many researchers agree that a way to overcome the performance anomaly and the inter-flow blocking problems might be a smart scheduling algorithm to be deployed at the AP. Indeed, several schedulers for centralized wireless networks have already been proposed in literature [5][6][7]. Most of them rely on a model of the wireless channel. The links between the AP and the user devices are independent of each other and subject to bursty errors according to a two-state Markov model: link quality is either good (i.e. error-free) or bad (faulty). Unfortunately, this model is sometimes far from the actual channel behaviour, and a system based on it can easily lose its gain. For that reason, a more reliable solution would be centering scheduling decisions on a real measure of the link state.

Starting from these observations, we have designed a centralized scheduling algorithm able to take into account the actual channel behaviour. The main innovation of our scheduler is the way it measures the link quality. This is not appraised with usual metrics, such as signal-to-noise ratio, but is quantified as the time needed to deliver a frame to the destination. Hence, the resource to share is not the total capacity of the channel, but the time the channel is in use. We will show that this approach leads to the important property of flow isolation.

The paper is organized as follows. The scheduler is described in the next Section and evaluated in Section 3. In particular, after an outline of the testbed configuration, Subsection 3.2 introduces the simulation methodology and the obtained results and Subsection 3.3 presents the experimental trial. A thorough discussion of the work and its outcome can be found in Section 4. Finally Section 5 concludes the paper.

2   Description of the DTT Scheduler

The architecture of the DTT scheduler is depicted in Figure 1. The whole framework is inserted on top of the MAC layer, which is in no way modified. A classifier splits outgoing traffic into several queues, on the basis of the destination MAC address. Hence all frames held in the same queue are addressed to the same station. A "bucket" is associated to each queue to account for the over-the-air time of the previous transmissions. As an example, consider a network with three users (refer again to Figure 1). The scheduler will therefore create a queue and a bucket for each associated station (left, center, right). At the end of every frame transmission, the scheduler computes the Cumulative Frame Transmission Time (CFTT). The CFTT comprises all the time spent for the transmission, including all retransmission attempts, backoff and idle periods. The CFTT is also produced when the retry limit is reached with a transmission failure. Given this definition, it can be seen that the CFTT, embracing all the factors that limit the maximum frame rate, is a deterministic and real measure of the link state.

The CFTT is then used to drain the bucket associated to the destination of the transmitted frame. Let us assume that the MAC layer has just completed a transmission of a frame for the station associated to the queue on the right. Then the rightmost bucket is drained with CFTT tokens. Next, this same value is equally divided by the number of non-empty queues and the result loads the related buckets. The bucket whose frame has just been sent, if non-empty, is included in this count. This is needed to give all the queued frames the same treatment. All the buckets coupled with an empty queue are cleared (set to zero) to avoid that some stations, idle for a long period of time, keep a credit/debit that would reduce short-term fairness once they have some new frames to transmit. In our example all queues are non empty, hence the CFTT is divided by three and each bucket is added CFTT/3 tokens. Afterwards, the scheduler picks the next frame from the queue whose associated bucket is the fullest (the one on the left of Figure 1) and hands it over to MAC layer. Only one frame at a time is sent to MAC, and the next frame is not sent until the previous transmission is over. This allows the scheduler to make a precise computation of the CFTT and avoids the MAC buffer to hold any other frame but the one under delivery.

A few things are worth noting. First, the tokens are not related to transmission times with complex formulae, but with a simple and direct one-to-one relationship. Thus they are exactly a transmission time, or a fraction of that. Second, the tokens are an actual measure (not an estimate, nor a prediction) of the channel quality. More retransmissions, possibly at lower bit rates, are needed to deliver the frame to the stations whose channel quality is poor. As a consequence, such destinations get their buckets emptied by larger amounts of

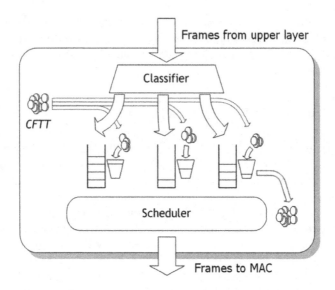

Fig. 1. The architecture of the DTT scheduler

tokens, thus having to wait longer before being chosen for the next transmission. On the contrary, easily reachable destinations get their buckets drained slightly and so they need to be idle for shorter intervals. Under these rules, it is clear that the bucket with more tokens is also the one whose associated queue has transmitted less. The name of the scheduler, Deficit Transmission Time (DTT), aims at reminding just this concept.

3   Performance Evaluation

The proposed scheduler has been evaluated via simulation and experimental trials. The same general scenario, described in the next Subsection, has been used for both kinds of test. The simulation mainly addressed aspects that are difficult to reveal or analyse through a real testbed. In particular, Subsection 3.2 concentrates on the relation between time on air and retransmissions. A short outline of the simulation tool is also given. Then Subsection 3.3 presents the experimental results.

3.1   Description of the Test-Bed

All the trials have been performed with the reference scenario of Figure 2. One access point is connected with a wired link to a server that generates UDP and TCP traffic. The AP then transmits data packets toward two or three stations, depending on the specific try. Traffic is only in the downlink direction, from the AP to the stations. The only exceptions are TCP control packets sent back from the stations to the server. To create various channel conditions, stations are placed at different distances from the AP and in most cases move around. The experimental trials have been run in a typical office environment, whereas the simulation assumed free space propagation.

All stations are equipped with IEEE 802.11b network cards, providing a maximum theoretical throughput of 11 Mbps. For the simulation, a bit rate adjustment strategy has been implemented at MAC layer. In case a frame transmission fails, the bit rate is decreased to 5.5 Mbps, then 2 Mbps and, finally, 1 Mbps. This last value is kept until an ACK is received or the retransmission limit is reached. An analogous strategy is also running on the laptop computers used in the experiment. The RTS/CTS mechanism is disabled in all cases.

Further details are then given when describing each specific experiment.

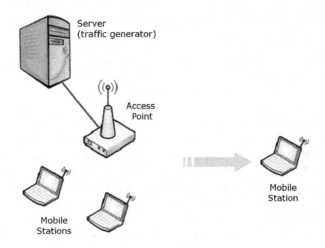

Fig. 2. Reference test-bed for simulation and experimental trials

3.2   Simulation Analysis

We have chosen to employ the OMNeT++ simulator, version 3.0b1 [8], which we have integrated with the Mobility Framework (version 1.0a3) developed at the Technical University of Berlin [9], and with an accurate 802.11b MAC layer, which we have built from scratch. Given that both the simulator and its parts are not yet well established in literature, we carried out some validation tests, comparing the results with known models. Specifically, our baselines were an analytic formula for the maximum achievable throughput with a single transmitting station [10] and Bianchi's performance study [11].

As to the first model, the maximum observed difference between the theoretical value and the simulation is in the order of 0.1%, which can be considered negligible. A very similar behaviour has been observed with regard to Bianchi's model. Figure 3 presents the results for a network of 10 stations working in

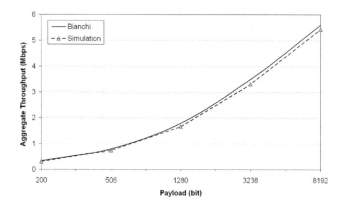

Fig. 3. Validation of the simulation tool: throughput versus payload size for a network of 10 stations transmitting at 11 Mbps

saturation conditions. As it can be seen, the simulator matches pretty closely the theoretical values. Therefore we can conclude that the accuracy level of the employed tool is enough to guarantee reliable trials.

Simulation has been used to examine the correlation between time on air and number of frame retransmissions, for both a simple FIFO based AP and our scheduler. The test was run with two stations, both static, and each receiving a continuous UDP stream of 5 Mbps, with packets of 1440 bytes (same traffic of the experimental tests). The first station (say "A") is very close to the AP and is almost always reached at the first attempt; the other station (say "B") suffers poor channel conditions, and often needs a high number of retries. The time on air is updated after the completion of each transmission cycle, being each increase computed in the same way as described in Section 2 for the CFTT. In other words, each increase is the CFTT of the last frame. The retransmission limit has been set to 4, as suggested in the standard for the used frame length.

Figures 4 and 5 plot the total time on air (lines, left axis) and the number of retries (points, right axis). The simulations run for 60 seconds, but, to have a better insight of the events, only the first 250 ms are shown. In both figures, the time on air looks like a flight of stairs, whose steps are very high for B and very low for A. In correspondence of each step, there is a point (cross or diamond) referring to the number of retries for that frame. The bigger the number of retries, the worst the quality of the link, the higher the step. This is a confirmation of the goodness of the CFTT in accounting for the channel behaviour. By the way, when the number of retries is 4, the frame has been dropped. Note that the relationship between the height of the step and the number of retries is not linear. This is because the CFTT also includes the backoff periods, which are aleatory.

Some more things are worth nothing. The first is that, in Figure 4, the stairs for B are much steeper than those for A, while the number of steps is roughly the same. This means that the FIFO discipline alternates transmissions toward the two stations, but delivering a frame to B takes much longer than

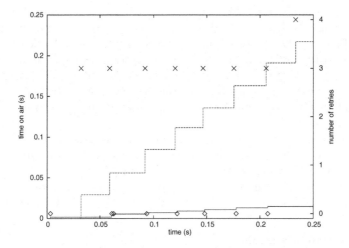

Fig. 4. Detail of time on air (lines) and number of transmission retries (points) for the FIFO discipline. The solid line and the diamonds refer to the nearest node (A), the dashed line and the crosses refer to the farthest node (B).

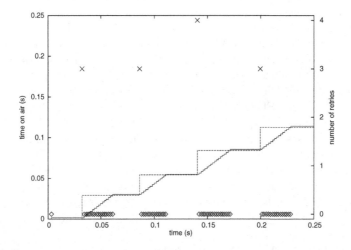

Fig. 5. Detail of time on air (lines) and number of transmission retries (points) for the DTT scheduler. The solid line and the diamonds refer to the nearest node (A), the dashed line and the crosses refer to the farthest node (B).

delivering it to A. Thus, FIFO allows the station in the bad position to occupy the channel most of the time. We can see that the time on air for B is almost 90% of the total. Clearly, since most of this time is wasted in transmission failures and control procedures, we can only expect a very low throughput. On the contrary (see Figure 5), the DTT compensates this unfairness sending more frames to A. For example, at 0.14 seconds, a frame addressed to B is dropped after four retransmissions. This corresponds to an overall channel occupation time of around 30 ms, that includes the time on air, the expired timeouts and the backoff periods. On the other hand, delivering a frame to A takes less than 2 ms. The disparity is evident. Thus, after the far station has received its frame, the DTT scheduler may let the AP transmit around 15 frames to the near station. B can receive its next frame once the allocated times have reached the same level (at around 0.2 s). That is how A's stairs achieves the same steepness of B's, but with much more steps.

Secondly, far less points (diamonds in particular) appears in Figure 4 in comparison to Figure 5. That means that far less frames have been transmitted. Therefore, even without drawing the throughput, we can infer that the FIFO discipline produces a (much) lower aggregate throughput than DTT. This statement will be proved in the next Section, when describing the outcome of the experiments.

3.3   Experimental Trials

For the experimental measures, we have built a software framework to embed in a prototype AP. The scheduler is implemented as a Linux kernel module. It intercepts the packets arriving at the device driver, and stores them internally. It dynamically creates and manages as many queues and buckets as the number of registered stations. The packets are then sent back to the driver one at a time, according to the scheduling decisions. The driver finally passes each frame to the physical device (the WLAN card), which dispatches it over the medium. The driver has also been modified to notify the scheduler of completed frame transmissions and reached retry limits. This is necessary to compute the CFTT.

The scheduler has been installed on a laptop computer, that acts as the prototype AP. For the FIFO discipline we used a commercial AP, that natively implements a single FIFO queue. In the prototype AP, we have also reduced the timeout to force disassociation to 30 seconds (from the default 6 minutes) to have a faster response of the system. This is not strictly related to the DTT scheduler, but it is an optimization that aims at quickly releasing the bandwidth of stations that have clearly become unreachable. The commercial AP is employed with no modifications. UDP traffic has been created with the MGEN traffic generator [12]. Packets are 1440 bytes long. TCP traffic has been produced via a simple file transfer.

In a first try, the AP casts UDP traffic towards two stations. Each UDP downlink flow is at 5 Mbps, therefore the network works in saturation conditions. At the beginning all stations are in a good position. Then, each of them alternatively moves away from the AP, and the quality of the link starts degrading until the AP decides to disassociate it. After a while, the station re-enters in the AP coverage area and reassociates.

Figure 6 plots the throughput seen by two stations when the commercial AP is employed. In this figure the anomaly of 802.11 is clearly visible. As long as the two stations are both close to the AP, they equally share the available bandwidth. However, once one station starts moving away (at around 70 s), the other, that still has a good link, is dragged into bandwidth shortage. Only when

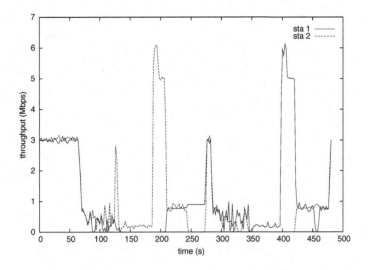

Fig. 6. Throughput seen by two stations receiving UDP traffic with the commercial AP

the far station is disassociated (at 180 s), the other can exploit the full potential of its link. Note the 6 Mbps peaks in the throughput: these are present in the following graphs as well, and are merely due to the backlogged packets.

The improvement introduced by the DTT scheduler is visible in Figure 7. The scenario is the same as before. Again, no difference exists while the stations are close to the AP. Then, when a station is brought progressively farther, the other does not suffer in any way and its throughput remains constant. It can only be noticed a small increment in the fluctuations of throughput that occur when the far station is about to be disassociated (at around 180 s and 380 s). In that case, all frames reach the retransmission limit, thus occupying the channel for the longer time possible. As it happens for the FIFO policy, once the far station is disassociated, the close one gets all the available bandwidth.

Figure 8 presents the outcome for a slightly more complex network. Three terminals have been moved alternatively closer and farther from the AP. As it can be noted, the behaviour of the system is similar to what previously described. The scheduler constantly keeps the throughput of nearby stations to high levels, penalizing the stations that go away. This result definitely increases the confidence on the goodness of DTT for more complex scenarios. Proving large scale scalability, however, is outside of the scope of the paper (also consider that the set of possible patterns of movements, timings and traffic load is extremely vast). The interested reader may refer to [14], which reports the results of a simulation analysis for a large number of VoIP connections.

We have then examined the behaviour of the system with TCP traffic. Two stations are still the sink of two UDP flows, while a third station is the destination of a file transfer. As usual, all the stations go in turn far from the AP. Figure 9 and 10 refers to the commercial AP and the DTT scheduler, respectively. Note

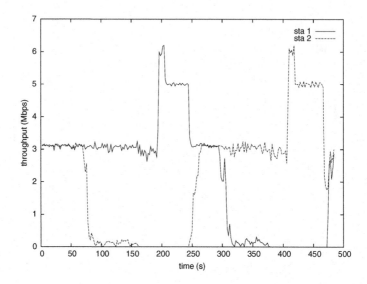

Fig. 7. Throughput seen by two stations receiving UDP traffic with the DTT scheduler

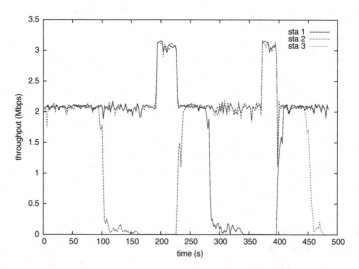

Fig. 8. Throughput seen by three stations receiving UDP traffic with the DTT scheduler

that for the commercial AP we had to lower the rate of the UDP flows to 1 Mbps, i.e. well under the saturation threshold. This is because the TCP session could not even start when injecting the usual 5 Mbps UDP traffic per station. The reason is that when the unique queue gets saturated, TCP starts the congestion control procedures, thus reducing its throughput. UDP traffic however keeps its packet rate constant and quickly monopolizes the queue, eventually causing TCP to starve.

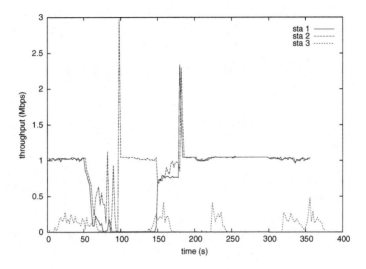

Fig. 9. Throughput seen by two stations receiving UDP traffic (1 & 2) and one station receiving TCP traffic (3) with the commercial AP

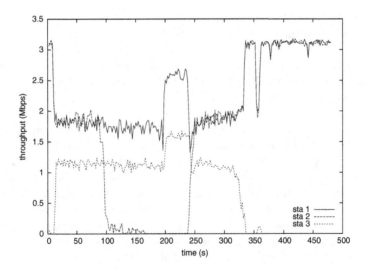

Fig. 10. Throughput seen by two stations receiving UDP traffic (1 & 2) and one station receiving TCP traffic (3) with the DTT scheduler

In spite of the reduced load, the TCP session still has troubles even in sustaining itself. Furthermore, when one of the two UDP-receiving stations moves away, the throughput of TCP falls to zero. In this scenario the impact of our scheduler is even more impressive. The network can handle the original 5 Mbps UDP flows, granting each of them one third of the available bandwidth. Thus each UDP flows settles at slightly less than 2 Mbps, while the TCP settles at

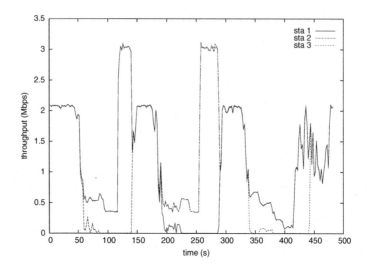

Fig. 11. Throughput seen by three stations receiving UDP traffic with a round robin scheduler

around 1.25 Mbps. Moreover, as expected, the TCP session is not influenced by the movements of the other stations and vice versa.

The last thing to point out about this test is the presence of a hidden uplink flow. This flow is made of all the TCP acknowledgement packets sent by the TCP station to the AP. The effect of this flow is twofold. It reduces the overall available bandwidth (the sum of all the flows is clearly less than the 6.2 Mbps registered in the previous tests) and produces some more fluctuations in the throughput. Both effects disappear as soon as the TCP station moves away (at around 320 s) and the throughput stabilizes at the same levels of Figure 7.

Finally we present the results for a "side test" showing how the presence of multiple queues is not sufficient to prevent the performance anomaly. In the prototype AP, we substituted the DTT scheduler with a simple round robin discipline. Queues are always served in the same order, regardless of the state of the channel and of previous history. Figure 11 plots the throughput for a three station scenario. If we compare this plot with Figure 6 for the commercial AP, we can note just a marginal improvement for the stations near the AP. The undesirable anomaly induced by the far node is still unequivocally present.

4   Discussion

From the trials, it has clearly emerged that the presence of just one station with a poor link to the AP damages all the stations in the network. As mentioned in Section 1, the FIFO-driven AP tries to supply all stations with the same bandwidth. Unfortunately this try gives no benefits neither to the farthest users, whose connection is hampered by the propagation conditions, nor to the other users, whose throughput is brought to the values of the worst station. This is the well known "performance anomaly". We have shed light on it from two different points of view: simulative and experimental (see Figures 4 and 6). From the first, we have highlighted that letting the worst user control the channel results in a high degree of unfairness. In particular, it can happen that, in the worst conditions, the poorest link uses (and wastes) up to 90% of the bandwidth. Hence it was rather easy to infer that network efficiency could only be reduced. The experiments confirmed our deduction. Finally, we have also seen that TCP traffic is very sensitive to this problem (Figure 9).

We have then shown that using multiple queues does improve the performance of the system. However, if the algorithm to choose the next frame to transmit is not smart enough, the improvement is quite marginal. This is the case of the round-robin discipline (Figure 11). The increased complexity does not yield much better results than the original system. Consequently, inserting an "intelligent" scheduler on top of the 802.11 card is a necessary step to significantly improve network capacity. The DTT is such a scheduler.

Figures 7, 8, and 10 prove that the DTT can separate the links toward each station. Therefore, while the far users see their bandwidth severely reduced, the closer stations can still perceive the channel in a good state, thus being able to fully exploit their links. The improvement is noteworthy, and becomes impressive when applied to TCP traffic (Fig. 10). A TCP connection can be kept at high throughput levels from the start to the finish, even if other bandwidth-hungry flows are loading the network. This is true not only under the performance anomaly scenario, but also in ideal conditions, i.e. when all stations have a perfect link to the AP (and the same transmission rate). As mentioned in Section 3.3, the inter-flow blocking brought by the unique FIFO queue induces the TCP to starve under high network loads. Since the DTT splits the traffic in several queues, it can equally divide the bandwidth among all stations. The TCP benefits from this strategy as it is not influenced by the traffic injected by the other flows.

We have already mentioned that, when employing TCP traffic, some packets (the acknowledgements, ACKs) go in the uplink direction. The number and size of ACKs is limited, and the traffic is strongly unbalanced towards the downlink (that is much more crowded than the uplink). This model is also pretty close to real conditions, as most applications (e.g. browsing the Internet, downloading files) generates much more traffic in the downlink direction. We have seen that the DTT still works fine. The confirmation is in Figure 10. The effect of the ACK packets is in the fluctuations in the throughput (besides the reduction in the overall bandwidth, of course).

The remarkable performance of DTT can be explained with the principle that drove its design. Radunovic et al. [13] have found that a desirable objective for network planning should be achieving "proportional fairness" in bandwidth usage. Proportional fairness is a metric that represents a good compromise between two extreme goals: maximum network efficiency (i.e. only the best link is used) and maximum fairness (i.e. equal average rate to all flows). By the way, maximum fairness is the goal of the basic 802.11 strategy. Furthermore, in a multi rate environment like the one generated by different quality of the links, proportional fairness is realized when all the stations use the channel for the same time [3]. A corollary of this proposition is that the flows are isolated: each station gets the maximum of its bandwidth share regardless of the others. And this is exactly what the DTT achieves.

5   Conclusions

The paper has firstly presented a simulation analysis that brought to light the phenomena leading to the performance anomaly and the inter-flow blocking problems of 802.11 networks. Then, starting from these findings, we have proposed the DTT, a simple centralized channel-aware wireless scheduler. The scheduler is based on an indirect but reliable measure of the channel quality: gross frame transmission times. This measure is used to take decisions on the frame to be transmitted next. The final goal is to grant each flow the same amount of channel occupancy time. This allows the DTT to isolate the different traffic flows, letting each flow obtain its downlink channel time occupancy share irrespective of the radio channel quality experimented by the others. In order to prove its feasibility, we have developed a Linux-based prototype AP based on the DTT scheduler. The outcome of the experimental trials has confirmed the efficiency of the proposed solution. In particular, the experimental results pointed out that a system based on the DTT can brightly overcome the well-known performance anomaly of IEEE 802.11 networks and reduce the negative effects of the inter-flow blocking problem at the AP queue.

The presented scheduler has therefore multiple advantages. It runs a simple algorithm, which does not need complex channel modelling or heavy computations. We can therefore envision that it could be hosted on all 802.11 based devices. Moreover it is transparent to both the applications and the network interface cards, thus allowing to use all the deployed hardware without modifications. A simple software/firmware upgrade would be enough to make the APs far more efficient.

Finally, with the introduction of some weights when distributing the tokens, the DTT may offer a suboptimal solution to the downlink traffic differentiation issues of legacy 802.11b APs. Further studies are also planned to change the nature of DTT from centralized to distributed. This will allow an extension of its appealing features to all traffic flows, i.e. in both the downlink and uplink directions. This can be very useful when non-802.11e systems are expected to support delay-sensitive services, such as VoIP.

References

1. ANSI/IEEE Std 802.11, 1999 Edition. Part 11: Wireless LAN Medium Access Control (MAC) and Physical Layer (PHY) specifications.
2. S. Pilosof, R. Ramjee, D. Raz, Y. Shavitt, P. Sinha, *Understanding TCP Fairness over Wireless LAN*, Proc. of IEEE Infocom 2003, San Francisco, April 2003.

3. L. B. Jiang, S. C. Liew, *Proportional Fairness in Wireless LANs and Ad Hoc Networks*, IEEE Wireless Communications and Network Conference, March 2005.
4. M. Heusse, F. Rousseau, G. Berger-Sabbatel, A. Duda, *Performance Anomaly of 802.11b*, Proc. of IEEE Infocom 2003, San Francisco, April 2003.
5. Y. Cao, V.O.K. Li, *Scheduling algorithms in broadband wireless networks*, Proceedings of the IEEE, Volume 89, Issue 1, Jan. 2001, pp. 76-87.
6. P. Bhagwat, A. Krishna, and S. Tripathi, *Enhancing throughput over wireless LANs using channel state dependent packet scheduling*, Proc. of InfoCom 1996, March 1996, pp. 1133-1140.
7. X. Liu, E. K. P. Chong, N. B. Shroff, *Opportunistic Transmission Scheduling With Resource-Sharing Constraints in Wireless Networks*, IEEE Journal on Selected Areas in Communications, Vol. 19, Issue 10, Oct. 2001, pp. 20532064.
8. The OMNeT++ discrete event simulation system. Available at *http://www.omnetpp.org*.
9. The Mobility Framework for OMNeT++. Available at *http://mobility-fw.sourceforge.net/hp/index.html*.
10. R. G. Garroppo, S. Giordano, S. Lucetti, F. Russo, *IEEE 802.11b Performance Evaluation: Convergence of Theoretical, Simulation and Experimental Results*, Networks 2004, Wien, Vol. 1, pp. 405-410.
11. G. Bianchi, *Performance analysis of the IEEE 802.11 distributed coordination function*, IEEE Journal on Selected Areas in Communications, Volume 18, Issue 3, March 2000, pp. 535547.
12. B. Adamson and H. Greenwald, *MGEN User's and Reference Guide*, 2004. Available at *http://mgen.pf.itd.nrl.navy.mil/mgen.html*.
13. B. Radunovic, J. Le Boudec, *Rate Performance Objectives of Multihop Wireless Networks*, IEEE/ACM Trans. on Mobile Computing, Vol. 3, Issue 4, pp. 334349, Oct. 2004.
14. R. G. Garroppo, S. Giordano, S. Lucetti and L. Tavanti, *A measurement-based channel aware scheduler to lessen VoIP capacity degradation in 802.11 networks*, submitted to ICC 2006 and available at: *http://netgroup-serv.iet.unipi.it/reports/dtt-voip-icc06.pdf*.

Subnet Formation and Address Allocation Approach for a Routing with Subnets Scheme in MANETs*

Johann López, José M. Barceló, and Jorge García-Vidal

Technical University of Catalonia (UPC), Department of Computer Architecture,
C/Jordi Girona 1-3, 08034 Barcelona, Spain
{johannl, joseb, Jorge}@ac.upc.edu
http://recerca.ac.upc.edu/XARXES/CompNet/

Abstract. Due to MANET topological routing algorithms are not scalable respect to the number of nodes in the network, we evaluate the potential use of a subnet structure in MANETs. We show scenarios in which a MANET with subnet structure is applicable, present the main technical challenges for the application of this structure and show that a reduction of routing overhead from a factor of N^2 to N^2/k (being N the number of nodes and k the number of subnets) is reachable. In this paper we propose a Subnet Formation and Address Allocation mechanism and evaluate analytically the influence of this proposal on the overhead generated. This solution is only one of the many challenges to fix for putting in use a MANET with subnets structure.

1 Introduction

During the past few years the research efforts in the area of communications have been increased. And more recently an important part of these efforts have been focused on the Mobile Ad-hoc Networking (MANET) [1]. A MANET is mainly a wireless network without infrastructure, in which the nodes must behave simultaneously as a host and as a router.

One of the main research issues has been the routing. Routing in MANETs can be classified in topology based routing, and Position based routing approaches. The latter determines relative or absolute positions (e.g. GPS) of the nodes in the network. On the other hand, the former approach determines the routes according to topological information to achieve connectivity. Two of the main protocols obtained in the routing area are the well-known AODV [2] (reactive) and the OLSR [3] (proactive) topology based protocols.

One of the main drawbacks of the topological based approaches is the scalability in reaction to the number of nodes (limiting factor). In MANET every node in the network requires to participate as a router and the topological protocols rely on flooding of the control packets through the entire network to create and maintain routes. If the number of nodes grows largely, the number of control packets will increase drastically, increasing the overhead in the network, consuming the scarce bandwidth in the network, and

---

* This research was supported by the Spanish Ministry of Education and Science under the CICYT TEC2004-06437-C05-05 project and by the European NoE EuroNGI project.

therefore reducing the throughput. Without taking into account the mobility of the nodes, this scenario is something similar to what happened to the ARPAnet at the beginning.

The logical solution to reduce this routing overhead could be having a structure like the one defined in Internet, in which the nodes are aggregated into subnets to be handled as a single entity for routing purposes. Unfortunately, the difficulty to apply this subnetting structure in MANETs is high, due to their dynamic and distributed nature. However, there are scenarios in MANETS in which the nodes can be grouped following physical or environmental constraints to apply the aforementioned structure. These formed groups can be considered subnets of a MANET, giving the chance of representing multiple routes of a large number of nodes by a single route. Since the routing information is cutting down, a reduction in the overhead may be obtained [5]. Some examples of the mentioned scenarios are the Wireless Mesh Networks and the wireless emergency networks [4].

The main challenges for applying this subnetting structure are: the address allocation under mobility scenarios, the dynamic creation and removal of subnets, and finally the maintenance of the already established sessions when a node moves from one subnet to other (mobility between subnets).

In this paper we propose a mechanism for the subnet formation and address allocation for the mentioned structure (MANET with subnets). In addition we present a preliminary analytical evaluation to know its influence on the overhead estimation produced by routing with subnets structure. We particularly obtain the cost (in number of packets) generated by the change of subnets factor.

The rest of the paper is organized as follows: a generic description of the MANET with a subnetting structure and an analytical evaluation of the expected overhead for such structure are given in section 2. Section 3 shows the related work and previous attempts of address allocation mechanisms for MANETs. Then, we present the basic idea and a description of the proposed mechanism in section 4. Analytical evaluation of the influence of the proposed approach on the overhead is presented in section 5. Finally, we have the conclusions and future work.

2   Subnetting Structure Description and Overhead Estimation

We are proposing a structure that takes advantage of the fact that currently the nodes in a MANET can be grouped following physical or environmental constraints.

2.1   Structure Description

Figure 1 shows the scenario in which our proposal is based. Nodes form an area of size A around a leader node, which is a node with some extra capabilities (e.g. transmission rate, power supply, speed of movement, etc). The formed area will correspond to an IP subnet of dynamic size, e.g. based on the number of nodes attached to the area; it means that the nodes in that area will share the same IP address prefix (IP addresses are used like host locators). And when a node moves from one area to another has to acquire a new IP address corresponding to the new IP subnet.

The aforementioned description of our scenario shows clearly the main challenges that must be solved to apply a structure with subnets. They are: the subnet formation and address acquisition, the intra-subnet routing and the inter-subnet routing, and the mobility of nodes between subnets. We can take advantage of the extra capabilities of the leader node to solve these technical issues efficiently, see figure 2. The Mobility of the nodes into the subnet is not a critical issue since it could be handled by the current proposed MANET routing protocols (AODV, or OLSR), however a mobility management between subnets is necessary. Additionally, some enhancements to the current MANET routing protocol are needed to allow address aggregation mechanisms, and interaction between them and the subnet formation and address allocation mechanism.

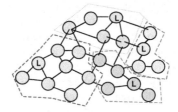

Fig. 1. MANET with nodes grouped to form subnets

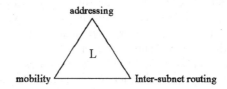

Fig. 2. The nodes with extra capabilities are the corner stone to solve efficiently the technical issues of applying subnets in MANETs

In this paper we focus on the solution of the subnet formation and address allocation issue, and let the solution of the other challenges for a future work.

2.2 Overhead Estimation

We use some well-known analytical models of reactive and proactive routing protocols [10], hierarchical routing [12], and cellular systems [11] to validate the overhead of the proposed routing structure. The model for MANET routing protocols let us estimate the control overhead generated in a fixed network case, and the control overhead for a mobile case. After that, we apply some hierarchical routing (subnetting) parameters to the model, estimating the new control overhead for a fixed network case. Then, with the expressions obtained and the cellular system models we can estimate the control overhead generated by the subnetting and the mobility.

In hierarchical routing any node keeps complete routing information about nodes that are close to it, and lesser information about nodes located further away from it. The reduction of the routing information is achieved partitioning the network (creating subnets). We propose to form subnets with a 2 level hierarchical clustering based scheme [12], assuming all the nodes are uniformly distributed in the network and into each subnet for the scope of this analysis.

To guarantee full connectivity in the network one node at least must maintain a route to each node into the same subnet, and a route to each subnet in the network. From this, the network must have $(k-1)+N/k$ routes per node (where k is the number of subnets in the network, and N is the number of nodes in the network). Therefore, the first advantage in subnetting is the reduction of the routing table and the saving in the look up algorithm.

2.2.1 For Reactive Protocols

We use the parameters defined in [10] to model the network: the number of nodes N, the average live time of a link T_b ($T_b = 1/\mu$, where μ is the link breakage rate) to model the mobility, the average length of a route L which depends mainly of the shape of the network. Additionally, the model assumes that μ and L remain constants, and the network always remains connected.

The parameters that model the reactive protocols are: the average number of route creation λ (Route Requests), and the average number of active routes per node a, such active route is a pair where the source continuously sends packets to the destination; the average number of emissions for a route request (could include the route reply messages) B_r, and the route request optimization factor o_r, which depends on the network and the traffic parameters ($o_r = B_r/N$). For a pure flooding protocol, if we include the Route Reply from the destination, we get that; $o_r = 1 + j / N$, where j is the number of reply messages.

When we introduce subnets to the reactive protocol reactive protocol model, we include the average number of route creation λ_I by a node to other nodes into the same subnet, the average number of route creation λ_E by a node to other subnets, and the average length of a route q to another subnet.

Applying these new parameters to the model obtained in [10] for a fixed network case, we have $N\lambda_I$ route requests for routes to nodes into the same subnet produced each second, and $N(k-1)\lambda_E$ route requests per second for routes to nodes located in other subnets. Therefore, the overhead generated by these requests can be expressed by

$$o_r \lambda_I \frac{N^2}{k} + o_r \lambda_E (k-1)N\left(\frac{N}{k}+q\right) + S \tag{1}$$

Where S represents the cost of finding out the routes to other subnets $S=(k-1)2N/k$. Assuming that the probability of having a route to a subnet is much higher (cache probability ≈ 1) than having a route to a particular node, this cost is only paid few times, therefore during a period of time long this value will be small (because is not a rate). Since the q value is very small compared with the number of nodes N in the network, and S is constant during the time, we consider these two values does not dominate the overhead (are not relevant) for our analysis. From this we have

$$O(N) \approx o_r \lambda_I \frac{N^2}{k} + o_r \lambda_E (k-1)\frac{N^2}{k} \tag{2}$$

Since the nodes are uniformly distributed, and assuming that λ_I and λ_E are independent from each other and have the same probability occurrence, we can represent $\lambda = \lambda_I + (k-1)\lambda_E$. Expressing (4) in terms of λ we obtain

$$O(N) \approx o_r \lambda \frac{N^2}{k} \tag{3}$$

Now, to model the overhead due to the mobility we divide it in two components

$$O(N) = O_s(N) + O_H(N) \tag{4}$$

The first term $O_S(N)$ represents the overhead due to the mobility of the nodes into the subnet. And the second one $O_H(N)$ represents the overhead due to the change of subnet. This overhead is produced because each time that a node changes of subnet, it must change its address. The detailed process to obtain $O_H(N)$ is explained detailed in section 5.1.

Since the link breakage is assumed in our model like the main component of the overhead in reaction to mobility, after adding subnets to the reactive protocol model we will have two cases. The first case appears when the broken link corresponds to a link between two nodes that are into the same subnet, and for this case the route repair will be local into the subnet. In that case a flooding in the subnet is enough to repair the route, therefore, it is not necessary to repair from the source. The second one is presented when the broken link corresponds to a link between two nodes that are located in different subnets. For this case the route has to be repaired from the source of the route. If we have aNL active links in the network; the overhead $O_S(N)$ due to mobility could be represented by

$$o_r \mu a L \frac{N^2}{k} \leq O_s(N) \leq o_r \mu a L N^2 \tag{5}$$

Due to the difficult to quantify exactly the emissions of control packets in reaction to mobility, we decided to express it between two quotes, corresponding each one to the previous cases (the best and worst). We have to note that often several routes have identical destinations and the majority can be repaired locally, meaning that the overhead will be close to the lower bound the mayor part of the time

2.2.2 For Proactive Protocols

For the proactive model we define, [10]: the packets for proactively discovering the local topology (hello packets) emitted by a node per second h_p, the topology broadcast packets emitted by a node during a second for allowing global knowledge of the topology t_p. These parameters are expressed in terms of rates. To react to topological changes the active next hop AN_p is defined; it corresponds to the average number of active links per node, and it is used to evaluate what topology changes may trigger additional control traffic. Since proactive protocols can take advantage from their knowledge of the topology in order to optimize broadcasting, a broadcast optimization factor o_p is denoted ($o_p = B_p/N$), where B_p denotes the average number of emissions to achieve a topology broadcast.

When we add subnets, a mechanism to find out the routes to reach other subnets is needed. Within the scope of this study we introduce the parameter φ to represent the cost of finding out these routes, and leaving the description and evaluation (identify the value of the parameter φ) of this mechanism for a future study.

With the proactive protocol, each node emits h_p hello messages per second, and now each t_p is emitted to the nodes that are close to it (to all the members of the subnet). The overhead generated is given by

$$O(N) = h_p N + o_p t_p \frac{N^2}{k} + \varphi \qquad (6)$$

In addition, the parameter φ includes the cost of emitting the routes to other subnets to each node. Despite of all this routing information have a cost, we can expect this cost is much lower compared to the overhead without hierarchical routing, because this cost does not depend of a N^2 factor like in the proactive and reactive protocols, and because the procedure can take advantage of the partial knowledge of the topology and the characteristics of the scenario.

The overhead generated in reaction to mobility is represented by the expression (4) where the second component $O_H (N)$ is calculated in section 5.1, and the component $O_s (N)$ will be expressed by

$$O_s(N) = o_p \mu A N_p \frac{N^2}{k} + \varphi \qquad (7)$$

The first part corresponds to the overhead generated by a link breakage, such that the topology is only updated locally. Here is evident that a local topology change does not have to generate control overhead in the entire network, because certainly the nodes located further away are not affected by these changes. The main idea behind this assumption is that if a node knows how to reach a subnet, it is not necessary to know how the topology in that subnet is. This assumption is similar to the idea of Internet in which an Autonomous System (AS) does not know how is organized another AS and only knows how to reach that AS. Again, we have the parameter φ in the second part of the expression, to represent the overhead generated in reaction to a link breakage between subnets.

A complete description of the analytical evaluation is given in [14]. Table 1 summarizes the results obtained in [14] and shows the comparison between the overhead model for currents MANET (reactive and proactive) protocols with a flat structure, see [10]; and the models obtained for the same protocols applying a structure with subnets.

Here we notice the $g\eta N$ term placed in the subnet columns. This term represents the overhead generated due to the change of subnet, and we remark it because it is directly related with the address allocation mechanism and it will be referred in section 5 again.

We would like to emphasize that after adopting the structure with subnets the dominant term of the overhead expressions is reduced from $O(N^2)$ to $O(N^2/k)$. In addition we note that reaching this overhead reduction implies a cost represented by a higher complexity of the network an extra generation of control packets. However, we estimate that the reduction of the overhead is so high that this cost could be amortized by the new structure while keeping an important reduction. Here, it is obvious that a trade off between the number of subnets and the cost (network complexity) must be reached. But this issue is for a future work.

Table 1. Comparison of the overhead model for reactive and proactive routing protocols with a flat structure against the same protocol with subnets structure. The first row corresponds to the fixed case models, while the second row corresponds to the models with mobility.

Reactive Protocol		Proactive protocol	
Flat Structure	With Subnets	Flat Structure	With Subnets
$o_r \lambda N^2$	$\approx o_r \lambda \dfrac{N^2}{k}$	$h_p N + o_p t_p N^2$	$\approx h_p N + o_p t_p \dfrac{N^2}{k} + \varphi$
$o_r \mu a L N^2$	$\approx o_r \mu a L \dfrac{N^2}{k} + g\eta N$	$o_p \mu A N_p N^2$	$\approx o_p \mu A N_p \dfrac{N^2}{k} + \varphi + g\eta N$

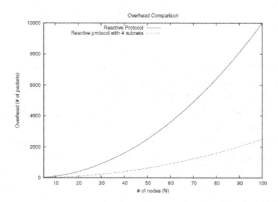

Fig. 3. Overhead comparison between a reactive protocol and the same protocol with subnets

Figure 3 reveals clearly the magnitude of the expected overhead reduction when a structure with subnets is used. This figure shows a comparison of the overhead obtained for a reactive protocol (fixed case) with a flat structure against the overhead obtained for the same protocol applying a structure with subnets. These results justify our current efforts in the subnetting integration to MANETs.

Additionally, a reduction of the topology packets (bandwidth) for the case of proactive protocols, and a reduction in the delay incurred to acquire a route for the case of reactive protocols could be expected.

3   Related Work

There are proposals on layer 2 mobility and layer 2/3 cluster election mechanisms (e.g. [24]). However, we have centred our efforts in L3 configuration mechanisms.

The available address configuration mechanisms for ad-hoc networks can be static or dynamic. For the static approach the nodes have a manual or predefined address. This simple mechanism works well in non-mobile environments. However, in a mobile environment (like in MANETs) dynamic address allocation approaches are more desirable. The dynamic approaches can be divided in stateless, which do not maintain any allocation table (e.g. Duplicate Address Detection) or stateful, which maintain an either dynamic or static allocation table (e.g. DHCP).

Reference [13] gives an overview of the challenges of address auto-configuration in MANETs, present current approaches, and discusses their advantages and drawbacks. Some of the issues presented in [13] to take into account during the address auto-configuration is: the management of the resource address space, the latency of the configuration mechanism must be low, and the network partition and merging. From the correct use of the address space, depends on the allocation of a unique network address. Eventually the corresponding address may be de-allocated when a node leaves the network (or the address could have a time to live). A small address space is more efficient in terms of energy and bandwidth, which represents another advantage of the dynamic addresses. The configuration process should be fast, because without an address the node cannot participate in unicast communications. Although the network partitioning and merging is the major challenge in address configuration, in our scenario this issue is not a challenge because the subnets are assumed static (leader nodes static) and not overlapped. It means, each time that a node leaves its current subnet, it can attach to a closer subnet (another leader node).

Regardless of the fact that the main address configuration approaches for MANET are referenced in [13] we will give a short description of the more relevant. ZERO conf [15] is a stateful, with a central allocation table, and IPv6 approach. The initiator serves as Address Agent (AA), constructing and assigning addresses to the unconfigured nodes. The address is based on its own MAC address and the MAC address of the requester. The initiator is dynamically elected and this node maintains the allocation table, containing already assigned Ipv6 addresses, corresponding MAC addresses, and life times. The main drawback of this approach is the high consume of bandwidth due to the overhead generated (flooding large messages periodically).

MANET conf [8] is a stateful approach, which uses a common distributed allocation table (cdat). It is one of the first auto-configuration proposals for MANETs. A new node entering to the network (requester) chooses an already configured node as the initiator which performs address allocation in its behalf. All other nodes know a route to the initiator and can forward their responses to it. If the proposal is accepted by all the member of the MANET, the proposed address is assigned to a newly arrived node. Otherwise, another candidate IP address is chosen and the process is repeated. Ultimately, the initiator conveys the result of the address allocation operation to the requester. Even if the requester moves, except for the initiator none of the nodes have to track the requester. Thus, the initiator acts as a proxy for the requester until an IP address is assigned and packets can be routed to the requester. Despite of the main drawbacks of this approach are related with the network partitioning and merging issues and this drawback is not relevant for our interests, this approach requires a flooding based synchronization process to inform about new assigned address, it would consume a large amount of bandwidth.

The IP Address Assignment using Binary Split [7] is a stateful approach which uses a multiple distributed allocation table (mdat). In this approach every node has a disjoint set of IP addresses that it can assign to a new node without consulting any other node in the network. In addition to the address, the initiator assigns half of its allocation table to the requester (arriving node). Nodes synchronize periodically to keep record of IP address assignment in the entire network and to detect IP address leaks. This synchronization procedure requires periodic and reliable flooding, at the cost of higher protocol overhead.

Prophet [16] is a stateful approach with a multiple distributed allocation function. Each node maintains a function f(n) and a state value to generate a sequence of numbers. This function generates the same number only at very large intervals, and the probability that f(n) returns to the same number for two different state values is very low. The initiator use f(n) to generate an address. Address conflicts are prohibited by calculating potential future allocations using f(n). The initiator updates its State value, and assigns the address a state value and a list of predicted conflicts to the requester, which can now act as an initiator itself to configure un-configured nodes. The main problem is to find a function that can fulfil the requirements (for a realistic size). Even in IPv6, the 64 bit interface ID space is exhausted after 64 assignment by the first node, and f(n) may generate duplicate addresses.

The IPv6 autoconf [6] is a stateless approach, which uses Duplication Address Detection (DAD) with limited flooding. It is a hierarchical approach based on so-called leader nodes. These leader nodes are responsible for paths of the address configuration of other nodes. During the DAD, flooding is needed. However, in order to limit the flooding to a bounded area, broadcast links are "emulated". Each node defines its broadcast link, called scope, as the group of nodes, which are less or equal than rs hops away. A hierarchy is established by the leader nodes that configure a group of nodes by issuing Router Advertisements. The Random Source ID (RS-ID) option is defined for the Neighbour Discovery messages. An address conflict is recognized if a node receives a Neighbour Solicitation message with its address and a RS-ID that the node has never used. This mechanism is based on the IPv6 Stateless address auto-configuration [9], and basically an extension of the Neighbour Discovery Protocol (NDP) to make it applicable to MANET. This mechanism is too complex, and consumes long time before a node can transmit data (high latency). Furthermore, it does not avoid the flooding to the entire network. Although of the drawbacks, some issues of this approach are useful for our work.

The Proactive Auto-configuration (PAA) [17] is a stateless approach, which uses strong DAD mechanism. It is integrated with the routing protocol (OLSR). PAA takes advantage of the fact that nodes are already members of a MANET domain, running a proactive protocol, and already have a relatively complete understanding of the topology. The nodes are well suited to allocate IP addresses that have a high probability of currently not being used by any other node in the network. PAA also performs strong DAD to ensure that no other node is currently configured or in process of configuring itself with a duplicate address. This is done by flooding the entire network, and the underlying routing protocol is used for it. The approach defines a client and server mode. An un-configured node will run the PAA client mode to contact already configured nodes, which run the PAA server mode. The proxy solution works well in terms of bandwidth, at the cost of mobility (reliability). Since the broadcast solution relies on flooding, it generates a large overhead, but allowing high degree of mobility.

The Hybrid Centralized Query Based Auto-configuration HCQA[18] is an hybrid approach (performs DAD with a centrally maintained allocation table). In HCQA a node selects an address by itself and verifies it uniqueness with the QDAD. If the DAD is successful, it configures the address and registers it with a dynamically elected Address Authority (AA), which inserts the new address into its allocation table. This AA is also able to defend an already allocated address on behalf of the other node by sending an AREP message. This approach fulfils many of the particularities existent in our scenario. This approach has a short latency, but the overhead is still large during the initiation.

Despite of the diverse and large amount of proposed approaches for address auto-configuration in MANETs none of them satisfy the requirements and characteristics of our scenario. And the reason is that these approaches are not thought to take into account the subnet formation and maintenance. Now is evident the need of an approach that fulfils the requirements and takes advantage of the particularities of our proposed scenario.

4   Subnet Formation and Address Allocation

Our proposal is made basically, taking the some of the former mechanisms that better satisfies the requirements of our scenario. This proposal is a hybrid approach, where Duplicate Address Detection works in conjunction with a multi-central allocation table. Each of these tables is located in a leader node. Additionally it may be used either with IPv4 or IPv6.

Since the subnetting relies on the relationship of the addresses of the nodes, the subnet formation is composed of a grouping and address allocation mechanism. We now explain a grouping and address acquisition procedure.

4.1   Grouping the Nodes

To group the nodes some assumptions are made. One leader node is fixed for each subnet. This leader is designated and configured statically. In any case, a distributed cluster-head election mechanism can also be introduced. Every node knows each of its one-hop neighbours, using a hello message exchange protocol. The subnet is formed around the leader node. It means that each node will be configured with the same address prefix and register its address with the leader node, which is closer (in distance terms) to it. The metric used to determine the distance is the number of hops (nodes) needed to communicate the node to the leader. The mechanism defined in the leader nodes to inform their prefix is explained later. Here it is evident that the leader node must be a node with some extra capabilities, like low mobility, higher computational power, energy supply, etc. An example of a leader node could be a node that resides in a truck or another kind of vehicle.

4.2   Address Configuration

Figure 4 illustrates the message format defined during the entire procedure. The message is sent over UDP, which is encapsulated in IP (v4 or v6). The fields correspond to the information needed by the nodes to complete successfully the configuration procedure. The Distance to L indicates how far away (# of hops) is located the node that generates the message from its Leader. The Leader ID announces the subnet prefix. The Sequence Number identifies the same messages generated by different nodes within the same coverage area. The Solicited Target Address informs the requested address during the duplicate address detection phase. The type field identifies the type of message. We have defined 4 types (hello request, hello reply, duplicated address detection and address confirmation or rejection) of messages. Finally we have specified an optional field for future enhancements (e.g. to announce the time to live of the requested address).

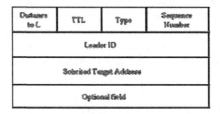

Fig. 4. Message format used during the address configuration and subnet formation process

The address configuration process is composed by three stages: the leader configuration and detection, the node address construction, and the duplicated address detection.

4.2.1 Leader Detection and Selection

Once the leader node is designated (statically or dynamically), it begins the procedure broadcasting Hello (beacon) messages. These hello messages are broadcasted periodically, such that a node located one–hop away from the leader listens these beacon messages, acquiring the information needed from them to decide the membership to a subnet. When a new node starts up or arrives to the network it will broadcast a hello request message.

With the information obtained from the hello messages, a node chooses the Leader that is closer to it. Since each leader identifies the different available subnets in a defined area, and the node aggregation relies on the relationship of their addresses, the node takes the subnet prefix of the received message.

4.2.2 Node Address Construction

Once a leader is chosen, the node constructs a tentative address that is based on the subnet prefix and the interface identifier. The interface identifier could be calculated from the MAC-address of an IEEE 802.x interface. The Extended Universal Identifier defined by IEEE cannot be guaranteed due to different causes (e.g. manufacturers using unregistered 802.x addresses). For this reason a duplication address detection phase is needed.

4.2.3 Duplicate Address Detection

After that, the node issues an address duplication detection message addressed to the leader and with the well-known unspecified address as source IP address. The tentative address is used as Solicited Target Address. Once this message arrives to the leader, it looks up within its database to verify if the tentative address is already assigned or not. If the address is available, the Leader replies with an address confirmation message to the requesting node including a time to live for this tentative address. Otherwise the leader node replies with a deny message. When the node receives the confirmation message, it configures the tentative address as its local address. After configuration, the node begins to forward hello messages in order to extent the coverage of the subnet.

Figure 5 summarizes the address configuration approach.

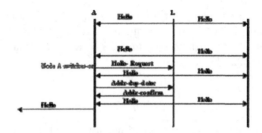

Fig. 5. Message exchange of the address configuration process

The procedure is susceptible for future enhancements. An important and needed enhancement for our approach will be the integration with the routing protocol, with the objective of reducing the overhead generated by both protocols (e.g. sharing the hello messages exchange mechanism).

5 Performance Evaluation

Certainly, as we explained in section 2.1, when the network is divided in subnets, we are introducing a new disturbing factor, which is the movement of nodes between subnets. Now, the nodes moving to others subnets must reconfigure their current IP address with a new one corresponding to the new IP subnet.

In table 1, we obtained analytically an estimation of the overhead produced, when one node moves to another subnet, and that estimation was represented by the term $g\eta N$. Here, we explain how this term affects the analytical expressions.

5.1 Obtaining the $g\eta N$ Term

In a subnet the nodes are grouped according to its proximity (number of hops) to a leader node, and they will cover an area (the subnet scope) of variable size. If we assume a subnet (area) of fixed size, the change of subnet looks similar to the change of cell in a cellular system.

For the scope of this analysis, we are particularly interested in calculating the probability of subnet (area) boundary crossing. According to [19], an approximate evaluation for cellular system performance is obtained through models based on fluid flow assumptions. The following conditions are needed to derive a simple expression:

- The nodes and their traffic are uniformly distributed over a given subnet (area or cell).
- The nodes have a mean velocity of v and their directions of movements are uniformly distributed over $[0,2\pi]$

Under these conditions the subnet crossover rate η is given by,

$$\eta = v\frac{P}{\pi S} \tag{8}$$

Where P corresponds to the perimeter of the subnet, and S is the area of the subnet.

We denote the time spent by a node within a given subnet (dwell time) [20], [21]by the random variable T_h. The mean dwell time $E(T_h)$ can be calculated by knowing the subnet crossover rate [22], [23], that is

$$E(T_h) = \frac{1}{\eta} \tag{9}$$

which corresponds to the average number of handoffs. Additionally, the dwell time is assumed exponentially distributed (the residing time of a node in the actual subnet is not related with the residing time of the same node in a previous subnet, memory less system). So, the probability of subnet boundary crossing is given by

$$P(T_h) = \eta e^{-\eta t} \tag{10}$$

If our Address Acquisition procedure generates g packets in average, and if we have N/k nodes per subnet, we will have $kh\eta(N/k)$ packets in average due to the change of subnet in the entire network. Now, we can represent the overhead due to change of subnet by

$$O_H(N) = g\eta N \tag{11}$$

5.2   Calculating the Number of Configuration Packets

Each time that a node changes of subnet, it has to replace its current IP address by another one corresponding to the new IP subnet, therefore, the address allocation mechanism has a huge influence on the overhead produced.

As the address allocation is tied with the subnet formation mechanism, we have obtained the number of packets (overhead) generated for each mechanism.

5.2.1   Subnet Formation Overhead
If we represent the rate of the hello messages generated by the leader nodes by β, when the network starts up, we will have βk packets per second, where k is the

number of subnets in the network and it is exactly the same that the number of leader nodes in the network.

After all nodes in the MANET get configured, $\beta(k+N)$ packets per second are generated in the network for the subnet maintenance.

Since the hello emission process will be integrated with the routing protocol for the local topology discovery procedure in a future enhancement, the overhead produced by this mechanism is not considered in the analysis of the next section, because from now this overhead is counted as part of the overhead generated by the routing protocol.

5.2.2 Address Configuration Overhead

Due to the explanation presented in last section, the overhead produced by this mechanism is basically the exchange of DAD and address confirmation messages, between the requesting node and the leader node.

The average number of hops from a node to its leader node into a subnet is represented by d_k ($2d_k$ = average diameter of the subnet), and ω represents the average number of lost packets due to the node density and the traffic load in the network, such that if the node density increases, the packet loss also increases.

This mechanism will generate $2d_k N/K + 2d_k\omega$ configuration packets in a subnet. The total number of configuration packets in the network can be expressed by

$$2d_k N + 2d_k \omega \tag{12}$$

Replacing (12) in (11) we obtain that the influence on the address configuration mechanism on the overhead produced by the change of subnet factor can be expressed by

$$O_H(N) = \eta(2d_k N + 2d_k \omega) \tag{13}$$

Since the parameter d_k has a direct connection with the number of subnets in the network, its value is reduced as the number of subnets in the network increases. From the expression (13) we can observe that the   impact of the address configuration mechanism over the overhead is low.

6 Conclusions

We have proposed and presented a subnetting structure for MANETs, with the objective of reducing the overhead generated by the topological routing protocols. Moreover, we have identified the main challenges to solve for making that proposal viable. And lastly we have proposed and evaluated the influence of a Subnet Formation and Address Allocation approach on the overhead. This is only one of the many challenges to solve before putting in use a routing with subnets scheme in a MANET.

We notice that this study presents only a partial solution for the Subnet Formation and address allocation question but the remaining challenges continues unsolved. Our current and future efforts are addressed to solve these unsolved challenges. Actually, we are optimizing the presented approach, including some enhancements like the integration with the routing protocol, to share the hello message exchange mechanism to reduce the overhead generated. The focus of our future work is to solve the mobility of nodes between subnets, the intra-subnet routing, and the inter-subnet routing (modifications to the existent routing protocols).

References

1. Mobile Ad-hoc Networks working group IETF: http://www.ietf.org/html.charters/manet-charter.html.
2. C. Perkins, E. Belding-Royer, and S. Das. Ad hoc Vector (AODV) Routing. RFC 3561, July 2003.
3. T. Clausen and P. Jacquet, "Optimized Link State Routing Protocol", RFC 3626, October 2003.
4. H. Aiache et al, "WIDENS System Specification", Deliverable 2.2, IST WIDENS, June 2004
5. C. Shiflet, E. M. Belding-Royer and C. E. Perkins. "Address Aggregation in Mobile Ad hoc Networks." Proceedings of the IEEE International Conference on Communications (ICC), Paris, France, June 2004.
6. K. Weniger, M. Zitterbart. "IPv6 Auto configuration in Large Scale Mobile Ad-Hoc Networks", Proceedings of European Wireless 2002, Florence, Italy, Feb. 2002.
7. M. Mohsin, R. Prakash. "IP Address Assignment in a Mobile Ad Hoc Network", IEEE Military Communications Conference (MILCOM 2002), volume 2, pp. 856-861, October 2002.
8. S. Nesargi, R. Prakash. "MANETconf: Configuration of Hosts in a Mobile Ad Hoc Network". Proceedings of INFOCOM, 2002.
9. S. Thomson and T. Narten, "IPv6 Stateless Address Auto configuration" in RFC2462 (December 1998).
10. L. Viennot, P. Jacquet, T. H. Clausen, "Analyzing control traffic overhead versus mobility and data traffic activity in mobile Ad-Hoc network protocols," presented at ACM Wireless Networks journal (Winet), 2004.
11. B. Jabbari, "Teletraffic aspects of evolving and next-generation wireless communication networks," Personal Communications, IEEE [see also IEEE Wireless Communications], vol. 3, pp. 4, 1996.
12. L. Kleinrock, F. Kamoun, "Hierarchical Routing for Large Networks: Performance Evaluation and Optimization," Computer Networks, Vol. 1, pp. 155-174, 1977.
13. K. Weniger, M. Zitterbart, "Address Autoconfiguration in Mobile Ad Hoc Networks: Current Approaches and Future Directions", IEEE Network Magazine Special issue on 'Ad hoc networking: data communications & topology control', Jul 2004.
14. J. López, J. M. Barceló, J. García-Vidal, "Analysing the overhead in Mobile ad-hoc network with a hierarchical Routing structure", International Working Conference Performance Modelling and Evaluation of Heterogeneous Networks' (HET-NETS'05), June 2005.
15. M. Günes and J. Reibel, "An IP Address Configuration Algorithm for Zeroconf Mobile Multihop Ad Hoc Networks," Proc. International Workshop Broadband Wireless Ad-Hoc Networks and Services, Sophia Antipolis, France, Sept. 2002.
16. H. Zhou, L. M. Ni, and M. W. Mutka, "Prophet Address Allocation for Large Scale Manets," Proc. IEEE INFOCOM 2003, San Francisco, CA, Mar. 2003.
17. Andreas Tønnesen, Andreas Hafslund, Paal Engelstad, IP Address Autoconfiguration for Proactive Mobile Ad Hoc Networks, Proc. ICC, Paris, June 2004.

18. Y. Sun and E. M. Belding-Royer, "Dynamic Address Configuration in Mobile Ad-Hoc Networks," UCSB tech. rep. 2003-11, Santa Barbara, CA, June 2003.
19. B. Jabbari, "Teletraffic aspects of evolving and next-generation wireless communication networks," Personal Communications, IEEE [see also IEEE Wireless Communications], vol. 3, pp. 4, 1996.
20. D. Hong and S S Rappaport, "Traffic Model and Performance Analysis for Cellular Mobile Radio Telephone Systems with Prioritized and Non-prioritized Hand-off Procedures," IEEE Trans Vehfc Tech, vol 35,no 3, Aug 1986, pp. 77-92.
21. S. S. Rappaport, "The Multiple-Call Hand-off Problem in High-Capacity Cellular Communications Systems," IEEE Trans. Vehic. Tech., Aug. 1991, vol. 40, no. 3, pp. 546-57.
22. G. Morales-Andres and M. Villen-Altamirano, "An Approach to Modelling Subscriber Mobility in Cellular Radio Networks," Telecom Forum87, Geneva, Switzerland, Nov. 1987.
23. R. Thomas, H. Gilbert, and G. Maziotto, "Influence of the Moving of the Mobile Stations on the Performance of a Radio Mobile Cellular Network," Proc. 3rd Nordic Seminar on Digital Land Mobile Radio Comm., Sept. 1988.
24. J. Y. Yu, P.Chong, "a Survey Of Clustering Schemes for Mobile Ad hoc Networks", IEEE Communications Surveys & Tutorials,First Quarter 2005.

The State of the Art in Cross-Layer Design for Wireless Sensor Networks

Tommaso Melodia, Mehmet C. Vuran, and Dario Pompili

Broadband and Wireless Networking Laboratory,
School of Electrical & Computer Engineering,
Georgia Institute of Technology, Atlanta, GA 30332
{tommaso, mcvuran, dario}@ece.gatech.edu

Abstract. The literature on cross-layer protocols, protocol improvements, and design methodologies for wireless sensor networks (WSNs) is reviewed and a taxonomy is proposed. The communication protocols devised for WSNs that focus on cross-layer design techniques are reviewed and classified, based on the network layers they aim at replacing in the classical open system interconnection (OSI) network stack. Furthermore, systematic methodologies for the design of cross-layer solution for sensor networks as resource allocation problems in the framework of non-linear optimization are discussed. Open research issues in the development of cross-layer design methodologies for sensor networks are discussed and possible research directions are indicated. Finally, possible shortcomings of cross-layer design techniques such as lack of modularity, decreased robustness, and instability are discussed, and precautionary guidelines are presented.

1 Introduction

There exist exhaustive amount of research to enable efficient communication in wireless sensor networks (WSNs) [1]. Most of the proposed communication protocols improve the energy efficiency to a certain extent by exploiting the collaborative nature of WSNs and its correlation characteristics. However, the main commonality of these protocols is that they follow the traditional layered protocol architecture. While these protocols may achieve very high performance in terms of the metrics related to each of these individual layers, they are not jointly optimized to maximize the overall network performance while minimizing the energy expenditure. Considering the scarce energy and processing resources of WSNs, joint optimization and design of networking layers, i.e., cross-layer design, stands as the most promising alternative to inefficient traditional layered protocol architectures.

Accordingly, an increasing number of recent papers have focused on the cross-layer development of wireless sensor network protocols. In fact, recent papers on WSNs [13][18][31] reveal that cross-layer integration and design techniques result in significant improvement in terms of energy conservation. Generally, there are

M. Cesana, L. Fratta (Eds.): Wireless Syst./Network Architect. 2005, LNCS 3883, pp. 78–92, 2006.
© Springer-Verlag Berlin Heidelberg 2006

three main reasons behind this improvement. First, the stringent energy, storage, and processing capabilities of wireless sensor nodes necessitate such an approach. The significant overhead of layered protocols results in high inefficiency. Moreover, recent empirical studies necessitate that the properties of low power radio transceivers and the wireless channel conditions be considered in protocol design. Finally, the event-centric approach of WSNs requires application-aware communication protocols.

Although a consistent amount of recent papers have focused on cross-layer design and improvement of protocols for WSNs, a systematic methodology to accurately model and leverage cross-layer interactions is still missing. With this respect, the design of networking protocols for multi-hop wireless ad hoc and sensor networks can be interpreted as the distributed solution of resource allocation problems at different layers. However, while most of the existing studies decompose the resource allocation problem at different layers, and consider allocation of resources at each layer separately, we review recent literature that has tried to establish sound cross-layer design methodologies based on the joint solution of resource allocation optimization problems at different layers.

Several open research problems arise in the development of systematic techniques for cross-layer design of WSN protocols. In this paper, we describe the performance improvement and the consequent risks of a cross-layer approach. We review literature proposing precautionary guidelines and principles for cross-layer design, and suggest some possible research directions. We also present some concerns and precautionary considerations regarding cross-layer design architectures. A cross-layer solution, in fact, generally decreases the level of modularity, which may loose the decoupling between design and development process, making it more difficult to further design improvements and innovations. Moreover, it increases the risk of instability caused by unintended functional dependencies, which are not easily foreseen in a non-layered architecture.

The paper is organized as follows. In Section 2, we overview the communication protocols devised for WSNs that focus on cross-layer design techniques. We classify these techniques based on the network layers they aim at replacing in the classical OSI network stack. Moreover, a new communication paradigm, i.e., cross-layer module, is introduced. In Section 3, we discuss the resource allocation problems that relate to the cross-layer design and the proposed solutions in WSNs. Based on the experience in cross-layering in WSNs, in Section 4 we list the potential open problems that we foresee for WSNs. Then, we stress some reservations about cross-layer design by discussing its pros and cons in Section 5, and conclude the paper in Section 6.

2 Cross-Layer Protocols for Wireless Sensor Networks

The experience gained through both scientific studies and experimental work in WSNs revealed important interactions between different layers of the network stack. These interactions are especially important for the design of communication protocols for WSNs.

As an example, in [15], the effect of wireless channel on a simple communication protocol such as flooding is investigated through testbed experiments. Accordingly, the broadcast and asymmetric nature of the wireless channel results in a different performance than that predicted through unit disk graph models (UDG). Similarly, in [38], the experimental studies reveal that the perfect-reception-within-range models can be misleading in performance evaluations due to the existence of *transitional region* in low power links. Moreover, in [26], guidelines for physical-layer-driven protocol and algorithm design are investigated. These existing studies strongly advocate that communication protocols for WSN need to be re-designed considering the wireless channel properties. Similarly, as pointed out in [31], the interdependency between local contention and end-to-end congestion is important to be considered in protocol design. The interdependency between these and other network layers call for adaptive cross-layer mechanisms for efficient data delivery in WSNs.

In addition to the wireless channel impact and cross-layer interactions, spatio-temporal correlation is another significant characteristic of sensor networks. Dense deployment of sensor nodes results in the sensor observations being highly correlated in the space domain. Similarly, the nature of the energy-radiating physical phenomenon yields temporal correlation between each consecutive observation of a sensor node. Exploiting the spatial and temporal correlation further improves energy efficiency of communication in WSNs [30].

Next, we overview representative communication protocols that are relevant to the cross-layering philosophy. Moreover, we overview a single module solution for efficient communication in WSNs.

2.1   Existing Work

Cross-layer approach has so far been used in two main context in WSNs. In many papers, the cross-layer *interaction* is considered, where the traditional layered structure is preserved, while each layer is informed about the conditions of other layers. However, the mechanisms of each layer still stay intact. On the other hand, there is still much to be gained by rethinking the mechanisms of network layers in a unified way so as to provide a single communication module for efficient communication in WSNs. In this section, we also focus on the cross-layer *module* design, where functionalities of multiple traditional layers are melted into a functional module.

In the following, the literature of WSN protocols with cross-layer principles are surveyed. We classify these studies in terms of interactions or modularity among physical (PHY), medium access control (MAC), routing, and transport layers.

MAC + PHY: In [17], the energy consumption analysis for physical and MAC layers is performed for three different MAC protocols. The authors provide analysis of energy consumption and conclude that single-hop communication can be more efficient if real radio models are used. Although this is an interesting result, the analysis is based on a linear network, which may not be practical in realistic scenarios.

A cross-layer solution among MAC layer, physical phenomenon, and the application layer for WSNs is proposed in [32]. The spatial correlation in the observed physical phenomenon is exploited for medium access control. Based on a theoretical framework, it is shown that a sensor node can act as a representative node for several other sensor nodes. Accordingly, a distributed, spatial correlation-based collaborative medium access control (CC-MAC) protocol is proposed. Simulation results show that exploiting spatial for medium access results in high performance in terms of energy, packet drop rate, and latency.

MAC + Routing: In many work, the *receiver-based* routing is exploited for MAC and routing cross-layer modularity. In this approach, the next hop is chosen as a result of the contention in the neighborhood. Receiver-based routing has been independently proposed in [28], [35], and [36]. In [35] and [36], the authors discuss the energy efficiency, latency, and multihop performance of the algorithm. In [37], the work in [35] and [36] is extended for a single radio node. In [28], the receiver-based routing is also analyzed based on a simple channel model and lossless links. Moreover, the latency performance of the protocol is presented based on different delay functions and collision rates. Although the authors provide insightful results for the receiver-based routing, the impact of physical layer is not considered in the protocol operation. Similarly in [14], the routing decision is performed as a result of successive *competitions* at the medium access level. More specifically, the next hop is selected based on a weighted progress factor and the transmit power is increased successively until the most efficient node is found. Moreover, on-off schedules are used. The performance evaluations of all these propositions present the advantages of cross-layer approach at the routing and MAC layers.

A joint scheduling and routing scheme is proposed in [27] for periodic traffic in WSNs. In this scheme, the nodes form distributed on-off schedules for each flow in the network while the routes are established such that the nodes are only awake when necessary. Since the traffic is periodic, the schedules are then maintained to favor maximum efficiency. The authors also investigate the trade-off between on-off schedules and the connectivity of the network.

The usage of on-off schedules in a cross-layer routing and MAC framework is also investigated in [18]. In this work, a TDMA-based MAC scheme is devised, where nodes distributively select their appropriate time slots based on local topology information. The routing protocol also exploits this information for route establishment. In [18], the authors advocate the usage of cross-layer interaction through comparative simulations with a strict layered approach.

WSNs are characterized by multiple flows from closely located nodes to a single sink. However, if this fact is not considered in route establishment, potential interfering routes can be established. In [13], this effect of broadcast nature of MAC on routing is investigated. In this work, MAC interference between routes is minimized by constructing *interference-aware* routes. The routes are constructed using *node codewords* that indicate the interference level of nodes and each packet contains a *route indicator* for route establishment. As a result, the routes are constructed to minimize the interference among them.

Routing + PHY: A cross-layer optimization of network throughput for multi-hop wireless networks is presented in [34]. The authors split the throughput optimization problem into two sub-problems, i.e., multi-hop flow routing at the network layer and power allocation at the physical layer. The throughput is tied to the per-link data flow rates, which in turn depend on the link capacities and hence, the per-node radio power level. On the other hand, the power allocation problem is tied to interference as well as the link rate. Based on this solution, a CDMA/OFDM based solution is provided such that the power control and the routing are performed in a distributed manner.

In [25], new forwarding strategies for geographic routing are proposed based on the results in [38]. The authors provide expressions for the optimal forwarding distance for networks with automatic repeat request (ARQ) and without ARQ. Moreover, two forwarding strategies for these cases are provided. The forwarding algorithms require the packet reception rate of each neighbor for determination of the next hop and construct routes accordingly. Although the new forwarding metrics illustrate the advantages of cross-layer forwarding techniques in WSNs, the analysis for the distribution of optimal hop distance is based on a linear network structure.

Transport + PHY: In [8], a cross-layer optimization solution for power control and congestion control is considered. The authors provide analytical analysis of power control and congestion control, and the trade-off between layered and cross-layer approach is presented as discussed in Section 3. Based on this framework, a cross-layer communication protocol based on CDMA is proposed, where the transmission power and the transmission rate is controlled. However, the proposed solutions only apply to CDMA-based wireless multihop networks, which may not apply to WSNs that CDMA technology may not be feasible.

3-Layer Solutions: In addition to the proposed protocols that focus on pairwise cross-layer interaction, more general cross-layer approaches among three protocol layers exist. In [22], the optimization of transmission power, transmission rate, and link schedule for TDMA-based WSNs is proposed. The optimization is performed to maximize the network lifetime, instead of minimizing the total average power consumption. In [11], joint routing, MAC, and link layer optimization is proposed. The authors consider a variable-length TDMA scheme and MQAM modulation. The optimization problem considers energy consumption that includes both transmission energy and circuit processing energy. Based on this analysis, it is shown that single-hop communication may be optimal in some cases where the circuit energy dominates the energy consumption instead of transmission energy. Although the optimization problems presented in the paper are insightful, no communication protocol for practical implementation is proposed. Moreover, the transport layer issues such as congestion and flow control are not considered.

2.2   Cross-Layer Module (XLM) for Wireless Sensor Networks

The cross-layer approach emerged recently still necessitates a unified cross-layer communication protocol for efficient and reliable event communication that considers transport, routing, and medium access functionalities with physical layer (wireless channel) effects for WSNs. Here, we overview a new communication paradigm, i.e., cross-layer module (XLM) for WSNs [3]. XLM replaces the entire traditional layered protocol architecture that has been used so far in WSNs.

The basis of communication in XLM is built on the *initiative* concept. The initiative concept constitutes the core of XLM and implicitly incorporates the intrinsic functionalities required for successful communication in WSN. A node initiates transmission by broadcasting an RTS packet to indicate its neighbors that it has a packet to send. Upon receiving an RTS packet, each neighbor of a node decides to participate in the communication through *initiative determination*. Denoting the initiative as $\mathcal{I}$, it is determined as follows:

$$
\mathcal{I} =
\begin{cases}
1, \text{ if}
\begin{cases}
\xi_{RTS} \geq \xi_{Th} \\
\lambda_{relay} \leq \lambda_{relay}^{Th} \\
\beta \leq \beta^{max} \\
E_{rem} \geq E_{rem}^{min}
\end{cases} \\
\\
0, \text{ otherwise}
\end{cases}
\tag{1}
$$

where ξ_{RTS} is the received SNR value of the RTS packet, λ_{relay} is the rate of packets that are relayed by a node, β is the buffer occupancy of the node, and E_{rem} is the residual energy of the node, while the terms on the right side of the inequalities indicate the associated threshold values for these parameters, respectively. The initiative, $\mathcal{I}$, is set to 1 if all four conditions in (1) are satisfied. The first condition ensures that reliable links be constructed for communication. The second and third conditions are used for local congestion control in XLM. The second condition prevents congestion by limiting the traffic a node can relay. The third condition ensures that the node does not experience any buffer overflow. The last condition ensures that the remaining energy of a node E_{rem} stays above a minimum value, E_{rem}^{min}.

The cross-layer functionalities of XLM lie in these constraints that define the *initiative* of a node to participate in communication. Using the initiative concept, XLM performs local congestion control, hop-by-hop reliability, and distributed operation. For a successful communication, a node first initiates transmission by broadcasting an RTS packet, which serves as a link quality indicator and also helps the potential destinations to perform receiver-based contention. Then, the nodes that hear this initiation perform initiative determination according to (1). The nodes that decide to participate in the communication contend for routing of the packet by transmitting CTS packets. The waiting times for the CTS packet transmission is determined based on the advancement of a node for routing [3]. Moreover, the local congestion control component of XLM ensures energy efficient as well as reliable communication by a two-step congestion control. Analytical performance evaluation and simulation experiment results show that XLM significantly improves the communication performance and outperforms the traditional layered protocol architectures in terms of both network performance and implementation complexity.

3 Cross-Layer Resource Allocation

The design of networking protocols for multi-hop wireless ad hoc and sensor networks can be interpreted as the distributed solution of resource allocation problems at different layers. Resource allocation in the context of multi-hop wireless networks has been extensively studied in the last few years, typically with the objectives of maximizing the network lifetime [6], minimizing the energy consumption [23], and maximizing the network capacity [24]. However, most of the existing studies decompose the resource allocation problem at different layers, and consider allocation of the resources at each layer separately. Resource allocation problems are treated either heuristically, or without considering cross-layer interdependencies, or by considering pairwise interactions between isolated pairs of layers.

A typical example of the *tight coupling* between functionalities handled at different layers is the interaction between the congestion control and power control mechanisms [8]. The congestion control regulates the allowed source rates so that the total traffic load on any link does not exceed the available capacity. In typical congestion control problems, the capacity of each link is assumed to be fixed and predetermined. However, in multi-hop wireless networks, the attainable capacity of each wireless link depends on the interference levels, which in turn depend on the power control policy. Hence, congestion control and power control are inherently coupled and should not be treated separately when efficient solutions are sought.

Furthermore, the physical, medium access control (MAC), and routing layers together impact the contention for network resources. The physical layer has a direct impact on multiple access of nodes in wireless channels by affecting the interference at the receivers. The MAC layer determines the bandwidth allocated to each transmitter, which naturally affects the performance of the physical layer in terms of successfully detecting the desired signals. On the other hand, as a result of transmission schedules, high packet delays and/or low bandwidth can occur, forcing the routing layer to change its route decisions. Different routing decisions alter the set of links to be scheduled, and thereby influence the performance of the MAC layer.

Several papers in the literature focus on the joint power control and MAC problem and/or power control and routing issues, although most of them study the interactions among different layers under restricted assumptions. In Section 3.1, we report a set of significative examples. In Section 3.2, we describe previous work that dealt with cross-layer design of multi-hop wireless networks within an optimization framework. In Section 3.3, we discuss a general framework for describing cross-layer optimization problems.

3.1 Related Work: Pairwise Interactions

In [12], the problem of scheduling maximum number of links in the same time slot is studied. The objective of the paper is to develop a power control based multiple access algorithm for contention-based wireless ad hoc networks, so that the network maximum per-hop throughput is achieved.

In [10], the problem of joint routing, link scheduling, and power control to support high data rates for broadband wireless multi-hop networks is analyzed. In particular, the work focuses on the minimization of the total average transmission power, subject to given constraints regarding the minimum average data rate per link, as well as peak transmission power constraints per node.

In [20], the joint power control and scheduling problem is addressed under the assumption that the session paths are already given. This work aims at satisfying the rate requirements of the sessions not only in the long term, as considered in [10], but also in the short term, in order to prevent the sessions with low jitter or bounded delay requirement from suffering from the ambiguity of the long term guarantees. The need for close interactions between these layers is demonstrated, and it is pointed out that independent decisions at different layers for achieving a local objective would deteriorate the performance of other layers.

3.2   Related Work: Optimization Frameworks

Recent studies, and in particular the pioneering work by Low [21] and Chiang [8], have demonstrated the need to integrate various protocol layers into a coherent framework, to help provide a unified foundation for the analysis of resource allocation problems, and to develop systematic techniques for cross-layer design of multi-hop wireless networks. These results are built on recently developed nonlinear optimization theory for the design of communication systems. In particular, convex optimization [5] and geometric programming [9] optimization techniques have been recently proposed and investigated. The objective is to develop a framework that accurately models every aspect of the layered network architecture, resulting in new theoretical results and in practical new design perspectives.

The main technique used in these papers is the method of dual decomposition for convex optimization problems. The technique of dual decomposition has been used by Low in [21], where parameters describing congestion are interpreted as primal and dual optimization variables, while the TCP protocol is interpreted as a distributed primal-dual protocol solving a distributed utility maximization problem. In [8], transmitted power levels and congestion window sizes are jointly optimized. The amount of bandwidth supplied to the upper layers is nonlinearly coupled to the bandwidth demanded by the congestion control through a dual variable. In [7], the cross-layer design of congestion control, routing, and scheduling are jointly tackled by extending the framework of utility maximization introduced in [8]. In [33], a primal-dual method is proposed for distributed solution of a joint source coding, routing, and channel coding. In [34], an optimization framework is proposed that jointly optimizes routing and power allocation by also relying on network coding techniques.

3.3   A General Framework for Cross-Layer Design Problems

As discussed above, the current trend is to formulate increasingly complex cross-layer resource allocation problems in multi-hop wireless networks as optimization problems. While details of the model are dependent on the particular problem being dealt with, it is possible to outline a general framework where particular problems can fit by specifying the form of particular functions. We build on the framework proposed in [8] and further specify it, for example by including latency bounds. Hence, we introduce the following notations that are used in the general formulation:

- $\mathbf{r} = [r_1, r_2, .., r_s, .., r_{|\mathcal{S}|}]$ is the vector whose generic element r_s represents the bit rate assigned to source $s \in \mathcal{S}$;
- $\mathbf{p} = [p_1, p_2, .., p_j, .., p_{|\mathcal{N}|}]$ is the transmission power vector, where the generic element p_j is the transmission power assigned to node $j \in \mathcal{N}$;
- $\mathbf{F} = [f_{ij}^s]$ is a binary matrix that represents the routing decisions, where the generic element f_{ij}^s equals 1 iff link (i, j) is part of the end-to-end path associated with source s;
- $\mathbf{P}^e = [P_1^e, P_2^e, .., P_j^e, .., P_{|\mathcal{N}|}^e]$ is a vector whose generic element P_j^e represents the decoding error probability desired by node $j \in \mathcal{N}$;
- $d_{ij}()$ is the delay expression associated to link (i, j), that models the specific physical and MAC layer, and their interaction with the routing and congestion control functions;
- $l_{ij}()$ is the capacity expression associated with link (i, j), that depends on the physical layer characteristics;
- B^s is the delay bound associated with source s;
- $\mathcal{U}_s$ and $\mathcal{V}_j$ are utility functions in the objective function, which model the desired optimality characteristics of the network, according to the application requirements.

The problem can be cast as follows:

$\mathbf{P}^{Opt}$: Cross-layer Resource Allocation

$$Given: \quad P_s^e, d_{ij}(), l_{ij}(), B^s$$
$$Find: \quad \mathbf{r}, \mathbf{F}, \mathbf{p}$$
$$Minimize: \sum_{s \in \mathcal{S}} \mathcal{U}_s(r_s) + \sum_{j \in \mathcal{N}} \mathcal{V}_j(p_j) \tag{2}$$
$$Subject\ to:$$

$$\sum_{s \in \mathcal{S}} f_{ij}^s \cdot r_s \leq l_{ij}(\mathbf{P}^e, \mathbf{p}); \tag{3}$$

$$\sum_{(i,j) \in \mathcal{E}} f_{ij}^s \cdot d_{ij}(\mathbf{r}, l_{ij}(\mathbf{P}^e, \mathbf{p})) \leq B_s; \tag{4}$$

$$\mathbf{F} \in \mathcal{F}_{feas}(\mathbf{r}); \ \mathbf{r} \in \mathcal{R}_{feas}; \ \mathbf{p} \in \mathcal{P}_{feas}. \tag{5}$$

The above formulation jointly models problems at different layers in a cross-layer fashion. The optimization variables, whose values have to be jointly determined, are associated to different resources at different layers of the protocol stack. The *transport problem* consists of deciding the bit rate vector $\mathbf{r}$ to be assigned to the set of sources in the network. The *routing problem* consists of determining the routing matrix $\mathbf{F}$ according to which the sources route their data flows. The *physical problem* consists of selecting the optimal transmission power vector $\mathbf{p}$ that the set of sources should use. The above variables have to be jointly selected in order to maximize the objective function in (2). In particular, (2) maximizes the sum of the utilities of each source $s \in S$ and of each node $j \in \mathcal{N}$, according to the utility functions $\mathcal{U}_s$ and $\mathcal{V}_j$, respectively. While the former increases with increasing bit rates granted to each source, the latter increases with decreasing power assigned to each node. Constraint (3) imposes that the resource utilized on each link be lower than the link capacity, which depends on the desired decoding error probability vector and on the used transmission powers. Constraint (4) forces the end-to-end delay of each source to be bounded by the maximum tolerated delay. The delay on each link can be expressed as a function of the assigned vector rate and link capacity. Constraints (5) impose limitations on the routing decisions, the available bit rates, and the selectable transmission powers, respectively, considering the MAC and physical constraints. Specifically, in the routing decision an end-to-end path is considered feasible if it is composed only of links connecting adjacent nodes. Moreover, concurrent transmissions are considered feasible if the generated interference is within certain bounds.

4   Open Research Problems

As explained in Sections 2 and 3, there exists some research on cross-layer interactions and design in developing new communication protocols. However, there is still much to be gained by rethinking the protocol functions of network layers in a unified way so as to provide a single communication module for efficient communication in WSNs. In other words, the cross-layer approach emerged recently, still necessitates a unified cross-layer communication protocol for efficient and reliable event communication that considers transport, routing, and medium access functionalities with physical layer (wireless channel) effects for WSNs.

There are several open research problems toward the development of systematic techniques for cross-layer design of wireless sensor network protocols:

Identify Adequate Utility Functions: A thorough study is needed to identify utility functions that: i) represent the desired global design objectives of sensor networks, such as minimal energy consumption and maximum network lifetime; ii) exhibit particular properties, e.g., convexity, that allow finding a unique global optimum with efficient methods and developing distributed implementations.

Improved Understanding of Energy Consumption: Existing studies on cross-layer optimization are mostly focused on jointly optimizing functionalities at different layers, usually with the overall objective of maximizing the network throughput. Conversely, in WSNs the ultimate objective is usually to minimize the energy consumption and/or to maximize the network lifetime. Hence, further study is needed to develop models and methodologies suitable to solve energy-oriented problems.

Accurate Delay Modeling: There is a need to develop sound models to include in the above framework an accurate description of the end-to-end delay as results from the interaction of the different layers. This is particularly important for the design of sensor network protocols for monitoring applications that require real-time delivery of event data, such as those encountered in wireless sensor and actor networks (WSAN) [2].

Connectivity with Realistic Physical Layer: Connectivity in wireless networks has been previously studied [16][4], i.e., stochastic models have been developed to determine conditions under which a network is connected. These results, however, cannot be straightforwardly used, as they are based on the so-called unit disk graph communication model. However, recent experimental studies have demonstrated that the effects of the impairments of the wireless channel on higher-layer protocols are not negligible, as the availability of links further fluctuates because of channel fading phenomena that affect the wireless transmission medium. Furthermore, mobility of nodes is not considered. In fact, due to node mobility and node join and leave events, the network may be subject to frequent topological reconfigurations. Thus, links are continuously established and broken. For the above reasons, new analytical models are required to determine connectivity conditions that incorporate mobility and fading channels.

Cross-Layer Network Simulators: Current discrete-event network simulators such as OPNET [39], NS-2 [40], J-Sim [41], GloMoSim [42] may be unsuitable to implement a cross-layer solution, since their inner structure is based on a layered architecture, and each implemented functionality run by the simulator engine is tightly tied to this architecture. Hence, implementing a cross-layer solution in one of these simulators may turn into a non-trivial task. For this reason, there is a need to develop new software simulators that are based on a new developing paradigm so as to ease the development and test of cross-layer algorithmic and protocol solutions.

5   Precautionary Guidelines in Cross-Layer Design

In Section 4, we described several open research problems toward the development of systematic techniques for cross-layer design of wireless sensor network protocols. In this section, we describe possible risks raising when a cross-layer approach is followed, and propose precautionary guidelines and principles for cross-layer design beyond the open research issues presented in Section 4.

As stressed in Sections 2 and 3, the increased interactions and dependencies across layers turn into an interesting optimization opportunity that may be worth exploiting. Following this intuition, many cross-layer design papers that explore a much richer interaction between parameters across layers have been proposed in the recent past. While, however, as an immediate outcome most of these cross-layer suggestions may yield a performance improvement in terms of throughput or delay, this result is often obtained by decreasing the *architecture modularity*, and by loosing the logical separation between designers and developers. This abstraction decoupling is needed to allow the former to understand the overall system, and the latter to realize a more efficient production. For these reasons, when a cross-layer solution is proposed, the system performance gain needs to be weighed against the possible longer-term downfalls raised by a diminished degree of modularity.

In [19], the authors reexamine holistically the issue of cross-layer design and its architectural ramifications. They contend that a good architectural design leads to *proliferation* and *longevity* of a technology, and illustrate this with some historical examples, e.g., John von Neumann's architecture for computer systems, at the origin of the separation of software and hardware; the layered OSI architecture for networking, base of the current Internet architecture success; Shannon's architecture for communication systems, motivating the nonobvious separation of source and channel coding; last but not least, the plant controller feedback paradigm in control systems, providing universal principles common to human engineered systems as well as biological systems.

Although the concerns and cautionary advice expressed in [19] about cross-layer design are sound and well motivated, the layered-architecture, which turned to be a successful design choice for wired networks, may need to be carefully rethought for energy-constrained WSNs, where the concept itself of 'link' is labile, and many different effective transmission schemes and communication paradigms are conceivable.

This is also the conclusion drawn in [29], where the pros and cons of cross-layer design approach are evaluated. In [29], cross-layer design to improve reliability and optimize performance is advocated, although the design needs to be cautiously developed to provide long-term survivability of cross-layer architectures. In the following, we present some concerns and precautionary considerations, which need to be considered when a cross-layer design architecture is proposed, and suggest some possible research directions.

Modularity: In the classical layered design approach, a system architecture is broken down into *modular components*, and the *interactions* and *dependencies* between these components are systematically specified. This design philosophy allows to break complex problems into easier subproblems, which can then be solved in *isolation*, without considering all the details pertaining the overall system. This approach guarantees the inter-operability of subsystems in the overall system once each subsystem is tested and standardized, leading to quick proliferation of technology and mass production. Conversely, a cross-layer design approach may loose the decoupling between design and development process, which may impair both the design and the implementation development and slow the innovation down.

System Enhancement: Design improvements and innovations may become difficult in a cross-layer design, since it will be hard to assess how a new modification will interact with the already existing solutions. Furthermore, a cross-layer architecture would be hard to upkeep, and the maintaining costs would be high. In the worst cases, rather than modifying just one subsystem, the entire system may need to be replaced. For these reasons, we advocate keeping some degree of modularity in the design of cross-layer solutions. This could be achieved by relying on functional entities - as opposed to layers in the classical design philosophy - that implement particular functions. This would also have the positive consequence of limiting the duplication of functions that often characterizes a layered design. This functional redundancy is, in fact, one the cause for poor system performance.

Instability: In cross-layer design, the effect of any single design choice may affect the whole system, leading to various negative consequences such as instability. This is a non trivial problem to solve, since it is well known from control theory that stability is a paramount issue. Moreover, the fact that some interactions are not easily foreseen makes cross-layer design choices even trickier. Hence, great care should be paid to prevent design choices from negatively affecting the overall system performance. To this purpose, there is a need to integrate and further develop control theory techniques to study stability properties of system designed following a cross-layer approach. Dependency graphs, which may be used to capture the dependency relation between parameters, could be valuable means to prove stability, although hard to implement in some cases.

6   Conclusions

In this paper, we reviewed and classified literature on cross-layer protocols, improvements, and design methodologies for wireless sensor networks (WSNs). We overviewed the communication protocols devised for WSNs that focus on cross-layer design techniques. We classified these techniques based on the network layers they aim at replacing in the classical OSI network stack. Furthermore, we discussed systematic methodologies for the design of cross-layer solutions for sensor networks as resource allocation problems in the framework of non-linear optimization. We outlined open research issues in the development of cross-layer methodologies for sensor networks and discussed possible research directions.

A cross-layer design methodology for energy-constrained wireless sensor networks is an appealing approach as long as cross-layer interactions are thoroughly studied and controlled. As pointed out in this paper, no cross-layer dependency should be left unintended, since this may lead to poor performance of the entire system.

References

1. I. F. Akyildiz, W. Su, Y. Sankarasubramaniam, Y., and E. Cayirci, "Wireless Sensor Networks: A Survey", Computer Networks (Elsevier) Journal, Vol. 38, No. 4, pp. 393-422, March 2002.
2. I. F. Akyildiz, and I. H. Kasimoglu, "Wireless Sensor and Actor Networks: Research Challenges," Ad Hoc Networks Journal (Elsevier), Vol. 2, No. 4, pp. 351-367, October 2004.
3. I. F. Akyildiz, M. C. Vuran, and O. B. Akan, "A Cross-Layer Protocol for Wireless Sensor Networks," in Proc. CISS '06, Princeton, NJ, March 2006.

4. Christian Bettstetter, "On the Minimum Node Degree and Connectivity of a Wireless Multihop Network," In Proc. ACM Intern. Symp. on Mobile Ad Hoc Networking and Computing (MobiHoc), Lausanne, Switzerland, pp. 80-91, June 9-11, 2002

5. Stephen Boyd, and Lieven Vandenberghe, "Convex Optimization," Cambridge University Press, March 2004.

6. J. H. Chang, and L. Tassiulas, "Energy conserving routing in wireless ad hoc networks," in *Proc. IEEE INFOCOM 2000*, March 2000, pp. 22–31.

7. L. Chen, S. H. Low, M. Chiang, and J. C. Doyle, "Optimal Cross-layer Congestion Control, Routing and Scheduling Design in Ad Hoc Wireless Networks, " submitted for publication.

8. M. Chiang, "Balancing transport and physical Layers in wireless multihop networks: jointly optimal congestion control and power control," *IEEE JSAC*, vol. 23, no. 1, pp. 104 116, Jan. 2005.

9. M. Chiang, "Geometric programming for communication systems", Short monograph in Foundations and Trends in Communications and Information Theory, vol. 2, no. 1-2, pp. 1-154, July 2005.

10. R. Cruz and A. Santhanam, "Optimal routing, link scheduling and power control in multi-hop wireless networks," in *Proceedings of INFOCOM'03*, San Francisco, USA, Mar. 2003, pp. 702–711.

11. S. Cui, R. Madan, A. Goldsmith, S. Lall, "Joint routing, MAC, and link layer optimization in sensor networks with energy constraints," in *Proc. IEEE ICC '05*, vol. 2, pp. 725 - 729, May 2005.

12. T. ElBatt and A. Ephremides, "Joint Scheduling and Power Control for Wireless Ad-hoc Networks," in *Proceedings of INFOCOM'02*, New York, June 2002.

13. Fang, Y., McDonald, B., "Dynamic codeword routing (DCR): a cross-layer approach for performance enhancement of general multi-hop wireless routing," 2004.

14. D. Ferrara, et. al., "MACRO: An Integrated MAC/Routing Protocol for Geographical Forwarding in Wireless Sensor Networks," in *Proc. IEEE Infocom '05*, vol. 3, pp. 1770 - 1781, March 2005.

15. D. Ganesan, et. al., "An empirical study of epidemic algorithms in large scale multihop wireless networks," Technical Report, Intel Research, 2002.

16. Gupta, P. and Kumar P. R., "Critical power for asymptotic connectivity in wireless networks," Stochastic Analysis, Control, Optimization and Applications: a volume in honor of W. H. Fleming, W. M. McEneaney, G. Yin and Q. Zhang, Birkhauser, Boston, 1998.

17. J. Haapola, Z. Shelby, C. Pomalaza-Raez, P. Mahonen, "Cross-layer energy analysis of multi-hop wireless sensor networks," in *EWSN '05*, pp. 33 - 44, 2005.

18. L. van Hoesel, T. Nieberg, J. Wu, and P. J. M. Havinga, "Prolonging the lifetime of wireless sensor networks by cross-layer interaction," *IEEE Wireless Communications*, vol. 11, no. 6, pp. 78 - 86, Dec. 2004.

19. V. Kawadia and P.R. Kumar, "A Cautionary Perspective On Cross-Layer Design," IEEE Wireless Communications Magazine, February 2005.

20. U. C. Kozat, I. Koutsopoulos, and L. Tassiulas, "A Framework for Cross-layer Design of Energy-efficient Communication with QoS Provisioning in Multi-hop Wireless Networks," in *Proceedings of INFOCOM'04*, Honk Kong, Mar. 2004.

21. S. H. Low, "A Duality Model of TCP and Queue Management Algorithms," IEEE/ACM Transactions on Networking, vol 11, no. 4, pp. 525-526, August 2003.

22. R. Madan, S. Cui; S. Lall, A. Goldsmith, "Cross-layer design for lifetime maximization in interference-limited wireless sensor networks," in *Proc. IEEE INFOCOM '05*, vol. 3, pp. 1964 - 1975, March 2005.

23. T. Melodia, D. Pompili, and I. F. Akyildiz, "On the interdependence of distributed topology control and geographical routing in ad hoc and sensor networks," *Journal of Selected Areas in Communications*, vol. 23, no. 3, pp. 520–532, Mar. 2005.

24. Bozidar Radunovic, Jean-Yves Le Boudec, "Rate Performance Objectives of Multihop Wireless Networks," IEEE Transactions on Mobile Computing, vol. 03, no. 4, pp. 334-349, October 2004.

25. K. Seada, M. Zuniga, A. Helmy, B. Krishnamachari, "Energy-efficient forwarding strategies for geographic routing in lossy wireless sensor networks," in *ACM Sensys '04*, November 2004.

26. E. Shih, et. al., "Physical Layer Driven Protocol and Algorithm Design for Energy-Efficient Wireless Sensor Networks," in *Proc. ACM MOBICOM '01*, July 2001.

27. M. L. Sichitiu, "Cross-layer scheduling for power efficiency in wireless sensor networks," 2004.

28. P. Skraba, H. Aghajan, A. Bahai, "Cross-layer optimization for high density sensor networks: Distributed passive routing Decisions," in *Proc. Ad-Hoc Now'04*, Vancouver, July 2004.

29. S. Toumpis and A.J. Goldsmith, "Performance, Optimization, and Cross-Layer Design of Media Access Protocols for Wireless Ad Hoc Networks," in *Proc. ICC*, Seattle, Washington, USA, May 2003.

30. M. C. Vuran, O. B. Akan, and I. F. Akyildiz, "Spatio-Temporal Correlation: Theory and Applications for Wireless Sensor Networks," Computer Networks Journal (Elsevier), Vol. 45, No. 3, pp. 245-261, June 2004.

31. M. C. Vuran, V. B. Gungor, and O. B. Akan, "On the interdependency of congestion and contention in wireless sensor networks," in *Proc. SENMETRICS '05*, July 2005.

32. M. C. Vuran, and I. F. Akyildiz, "Spatial Correlation-based Collaborative Medium Access Control in Wireless Sensor Networks," *to appear in IEEE/ACM Transactions on Networking*, June 2006.

33. W. Yu and Jun Yuan, "Joint Source Coding, Routing, and Resource Allocation for Wireless Sensor Networks," in Proc. of IEEE International Conference on Communications (ICC), May 2005.

34. J. Yuan, Z. Li, W. Yu, B. Li, "A Cross-Layer optimization framework for multicast in multi-hop wireless networks wireless internet," in *Proc. WICON '05*, pp. 47 - 54, July 2005.

35. M. Zorzi, R. Rao, "Geographic random forwarding (GeRaF) for ad hoc and sensor networks: multihop performance," *IEEE Trans. Mobile Computing*, vol. 2, no. 4, pp. 337- 348, Oct.-Dec. 2003.

36. M. Zorzi, R. Rao, "Geographic random forwarding (GeRaF) for ad hoc and sensor networks: energy and latency performance," *IEEE Trans. Mobile Computing*, vol. 2, no. 4, pp. 349 365, Oct.-Dec. 2003.

37. M. Zorzi, "A new contention-based MAC protocol for geographic forwarding in ad hoc and sensor networks," in *Proc. IEEE International Conference on Communications*, vol. 6, pp. 3481 - 3485, June 2004.

38. M. Zuniga, B. Krishnamachari, "Analyzing the transitional region in low power wireless links," in *Proc. IEEE SECON '04*, pp. 517 - 526, Oct. 2004.

39. OPNET, http://www.opnet.com/

40. NS-2, http://www.isi.edu/nsnam/ns/

41. J-Sim, http://www.j-sim.org/

42. GloMoSim, http://pcl.cs.ucla.edu/projects/glomosim/

Modelling Restricted Accessibility for Wireless Multi-service Systems

Villy B. Iversen

COM Center, Building 345v, Technical University of Denmark,
DK-2800 Kgs. Lyngby, Denmark
fax: (+45) 4593 6581
vbi@com.dtu.dk

Abstract. Some fundamental aspects of restricted availability and accessibility for multi-rate traffic are clarified. In classical teletraffic models all connections have the same bandwidth demand. In service-integrated systems each service has individual bandwidth requirement. For example in CDMA systems we may experience blocking (outage) even if the nominal capacity of a cell has not been fully used, because the actual capacity depends on interference from neighboring cells. Therefore, calls will experience individual accessibility. This paper presents a new theory and model for this problem. The model preserves the reversibility and insensitivity and generalizes the basic knowledge of classical teletraffic models. The theory is illustrated by a WCDMA traffic model.

Keywords: Restricted accessibility, wireless, CDMA, blocking, multi-slot traffic, processor sharing.

1 Introduction

In systems with full accessibility a call attempt has access to any idle channel. In systems with restricted accessibility a call attempt may be blocked even if some channels are idle. With accessibility $k \leq n$ a call attempt has access to k out of n channels. Limited accessibility was usual in classical telecommunication systems due to the limited capacity of switching equipment. An extensive theory of gradings was established to increase the utilization and at the same time minimize the amount of switching equipment. With the advent of digital switches these problems were eliminated and it became improper to deal with limited access even though these problems still appear in e.g. satellite communication.

In new generation systems as CDMA we have restricted accessibility. Due to interference from own cell and neighboring cells a call may be blocked even though the maximum number of channels or bandwidth has not been occupied. In such system new calls will experience blocking probabilities which depend on both the bandwidth required and the state of the system.

2 Availability

To acquire a deeper understanding of the issues we first consider the availability of a system. The availability of a system is the proportion of time the system is

M. Cesana, L. Fratta (Eds.): Wireless Syst./Network Architect. 2005, LNCS 3883, pp. 93–102, 2006.
© Springer-Verlag Berlin Heidelberg 2006

available. Thus accessibility concerns the capacity of a system (space) whereas availability concerns the reliability (time). The following considerations are elementary but important for understanding accessibility for multi-rate models. We may assume a system has a constant rate γ of becoming unavailable. The time to next break-down of the system is then exponentially distributed with rate γ. If we consider a time interval of constant length τ, then the probability of observing unavailability during this interval is:

$$b = 1 - e^{-\gamma \tau},$$

i.e. the probability of at least one breakdown before time τ has elapsed. The probability that the system is fully available during the time τ is:

$$a = 1 - b = e^{-\gamma \tau}.$$

The probability that the system is fully available during two non-overlapping time intervals, each of duration τ, becomes:

$$a_2 = a^2 = e^{-\gamma 2\tau}.$$

If the rate of becoming unavailable is time-dependent, then we have to replace γt by

$$\bar{\gamma}(t) = \int_0^t \gamma(u)\, \mathrm{d}u \tag{1}$$

assuming that we start observations at time $t = 0$. The probability that the system is fully available during a total time subdivided into l non-overlapping periods becomes:

$$\begin{aligned}
a_{0,l} &= a_{0,1} \cdot a_{1,2} \cdot \ldots \cdot a_{l-1,l} \\
&= e^{-\bar{\gamma}_{0,1}} \cdot e^{-\bar{\gamma}_{1,2}} \cdot \ldots \cdot e^{-\bar{\gamma}_{l-1,l}} \\
&= e^{-\bar{\gamma}_{0,l}}
\end{aligned} \tag{2}$$

where

$$\bar{\gamma}_{i-1,i} = \int_{i-1}^i \gamma(u) \cdot \mathrm{d}u$$

3   Accessibility

The above elucidation of availability is easy to comprehend. We now consider accessibility in a similar way. We change from availability in time to accessibility in space, i.e bandwidth. Instead of considering the availability during a certain time period we consider the accessibility to a certain bandwidth. First we split the total bandwidth into n bandwidth units (slot, channels) of equal capacity. Let us consider a system with limited accessibility where the blocking probability b (or the accessibility $a = 1 - b$) of a single-slot call is constant, independent of the state. The probability that a single-slot call attempt is blocked is equal to b. Using the analogy with availability, a multi-slot call requiring d slots has the probability of being accepted equal to:

$$a_d = 1 - b_d = a^d = (1-b)^d$$
$$= e^{\ln a \cdot d} \tag{3}$$

In comparison with the availability model, the rate of becoming non-accessible is thus $-\ln a$ per bandwidth unit. A d–slot call is only accepted if each of the d individual bandwidth units are accepted one-by-one.

3.1   State or Usage Dependent Blocking Probability

In general the rate of becoming non-accessible is not constant, but increases with the state of the system or the utilization of the bandwidth. Let us consider a system with the total bandwidth n. As an example we assume the rate of becoming non-accessible is linearly increasing from 0 to 1 in the bandwidth interval $(0, n)$. Thus in state k the rate is k/n. If we split the total bandwidth into n channels, each of one bandwidth unit, then the blocking probability for a new call attempt when k channels are busy becomes $b_{k,k+1} = 1 - a_{k,k+1}$ where:

$$a_{k,k+1} = \exp\left\{-\int_k^{k+1} \frac{x}{n}\, dx\right\} = \exp\left\{-\frac{2k+1}{2n} \cdot 1\right\}$$

This is the classical accessibility model where all channels have the same bandwidth. Now let us consider multi-rate traffic. In the above example we split the total bandwidth into $2n$ channels. Then the example above corresponds to a 2-slot call attempt arriving in state $2k$ requiring 2 channels, and a natural requirement for the model considered is that the blocking probability should be the same (to get the same total integral we have to scale x by a factor $1/2$):

$$a_{2k,2k+2} = \exp\left\{-\int_{2k}^{2k+2} \frac{x}{2}\frac{1}{n}\, d\frac{x}{2}\right\} = \exp\left\{-\frac{2k+1}{2n}\right\}$$

The accessibility for accepting two single slot calls in state $2k$ becomes:

$$a_{2k,2k+1} \cdot a_{2k+1,2k+2} = \exp\left\{\int_{2k}^{2k+1} \frac{x}{2}\frac{1}{n}\, d\frac{x}{2}\right\} \cdot \exp\left\{\int_{2k+1}^{2k+2} \frac{x}{2}\frac{1}{n}\, d\frac{x}{2}\right\}$$

$$= \exp\left\{-\frac{4k+1}{8n}\right\} \cdot \exp\left\{-\frac{4k+3}{8n}\right\}$$

$$= \left\{-\frac{2k+1}{2n}\right\}$$

$$= a_{2k,2k+2}$$

q.e.d.

The probability that a 2-slot call is blocked is thus equal to the probability that two single slot calls are blocked.

In general the probability that a call requiring the bandwidth w is accepted in state k becomes:

$$a_w = \int_k^{k+w} \gamma(x)\mathrm{d}x$$

Thus we have derived the blocking probability for a continuous bandwidth demand.

4   Reversibility

A fully accessible system with multi-rate traffic (Poisson arrival process) is reversible, has product-form and is insensitive to the holding time distribution [2]. In Fig. 1 we show an example with two traffic streams. Flow clockwise is equal to flow counter-clockwise (Kolmogorov cycles) and thus the diagram is reversible and it also has product-form. We may calculate the state probabilities using Fortet & Grandjean's (Kaufman [6] & Robert's [7]) algorithm or the convolution algorithm [2].

In Fig. 2 we show the state transition diagram for a system with limited accessibility, where we have introduced the blocking probabilities derived above. Still the diagram is reversible and insensitive, but the product-form has been lost. The acceptance probability is defined as $1 - b_x$, where b_x is the blocking probability in state x. When b_x is greater than zero, then we may choose b_x so

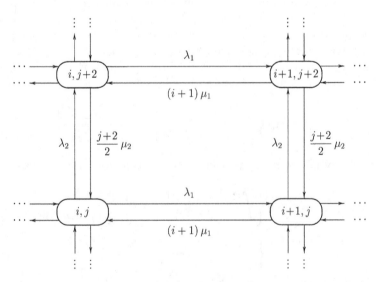

Fig. 1. State-transition diagram for a multi-rate traffic loss system. In this example the arrival processes are Poisson processes (λ_1, λ_2), and the slot sizes are $d_1 = 1$, $d_2 = 2$, respectively. The process is reversible as the flow clockwise equals the flow counter-clockwise.

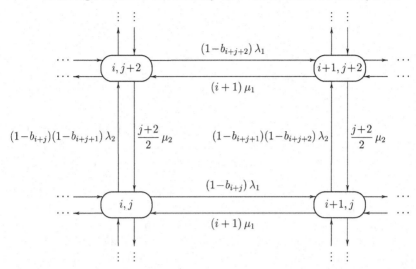

Fig. 2. State-transition diagram with state-dependent blocking probabilities for the loss system in Figure 1. The process is reversible as the flow clockwise equals the flow counter-clockwise.

that the diagram is still reversible, but the product form will be lost. For a d–lot call we have to choose the passage factor in state x equals to number of channels occupied in the cell.

$$1 - b_{x,d} = \prod_{j=x}^{x+d-1} (1 - b_j)$$
$$= (1 - b_x)(1 - b_{x+1}) \ldots (1 - b_{x+d-1}) \qquad (4)$$

We notice that $b_x = b_{x,1}$. This corresponds to that a d–slot call chooses one single channel d times, and the call is only accepted if all d channels are successfully obtained. This is a requirement in agreement with the previous sections, and it can be shown to be a necessary and sufficient condition for maintaining the reversibility of the process.

Due to reversibility we have local balance and may calculate all state probabilities expressed by state $(0,0)$, then normalize the state probabilities, and finally obtain the performance measures.

The theory above is general and in the following we apply it to classical teletraffic models.

5   Delbrouck's Algorithm for Loss Systems Generalized

Delbrouck's algorithm [1] is a generalization of Kaufman & Roberts algorithm (Fortet & Grandjeans's algorithm [2]). If we denote the state probability of state x relative to state 0 by $q(x)$, then Delbrouck's algorithm can be written as [1]:

$$q(x) = \begin{cases} 0 & x < 0 \\ 1 & x = 0 \\ \displaystyle\sum_{i=1}^{N} \frac{1}{x} \cdot \frac{d_i\,\lambda_i}{\mu_i\,Z_i} \sum_{j=1}^{\lfloor x/d_i \rfloor} q(x - jd_i)\left(\frac{Z_i - 1}{Z_i}\right)^{j-1} & x = 1, 2, \cdots, n \end{cases} \tag{5}$$

where $\lfloor x/d_i \rfloor$ denotes the integer part of x_i/d_i. If $\lfloor x/d_i \rfloor$ is less than one, then in usual way the sum is defined as zero. N is the total number of traffic streams, n is the number of channels. For traffic stream i, the arrival rate is $\lambda_i(j)$, where j is the number of connections of type i. One connection requires d_i channels. The mean service time for stream i is μ_i^{-1}. Traffic stream i is characterized by the mean value A_i and peakedness Z_i. For a Poisson arrival process $A_i = \lambda_i/\mu_i$ is the offered traffic measured in number of connections, and the peakedness is one. For a state-dependent Poisson arrival process the offered traffic is $A_i = S(1 - Z_i)$, where S_i is the number of traffic sources. The peakedness is $Z_i = 1/(1 + \beta_i)$, where $\beta_i = \gamma_i/\mu_i$, and γ_i is the arrival rate of an idle source. For the Binomial (Engset) case we have a positive number of sources and the arrival rate when x_i sources are busy is $(S_i - x_i)\,\gamma_i$. For the Pascal case the arrival rate when x_i sources are busy is $(S_i + x_i)\,\gamma_i$. Mathematically, we can deal with Pascal traffic using the same formulæ as for Engset by letting S_i and β_i be negative. For Engset traffic peakedness is less than one (smooth traffic), whereas for Pascal traffic peakedness is greater than one (bursty traffic). The total number of busy channels, i.e. global state is denoted by x. The relative global state probabilities are $q(x)$. For each iteration, the computation need to consider $\lfloor x/d_i \rfloor$ previous global states, except for Poisson arrival processes where we only need one previous state.

Including state-dependent blocking probabilities we can rewrite (5) as follows [5]:

$$p(x) = \begin{cases} 0 & x < 0 \\ p(0) & x = 0 \\ \displaystyle\sum_{i=1}^{N} p_i(x) & x = 1, 2, \ldots, n \end{cases} \tag{6}$$

where   (7)

$$p_i(x) = \left\{ \frac{d_i}{x} \cdot \frac{S_i\gamma_i}{\mu_i} \cdot p(x - d_i) - \frac{x - d_i}{x} \cdot \frac{\gamma_i}{\mu_i} \cdot p_i(x - d_i) \right\} \cdot (1 - b_{x-d_i,d_i}) \,. \tag{8}$$

We are thus able to obtain the exact global state probabilities for a system with global-state dependent blocking probabilities as they appear in e.g. CDMA systems, even if the system does not have a product-form. In the above equations $p_i(x)$ is the contribution of traffic stream i to state $p(x)$. Thus an important observation is that the carried traffic in state x for traffic stream i is

$$y_i(x) = x \cdot p_i(x) \,. \tag{9}$$

We should normalize both state probabilities and carried traffic after each step in the iteration (increase of number of channels by one) to avoid numerical problems [2]. The normalization constant always is greater than one and therefore the algorithm is numerically very accurate [5].

It is obvious that (8) requires much less computation times and memory than (5) since it only need at most d_i previous global state probabilities $q(x)$ and d_i previous values δ_i of traffic stream i. It is like a sliding window for each iteration step.

The relative state probabilities should be normalized to obtain the absolute state probabilities. An very effective and accurate algorithm, which also evaluates the performance of each traffic stream is described in (Iversen [5]) and applied below.

6   Channel Reservation

The model operates with global state probabilities and therefore adapts itself to access control strategies based on global states as channel reservation, called guard channels in some systems. For each traffic stream we may introduce a channel reservation parameter r_i. If less then r_i channels are idle, then calls of type i are blocked. Thus we let $p_i(x) = 0$ for $x = n - r_i + 1, n - r_i + 2, \ldots, n$. The global state probabilities $p(x)$, $x > n - r_i$, will be modified and also the following $p_i(x)$ will be modified. The process is no longer reversible, and the solution will in general be an approximation. The approximation is natural and is being investigated further. The fist result are very promising.

7   WCDMA Case Study

We consider an example described in [3] with 4 different services with parameters shown in table 1. The offered traffic A is given in number of connections, and the bandwidth demand d in number of bandwidth units. The number of bandwidth units is 284. For a system with full accessibility the performance measures are shown in table 2. We consider three congestion measures:

- The time congestion E is the proportion of time a service is blocked,
- The call congestion B is the proportion of call attempts which are blocked,

Table 1. Input parameters for the case considered. A is offered traffic, Z peakedness and d bandwidth requirement in channels. The total number of bandwidth units is 284.

Class i	A_i	Z_i	d_i
1	20.00	2.00	2.00
2	10.00	1.00	4.00
3	4.00	0.40	10.00
4	2.50	0.25	16.00

Table 2. Performance measures for the parameters given in table 1 and with full accessibility

Class	Time cong. E	Traffic cong. C	Call Cong. B	Carried Traffic
1	0.010133	0.022239	0.011245	58.665650
2	0.021220	0.021220	0.021220	58.726826
5	0.060565	0.018243	0.044394	58.905396
6	0.109536	0.015518	0.059312	59.068904
Total		0.019305		235.366777

Table 3. Performance measures for the parameters given in table 1 and with state-dependent blocking

Class	Time cong. E	Traffic cong. C	Call Cong. B	Carried Traffic
1	0.262984	0.418228	0.264405	34.906318
2	0.458604	0.458604	0.458604	32.483784
5	0.789709	0.594068	0.785346	24.355907
6	0.920837	0.735190	0.917391	15.888620
Total		0.551522		107.634629

– The traffic congestion C is the proportion of offered traffic which is blocked, where we define the offered traffic as the traffic carried when the capacity is unlimited.

For Poisson arrival processes ($Z = 1$) we have the *PASTA*–property and the three measures are identical. In all other cases the traffic congestion is the most relevant. The carried traffic is measured in channels. We notice that the four services have almost the same traffic congestion because $Z \cdot d = 4$ is constant.

In Table 3 the same model is considered with state dependent blocking. The state-dependent blocking probability is log-normal distributed as we usually describe the neighboring cell interference by a log-normal distribution. We introduce log-normal random process to describe neighbor cell interference with parameters:

$$\mu = \frac{i}{i+1} \cdot n \tag{10}$$

$$\sigma = \mu$$

The cell capacity in channels is n. The mean value of the interference process μ is equal to the average capacity lost in our cell due to the neighboring cell interference. The standard deviation σ is chosen to be equal to the μ as proposed by (Staehle & Mäder [8]).

Then b_x is expressed as the probability that the neighbour cell interference is greater than the available capacity in the current cell ($n - x$):

$$b_x = P(x' > n - x)$$

$$= 1 - P(x' < n - x)$$
$$= 1 - D(n - x)$$

Here $D(x)$ is the cumulative distribution function of the log-normal distribution:

$$D(x) = \frac{1}{2}\left\{1 + \text{erf}\left(\frac{\ln(x) - M}{S\sqrt{2}}\right)\right\} \tag{11}$$

where M and S are corresponding parameters of normal distribution and are obtained from μ and σ^2 by the following calculations:

$$M = \ln\left\{\frac{\mu^2}{\sqrt{\mu^2 + \sigma^2}}\right\}$$

$$S = \ln\left\{1 + \frac{\sigma^2}{\mu^2}\right\}$$

We choose the other cell interference factor $i = 0.70$ and the cell capacity $n = 284$ (bandwidth unit $= 13.5$ kcps). Then the interference process mean value and standard deviation are both 100.7. For $x \leq 96$ there is no blocking, and for $x = 284$ the blocking probability is of course one. The results in table 3 show that in particular broadband services experience a larger blocking. It also shows at big difference between the three performance measures for non-Poisson traffic. From traffic engineering point of view the traffic congestion is the most important.

8   Conclusions and Further Work

A full accessible system with multi-rate state dependent Poisson arrival process (BPP traffic) is reversible, has product-form and is insensitive to the holding time distribution [2]. With limited accessibility, the process is still reversible and insensitive, but the product-form has been lost. The limited accessibility is expresses as a state-dependent blocking probability. We show the a d–slot call has the same blocking probability as d single-slot calls. So the blocking probability of a call depends both on the state of the system and the bandwidth required. Due to reversibility we have local balance and may calculate all state probabilities by a new effective algorithm and derive time, call, and traffic congestion, the most important performance measure being traffic congestion. We may also include channel reservation in a simple way, and thus give priority to some traffic streams. The model can be generalized to delay systems using the concept departure blocking. The only feasible model using this is a special generalization of Processor Sharing models to multi-rate traffic [5].

References

1. Delbrouck, L.E.N.: On the steady-state distribution in a service facility carrying mixtures of traffic with different peakedness factor and capacity requirements, IEEE Transactions on Communications, Vol. COM-31, 1983 : 11, 1209–1211.

2. Iversen,Villy B.: Teletraffic Engineering and Network Planning. COM, Technical University of Denmark. March 2005. 350 pp. Available at www.com.dtu.dk/education/34340/material/telenook.pdf.
3. Iversen, V.B. & Benetis, V. & Ha, N.T. & Stepanov, S.: Evaluation of Multi-service CDMA Networks with Soft Blocking . ITC 16th Specialist Seminar on Performance Evaluation of Mobile and Wireless Systems, Antwerp, Belgium, August 31 – September 2, 2004. 8 pp.
4. Iversen, Villy B. & Stepanov, S.N.: The Unified approach for Teletraffic Models to convert Recursions for global State probabilities into Stable Form. ITC19, 19th International teletraffic Congress, Beijing 2005.
5. Iversen, Villy B.: Evaluating multi-rate loss systems with applications to generalized Processor sharing. EuroNGI Workshop, Paris, France, December 7–9, 2005. Submitted for publication. 12 pp.
6. Kaufman, J.S. (1981): Blocking in a shared resource environment. IEEE Transactions on Communications, Vol. COM–29 (1981) : 10, 1474–1481.
7. Roberts, J.W. (1981): A service system with heterogeneous user requirements – applications to multi–service telecommunication systems. *Performance of data communication systems and their applications*. G. Pujolle (editor), North–Holland Publ. Co. 1981, pp. 423–431.
8. Staehle, D. & Mäder, A.: *An analytic approximation of the uplink capacity in a UMTS network with heterogeneous traffic*. Proceedings of ITC 18, Berlin September 2003, pp. 81-91. Elsevier 2003.

A Low Computation Cost Algorithm to Solve Cellular Systems with Retrials Accurately

Mª. José Doménech-Benlloch, José Manuel Giménez-Guzmán,
Jorge Martínez-Bauset, and Vicente Casares-Giner

Department of Communications, Universitat Politècnica de València, UPV,
ETSIT Camì de Vera s/n, 46022, València, Spain
{mdoben, jogiguz}@doctor.upv.es
{jmartinez, vcasares}@dcom.upv.es

Abstract. This paper proposes an approximate methodology for solving Markov models that compete for limited resources and retry when access fails, like those arising in mobile cellular networks. We limit the number of levels that define the system by aggregating all levels beyond a given one in order to manage curse of dimensionality issue. The developed methodology allows to balance accuracy and computational cost. We determine the relative error of different typical performance parameters when using the approximate model as well as the computational savings. Results show that high accuracy and cost savings can be obtained by deploying the proposed methodology.

1 Introduction

A common assumption when evaluating the performance of communication systems is that users that do not obtain an immediate service leave the system without retrying. However, due to the increasing number of users and the complexity of current systems the impact of retrials is no longer negligible.

This perception has triggered an increasing interest in introducing the phenomenon of retrials in telecommunication systems. Different models have been proposed to evaluate the impact of blocked subscribers retrying after a relative short delay, both in wire line telephone networks [1] and in cellular networks [2]. The retrial phenomenon can also be observed in web browsing, where users try to reload a web page in case of congestion. Retrials do not only appear as a consequence of user behavior, but also due to the operation of some protocols like random access protocols [3]. For an interesting overview of the retrial phenomenon, please refer to [4] and references therein.

In real systems, the population can be very large or even infinite, so the numerical computation can become extremely large in terms of memory space and CPU time, or even impossible in many cases. So approximate methodologies are needed like the one proposed in [5], which is studied in a mobile cellular network scenario. It is based on grouping states according to the presence or not of users in the retrial orbit. Our work is motivated by the perception that this seems a gross approximation in overloaded systems, where retrials are specially

M. Cesana, L. Fratta (Eds.): Wireless Syst./Network Architect. 2005, LNCS 3883, pp. 103–114, 2006.

critical. As it will be shown later, the precision with which common performance parameters are estimated can be quite poor. Our proposal makes it possible a gradual transition from the model in [5] towards the exact model.

The rest of the paper is structured as follows. Section 2 describes the exact model and defines the performance parameters, comparing it with the approximation proposed in [5]. Section 3 introduces the novel approximation of the Markov model and Section 4 presents its numerical evaluation. Finally, a summary of the paper and some concluding remarks are given in Section 5.

2   System Model

As in [5], the system under study is a mobile cellular network with customer retrials. This system can be modeled by Fig. 1, where a group of M users contend for C servers, requesting an exponentially distributed service time with rate μ. When a user accesses the system and finds all servers busy, it joins the retrial orbit and retries after an exponentially distributed time with rate μ_r. The retry is successful if it finds a free server. Otherwise, the user returns to the retrial orbit with probability $(1 - P_i)$ or leaves the system with probability P_i. The implicit assumption of geometric distribution for the number of retrials is a first order approximation to more exact models like the one proposed in [6]. The arrival process is modeled as an state-dependent Poisson process with rate $\lambda(k, m) = (M - k - m)\lambda$, being λ the individual user arrival rate when idle, and k (m) the number of users in service (in the retrial orbit).

The most common performance parameter used in queueing systems is the blocking probability, which is defined as the probability of having all servers occupied. Notwithstanding, other performance parameters can describe the behaviour of retrial systems more accurately. That performance parameters are the immediate service probability (P_{is}), the delayed service probability (P_{ds}) and the non-service probability (P_{ns}). Obviously, it must be met that $P_{is} + P_{ds} + P_{ns} = 1$.

The computation of such performance parameters can be done in terms of the next rates. Let us denote by R_o the mean offered user rate, by $R_{1,s}$ the mean first attempt successful rate and by $R_{1,f}$ the mean first attempt failure rate. It is

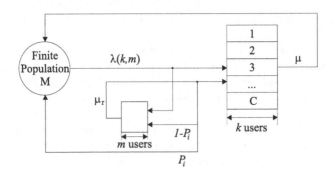

Fig. 1. System Model

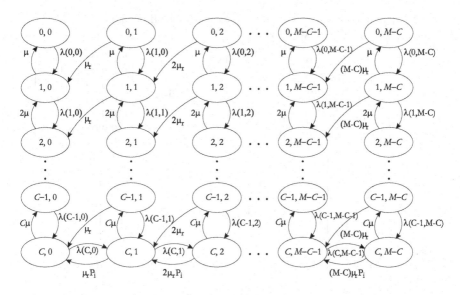

Fig. 2. Exact Markov model

obvious that, $R_o = R_{1,s} + R_{1,f}$. Let us also denote by R_r the mean retrial rate, by $R_{r,s}$ the mean successful retrial rate, and by $R_{r,f}$ the mean failure retrial rate. It is also obvious that, $R_r = R_{r,s} + R_{r,f}$. Finally, let us denote by R_{ab} the mean abandon rate, which can be expressed as $R_{ab} = P_i R_{r,f}$. The performance parameters are defined by the following expressions

$$P_{is} = \frac{R_{1,s}}{R_o}; P_{ds} = \frac{R_{r,s}}{R_o}; P_{ns} = \frac{R_{ab}}{R_o} \tag{1}$$

2.1 Exact Markov Model

The retrial system described in Fig. 1 can be modeled as a Markov process with the state space defined as $S := \{(k,m) : 0 \le k \le C; 0 \le m \le M - C\}$, where k is the number of occupied servers and m the number of users in the retrial orbit. The state-transition diagram is shown in Fig. 2.

The infinitesimal generator matrix (2) presents a tridiagonal structure whose elements are also matrices. This is the classical structure of a QBD process [7].

$$\mathbf{Q} = \begin{bmatrix} \mathbf{D}_0 & \mathbf{L}_0 & \ldots & 0 & 0 \\ \mathbf{M}_1 & \mathbf{D}_1 & \ldots & 0 & 0 \\ 0 & \mathbf{M}_2 & \ldots & 0 & 0 \\ \vdots & \vdots & \ddots & \vdots & \vdots \\ 0 & 0 & \ldots & \mathbf{L}_{M-C-2} & 0 \\ 0 & 0 & \ldots & \mathbf{D}_{M-C-1} & \mathbf{L}_{M-C-1} \\ 0 & 0 & \ldots & \mathbf{M}_{M-C} & \mathbf{D}_{M-C} \end{bmatrix} \tag{2}$$

where $\mathbf{M}_m$, $\mathbf{D}_m$ and $\mathbf{L}_m$, are square matrices with dimension $(C+1)(C+1)$. As an example, for $C = 5$ we have

$$\mathbf{M}_m = \begin{bmatrix} 0 & m\mu_r & 0 & 0 & 0 & 0 \\ 0 & 0 & m\mu_r & 0 & 0 & 0 \\ 0 & 0 & 0 & m\mu_r & 0 & 0 \\ 0 & 0 & 0 & 0 & m\mu_r & 0 \\ 0 & 0 & 0 & 0 & 0 & m\mu_r \\ 0 & 0 & 0 & 0 & 0 & m\mu_r P_i \end{bmatrix} \qquad \mathbf{L}_m = \begin{bmatrix} 0 & 0 & 0 & 0 & 0 & 0 \\ 0 & 0 & 0 & 0 & 0 & 0 \\ 0 & 0 & 0 & 0 & 0 & 0 \\ 0 & 0 & 0 & 0 & 0 & 0 \\ 0 & 0 & 0 & 0 & 0 & 0 \\ 0 & 0 & 0 & 0 & 0 & \lambda(5,m) \end{bmatrix}$$

$$\mathbf{D}_m = \begin{bmatrix} * & \lambda(0,m) & 0 & 0 & 0 & 0 \\ \mu & * & \lambda(1,m) & 0 & 0 & 0 \\ 0 & 2\mu & * & \lambda(2,m) & 0 & 0 \\ 0 & 0 & 3\mu & * & \lambda(3,m) & 0 \\ 0 & 0 & 0 & 4\mu & * & \lambda(4,m) \\ 0 & 0 & 0 & 0 & 5\mu & * \end{bmatrix}$$

The asterisks that appear in $\mathbf{D}_m$ are the negative values that make the sum of every row of $\mathbf{Q}$ equal to zero.

The stationary state probability vector π can be obtained by solving $\pi\mathbf{Q} = \mathbf{0}$ with the normalization condition $\pi\mathbf{e} = \mathbf{1}$. Note that $\mathbf{e}$ is the common all ones transposed vector.

The blocking probability can be computed as

$$BP = \sum_{m=0}^{M-C} \pi(C,m)$$

And the rest of the performance parameters can be determined by using the following expressions

$$R_o = \sum_{k=0}^{C} \sum_{m=0}^{M-C} \lambda(k,m)\pi(k,m) \qquad R_r = \sum_{k=0}^{C} \sum_{m=0}^{M-C} m\mu_r\pi(k,m)$$

$$R_{1,s} = \sum_{k=0}^{C-1} \sum_{m=0}^{M-C} \lambda(k,m)\pi(k,m) \qquad R_{r,s} = \sum_{k=0}^{C-1} \sum_{m=0}^{M-C} m\mu_r\pi(k,m)$$

$$R_{1,f} = \sum_{m=0}^{M-C} \lambda(C,m)\pi(C,m) \qquad R_{r,f} = \sum_{m=0}^{M-C} m\mu_r\pi(C,m)$$

2.2   Previous Approximate Markov Models

In [5] a boolean variable is defined to indicate the presence ('1') or absence ('0') of blocked users with option to retry. Then, the approximation is done by aggregating all the columns of the exact model beyond the first one, i.e. aggregating states depending on the presence or not of users in the retrial orbit.

We evaluated the error introduced by this approximation in a mobile cellular network scenario, which parameters are similar to the ones used in [5], being

M	120 users
C	30 servers
μ	$1/180s^{-1}$
ρ $(\rho = \frac{\lambda}{\lambda+\mu})$	$0.14 - 0.44$
μ_r	$0.1s^{-1}$
P_i	0.5

The results for the exact Markov model are presented in Fig. 3(a), where we show the evolution of the different performance parameters as ρ increases. As can be seen, retrials become important when the system is overloaded, i.e. when the blocking probability is, for example, over 10% ($\rho \simeq 0.22$).

In Fig. 3(b) we evaluate the relative error in the performance parameters when using the approximate methodology, defined by $\mid \Gamma^{exact} - \Gamma^{approx} \mid / \Gamma^{exact}$, where $\Gamma \in \{BP, P_{is}, P_{ds}, P_{ns}\}$. As shown, the blocking probability computed by the approximate model is close to its exact value. However, the relative error in the rest of the performance parameters is not negligible when the mean number of users in the retrial orbit is significant, i.e. in overloaded systems.

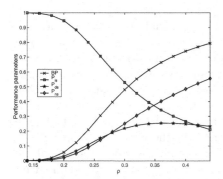

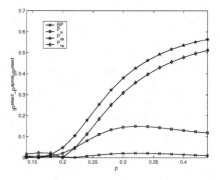

(a) Results of the exact Markov model.   (b) Relative errors respect to the exact.

Fig. 3. Results of the exact model and relative errors of the approximate model

3   Novel Approximate Markov Model

We propose a novel approximate Markov model that is able to improve the accuracy of the model proposed in [5], with a relatively small additional computation cost. This novel model can be considered a generalization of [5], being the aggregation done when there are Q or more users in the retrial orbit. The value of Q is tunable from $Q = 1$ (as proposed in [5]) to $Q = M - C$ (exact model), increasing both accuracy and computation cost as we increase Q.

The generic definition of the state space of that Markov process is $S := \{(k, m) : 0 \le k \le C; 0 \le m \le Q\}$, where k is the number of occupied servers and

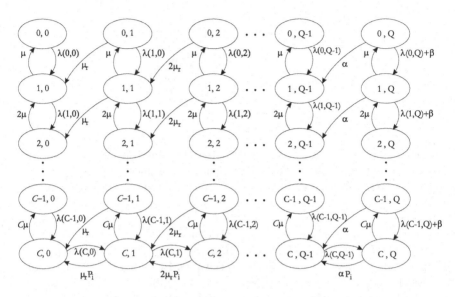

Fig. 4. Approximate Markov model

m (when $m < Q$) is the number of users in the retrial orbit. The set of states (k, Q) corresponds to the situation where Q or more users are in the retrial orbit. Fig. 4 shows the state transition diagram of the proposed approximate model. The first $Q - 1$ columns are exactly the same as the first $Q - 1$ columns in Fig. 2. For column Q we approximate the new users arrival rate by $\lambda(k, Q) = (M - k - \overline{m})\lambda$, where $\overline{m}$ denotes the average number of users in the retrial orbit when it holds Q or more users. When a user in the retrial orbit executes a successful retrial, then the number of users in the orbit can drop below Q with probability $(1 - p)$ or not with probability p. Therefore, the retrial rate in states (k, Q) could be split in two contributing rates α and β. The first one corresponds to transitions from (k, Q) to $(k + 1, Q - 1)$ and is approximated by $\alpha = \overline{m}\mu_r(1 - p)$. The second one corresponds to transitions from (k, Q) to $(k + 1, Q)$, and is approximated by $\beta = \overline{m}\mu_r p$. Parameters $\overline{m}$ and p must be conveniently estimated from the model.

The infinitesimal generator of the proposed model **Q** presents the same structure as the exact model infinitesimal generator changing the limits from $(M - C)$ to Q. Matrices $\mathbf{M}_Q$ and $\mathbf{D}_Q$ are different from those defined in the exact model. As an example, for $C = 5$ we have

$$\mathbf{M}_Q = \begin{bmatrix} 0 & \alpha & 0 & 0 & 0 & 0 \\ 0 & 0 & \alpha & 0 & 0 & 0 \\ 0 & 0 & 0 & \alpha & 0 & 0 \\ 0 & 0 & 0 & 0 & \alpha & 0 \\ 0 & 0 & 0 & 0 & 0 & \alpha \\ 0 & 0 & 0 & 0 & 0 & \alpha P_i \end{bmatrix} \qquad \mathbf{D}_Q = \begin{bmatrix} * & \lambda(0, \overline{m}) + \beta & \ldots & & 0 \\ \mu & * & \ldots & & 0 \\ 0 & 2\mu & \ldots & & 0 \\ 0 & 0 & \ldots & & 0 \\ 0 & 0 & \ldots & \lambda(4, \overline{m}) + \beta \\ 0 & 0 & \ldots & & * \end{bmatrix}$$

The rates defined in Section 2 can now be rewritten as

$$R_o = \sum_{k=0}^{C} \sum_{m=0}^{Q} \lambda(k,m)\pi(k,m) \qquad R_r = \sum_{k=0}^{C} \sum_{m=0}^{Q-1} m\mu_r \pi(k,m) + \overline{m}\mu_r \sum_{k=0}^{C} \pi(k,Q)$$

$$R_{1,s} = \sum_{k=0}^{C-1} \sum_{m=0}^{Q} \lambda(k,m)\pi(k,m) \qquad R_{r,s} = \sum_{k=0}^{C-1} \sum_{m=0}^{Q-1} m\mu_r \pi(k,m) + \overline{m}\mu_r \sum_{k=0}^{C-1} \pi(k,Q)$$

$$R_{1,f} = \sum_{m=0}^{Q} \lambda(C,m)\pi(C,m) \qquad R_{r,f} = \sum_{m=0}^{Q-1} m\mu_r \pi(C,m) + \overline{m}\mu_r \pi(C,Q)$$

Parameters p and $\overline{m}$ can be estimated as described below. Balancing the probability flux crossing each vertical cut of the state transition diagram produces the following set of equations

$$\lambda(C,0)\pi(C,0) = \mu_r \sum_{k=0}^{C} \pi(k,1) - \mu_r \pi(C,1) + \mu_r P_i \pi(C,1)$$

$$\lambda(C,1)\pi(C,1) = 2\mu_r \sum_{k=0}^{C} \pi(k,2) - 2\mu_r \pi(C,2) + 2\mu_r P_i \pi(C,2) \tag{3}$$

$$\dots$$

$$\lambda(C,Q-1)\pi(C,Q-1) = \overline{m}\mu_r(1-p) \sum_{k=0}^{C} \pi(k,Q) - \overline{m}\mu_r(1-p)(1-P_i)\pi(C,Q)$$

Summing them we obtain

$$\sum_{m=0}^{Q-1} \lambda(C,m)\pi(C,m) = \sum_{m=0}^{Q-1} m\mu_r \sum_{k=0}^{C-1} \pi(k,m) + P_i \sum_{m=0}^{Q-1} m\mu_r \pi(C,m)$$
$$+ \overline{m}\mu_r(1-p) \sum_{k=0}^{C} \pi(k,Q) - \overline{m}\mu_r(1-p)(1-P_i)\pi(C,Q)$$

This equation can be rewritten as

$$\left[R_{1,f} - \lambda(C,Q)\pi(C,Q)\right] = \left[R_{r,s} - \overline{m}\mu_r \sum_{k=0}^{C} \pi(k,Q) + \overline{m}\mu_r \pi(C,Q)\right] +$$
$$+ \left[R_{ab} - \overline{m}\mu_r P_i \pi(C,Q)\right] + \overline{m}\mu_r(1-p) \sum_{k=0}^{C} \pi(k,Q) - \overline{m}\mu_r(1-p)(1-P_i)\pi(C,Q)$$

Given that $R_{1,f} = R_{r,s} + R_{ab}$ and after some algebra we get

$$\lambda(C,Q)\pi(C,Q) = \overline{m}\mu_r p \sum_{k=0}^{C} \pi(k,Q) - \overline{m}\mu_r p(1-P_i)\pi(C,Q) \tag{4}$$

From (3) and (4) we get

$$p = \frac{\lambda(C,Q)\pi(C,Q)}{\lambda(C,Q-1)\pi(C,Q-1) + \lambda(C,Q)\pi(C,Q)} \tag{5}$$

$$\overline{m} = \frac{\lambda(C, Q-1)\pi(C, Q-1) + \lambda(C, Q)\pi(C, Q)}{\mu_r[\sum_{k=0}^{k=C-1} \pi(k, Q) + P_i\pi(C, Q)]}$$

To find the values of p and $\overline{m}$ an iterative procedure must be followed. Starting with $p = 0$ and $\overline{m} = Q$ the stationary state probabilities $\pi(k, m)$ can be computed and the next values for p and $\overline{m}$ obtained. The procedure is repeated until the relative precision is less than, for example, 10^{-4}. In [5] the convergence of the iterative procedure was assumed. We evaluated a wide range of scenarios with different configuration parameters and the procedure converged in all cases.

4　Numerical Evaluation

This section has a two-fold objective. One is to evaluate the accuracy of our approach and the other is to evaluate the computation cost savings that can be obtained when referring to the exact model. The parameters used in the scenario under study are the ones presented in Section 2.

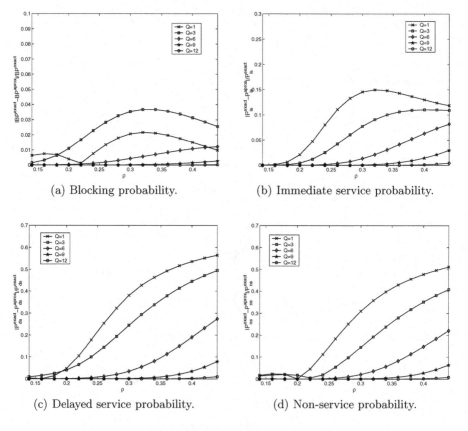

(a) Blocking probability.

(b) Immediate service probability.

(c) Delayed service probability.

(d) Non-service probability.

Fig. 5. Relative errors respect to the exact

4.1   Accuracy

In this section, we study the relative error in the performance parameters for approximate models with increasing complexity, i.e. with an increasing Q value.

In Fig. 5 we plot the relative error in the performance parameter values for different loads. In general, the relative error in all performance parameters decreases as we get closer to the exact model, i.e. as Q increases. Note again that using $Q = 1$ might not be a good choice because the relative error in P_{is}, P_{ds} and P_{ns} is not negligible.

It can be noted that the degree of success of approximations in systems with retrials is mainly dependent on the offered load. The reason of this behavior is that as more load is offered more users will be held in the retrial orbit. Therefore, using higher values for Q seems an intuitive choice. However the value of Q required for a given precision is much lower than $(M - C)$, that would constitute the exact solution. For example, in the worst scenario studied ($\rho = 0.44$), with $Q = 12$ we can get a relative error of less than 10^{-2} in the worst performance parameter while reducing the number of states more than 85%. In not so overloaded scenarios, the state space reduction is even higher.

As a conclusion, a rule of thumb to determine a suitable value for Q could be to try with a value around $Q \simeq 0.15(M - C)$, independently of the system load, although lower values would be probably enough. We have checked this rule in several scenarios and we found that it was a good choice in all of them.

4.2   Computation Costs

In this section we compare the computation costs, measured in floating-point operations (flops),[1] required to solve the exact and approximate models. Two different algorithms have been used, the GJL's proposed by Gaver, Jacobs and Latouche in [8] and the Servi's algorithm proposed in [9]. They provide the same solution but they need a different number of flops.

The scenario considered uses a load of $\rho = 0.22$, which is a typical overloaded scenario. For this scenario it is sufficient to consider $Q = 6$, as can be shown in Fig. 5. Fig. 6(a) shows the cost of each solving algorithm when applied to both the exact and the approximate models with a required relative precision of 10^{-4} for the computation of $\overline{m}$ and p. It is clear that the Servi's algorithm outperforms the GJL's algorithm for the range of Q values of interest. Note that the value of Q at which the costs of the approximate and exact models become equal is less than $M - C$, and from this point on the cost of the approximate model is higher than the cost of the exact model. This is due to the fact that the approximate model has an additional overhead associated to the iterative computation of $\overline{m}$ and p.

For Servi's algorithm, Fig. 6(b) displays the ratio of the costs of solving the approximate and the exact model. As shown, computation costs savings

---

[1] The numerical results and their associated computation cost have been obtained using Matlab. For this product, sums and subtractions require 1 flop if operators are real and 2 flops if complex, products and divisions require 1 flop if the result is real and 6 flops otherwise.

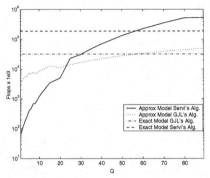

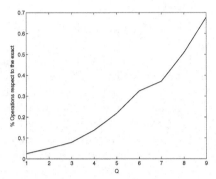

(a) Computation costs with different algorithms.

(b) Computation cost for the algorithm 0 proposed by Servi.

Fig. 6. Results of the exact model and relative errors of the approximate model

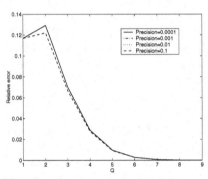

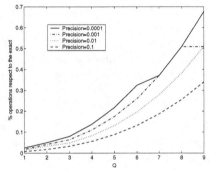

(a) Relative error of the performance parameter which exhibits the highest error (P_{ds}).

(b) Computation cost for the algorithm 0 proposed by Servi.

Fig. 7. Effect of using different precisions for the estimation of $\overline{m}$ and p

of approximately 99.6% are possible for $Q = 6$, which constitute a substantial performance gain while guaranteeing excellent precision.

Moreover, additional savings can be obtained when using a smaller precision for the estimation of $\overline{m}$ and p. Fig. 7(a) shows the variation of the relative error of the performance parameter which exhibits the highest error (P_{ds}) as a function of Q. It is clear that for values of Q higher than 6, it is enough to use rough estimations of $\overline{m}$ and p to achieve a negligible relative error for the values of the performance parameters. Fig. 7(b) shows the ratio of the costs of solving the approximate and the exact model as a function of Q. As observed, the computation cost can additionally be reduced by a factor of 2 for typical values of Q when using rough estimations of $\overline{m}$ and p.

5   Conclusions

We have proposed a novel methodology to determine the value of typical performance parameters in systems with retrials like mobile cellular networks. In these systems, repeated calls can have a negative impact on the performance and therefore its evaluation should not be neglected in the phases of design and planning. When the computation of the exact model might not be feasible due to the explosion of the state space, approximate methodologies are needed.

Our approximation methodology substantially improves the precision of previous approximations like [5], when estimating critical performance parameters. The computation cost can be reduced by two orders of magnitude when comparing to the exact model for a typical overloaded scenario. Additionally, it requires only a very small computation cost increase when compared to the model of [5].

We have noted that relative errors are very sensitive to the load offered to the system, being higher as load increases. We have shown that with a state space reduction of 85% respect to the exact model, our methodology is able to achieve accurate solutions, even in overloaded scenarios.

At present authors are extending this model by considering several retrial orbits. Here, the proposed methodology will allow to handle the state space explosion.

Acknowledgment

The authors express their sincere thanks to Jesús Artalejo and Vicent Pla for their insightful comments. This work has been supported by the Spanish Government and the European Commission through projects TIC2003-08272 and TEC2004-06437-C05-01 (30% PGE and 70% FEDER), by the Spanish Ministry of Education and Science under contract AP-2004-3332 and by the Universidad Politécnica de Valencia under Programa de Incentivo a la Investigación.

References

1. K. Liu, Direct distance dialing: Call completion and customer retrial behavior, *Bell System Technical Journal*, Vol. 59, pp. 295–311, 1980.
2. P. Tran-Gia and M. Mandjes, Modeling of customer retrial phenomenon in cellular mobile networks, *IEEE Journal on Selected Areas in Communications*, Vol. 15, pp. 1406–1414, October 1997.
3. D. J. Goodman and A. A. M. Saleh, The near/far effect in local ALOHA radio communications, *IEEE Transactions on Vehicular Technology*, Vol. 36, no. 1, pp. 19-27. February 1987.
4. J. Artalejo and G. Falin, Standard and retrial queueing system: A comparative analysis, *Revista Matemática Complutense*, vol 15, no. 1 pp. 101-129, 2002.
5. M. A. Marsan, G. De Carolis, E. Leonardi, R. Lo Cigno and M. Meo, Efficient Estimation of Call Blocking Probabilities in Cellular Mobile Telephony Networks with Customer Retrials, *IEEE Journal on Selected Areas in Communications*, Vol. 19, no. 2, pp. 332-346, February 2001.

6. E. Onur, H. Deliç, C. Ersoy and M. U. Çaglayan, Measurement-based replanning of cell capacities in GSM networks, *Computer Networks,* Vol. 39, pp. 749-767, 2002.
7. M. F. Neuts, *Matrix Geometric Solutions in Stochastic Models: An Algorithmic Approach,* The John Hopkins University Press, Baltimore, 1981.
8. D. P. Gaver, P. A. Jacobs and G. Latouche, Finite birth-and-death models in randomly changing environments, *Advanced Applied Probability,* Vol. 16, pp. 715-731, 1984.
9. L. D.Servi, Algorithmic Solutions to Two-Dimensional Birth-Death Processes with Application to Capacity Planning, *Telecommunication Systems,* Vol. 21:2-4, pp. 205-212, 2002.

An Afterstates Reinforcement Learning Approach to Optimize Admission Control in Mobile Cellular Networks

José Manuel Giménez-Guzmán, Jorge Martínez-Bauset, and Vicent Pla

Departamento de Comunicaciones, Universidad Politècnica de València, UPV,
ETSIT Camino de Vera s/n, 46022, València, Spain
jogiguz@doctor.upv.es
{jmartinez, vpla}@dcom.upv.es

Abstract. We deploy a novel Reinforcement Learning optimization technique based on afterstates learning to determine the gain that can be achieved by incorporating movement prediction information in the session admission control process in mobile cellular networks. The novel technique is able to find better solutions and with less dispersion. The gain is obtained by evaluating the performance of optimal policies achieved with and without the predictive information, while taking into account possible prediction errors. The prediction agent is able to determine the handover instants both stochastically and deterministically. Numerical results show significant performance gains when the predictive information is used in the admission process, and that higher gains are obtained when deterministic handover instants can be determined.

1 Introduction

Session Admission Control (SAC) is a key traffic management mechanism in mobile cellular networks to provide QoS guarantees. Terminal mobility makes it very difficult to guarantee that the resources available at the time of session setup will be available in the cells visited during the session lifetime, unless a SAC policy is exerted. The design of the SAC system must take into account not only packet level issues (like delay, jitter or losses) but also session level issues (like loss probabilities of both session setup and handover requests). This paper explores the second type of issues from a novel optimization approach that exploits the availability of movement prediction information. To the best of our knowledge, applying optimization techniques to this type of problem has not been sufficiently explored. The results provided define theoretical limits for the gains that can be expected if handover prediction is used, which could not be established by deploying heuristic SAC approaches.

In systems that do not have predictive information available, both heuristic and optimization approaches have been proposed to improve the performance of the SAC at the session level. Optimization approaches not using predictive information have been studied in [1, 2, 3, 4]. In systems that have predictive information available, most of the proposed approaches to improve performance are heuristic, see for example [5, 6] and references therein.

M. Cesana, L. Fratta (Eds.): Wireless Syst./Network Architect. 2005, LNCS 3883, pp. 115–129, 2006.

Our work has been motivated in part by the study in [5]. Briefly, the authors propose a sophisticated movement prediction system and a SAC scheme that taking advantage of movement prediction information is able to improve system performance. One of the novelties of the proposal is that the SAC scheme takes into consideration not only incoming handovers to a cell but also the outgoing ones. The authors justify it by arguing that considering only the incoming ones would led to reserve more resources than required, given that during the time elapsed since the incoming handover is predicted and resources are reserved until it effectively occurs, outgoing handovers might have provided additional free resources, making the reservation unnecessary.

In this paper we explore a novel Reinforcement Learning (RL) optimization technique based on afterstates learning, which was suggested in [7]. RL is a simulation based optimization technique in which an agent learns an optimal policy by interacting with an environment which rewards the agent for each executed action. We will show that when comparing afterstates learning with conventional learning, the former is able to find better solutions (policies) and with more precision (less dispersion).

We do a comparative performance evaluation of different scenarios that differ on the type of predictive information that is provided to the SAC optimization process, like only incoming, only outgoing and both types of handover predictions together. We also evaluate the impact that predicting the future handover instants either stochastically or deterministically have on the system performance.

The rest of the paper is structured as follows. In Section 2 we describe the models of the system and of the two prediction agents deployed. The optimization approaches are presented in Section 3. A numerical evaluation comparing the performance obtained when using different types of information and when handovers instants are stochastically or deterministically predicted is provided in Section 4. This later Section also includes a comparison of the performance of the two reinforcement learning approaches, i.e. afterstates and conventional learning. Finally, a summary of the paper and some concluding remarks are given in Section 5.

2   Model Description

We consider a single cell system and its neighborhood, where the cell has a total of C resource units, being the physical meaning of a unit of resources dependent on the specific technological implementation of the radio interface. Only one service is offered but new and handover session arrivals are distinguished, making a total of two arrival types.

For mathematical tractability we make the common assumptions. New and handover sessions arrive according to a Poisson process with rates λ_n and λ_h respectively. The duration of a session and the cell residence time are exponentially distributed with rates μ_s and μ_r respectively, hence the resource holding time in a cell is also exponentially distributed with rate $\mu = \mu_s + \mu_r$. Without loss of generality, we will assume that each session consumes one unit of resource and that only one session is active per mobile terminal (MT).

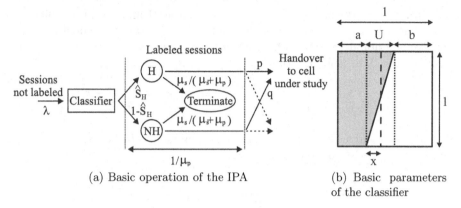

(a) Basic operation of the IPA

(b) Basic parameters of the classifier

Fig. 1. IPA and classifier models

We used a model of the prediction agent, given that the focus of our study was not the design of it.

2.1   Prediction Agent for Incoming Handovers

An active MT entering the cell neighborhood is labeled by the prediction agent for incoming handovers (IPA) as "probably producing a handover" (H) or the opposite (NH), according to some of its characteristics (position, trajectory, velocity, historic profile,...) and/or some other information (road map, hour of the day,...). After an exponentially distributed time, the actual destiny of the MT becomes definitive and either a handover into the cell occurs or not (for instance because the session ends or the MT moves to another cell) as shown in Fig. 1(a). The SAC system is aware of the number of MTs labeled as H at any time.

The model of the classifier is shown in Fig. 1(b) where the square (with a surface equal to one) represents the population of active MTs to be classified. The shaded area represents the fraction of MTs (S_H) that will ultimately move into the cell, while the white area represents the rest of active MTs. Notice that part of the MTs that will move into the cell can finish their active sessions before doing so. The classifier sets a threshold (represented by a vertical dashed line) to discriminate between those MTs that will likely produce a handover and those that will not. The fraction of MTs falling on the left side of the threshold ($\hat{S}_H$) are labeled as H and those on the right side as NH. There exists an uncertainty zone, of width U, which accounts for classification errors: the white area on the left of the threshold ($\hat{S}_H^e$) and the shaded area on the right of the threshold ($\hat{S}_{NH}^e$). The parameter x represents the relative position of the classifier threshold within the uncertainty zone. Although for simplicity we use a linear model for the uncertainty zone it would be rather straightforward to consider a different model.

As shown in Fig. 1(a), the model of the IPA is characterized by three parameters: the average sojourn time of the MT in the predicted stage μ_p^{-1}, the probability p of producing a handover if labeled as H and the probability q of producing a handover if labeled as NH. Note that $1 - p$ and q model the false-positive and non-detection probabilities respectively and in general $q \neq 1 - p$.

From Fig. 1(b) it follows that

$$1 - p = \frac{\hat{S}_H^e}{\hat{S}_H} = \frac{x^2}{2U(a+x)} \; ; \qquad q = \frac{\hat{S}_{NH}^e}{1 - \hat{S}_H} = \frac{(U-x)^2}{2U(1-a-x)}$$

Parameters a and b can be expressed in terms of S_H and U, being $a = S_H - U/2$ and $b = 1 - S_H - U/2$. Then

$$1 - p = \frac{x^2}{(U(2S_H - U + 2x))}; \quad q = \frac{(U-x)^2}{(U(2 - 2S_H + U - 2x))} \qquad (1)$$

Referring to Fig. 1(a), the value of the session rate entering the classifier λ is chosen so that the system is in statistical equilibrium, i.e. the rate at which handover sessions enter a cell (λ_h^{in}) is equal to the rate at which handover sessions exit the cell (λ_h^{out}). It is clear that

$$\lambda_h^{in} = \lambda S_H \frac{\mu_p}{\mu_p + \mu_s} \; ; \qquad \lambda_h^{out} = \frac{\mu_r}{\mu_r + \mu_s}[(1 - P_n)\lambda_n + (1 - P_h)\lambda_h^{in}]$$

where P_n (P_h) is the blocking probability of new (handover) requests.

Making $\lambda_h^{in} = \lambda_h^{out}$, substituting P_h by $P_h = (\mu_s/\mu_r) \cdot [P_{ft}/(1 - P_{ft})]$, where P_{ft} is the probability of forced termination of a successfully initiated session, and after some algebra we get

$$\lambda = (1 - P_n)(1 - P_{ft})\lambda_n(\mu_r/\mu_s + \mu_r/\mu_p)(1/S_H) \qquad (2)$$

2.2   Prediction Agent for Outgoing Handovers

The model of the prediction agent for outgoing handovers (OPA) is shown in Fig. 2. The OPA labels active sessions in the cell as H if they will produce a handover or as NH otherwise. The classification is performed for both handover sessions that enter the cell and new sessions that initiate in the cell, and are carried out by a classifier which model is the same as the one used in the IPA. The time elapsed since the session is labeled until the actual destiny of the MT becomes definitive is the cell residence time that, as defined, is exponentially distributed with rate μ_r. The fraction of sessions that effectively execute an outgoing handover is given by $S_H = \mu_r/(\mu_s + \mu_r)$. The OPA model is characterized by only two parameters $1 - p$ and q, which meaning is the same as in the IPA model. Note that $1 - p$ and q can be related to the classifier parameters by the expressions in (1).

In an earlier version of the IPA we were providing the optimization process only with state information of the neighboring cells but without any predictive information. We obtained that the gain was not significant, possibly because the information was not sufficiently specific. The authors in [8] reached the same

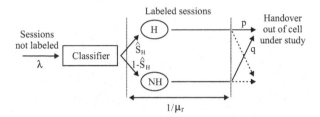

Fig. 2. Basic operation of the OPA

conclusion but using a genetic algorithm to find near-optimal policies. As it will be described in Section 4, here we are considering a circular-shaped cell of radio r and a holed-disk-shaped neighborhood with inner (outer) radio $1.0r$ $(1.5r)$ and providing the optimization process with predictive information of this sufficiently close neighborhood. This produces a significant gain. For the design of the OPA we were faced with the same dilemma but in this case we decided not to use more specific information. Defining a holed-disk-shaped neighborhood with outer (inner) radio r ($< r$) for the outgoing handovers and an exponentially distributed sojourn time in it, would had open the possibility of having terminals that could go in and out of this area, making the cell residence time not exponential. This would had increased the complexity and made the models with the IPA and with the OPA not comparable.

3   Optimizing the SAC Policy

We formulate the optimization problem as an infinite-horizon finite-state Markov decision process under the average cost criterion, which is more appropriate for the problem under study than other discounted cost approaches. When the system starts at state $\boldsymbol{x}$ and follows policy π then the average expected cost rate over time t, as $t \to \infty$, is denoted by $\gamma^\pi(\boldsymbol{x})$ and defined as: $\gamma^\pi(\boldsymbol{x}) = \lim_{t\to\infty} \frac{1}{t} E\left[w^\pi(\boldsymbol{x}, t)\right]$, where $w^\pi(\boldsymbol{x}, t)$ is a random variable that expresses the total cost incurred in the interval $[0, t]$. For the systems we are considering, it is not difficult to see that for every deterministic stationary policy the embedded Markov chain has a unichain transition probability matrix, and therefore the average expected cost rate does not vary with the initial state [9]. We call it the "cost" of the policy π, denote it by γ^π and consider the problem of finding the policy π^* that minimizes γ^π, which we name the optimal policy.

In our model the cost structure is chosen so that the average expected cost represents a weighted sum of the loss rates, i.e. $\gamma^\pi = \omega_n P_n \lambda_n + \omega_h P_h \lambda_h$, where ω_n (ω_h) is the cost incurred when the loss of a new (handover) request occurs and P_n (P_h) is the loss probability of new (handover) requests. In general, $\omega_n < \omega_h$ since the loss of a handover request is less desirable than the loss of a new session setup request.

Two optimization approaches have been explored: a dynamic programming (DP) approach and an automatic learning approach based on the theory of

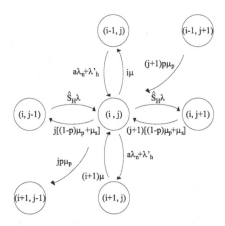

Fig. 3. State transition diagram

Reinforcement Learning [7]. DP gives an exact solution and allows to evaluate the theoretical limits of incorporating handover prediction in the SAC system, whereas RL tackles more efficiently the curse of dimensionality and has the important advantage of being a model-free method, i.e. transition probabilities and average costs are not needed in advance. In both approaches handover sessions have priority over new sessions and they are accepted as long as resources are available.

3.1 Dynamic Programming

We apply DP to the scenario that only considers the incoming handovers, in which case the system state space is $S := \{\boldsymbol{x} = (i,j) : 0 \leq i \leq C; \; 0 \leq j \leq C_p\}$, where i is the number of active sessions in the cell, j is the number of MTs labeled as H in the cell neighborhood and C_p is the maximum number of MT that can be labeled as H at a given time. We use a large value for C_p so that it has no practical impact in our results. At each state $(i,j), i < C$, the set of possible actions is defined by $A := \{a : a = 0, 1\}$, being $a = 0$ the action that rejects an incoming new session and $a = 1$ the action that accepts an incoming new session. The system can be described as a continuous-time Markov chain which state transition diagram is shown in Fig. 3, where $\lambda_h' = q\lambda(1 - \hat{S}_H)\mu_p/(\mu_p + \mu_s)$ denotes the average arrival rate of unpredicted handovers. It is converted to a *discrete time Markov chain* (DTMC) by applying uniformization. It can be shown that $\Gamma = C_p(\mu_p + \mu_s) + C(\mu_r + \mu_s) + \lambda + \lambda_n$ is an uniform upper-bound for the outgoing rate of all the states, being λ the input rate to the classifier. If $r_{\boldsymbol{xy}}(a)$ denotes the transition rate from state $\boldsymbol{x}$ to state $\boldsymbol{y}$ when action a is taken at state $\boldsymbol{x}$, then the transition probabilities of the resulting DTMC are given by $p_{\boldsymbol{xy}}(a) = r_{\boldsymbol{xy}}(a)/\Gamma$ ($\boldsymbol{y} \neq \boldsymbol{x}$) and $p_{\boldsymbol{xx}}(a) = 1 - \sum_{\boldsymbol{y} \in S} p_{\boldsymbol{xy}}(a)$. We define the incurred cost rate at state $\boldsymbol{x}$ when action a is selected by $c(\boldsymbol{x}, a)$, which can take any of the following values: 0 ($i < C$, $a = 1$), $\omega_n \lambda_n$ ($i < C$, $a = 0$) or $\omega_n \lambda_n + \omega_h(\lambda_h' + jp\mu_p)$ ($i = C$, $a = 0$).

If we denote by $h(\boldsymbol{x})$ the relative cost rate of state $\boldsymbol{x}$ under policy π, then we can write

$$h(\boldsymbol{x}) = c(\boldsymbol{x}, \pi(\boldsymbol{x})) - \gamma^\pi + \sum_{\boldsymbol{y}} p_{\boldsymbol{xy}}(\pi(\boldsymbol{x}))h(\boldsymbol{y}) \qquad \forall \boldsymbol{x} \qquad (3)$$

from which we can obtain the average cost and the relative costs $h(\boldsymbol{x})$ up to an undetermined constant. We arbitrarily set $h(0,0) = 0$ and then solve the linear system of equations (3) to obtain γ^π and $h(\boldsymbol{x})$, $\forall \boldsymbol{x}$. Having obtained the average and relative costs under policy π, an improved policy π' can be calculated as

$$\pi'(\boldsymbol{x}) = \arg\min_{a=0,1} \left\{ c(\boldsymbol{x}, a) - \gamma^\pi + \sum_{\boldsymbol{y}} p_{\boldsymbol{xy}}(a)h(\boldsymbol{y}) \right\}$$

so that the following relation holds $\gamma^{\pi'} \leq \gamma^\pi$. Moreover, if the equality holds then $\pi' = \pi = \pi^*$, where π^* denotes the optimal policy, i.e. $\gamma^{\pi^*} \leq \gamma^\pi \; \forall \pi$.

We repeat iteratively the solution of system (3) and the policy improvement until we obtain a policy which does not change after improvement. This process is called *Policy Iteration* [9, Section 8.6] and it leads to the average optimal policy in a finite —and typically small— number of iterations. Note that although the number of iterations is typically small each iteration entails solving a linear system of the same size as the state space, and thus the overall computational complexity can be considerably high.

3.2 Reinforcement Learning

We formulate the optimization problem as an infinite-horizon finite-state semi-Markov decision process (SMDP) under the average cost criterion. Only arrival events are relevant to the optimization process because no actions are taken at session departures. Additionally, given that no decisions are taken for handover arrivals (they are always accepted if enough free resources are available), then the decision epochs correspond only to the time instants at which new session arrivals occur. The state space for the scenario that only considers the incoming handovers is the same as defined when deploying DP, i.e. $S := \{\boldsymbol{x} = (x_0, x_{in}) : x_0 \leq C; x_{in} \leq C_p\}$, where x_0 and x_{in} represent, respectively, the number of active sessions in the cell and the number of sessions labeled as H in the cell neighborhood. The state space for the scenario that only considers the outgoing handovers is defined as $S := \{\boldsymbol{x} = (x_0, x_{out}) : x_{out} \leq x_0 \leq C\}$, where x_{out} represents the number of sessions labeled as H in the cell. The state space for the scenario that considers both the incoming and outgoing handovers is defined as $S := \{\boldsymbol{x} = (x_0, x_{in}, x_{out}) : x_{out} \leq x_0 \leq C; x_{in} \leq C_p\}$. At each decision epoch the system has to select an action from the set $A := \{a : a = 0, 1\}$, being $a = 0$ the action that rejects an incoming new session and $a = 1$ the action that accepts an incoming new session.

The cost structure is defined as follows. At any decision epoch, the cost incurred by accepting a new session request is zero and by rejecting it is ω_n. Further accrual of cost occurs when the system has to reject handover requests between two decision epochs, incurring a cost of ω_h per rejection.

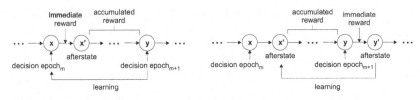

(a) Conventional learning.   (b) Afterstates learning.

Fig. 4. Reinforcement learning process

Intuitively, in systems as the one being considered, afterstates learning is based on the idea that what is relevant in the learning process is the state reached immediately after the action is taken. More specifically, all states at decision epochs in which the immediate actions taken drive the system to the same afterstate, would accumulate the same future cost if the same future actions are taken. The difference between conventional learning and afterstates learning is shown in Fig. 4.

In SMDPs actions occur at variable length time instants and therefore, state transition dynamics is specified not only by the state where an action was taken, but also by a parameter specifying the length of time since the action was taken. The Bellman optimality recurrence equations for a SMDP under the average cost criterion when learning is done at each decision epoch can be written as

$$h^*(\boldsymbol{x}) = \min_{a \in A_x} \{w(\boldsymbol{x}, a) - \gamma^* \tau(\boldsymbol{x}, a) + \sum_{\boldsymbol{y} \in S} p_{\boldsymbol{x}\boldsymbol{y}}(a) \min_{a' \in A_y} h^*(\boldsymbol{y}, a')\}$$

where $h^*(\boldsymbol{x}, a)$ is the average expected relative cost of taking the optimal action a in state $\boldsymbol{x}$ and then continuing indefinitely by choosing actions optimally, $w(\boldsymbol{x}, a)$ is the average cost of taking action a in state $\boldsymbol{x}$, $\tau(\boldsymbol{x}, a)$ is the average sojourn time in state $\boldsymbol{x}$ under action a (i.e. the average time between decision epochs) and $p_{\boldsymbol{x}\boldsymbol{y}}(a)$ is the probability of moving from state $\boldsymbol{x}$ to state $\boldsymbol{y}$ under action $a = \pi(\boldsymbol{x})$.

We deploy a modified version of the SMART algorithm [10] which follows an afterstates learning process using a temporal difference method (TD(0)). The pseudo code of the proposed algorithm is shown in the box below. In systems where the number of states can be large, RL based on afterstates learning tackles more efficiently the curse of dimensionality.

SMART with afterstates

1: Initialize $h(\boldsymbol{x}), \forall \boldsymbol{x} \in S$, arbitrarily (usually zeros)
2: Initialize γ arbitrarily (usually zeros)
3: Initialize $N(\boldsymbol{x}) = 0$, $W_T = 0$ and $T_T = 0$
4: Repeat forever:
        We denote by a the action taken in the current state $\boldsymbol{y}$, by $\boldsymbol{y}'_{reject}$
        ($\boldsymbol{y}'_{accept}$) the afterstate when the reject (accept) action is taken and
        by ω_{reject} the immediate cost when the request is rejected.

5:      Take action a:
6:          Exploration: random action
7:          *Greedy*: action selected from
$$\text{if } \left(h(\boldsymbol{y'}_{reject}) + w_{reject}\right) < h(\boldsymbol{y'}_{accept}) \text{ then}$$
$$a = reject$$
else
$$a = accept$$
8:      $\alpha = 1/(1 + N(\boldsymbol{x'}))$
        being α de learning rate, $\boldsymbol{x'}$ the previous afterstate and $N(\boldsymbol{x'})$ the number of
        times the afterstate $\boldsymbol{x'}$ has been updated:
9:      $h(\boldsymbol{x'}) \leftarrow (1 - \alpha)h(\boldsymbol{x'}) + \alpha\left[w_c(\boldsymbol{x'}, \boldsymbol{y}) + w(\boldsymbol{y}, a) + h(\boldsymbol{y'}) - \gamma\tau\right]$
        $N(\boldsymbol{x'}) \leftarrow N(\boldsymbol{x'}) + 1$
        being $w_c(\boldsymbol{x'}, \boldsymbol{y})$ the accrued cost when the system evolves from $\boldsymbol{x'}$ to $\boldsymbol{y}$, $w(\boldsymbol{y}, a)$
        the immediate cost of taking action a in state $\boldsymbol{y}$ and τ the time elapsed
        between decision epochs m and $m + 1$ (see Fig. 4(b)).
10:     if a is *greedy*:
11:         $W_T \leftarrow W_T + w_c(\boldsymbol{x'}, \boldsymbol{y}) + w(\boldsymbol{y}, a)$
12:         $T_T \leftarrow T_T + \tau$
13:         $\gamma \leftarrow W_T/T_T$
14:     $\boldsymbol{x'} \leftarrow \boldsymbol{y'}$

4   Numerical Evaluation

When introducing prediction, we evaluated the performance gain by the ratio $\gamma_{wp}^{\pi}/\gamma_p^{\pi}$, where γ_p^{π} (γ_{wp}^{π}) is the average expected cost rate of the optimal policy in a system with (without) prediction. We assume a circular-shaped cell of radio r and a holed-disk-shaped neighborhood with inner (outer) radio $1.0r$ ($1.5r$).

The values of the parameters that define the scenario are: $C = 10$ and $C_p = 60$, $\mu_r/\mu_s = 1$, $\mu_r/\mu_p = 0.5$, $\lambda_n = 2$, $\mu = \mu_s + \mu_r = 1$, $x = U/2$, $w_n = 1$, and $w_h = 20$. When deploying the IPA, $S_H = 0.4$. Note that in our numerical experiments the values of the arrival rates are chosen to achieve realistic operating values for $P_n(\approx 10^{-2})$ and $P_{ft}(\approx 10^{-3})$. For such values, we approximate (2) as $\lambda \approx 0.989\lambda_n(N_h + \mu_r/\mu_p)(1/S_H)$.

For the RL simulations, the ratio of arrival rates of new sessions to the cell neighborhood (ng) and to the cell (nc) is made equal to the ratio of their surfaces, $\lambda_{ng} = 1.25\lambda_{nc}$. The ratio of handover arrival rates to the cell neighborhood from the outside of the system (ho) and from the cell (hc) is made equal to ratio of their perimeters, $\lambda_{ho} = 1.5\lambda_{hc}$. Using the flow equilibrium property, we can write $\lambda_{ho} = (1 - P_n)(1 - P_{ft})(\mu_r/\mu_s)\lambda_{nc} \approx 0.989(\mu_r/\mu_s)\lambda_{nc}$. With regard to the RL algorithm, at the mth decision epoch an exploratory action is taken with probability p_m, which is decayed to zero by using the following rule $p_m = p_0/(1 + u)$, where $u = m^2/(\varphi + m)$. We used $\varphi = 1.0 \cdot 10^{12}$ and $p_0 = 0.1$. The exploration of the state space is a common RL technique used to avoid being trapped at local minima.

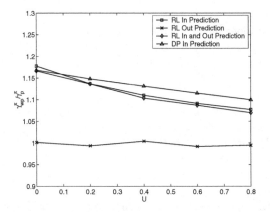

Fig. 5. Performance gain when using stochastic handover prediction

4.1   Stochastic Prediction

The prediction agents described in Sections 2.1 and 2.2 predict the time instants at which handovers will occur only stochastically and Fig. 5 shows the gain for different values of the uncertainty U when deploying such agents. When using RL, for each value of U we run 10 simulations with different seeds and display the averages. As observed, using incoming handover prediction induces a gain and that gain decreases as the prediction uncertainty (U) increases. From Fig. 5 it is clear that the knowledge of the number of resources that will become available is not relevant for the determination of optimum SAC policies, being even independent of the degree of uncertainty. This counter-intuitive phenomenon could be explained as follows.

Lemma 1. *Let X and Y be two independent and exponentially distributed rv with means $1/\mu_x$ and $1/\mu_y$, and $f_{(X,Y)}(x,y)$ its joint pdf, where $f_{(X,Y)}(x,y) = f_X(x)f_Y(y)$. Then the pdf of X conditioned on $X < Y$, is given by*

$$f_X(x|X < Y) = \frac{\int_x^\infty f_{(X,Y)}(x,y)dy}{\int_0^\infty \int_x^\infty f_{(X,Y)}(x,y)dydx} = \frac{f_X(x)\int_x^\infty f_Y(y)dy}{\int_0^\infty \int_x^\infty f_X(x)f_Y(y)dydx}$$

$$= (\mu_x + \mu_y)e^{-(\mu_x+\mu_y)x}$$

Now consider a perfect OPA, i.e. one with $p = 1$ and $q = 0$. Those sessions tagged as H will release the resources because they leave the cell —since we know this will happen before the session finishes— and hence, applying the result set in Lemma 1, the holding time of resources is exponentially distributed with mean $1/(\mu_r + \mu_s)$. Conversely, those sessions tagged as NH will release the resources because their sessions finish —since we know this will happen before the terminal leaves the cell— and hence the holding time of resources is exponentially distributed with mean $1/(\mu_r + \mu_s)$. Note that as the holding time of resources for H and NH sessions are identically distributed, having an imperfect OPA will not make any difference. On the other hand, if no out prediction is considered, an active session will release the resources because the session finishes or the terminal leaves the cell, whichever happens first, and therefore the holding time of resources is also exponentially distributed with mean $1/(\mu_r + \mu_s)$.

Therefore, if both the cell residence time and the session holding time are exponentially distributed, knowing whether a session will produce an outgoing handover or not does not provide, in theory, any helpful information to the SAC process. Additionally, the performance of the SAC should not be affected by the precision of the OPA.

4.2   Deterministic Prediction

In this section we evaluate the impact that more precise knowledge of the future handover time instants have on performance. Intuitively, it seems obvious that handovers taking place in a near future would be more relevant for the SAC process than those occurring in an undetermined far future. More precisely, in this is section both the IPA and OPA operate as before but the prediction will be made available to the admission controller, at most, T time units in advance the handover takes place. If the future handover is predicted less than T time units ahead of its occurrence the prediction is made available to the admission controller immediately, i.e. when the handover sessions enter the cell neighborhood or the cell and when new sessions are initiated. In that sense, the stochastic prediction can be seen as particular or limit case of the deterministic one when $T \to \infty$. A similar approach is used in [5], where authors predict the incoming and outgoing handovers that will take place in a time window of fixed size.

For the performance evaluation we use the scenarios, parameters and methodology described in Section 4.1, but now two uncertainty values are considered. In the first we set $U = 0.2$, which we consider it might be a practical value, while in the second, as a reference, we set it to $U = 0$. Figure 6 shows the variation of the gain for different values of T and U. As observed, there exists an optimum value for T, which is close to the mean time between call arrivals (λ^{-1}), although it might depend on other system parameters as well. As T goes beyond its optimum value, the gain decreases, probably because the temporal information becomes less significant for the SAC decision process. As expected, when $T \to \infty$ the gain is identical to the one in the stochastic prediction case. When T is lower than its optimum value the gain also decreases, probably because the system has not enough time to react. When $T = 0$ the gain is null because there is no prediction at all.

Figure 6 shows again that the information provided by the OPA is in general not relevant for the optimization process, except for a small interval around its optimal value, which is slightly above unity. For values of T close to its optimum, the gain is higher when using incoming and outgoing prediction together than when using only incoming handover prediction, and it is significantly higher than when stochastic time prediction is used.

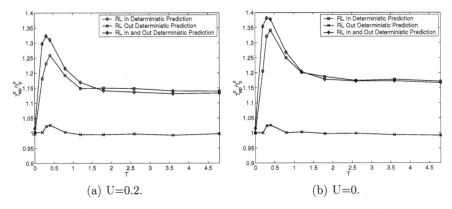

(a) U=0.2.   (b) U=0.

Fig. 6. Performance gain when using deterministic handover prediction

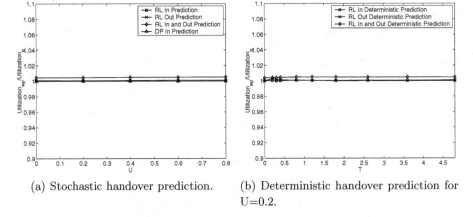

(a) Stochastic handover prediction.   (b) Deterministic handover prediction for U=0.2.

Fig. 7. Utilization gain when using handover prediction

Finally it is worth noting that the main challenge in the design of efficient bandwidth reservation techniques for mobile cellular networks is to balance two conflicting requirements: reserving enough resources to achieve a low forced termination probability and keeping the resource utilization high by not blocking too many new setup requests. Figure 7, which shows the ratio of the system resources utilization when not using prediction and when using prediction (utilization$_{wp}$/utilization$_p$) for both stochastic and deterministic prediction, justifies the efficiency of our optimization approach.

4.3   Comparison of Learning Techniques

In this section we evaluate the performance of the afterstates learning process. Figure 8 and Figure 9 compares the mean, the confidence interval and the relative width of the confidence interval (the ratio of the width to the mean) when

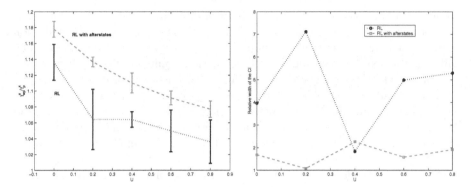

(a) Confidence interval of the gain when deploying input prediction.

(b) Relative width of the confidence interval when deploying input prediction.

Fig. 8. Comparison of the confidence intervals of the gain when deploying input prediction

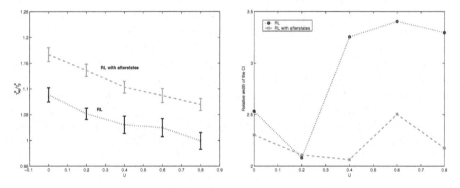

(a) Confidence interval of the gain when deploying input and output prediction.

(b) Relative width of the confidence interval when deploying input and output prediction.

Fig. 9. Comparison of the confidence intervals of the gain when deploying input and output prediction

deploying conventional learning and afterstates learning. As observed, the solutions obtained when deploying afterstates learning are better (the gain $\gamma_{wp}^{\pi}/\gamma_p^{\pi}$ is higher) and more precise (the relative width of the confidence interval is smaller).

5   Conclusions

In this paper we evaluate the performance gain that can be expected when the SAC optimization process is provided with information related to incoming, outgoing and incoming and outgoing handovers together, in a mobile cellular network scenario. The prediction information is provided by two types of prediction agents that label active mobile terminals in the cell or its neighborhood which will probably execute a handover. The prediction agents predict the future time instants at which handovers will occur either stochastically or deterministically.

The optimization problem is formulated as a Markov or semi-Markov decision process and two solving methods are used: dynamic programming and an afterstates based reinforcement learning approach. A general model of the prediction agents has been considered and as such it cannot be used neither to obtain results for specific systems nor to evaluate the added complexity of deploying a particular prediction method in operational systems. Nevertheless, the generality of the prediction model together with the optimization-based approach permit to obtain bounds for the gain of specific prediction schemes used in conjunction with SAC.

For the system model deployed, numerical results show that the information related to incoming handovers is more relevant than the one related to outgoing handovers. Additional performance gains can be obtained when more specific information is provided about the handover time instants, i.e. when their prediction is deterministic instead of stochastic. The gain obtained has been higher than 30% in the studied scenario even when the prediction uncertainty is 20%.

In a future work we will study the impact that a non-exponential resource holding time has on the performance of systems which deploy predictive information in the SAC process. As shown, when the resource holding time is exponential, deploying the OPA does not improve performance. We will also generalize the operation of the deterministic prediction agents by considering values for T independent for the IPA and for the OPA. Another aspect that deserves a closer study is the identification of the parameters that affect the optimum value of T and the study of its sensitivity.

Acknowledgments

This work has been supported by the Spanish Ministry of Education and Science (30% PGE, 70% FEDER) under projects TIC2003-08272 and TEC2004-06437-C05-01, and by the Universidad Politécnica de Valencia under "Programa de Incentivo a la Investigación".

References

1. R. Ramjee, R. Nagarajan, and D. Towsley, "On optimal call admission control in cellular networks," Wireless Networks Journal (WINET), vol. 3, no. 1, pp. 29–41, 1997.
2. N. Bartolini, "Handoff and optimal channel assignment in wireless networks," Mobile Networks and Applications (MONET), vol. 6, no. 6, pp. 511–524, 2001.
3. N. Bartolini and I. Chlamtac, "Call admission control in wireless multimedia networks," in Proceedings of IEEE PIMRC, 2002.

4. V. Pla and V. Casares-Giner, "Optimal admission control policies in multiservice cellular networks," in Proceedings of the International Network Optimization Conference (INOC), 2003, pp. 466–471.
5. W.-S. Soh and H. S. Kim, "Dynamic bandwidth reservation in cellular networks using road topology based mobility prediction," in Proceedings of IEEE INFOCOM, 2004.
6. Roland Zander and Johan M Karlsson, "Predictive and Adaptive Resource Reservation (PARR) for Cellular Networks," International Journal of Wireless Information Networks, vol. 11, no. 3, pp. 161-171, 2004.
7. R. Sutton and A. G. Barto, Reinforcement Learning. Cambridge, Massachusetts: The MIT press, 1998.
8. C. Yener, A. Rose, "Genetic algorithms applied to cellular call admission: local policies," IEEE Transaction on Vehicular Technology, vol. 46, no. 1, pp. 72–79, 1997.
9. M. L. Puterman, Markov Decision Processes: Discrete Stochastic Dynamic Programming. John Wiley & Sons, 1994.
10. T. K. Das, A. Gosavi, S. Mahadevan, and N. Marchalleck, "Solving semi-markov decision problems using average reward reinforcement learning," Management Science, vol. 45, no. 4, pp. 560–574, 1999.

Hierarchical Admission Control in Mobile Cellular Networks Using Adaptive Bandwidth Reservation

David Garcia-Roger, Mª. José Doménech-Benlloch, Jorge Martínez-Bauset, and Vicent Pla

Departamento de Comunicaciones, Universidad Politècnica de Valéncia , UPV,
ETSIT Camino de Vera s/n, 46022, Valéncia, Spain
Tel.: +34 963879733, Fax: +34 963877309
{dagarro, mdoben}@doctor.upv.es
{jmartinez, vpla}@dcom.upv.es

Abstract. We propose a novel adaptive reservation scheme designed to operate in association with the well-known Multiple Guard Channel (MGC) admission control policy. The scheme adjusts the MGC configuration parameters by continuously tracking the Quality of Service (QoS) perceived by users, adapting to any mix of aggregated traffic and enforcing a differentiated treatment among services during underload and overload episodes. We compare our adaptive scheme with two previously relevant proposals. The comparative performance evaluation carried out verifies that our scheme outperforms the two previous proposals in terms of both carried traffic and convergence speed to new operating conditions. Other key features of our scheme are its simplicity, its oscillation-free behavior, and its integrated strategy to deal with multiservice scenarios.

1 Introduction

This paper generalizes the novel session admission control (SAC) adaptive strategy introduced in [1], which operates in coordination with a well known trunk reservation policy named Multiple Guard Channel (MGC). It has been shown [2] that deploying trunk reservation policies in mobile networks allows the operator to achieve higher system capacity, i.e. to carry more traffic while meeting certain quality of service (QoS) objectives (bounds for new and handover blocking probabilities).

Two approaches are commonly proposed for the design of a SAC policy. The first considers system parameters like new and handover session arrival rates as stationary and pursues the design of a static SAC policy for the worst-case scenario. The second considers them as non-stationary and either uses historical information or, in order to track network conditions with more precision, estimates them periodically.

Our work is motivated in part by the fact that previous proposals like [3, 4] deploy long measurement windows to estimate system parameters, which make

M. Cesana, L. Fratta (Eds.): Wireless Syst./Network Architect. 2005, LNCS 3883, pp. 130–144, 2006.

the convergence period too long to cope with real operating conditions. Our scheme does not rely on measurement intervals to estimate the value of system parameters. Instead a probabilistic adjustment according to the last SAC decision is performed, that let us obtain a continuous adaptation of the configuration parameters of the SAC policy, assuring a high precision in the fullfillment of the QoS objectives. Our new scheme is considerably more advanced than the one described in [1], introducing a more sophisticated QoS management strategy which provides the network operator with more flexibility. The new scheme has three key features that enhance the scheme in [1]. First, it allows to enforce a differentiated treatment among streams (new and handover session arrivals) during underload and overload episodes. In the latter case, this differentiated treatment guarantees that higher priority streams will be able to meet their QoS objective possibly at the expense of lower priority ones. Second, the prioritization order of the streams can be fully specified by the operator. And third, the operator has the possibility of identifying one of the streams as best-effort, being it useful to concentrate on it the penalization that unavoidably occurs during overloads. Some of these features can be fully exploited in multiservice scenarios.

The main objective of this paper is to compare the performance of our scheme with the performance of the schemes reported in [3, 4] when operating in a single service scenario deploying an integer number of guard channels. This is the scenario for which [3, 4] where conceived. However, our scheme is more general because is has been designed to operate in multiservice scenarios as will be shown in the latter sections of this paper.

The remaining of the paper is structured as follows. Section 2 describes the model of the system and defines the relevant SAC policies. Section 3 describes the fundamentals of the adaptive scheme, introducing the policy adjustment strategy and how multiple arrival streams are handled. Section 4 describes the detailed operation of the scheme. Section 5 summarize some important details of the two other schemes and presents the comparative performance evaluation of our scheme with respect to these other schemes, both under stationary and nonstationary traffic conditions. Section 6 presents the extension for a multiservice scenario and Section 7 the performance evaluation of the scheme in different multiservice scenarios. Finally, Section 8 concludes the paper.

2   System Model and Relevant SAC Policies

We consider the homogeneous case where all cells are statistically identical and independent. Consequently the global performance of the system can be analyzed focusing on a single cell. Nevertheless, the proposed scheme could also be deployed in non-homogeneous scenarios.

In each cell a set of R different classes of users contend for C resource units, where the meaning of a unit of resource depends on the specific implementation of the radio interface. For each service, new and handover arrival requests are distinguished, which defines $2R$ arrival streams. For convenience, we denote by s_i the arrival stream i, $1 \leq i \leq 2R$. Additionally we denote by s_r^n (s_r^h), the arrival stream associated to service r new (handover) requests, $1 \leq r \leq R$. Therefore $s_r^n = s_r$ and $s_r^h = s_{r+R}$, $1 \leq r \leq R$.

Abusing from the Poisson process definition, we say that for any service r, new requests arrive according to a Poisson process with time-varying rate $\lambda_r^n(t)$. We consider that handover requests arrive according to a Poisson process with time-varying rate $\lambda_r^h(t)$. Although our scheme does not require any relationship between $\lambda_r^h(t)$ and $\lambda_r^n(t)$, for simplicity we will suppose that $\lambda_r^h(t)$ it is a constant fraction of $\lambda_r^n(t)$. Service r requests require b_r resource units per session. As each service has two associated arrival streams, if we denote by c_i the amount of resource units that an arrival stream requires for each session, then $b_r = c_r = c_{r+R}$, $1 \leq r \leq R$.

The duration of a service r session is exponentially distributed with rate μ_r^s. The cell residence (dwell) time of a service r session is exponentially distributed with rate μ_r^d. Hence, the resource holding time for a service r session in a cell is exponentially distributed with rate $\mu_r = \mu_r^s + \mu_r^d$.

We denote by P_i the perceived blocking probabilities for each of the $2R$ arrival streams, by $P_r^n = P_r$, the blocking probabilities for new requests and by $P_r^h = P_{R+r}$, the handover blocking probabilities, and the forced termination probability [5] $P_r^{ft} = P_r^h/(\mu_r^s/\mu_r^d + P_r^h)$ for $1 \leq r \leq R$. The QoS objective is expressed as upper bounds for the blocking probabilities, denoting by B_r^n (B_r^h) the bound for new (handover) requests. Let the system state vector be $n \equiv (n_1, n_2, \ldots, n_{2R-1}, n_{2R})$, where n_i is the number of sessions in progress in the cell initiated as arrival stream i requests. We denote by $c(n) = \sum_{i=1}^{2R} n_i c_i$ the number of busy resource units in state n.

In the case of a single service scenario, which is required to compare our scheme with previous solutions (see Section 5), we have that $R = 1$, so we can simplify the notation required. Thus we denote by P^n (P^h), eliminating the index that refers to the service, the probabilities P_1 (P_2), respectively. This notation can be extended to the rest of parameters. Furthermore, we can assume without loss of generality that each session (new or handover) only require one resource unit ($c = 1$).

Note that the proposed scheme is adaptive which means that if the offered load is above the system capacity, or the number of resource units decreases, or both simultaneously, the SAC system would react trying to meet the QoS objective for as many streams as possible. Therefore the proposed scheme is applicable to both fixed capacity systems (e.g. FDMA/TDMA) and systems limited by interference where capacity is variable (e.g. CDMA). For variable bit rate sources b_r resource units is exactly the effective bandwidth of the session [6, 7].

The definition of the SAC policies of interest is as follows: 1) *Complete-Sharing* (CS). A request is admitted provided there are enough free resource units available in the system; 2) *Multiple Guard Channel* (MGC). One configuration parameter is associated with each arrival stream i, $l_i \in \mathbb{N}$. An arrival of stream i in

Table 1. Definition of the scenario under study

C	50 (resource units)
$B^h\%$	1
λ^h	$0.2\lambda^n$ (s^{-1})
μ	$1/180$ (s^{-1})

state n, is accepted if $c(n) + c_i \leq l_i$ and blocked otherwise. Therefore, l_i is the amount of resources that stream i has access to and increasing (decreasing) it reduces (augments) P_i.

The single service scenario used for the comparison of our scheme with the schemes described in [3, 4], is the one defined in these two references and has been summarized in Table 1. A common assumption when defining a policy is that all handover requests are admitted provided that free resources are available (i.e. $l_2 = l^h = C$ or simply it does not exist like in [3, 4]), this is done because it is the stream with the highest priority.

3   Fundamentals of the Adaptive Scheme

Most of the proposed adaptive schemes deploy a reservation strategy based on *guard channels*, increasing its number when the QoS objective, P^h, is not met. The extension of this heuristic to an scenario with different streams would assume that adjusting the configuration parameter l_i only affects the QoS perceived by s_i (P_i) but has no effect on the QoS perceived by the other arrival streams. As an example, Fig. 1 shows the dependency of P^n and P^h on l^n and l^h. It has been obtained in the scenario introduced in Table 1 when deploying the MGC policy and when offering an arrival rate equal to $\lambda = 0.175$ s^{-1}. As shown, in general

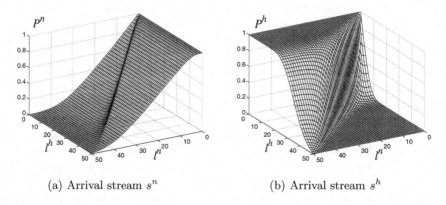

(a) Arrival stream s^n (b) Arrival stream s^h

Fig. 1. Dependency of the blocking probability with the configuration parameters

the correctness of such assumption is not justified (observe Fig. 1(b)) although it might be valid in some cases (observe Fig. 1(a)).

Our scheme has been designed to handle this difficulty and to fulfill two key requirements that have an impact on its performance: one is to achieve a convergence period as short as possible and the other is to enforce a certain response during underload and overload episodes. For these purposes we classify the different arrival streams into two generic categories: i) several "protected" streams, for which specific QoS objectives must hold; ii) one *Best-Effort Stream* (BES), with no specific QoS objective.

Therefore in a single service scenario, s^h due to its importance, must be a protected stream, and indeed it is the *Highest-Priority Stream* (HPS), defined as the last stream that gives up its QoS requirements. Conversely, s^n must be the *Lowest-Priority Stream* (LPS), defined as the first stream in giving up its QoS requirements. We study two treatments of the LPS. First, the LPS has a QoS objective, which must be met when possible (underload episodes). In this scenario our algorithm adapts both l^n and l^h. Second, when the LPS is a BES with no QoS objective. In this scenario our algorithm only adapts l^n. While the second treatment has received much attention in the literature (e.g. [3, 4]), to the best of our knowledge, the first treatment has not been proposed before.

3.1   Probabilistic Setting of the Configuration Parameters

A common characteristic of previous schemes like those in [3, 4] and [8, 9, 10] is that they require a time window (*update period*) at the end of which some estimates are produced. The design of this update period must achieve a trade-off between the time required to adapt to new conditions and the precision of estimates. The adaptive scheme we propose overcomes this limitation. The scheme tracks the QoS perceived by each arrival stream and performs a continuous adaptation of the configuration parameters of the SAC policy.

The operation of our scheme can be described as follow. Let us assume that the arrival processes are stationary and the system is in steady state. If the QoS objective for s_i is expressed as $B_i = b_i/o_i$ (a fixed upper bound for the blocking probability specified by the operator), where $b_i, o_i \in \mathbb{N}$, then it is expected that when $P_i = B_i$ the stream i will experience b_i rejected requests and $o_i - b_i$ admitted requests, out of o_i offered requests.

It seems intuitive to think that the adaptive scheme should not change the configuration parameters of those arrival streams meeting their QoS objective. Therefore, assuming integer values for the configuration parameters, like those of the MGC policy, we propose to perform a probabilistic adjustment each time a request is processed in the following way: i) accepted, do $(l_i \leftarrow l_i - 1)$ with probability $1/(o_i - b_i)$; ii) rejected, do $(l_i \leftarrow l_i + 1)$ with probability $1/b_i$.

The general operation of the proposed scheme is shown in Fig. 2. When a stream i request arrives, the SAC decides upon its admission or rejection and

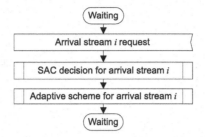

Fig. 2. Conceptual operation of the adaptive reservation scheme

this decision is used by the adaptive scheme to adjust the configuration of the SAC policy.

4   Operation of the SAC Adaptive Scheme

Figure 3(a) and 3(b) shows the operation of the SAC and the adaptive scheme. As shown in Fig. 3(a), to admit an arrival stream i request it is first checked that at least c_i free resource units are available. Note that once this is verified, HPS requests are always admitted, while the rest of streams must also fulfill the admission condition imposed by the MGC policy. Fig. 3(b) describes the adaptive scheme for the arrival stream i. Note that an initial distinction between a protected and a best-effort stream is needed. Clearly, a protected stream needs the adaptive scheme to work in association with the CAS in order to assure the QoS objectives. On the contrary, when the LPS is a BES, this stream does not need an adaptive scheme because it does not have QoS requirements.

To be able to guarantee that the QoS objective is always met, particularly during overloads episodes or changes in the load profile (i.e. the mix of aggregated traffic), the probabilistic adjustment described in Section 3.1 requires additional mechanisms. Two ways of adjustment are possible to change the policy configuration when the QoS objective for stream i is not met. The direct adjustment is to increase the configuration parameter l_i, but its maximum value is C, i.e. when $l_i = C$ full access to the resources is provided to stream i and setting $l_i > C$ does not provide additional benefits. In these cases, an indirect adjustment to help stream i is to limit the access to resources of lower priority streams by reducing their associated configuration parameters.

As shown in Fig. 3(d), upon a rejection the adaptive scheme uses first the direct adjustment and after exhausted it resorts to the indirect adjustment, in which case the adaptive schemes of the LPS must be conveniently disabled. Figure 3(c) shows the reverse procedure. Note that when the LPS is the BES its adaptive scheme is never enabled. Note also that we allow the values of the l_i parameters to go above C and below zero as a means to remember past adjustments.

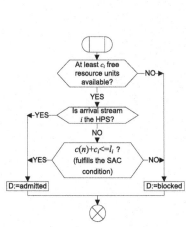

(a) Description of the *SAC for arrival stream i* block in Fig. 2

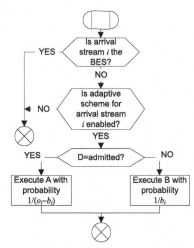

(b) Description of the *Adaptive scheme for arrival stream i* block in Fig. 2

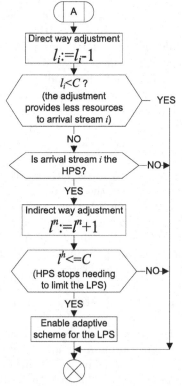

(c) Adjustment algorithm after an admission decision

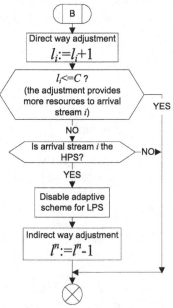

(d) Adjustment algorithm after a rejection decision

Fig. 3. Operation of SAC policy and adaptive scheme algorithm

5   Comparative Performance Evaluation

In this section we show the results of a comparative study between our scheme and the two proposed in [3, 4] for the scenario defined in Table 1. We will refer to the algorithm proposed in [3] as ZL and to the one in [4] as WZZZ, after its authors' initials. Details about them are now briefly described.

The adaptive scheme ZL has four parameters, namely α_u, α_d, N and τ. It operates as follows: i) after a blocked handover request, if it is detected that $P^h \geq \alpha_u B^h$, then l^n will be decreased by one ; ii) if for N consecutive handover requests it is found that $P^h \leq \alpha_d B^h$, then l^n will be increased by one.

This scheme (like the WZZZ scheme) estimates the ratio of the rejected to the total number of handovers requests during one update period τ of fixed length. However, this scheme ambiguously defines the *estimator*, i.e. how the measure of the ratio of the rejected to the total number of handovers requests is performed. This ambiguity leads the authors of [4] (private communication) to let $\tau \to \infty$ removing thus the dependency with respect to the τ parameter. This last choice is assumed for both the ZL and WZZZ schemes. Additionally, developing our comparative evaluation it was also found that both α_u and α_d parameters are not needed by the ZL scheme in order to obtain the desired performance ($P^h \leq B^h$). The suggested values in [3] are $\alpha_u = 0.9$ and $\alpha_d = 0.6$. Although these parameters succeed in their task of maintaining $\alpha_d B^h \leq P^h \leq \alpha_u B^h$, they also prevent P^h from reaching a steady-state regime, and therefore P^h keeps oscillating between the two boundary values. It was found that setting $\alpha_u = \alpha_d = 1.0$ allows the adaptive scheme to reach a steady-state regime in which $P^h = B^h$.

To minimize the number of parameters, improve system's adaptability to different traffic profiles, and improve system's response time, two new probability-based adaptive schemes based on the ZL scheme were proposed in [4]. We focus exclusively on the first one of them, given that the specification of the other one, as provided in [4], is not clear. The WZZZ scheme needs three parameters: α_u, α_d and P_{inc} (probability to decrease l^n). This scheme performs probabilistic adjustments only for each blocked handover request. The WZZZ scheme is slightly more complicated that the ZL scheme.

Our comparative work shows that as with the ZL scheme, both α_u and α_d are not needed either. The suggested value $P_{inc} = 0.2$ also seems to be counterproductive resulting in extremely low P^h and very high P^n. This is due to the fact that P_{inc} controls the speed at which the WZZZ scheme limits new requests the access to resources. Rather than the recommended $P_{inc} < 0.5$, a value of $P_{inc} = 1.0$ is shown to be a better choice. Besides, the fact that it only performs probabilistic adjustments for each blocked handover request (as opposed to the ZL scheme that performs adjustments for each offered handover request) leads the WZZZ scheme to achieve an even slower adaptation speed.

The comparative performance evaluation has been carried out using Möbius[TM] [11], which is a software tool that supports *Stochastic Activity Networks* (SANs) [12]. Möbius[TM] allows to simulate the SANs that model our system. Under certain conditions, the continuous-time Markov chains can be numerically solved. In particular the ZL and WZZZ are simulated while our adaptive scheme meets the conditions to be numerically solved.

For our scheme we deploy the implementation in which the LPS (s^n) is the BES. Additionally, some results of our scheme when the LPS is considered a protected stream are provided, in which case a value of $B^n = 10\%$ is assumed. We focus our study on the interval $\{\lambda : 0.15 \leq \lambda \leq 0.7\}$ (s^{-1}), approximately equivalent to $\{\lambda : 10 \leq \lambda \leq 40\}$ (min^{-1}) assumed in [3, 4]. This interval allows analyzing the schemes both in underload and overload conditions.

5.1   Performance Under Stationary Traffic

Figure 4 show the behavior of our scheme when the LPS is considered a protected stream with $B^n = 10\%$, and when it is a BES. Figure 4(a) shows how our scheme carries more traffic in the load region of interest, which is due to a more precise management of the guard channels. Figure 4(b) shows the variation of the handover blocking probability with the load. Note that when the LSP is a protected stream and an underload episode happens ($\lambda^n < 0.2\,s^{-1}$), the adaptive scheme sets l^n to a value lower than it would be necessary to met the QoS objective, i.e. a higher l^n value would still achieve $P^n \leq B^n$ and $P^h \leq B^h$. This behaviour is forced by the operation of the algorithm which tries to adjust l^n to achieve $P^n = B^n$. Therefore, during underload episodes operating in the mode "LSP is a protected stream" has advantages and disadvantages respect to the operation in the mode "LSP is the BES". The advantage is that P^h is lower and the disadvantage is that the system carries less traffic. As load increases, the QoS objective for s^h cannot longer be met increasing l^h (direct adjustment) and therefore the adaptive scheme of the LSP must be disabled to decrease l^n (indirect adjustment), which converts the LSP in a BES. In summary, the capability of our scheme to operate in two different modes provides the operator with additional flexibility to specify the QoS objective.

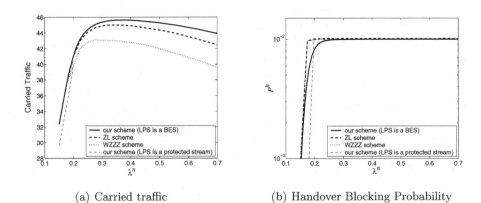

(a) Carried traffic   (b) Handover Blocking Probability

Fig. 4. Parameters with respect to the stationary load

5.2 Performance Under Nonstationary Traffic

To evaluate the performance in the transient regime of each scheme we first show their behavior after a step-type traffic increase from $\lambda^n = 0$ s^{-1} to $\lambda^n = 0.333$ s^{-1}. Before the step increase is applied the system is in the steady state regime, i.e. empty.

Figure 5(a) shows the transient behavior of the handover blocking probabilities. As observed, our scheme (either considering the LPS as a protected or as a BES) shows the fastest convergence speed. On the contrary, the ZL scheme (either with $N = 1$ or 10) shows a slower, oscillating behavior around B^h. So while our scheme needs only $t = 3400$ s to reduce P^h to a $\pm10\%$ interval around its objective ($B^h = 0.01$), the ZL scheme needs $t \approx 30000$ s, about ten times more to achieve the same. Note that the ZL scheme with $N = 10$ behaves slower than $N = 1$. Finally the WZZZ scheme ($P_{inc} = 0.2$) oscillates exactly as ZL but with an even more slowness.

As an initially empty system is improbable, a more realistic transient scenario is now discussed. We study the transient behavior after a step-type increase in the λ^h/λ^n ratio from 0.2 to 0.4 maintaining $\lambda^n = 0.417$ s^{-1}. Again, before the step increase is applied the system is in the steady state regime. As the WZZZ scheme has not a very competitive speed it is not included in this study. Figure 5(b) shows the transient behavior of P^h using our scheme when considering the LPS as a BES and the ZL scheme with $N = 1$. Again our scheme outperforms the ZL scheme in terms of speed and stability. Note that the convergence period will be even shorter when the offered load is above the system capacity thanks to the increase in the rate of probabilistic-adjustment actions.

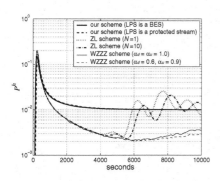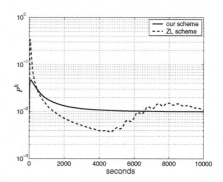

(a) Step-type traffic increase from $\lambda^n = 0$ s^{-1} to $\lambda^n = 0.333$ s^{-1}

(b) Step-type traffic increase from $\lambda^h/\lambda^n = 0.2$ to $\lambda^h/\lambda^n = 0.4$, with $\lambda^n = 0.417$ s^{-1}

Fig. 5. Transient behavior of the adaptive schemes in the presence of a step-type traffic increase

6   Multiservice Scenario

The extension of the heuristic used in the single service case to a multiservice scenario is based in the definition of a *priorization order*. In a multiservice scenario a network operator defines priorities for the protected streams in order to give a greater protection to the most important streams. We suppose that the operator can define priorities at its convenience. For MGC policy, if $\mathbf{s} = (s_1, s_2, \ldots, s_{2R})$ is the set of arrival streams, and the vector $\pi^* \in$ $\mathbf{\Pi}$, $\mathbf{\Pi} := \{(\pi_1, \ldots, \pi_i, \ldots, \pi_{2R}) : \pi_i \in \mathbb{N}, \ 1 \leq \pi_i \leq 2R\}$, is the order defined by

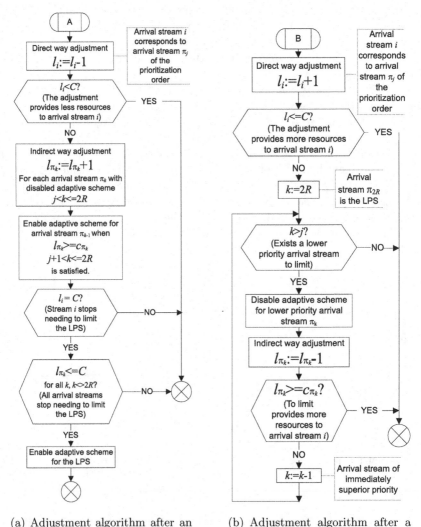

(a) Adjustment algorithm after an admission decision

(b) Adjustment algorithm after a rejection decision

Fig. 6. The adaptive algorithm for a multiservice scenario

the operator, $\mathbf{s}^* = (s_{\pi_1}, s_{\pi_2}, \ldots, s_{\pi_{2R}})$ is called the priorization order, being s_{π_1} y $s_{\pi_{2R}}$ the *Highest-Priority Stream* (HPS) and the *Lowest-Priority Stream* (LPS) respectively. If there is a BES, this stream will be the LPS in the priorization order.

We will also use the direct and indirect adjustments for the configuration parameters in a multiservice scenario. Thus every protected stream has its own adaptive scheme and changes to the indirect adjustment when the system cannot meet the QoS objective (e.g. during overload episodes or when there are changes in the load profiles). An additional mechanism disables the adaptive scheme of the lowest priority streams in the appropiate order, i.e. beginning with the LPS, when the fulfillment of the QoS objective of the highest priority streams is in danger. We also need to define the correct mechanism to enable the disabled streams when the risk of the non-fulfillment of the QoS objectives has vanished. Fig. 6 shows the complete adaptive algorithm for a multiservice scenario.

7   Performance Evaluation in a Multiservice Scenario

In this section we evaluate the system performance when associating our adaptive scheme to the MGC policy in a multiservice scenario. We have studied five different scenarios (A, B, C, D y E) which are defined in Table 2. The parameters in Table 2 have been selected to explore possible trends in the numerical results, i.e. taking scenario A as a reference, scenario B represents the case where the ratio c_1/c_2 is smaller, scenario C where f_1/f_2 is smaller, scenario D where B_1/B_2 is smaller and scenario E where B_1 and B_2 are equal. Note that the aggregated arrival rate of new requests is defined as $\lambda = \sum_{r=1}^{R} \lambda_r^n$, where $\lambda_r^n = f_i\lambda$. The system capacity is the maximum λ (λ_{max}) that can be offered to the system while meeting the QoS objective.

Finally, for all scenarios defined in Table 2 we assume the following prioritization order $\mathbf{s}^* = (s_2^h, s_1^h, s_2^n, s_1^n)$.

For each scenario we evaluated by simulation the performance of two implementations that differ in the treatment of the LPS (s_1^n), one in which it is a protected stream (refered as "implementation without *best-effort*") and one in which it is the BES (refered to "implementation with *best-effort*"). Due to space limitations, only a subset of the results will be presented.

Table 2. Studied scenarios

	b_1	b_2	f_1	f_2	$B_1^n\%$	$B_2^n\%$	$B_r^h\%$	λ_r^n	λ_r^h	μ_1	μ_2
A	1	2	0.8	0.2	5	1					
B	1	4	0.8	0.2	5	1					
C	1	2	0.2	0.8	5	1	$0.1B_r^n$	$f_r\lambda$	$0.5\lambda_r^n$	1	3
D	1	2	0.8	0.2	1	2					
E	1	2	0.8	0.2	1	1					

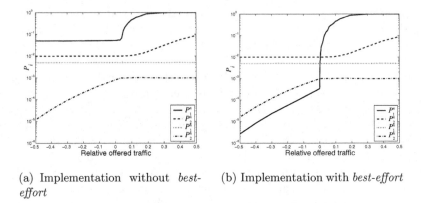

(a) Implementation without *best-effort*

(b) Implementation with *best-effort*

Fig. 7. P_i as a function of $(\lambda - \lambda_{max})/\lambda_{max}$ in stationary condition

7.1 Performance Under Stationary Traffic

Figure 7 shows the variation of the perceived blocking probabilities for scenario C with $C = 10$ resource units. When the LPS is a protected stream (Fig. 7(a)) it does not benefit from the capacity surplus during underload episodes and it is the first to be penalized during overload episodes. On the other hand, when the LPS is the BES (Fig. 7(b)) it benefits during underload episodes and, as before, it is the first to be penalized during overload episodes. In both implementations, note that s_2^n is also penalized when keeping on penalizing the LPS would be ineffective. Note also that during underload episodes $P_i = B_i$ is held for protected streams and therefore the system is setting l_i to a value lower than it would be necessary to met the QoS objective, i.e. a higher l_i value would still achieve $P_i \leq B_i$, but some streams (HPS and BES) benefit from this extra capacity.

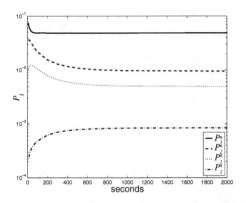

Fig. 8. Transient behavior of the blocking probabilities

7.2 Performance Under Nonstationary Traffic

In this section we study the transient regime after a step-type traffic increase from $0.66\lambda_{max}$ to λ_{max} is applied to the system in scenario A when the LPS is a protected stream. Before the step increase is applied the system is in the steady state regime.

Figure 8 shows the transient behavior of the blocking probabilities. As observed, the convergence period lasts around 1000 s, which is of the same order of magnitude than in the case of a single service scenario.

8   Conclusions

We developed a novel adaptive reservation scheme that operates in coordination with the Multiple Guard Channel policy. Three relevant features of our proposal are: its capability to handle multiple services, its ability to continuously track and adjust the QoS perceived by users and its simplicity.

We provide two implementations of the scheme. First, when the LPS has a QoS objective defined, which obviously must be met when possible. Second, when the LPS is treated as a best-effort stream and therefore obtains an unpredictable QoS, which tends to be "good" during underload episodes but is "quite bad" as soon as the system enters the overload region.

The comparative performance evaluation in single service scenarios shows that our scheme meets the QoS objective with an excellent precision while achieving both a higher carried traffic and an oscillation-free convergence period, which is 10 to 100 times shorter than the one achieved by other proposals. The performance evaluation in multiservice scenarios confirms that our scheme can handle satisfactorily the non-stationarity of a real network.

Future work will include the evaluation of the scheme when operating with other SAC policies, for example those for which the stationary probability distribution has a product-form solution. Another interesting extension would be to base the adjustment of the configuration parameters not only on the decisions of the SAC but also on predictive information, like movement prediction.

Acknowledgments

This work has been supported by the Spanish Ministry of Education and Science (30%) and by the EU (FEDER 70%) under projects TIC2003-08272, TEC2004-06437-C05-01 and under contract AP-2004-3332, and by the Generalitat Valenciana under contract CTB/PRB/2002/267.

References

1. D. Garcia-Roger, Mª Jose Domenech-Benlloch, J. Martinez-Bauset, V. Pla, "Adaptive Admission Control Scheme for Multiservice Mobile Cellular Networks", Proceedings of the 1st Conference on Next Generation Internet Networks (NGI2005), Roma, (Italy), 18-20 Apr. 2005.

2. D. García, J. Martínez, V. Pla, "Admission Control Policies in Multiservice Cellular Networks: Optimum Configuration and Sensitivity," Wireless Systems and Mobility in Next Generation Internet, Gabriele Kotsis and Otto Spaniol (eds.), Lecture Notes in Computer Science, vol. 3427, pp.121-135, Springer-Verlag 2005.
3. Y. Zhang, D. Liu, "An adaptive algorithm for call admission control in wireless networks", Proceedings of the IEEE Global Communications Conference (GLOBE-COM), pp. 3628-3632, San Antonio, (USA), Nov. 2001.
4. X.-P. Wang, J.-L. Zheng, W. Zeng, G.-D. Zhang, "A probability-based adaptive algorithm for call admission control in wireless network", Proceedings of the International Conference on Computer Networks and Mobile Computing (ICCNMC), pp. 197-204, Shanghai, (China), 20-23 Oct. 2003.
5. Y.B. Lin, S.Mohan, A. Noerpel, "Queueing priority channel assignment strategies for PCS hand-off and initial access", IEEE Transactions on Vehicular Technology, pp. 704-712, vol. 43, no. 3, Aug. 1994.
6. R. Guerin, H. Ahmadi, M. Naghshineh, "Equivalent capacity and its application to bandwidth allocation in highspeed networks", IEEE Journal on Selected Areas in Communications, pp. 968-981, vol. 9, no. 7, Sep. 1991.
7. J.S. Evans, D.Everitt, "Effective bandwidth-based admission control for multiservice CDMA cellular networks", IEEE Transactions on Vehicular Technology, pp. 36-46, vol. 48, no. 1, Jan. 1999.
8. O. Yu, V. Leung, "Adaptive Resource Allocation for prioritized call admission over an ATM-based Wireless PCN", IEEE Journal on Selected Areas in Communications, pp. 1208-1224, vol. 15, Sep. 1997.
9. P. Ramanathan, K. M. Sivalingam, P. Agrawal, S. Kishore, "Dynamic Resource Allocation Schemes During Handoff for Mobile Multimedia Wireless Networks", IEEE Journal on Selected Areas in Communications, pp. 1270-1283, vol. 17, no. 7, Jul. 1999.
10. O. Yu, S. Khanvilkar, "Dynamic adaptive QoS provisioning over GPRS wireless mobile links", Proceedings of the IEEE International Conference on Communications (ICC), pp. 1100-1104, vol. 2, New York, (USA), 28 Apr.- 2 May 2002.
11. Performability Engineering Research Group (PERFORM), Möbius^{TM}. User Manual. Version 1.8.0: http://www.perform.csl.uiuc.edu/mobius/manual/Mobius Manual.pdf.
12. J. F. Meyer, A. Movaghar, W. H. Sanders, "Stochastic activity networks: Structure, behavior, and application", Proceedings of the International Workshop on Timed Petri Nets, pp. 106-115, Torino, Italy, Jul. 1985.

Interference Estimation for the HSDPA Service in Heterogeneous UMTS Networks

Andreas Mäder and Dirk Staehle

Department of Distributed Systems, Institute of Computer Science,
University of Würzburg, Am Hubland, D-97074 Würzburg
{maeder, staehle}@informatik.uni-wuerzburg.de

Abstract. For the planning and deployment of the 3.5G enhancement of UMTS, the High Speed Downlink Packet Access, mobile telecommunication providers need to estimate the signal-to-interference-ratio of the HSDPA users. Although the received signal power is easy to calculate due the channel adaptive principle of HSDPA, the received interference includes the signal powers of the power controlled dedicated channel users and is therefore more challenging. Our contribution is a semi-analytical method to calculate the spatial distribution of the received interference. The method considers the interference generated in the own cell and in the surrounding cells including the load dependent interference coming from the dedicated channel users.

Keywords: Network planning, UMTS, 3.5G, HSDPA, other-cell interference.

1 Introduction

The *High Speed-Downlink Packet Access* (HSDPA) will provide up to 14.4Mbps in the downlink direction in UMTS networks. It is designed to satisfy the increasing demand for mobile wireless high speed access to the internet, and it is expected to be deployed by network operators in the very near future. The basic idea of HSDPA is to increase the packet data throughput by means of link adaptation and fast retransmission combining. The underlying transport channel of the HSDPA service is the *High Speed Downlink Shared Channel* (HS-DSCH) which is an evolution of the DSCH introduced in UMTS-Release'99. The HS-DSCH implements a combined time multiplexing/code multiplexing scheme. In contrast to the DSCH, the HS-DSCH relies on *Adaptive Modulation and Coding* (AMC) and uses a fixed spreading factor, fast scheduling with reduced TTIs (*Transmission Time Interval*) of 2ms and fast *Hybrid Automatic Repeat Request* (HARQ) on the physical layer. Another novelty is the introduction of the 16 QAM higher order modulation scheme. Together with the possible use of up to 15 codes for a single user, the maximum brutto data rate of 14.4Mbps can be achieved [1].

The concept of link adaptation makes fast power control as implemented for the dedicated channel (DCH) obsolete. DCH users receive the same signal-to-interference-and-noise ratio (SINR) regardless of their position in the coverage

M. Cesana, L. Fratta (Eds.): Wireless Syst./Network Architect. 2005, LNCS 3883, pp. 145–157, 2006.
© Springer-Verlag Berlin Heidelberg 2006

area of a NodeB. Fast power control tries especially to mitigate the effects of fast fading due to movement of the mobile. The HS-DSCH in contrast has a constant transmit power over long time periods and only adapts to long time effects like significant changes in the interference situation. The small TTIs enables it to react to a varying SINR due to fast fading with an appropriate *Transport Format and Resource Combination* (TFRC), which describes the modulation scheme and the code rate. In TTIs with low instantanous SINR, the NodeB chooses QPSK modulation with a low code rate, for higher SINRs, higher code rates and QAM16 is used. Another possibility is to serve only users with a high instantaneous SINR and postpone the scheduling of low SINR users until the radio condition has improved. In this way, the HSDPA service exploits the multi-user diversity which leads to a higher system throughput (see e.g. [2] or [3]).

Aside from fast fading, the signal quality of the HS-DSCH also depends on the distance between the NodeB antenna and the mobile. If the distance to the controlling NodeB is small, in mean the received SINR is high, resulting in a high mean data throughput. If the HSDPA users moves farther away from the controlling NodeB, more to the "edge" of the cell, the received power degrades due to a higher attenuation and at the same time, the received interference from other NodeBs increases, see e.g. [4]. This means that the NodeB is forced to choose lower TFRCs more often, and the user experiences a lower data through-put. The interference depends on the transmit powers of all NodeBs for the DCH users which in turn depends on the number of DCH users, i.e. on the DCH load.

The focus of this work is the calculation of the receieved mean interference and SINR over time, i.e. without the effects of slow and fast fading. Our system model considers the transmit power for the HSDPA users, the transmit power for the users with dedicated channels and the transmit power for the common and pilot channels. The model presented here is based on the semi-analytical approximate methods introduced in [5].

2   Problem Formulation and System Model

The SINR of an HSDPA user depends on the attenuation between the antenna and the MS and on the interference originating from non-HSDPA users and from surrounding NodeBs. The attenuation is subject to the plain pathloss and to several fading effects (multipath propagation, shadowing, etc.). The interference depends on the network layout and the position of the user, on the number of non-HSDPA users in the system and on the transmit powers for pilot and common channels. So, the interference in our terminology is the received power not originating from the HS-DSCH. In our work, we focus on the impact of the interference on the perceieved signal quality on a larger time scale. Therefore, we consider the attenuation in terms of the mean value over time, neglecting the effects of slow and fast fading. The question we want to answer is: What is the mean interference a HSDPA mobile sees depending on it's position in the network?

To answer this question, we need to know the total transmit powers at the NodeBs. We assume a heterogeneous network layout with a set of $\mathcal{L}$ NodeBs and partition the coverage area $\mathcal{F}$ in area elements f. Area elements which are within the coverage area of NodeB x are denoted as f_x. The transmit power $\hat{T}_x$ at the NodeB $x \in \mathcal{L}$ comprises a constant fraction $\hat{T}_x^c$ for the pilot signal and common signalling channels, a fraction $\hat{T}_x^d$ for the dedicated channels, and the HS-DSCH transmit power $\hat{T}_x^H$ which we assume as constant:

$$\hat{T}_x = \hat{T}_x^c + \hat{T}_x^H + \hat{T}_x^d. \tag{1}$$

Since the common channel and HS-DSCH power is constant, the main task is to calculate the transmit power T_x^d for the dedicated channel users. The (mean) received SINR in an area element f with attenuation $\hat{d}_{x,f}$ for an arbitrary user with transmit power P is

$$\hat{\gamma}_f = \frac{\hat{P}_x \hat{d}_{x,f}}{W\hat{N}_0 + \sum_{y \in \mathcal{Y}} \hat{T}_y \hat{d}_{y,f} + \alpha \hat{d}_{x,f}(\hat{T}_x - \hat{P}_x)}, \tag{2}$$

where W is the system chip rate of 3.84Mcps, $\hat{N}_0$ is the thermal noise power density, α is the orthogonality factor due to multipath propagation and the set $\mathcal{Y}$ is the set of NodeBs $\mathcal{L} \setminus x$. So e.g. for an HSDPA user with transmit power $\hat{T}_x^H$, the total received interference in the denominator of the SINR equation (2) consists of the thermal noise $W\hat{N}_0$, the other-cell interference $\sum_{y \in \mathcal{Y}} \hat{T}_y \hat{d}_{y,k}$ and the own-cell interference $\alpha \hat{d}_{x,k}(\hat{T}_x - \hat{T}_x^H)$.

3   Interference Model

The interferences generated by the NodeBs are mutually dependent, which means that the NodeB dedicated transmit powers depend on each other. We assume for our approximation that the dedicated transmit power is a lognormally distributed random variable, which eliminates the need for the calculation of the whole transmit power distribution. Instead, we only have to calculate the first two moments of the transmit powers. This is done by solving a matrix equation for the first and second moment exactly as described in [5], where also the different approximate methods are explained. In the next section, we want to give a short introduction to this method.

3.1   NodeB Transmit Powers with Dedicated Channels

For each area element f, we assume a Poisson distributed number of dedicated channel users offering a traffic intensity of a_f. The users can have different service classes s out of $\mathcal{S}$ service classes and the probability that class s is requested is denoted by p_s, such that $a_f = \sum_{s \in \mathcal{S}} p_s \cdot a_s$.

From the spatial traffic distribution wich is exemplarily shown in Fig. 1, the total traffic intensity at a NodeB can be calculated. In the figure, brighter colors indicate a lower and darker colors a higher traffic intensity. The triangles mark the NodeBs.

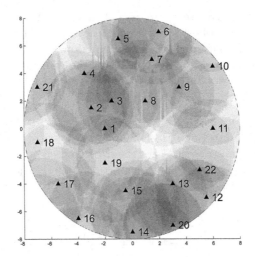

Fig. 1. Traffic intensities for DCH users in a heterogeneous network layout

The transmit power $\hat{T}_x^d$ for the dedicated channel users is the sum of all transmit powers $\hat{T}_{x,k}^d$ for the individual users k. The E_b/N_0 value of a user results from the multiplication of the SINR equation (2) with the processing gain $\frac{W}{R_k}$, with R_k as bit rate:

$$\hat{\varepsilon}_k = \frac{W}{R_k} \cdot \hat{\gamma}_k. \tag{3}$$

Note that we assume that mobile k belongs to an area element f. The individual transmit power is calculated by solving the target-E_b/N_0 equation (2) for $\hat{T}_{x,k}^d$. With the introduction of ω_k as *service load factors*, we get

$$\hat{T}_{x,k}^d = \omega_{0,k} W \hat{N}_0 + \sum_{y \in \mathcal{Y}} \omega_{y,k} \hat{T}_y + \omega_{x,k} \hat{T}_x \tag{4}$$

The service load factors ω_k in this equation depend on the target-E_b/N_0 values $\hat{\varepsilon}_k^*$ and the bit rate R_k and denote the load that one user with a specific service class adds to the total load at the NodeB. The load factors with an additional index also reflect the position of the mobile. The service load factors are defined as

$$\omega_k = \frac{\hat{\varepsilon}_k^* R_k}{W + \alpha \hat{\varepsilon}_k^* R_k} \quad \text{and} \quad \omega_{y,k} = \begin{cases} \omega_k \frac{1}{\hat{d}_{x,k}} & \text{if } y = 0 \\ \omega_k \alpha & \text{if } y = x \\ \omega_k \frac{d_{y,k}}{\hat{d}_{x,k}} & \text{if } y \neq x \end{cases} \tag{5}$$

We further define the total load at NodeB x as the sum over the service load factors for all mobiles:

$$\eta_x = \sum_{k \in x} \omega_k \quad \text{and} \quad \eta_{y,x} = \sum_{k \in x} \omega_{y,k} \tag{6}$$

Note that the load η_x must be lower than α^{-1}, which constitutes the pole capacity of the system. The load $\eta_{y,x}$ can be seen as the load at NodeB x inflicted by NodeB y due to it's position relative to NodeB x.

In the next step, we calculate the total required transmit power at the NodeB, which is the the sum over all dedicated channel transmit powers $\hat{T}_{x,k}^d$ plus the constant powers $\hat{T}_x^c$ and $\hat{T}_x^H$. If we solve for $\hat{T}_x$, we get

$$\hat{T}_x = (\hat{T}_x^c + \hat{T}_x^H)\frac{1}{1 - \eta_{x,x}} + W\hat{N}_0\frac{\eta_{0,x}}{1 - \eta_{x,x}} + \sum_{y \in \mathcal{Y}}\hat{T}_y\frac{\eta_{y,x}}{1 - \eta_{x,x}}. \tag{7}$$

We are now able to calculate the first two moments of the transmit powers. We assume that the locations are indepedent and identically distributed such that

$$E[\hat{\delta}_x] = E[\tfrac{1}{d_x}] = E[\tfrac{1}{d_{x,k}}] \quad \text{and} \quad E[\hat{\Delta}_{y,x}] = E[\tfrac{d_y}{d_x}] = E[\tfrac{d_{y,k}}{d_{x,k}}] \tag{8}$$

for all mobiles k. We further assume that the load η_x is independent of the attenuation ratios $\hat{\delta}$ and $\hat{\Delta}$, i.e.

$$E[\eta_{0,x}] = E[\eta_x] \cdot E[\hat{\delta}_x], \quad E[\eta_{y,x}] = E[\eta_x] \cdot E[\hat{\Delta}_{y,x}] \quad \text{and} \quad E[\eta_{x,x}] = E[\eta_x] \cdot \alpha. \tag{9}$$

Then, the equation for first moment of the dedicated channel transmit power becomes

$$\begin{aligned} E[\hat{T}_x] =&(\hat{T}_x^c + \hat{T}_x^H)E\left[\frac{1}{1 - \eta_x}\right]\alpha + W\hat{N}_0 E\left[\frac{\eta_x}{1 - \eta_x}\right]E[\hat{\delta}_x] \\ &+ \sum_{y \in \mathcal{Y}}E[\hat{T}_y]E[\hat{\Delta}_{y,x}]E\left[\frac{\eta_x}{1 - \eta_x}\right] \end{aligned} \tag{10}$$

If we consider Eq. (10) for all NodeBs in $\mathcal{L}$, we can solve the equation e.g. by formulating a matrix equation as in the original paper [5]. The same procedure, although slightly more complicated, can be applied for the calculation of the second moment.

3.2   Interference and Mean SINR for HSDPA Users

As result of the previous section, we have the first two moments of the NodeB transmit powers. Now we want to calculate the interference and the received SINR in the area of the network, which means that we look at an specific area element f and want to know the SINR for this element. This means, that we make the attenuation deterministic again and use the moments of the transmit powers to calculate the SINR.

The total interference seen by an HSDPA user in an area element f (i.e. the term in the denominator of Eq. (2)) is

$$\hat{I}_{x,f}^H = W\hat{N}_0\hat{\delta}_{x,f} + \sum_{y \in \mathcal{Y}}\hat{T}_{y,f}\hat{\Delta}_{y,f} + \alpha(\hat{T}_x^d + \hat{T}_x^c). \tag{11}$$

If we separate the interference originating from the constant part of the transmit powers from the dedicated channel interference, we may write Eq. (11) also as

$$\hat{I}^H_{x,f} = \hat{I}^{\text{const}}_{x,f} + \hat{I}^{\text{ded}}_{x,f}, \tag{12}$$

where $\hat{I}^{\text{const}}_x$ is the interference fraction originating from constant sources, i.e.

$$\hat{I}^{\text{const}}_{x,f} = W\hat{N}_0\delta_{x,f} + \alpha\hat{T}^c_x + \sum_{y\in\mathcal{Y}}(\hat{T}^c_y + T^H_y)\hat{\Delta}_{y,f} \tag{13}$$

and $\hat{I}^{\text{ded}}_x$ is the sum of all dedicated channel interferences:

$$\hat{I}^{\text{ded}}_{x,f} = \alpha\hat{T}^d_x + \sum_{y\in\mathcal{Y}}\hat{T}^d_y\hat{\Delta}_{y,f} \tag{14}$$

We assume now that the dedicated channel interferences are due to the power control error approximately lognormal distributed, see e.g. [6] or [7,8]. The total interference interference is therefore a sum of $|\mathcal{L}|$ lognormal distributed random variables plus the constant interference. Since the own-cell dedicated channel interference $\alpha\hat{T}^d_x$, and for positions at the the cell edge, a small subset of $\mathcal{L}$ is dominating $\hat{I}^{\text{ded}}_{x,f}$ for realistic values of the orthogonality factor, we model the total interference with a shifted lognormal distribution with scale and shape parameters μ_x, σ_x [9]. The parameters follow from the moments of the variable DCH transmit powers:

$$\mu_{x,f} = \ln(E[\hat{I}^{\text{ded}}_{x,f}] - \frac{1}{2}\sigma^2_{x,f}) \tag{15}$$

$$\sigma_{x,f} = \sqrt{\ln^2\left(\frac{\sqrt{E[(\hat{I}^{\text{ded}}_{x,f})^2] - (E[\hat{I}^{\text{ded}}_{x,f}])^2}}{E[\hat{I}^{\text{ded}}_{x,f}]}\right) + 1} \tag{16}$$

$$\tag{17}$$

The interference CDF and PDF follows as

$$A_{\hat{I}^H_{x,f}}(t) = \text{LN}_{\mu_{x,f},\sigma_{x,f}}(t - \hat{I}^{\text{const}}_{x,f}), \tag{18}$$

$$a_{\hat{I}^H_{x,f}}(t) = \text{LNpdf}_{\mu_{x,f},\sigma_{x,f}}(t - \hat{I}^{\text{const}}_{x,f}) \tag{19}$$

where LN denotes the lognormal CDF and LNpdf the lognormal PDF. Since we made the attenuation and therefore $\hat{\delta}_{x,f}$ and $\hat{\Delta}_{y,f}$ deterministic, we only need to calculate the moments of $\hat{I}^{\text{ded}}_{x,f}$:

$$E[\hat{I}^{\text{ded}}_{x,f}] = \sum_{y\in\mathcal{Y}} E[\hat{T}^d_y]\hat{\Delta}_{y,f} + \alpha\hat{E}[T^d_x] \tag{20}$$

and

$$E[(\hat{I}^{\text{ded}}_{x,f})^2] = \sum_{\substack{y_1,y_2\in\mathcal{Y}\\y_1\neq y_2}}\sum E[\hat{T}^d_{y_1}]E[\hat{T}^d_{y_2}]\hat{\Delta}_{y_1,f}\hat{\Delta}_{y_2,f} + \sum_{y\in\mathcal{Y}}E[(\hat{T}^d_y)^2]\hat{\Delta}^2_{y,f}$$

$$+ 2\alpha E[\hat{T}^d_x]\sum_{y\in\mathcal{Y}}E[\hat{T}^d_x]\hat{\Delta}_{y,f} + \alpha^2 E[(\hat{T}^d_x)^2]. \tag{21}$$

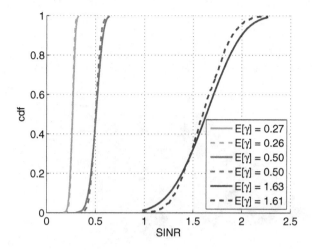

Fig. 2. CDF of the mean received SINR

The moments of the dedicated channel transmit powers $\hat{T}_x^d$ follow at once from $\hat{T}_x^d = \hat{T}_x - \hat{T}_x^c - \hat{T}_x^H$ and the fact that $\hat{T}_x^c$ and $\hat{T}_x^H$ are constant. Finally, the CDF of the mean SINRs in area element f can be calculated from the interference distribution as follows:

$$A_{\gamma_{x,f}^H}(t) = 1 - A_{\hat{I}_{x,f}^H}\left(\frac{\hat{T}_x^H}{t}\right). \tag{22}$$

The PDF is given by

$$a_{\gamma_{x,f}^H}(t) = \frac{1}{t^2} a_{\hat{I}_{x,f}^H}\left(\frac{\hat{T}_x^H}{t}\right). \tag{23}$$

Figure 2 shows the CDFs of the mean received SINRs for different area elements in the coverage area of NodeB 1 in the heterogenous network of Fig. 1. The HSDPA transmit power is 5000mW and the mean dedicated channel load η_x is 0.4 over all NodeBs. The SINRs correspond to the 25-, 50-, and 75-percentile of the attenuation distribution of the area elements. The dashed lines are the empirical CDFs originating from a Monte-Carlo simulation. The difference between the dashed and the solid lines show, that the analytical method overestimates the variance of SINR, although the abberation is in an acceptable order of magnitude.

4   Numerical Examples

In this section we present some numerical examples which show the effects of various system parameters on the interference and SINR distribution. We use the

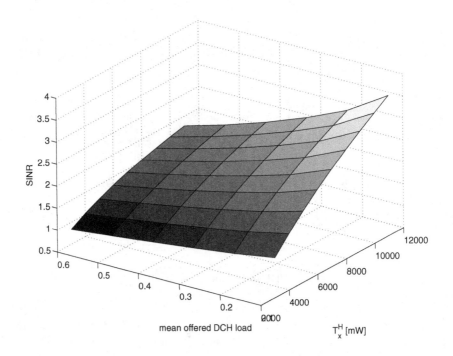

Fig. 3. SINR vs mean offered DCH load vs HSDPA transmit power

heterogeneous network as shown in Fig. 1 for our results. The scenarios consider two service classes for the dedicated channel users with 12.2kbps and 64kbps and a service probability of 0.5 for each service. We assume a deterministic propagation model as defined in [10] and limit the maximum transmit power of the NodeBs to 20W. If not stated otherwise, the side length of an area element is 100m.

In Fig. 3, the relation between SINR, mean offered DCH load and HSDPA transmit power is shown. On the lower two axes are the mean offered DCH load ranging from 0.1 to 0.6 and the HSDPA transmit power ranging from 3W to 11W. On the z-axis is the mean of the receieved SINR. For lower DCH loads, the plane is steeper for increasing HSDPA transmit powers than for higher DCH loads, since in this case the own- and other-cell interferences are also lower.

Figure 4 illustrates the mean shannon capacity (in Mbps) for the heterogeneous example network. We have chosen this measure because the HSDPA service operates near the shannon capacity for typical SINR values. In this scenario, the HSDPA transmit power is 5000mW and the mean load η_x for the dedicated channel users is 0.4. The maximum capacity of 9Mbps is reached in the vicinity of the (ommnidirectional) NodeB antennas. On the edges of the cells, the capacity is quite low because of the destructive influence of the other-cell interferences in this areas. We can also observe that on cells whith a small distance

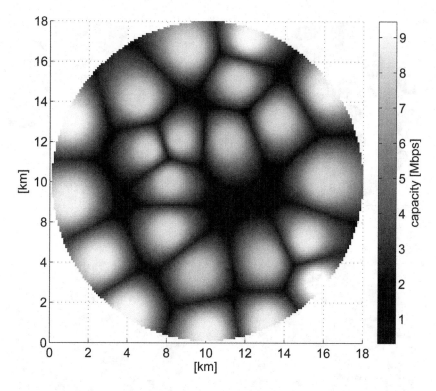

Fig. 4. Spatial shannon capacity

between the NodeBs the area with a high capacity is quite large and only begins to decline at the very near of the cell edge. This follows from the domination of the total interference by the own-cell interference term for a relatively large distance intervall.

The next four subfigures in Fig. 5 show the coverage areas for an increasing HSDPA transmit power, in this case for a DCH load of $\eta_x = 0.2$. We define the coverage area as an area where the received SINR reaches a certain target-SINR (corresponding to a TFRC) with a probability of 90%. The target-SINRs are −1dB, 1dB, 3dB, 5dB and 7dB. In the first subfigure with 2000mW HSDPA transmit power, the total coverage areas are small, and the higher target-SINRs are not reached in the coverage areas of the cells. If the transmit power is increased to 5000mW, the coverage area grows significantly, and in the centers of most cells the highest target-SINR is reached. If the HSDPA transmit power is increased further, the total coverage area does not grow to that extent as at the step from 2000mW to 5000mW, but the coverage area for the highest target-SINR grows strongly. For the highest transmit power of 12000mW, the gain in coverage is quite low in relation to the transmit power increase. This results suggest that due to the effects of the other-cell interference, high transmit powers are mostly to the benefit of the SINRs in the cell centers and therefore

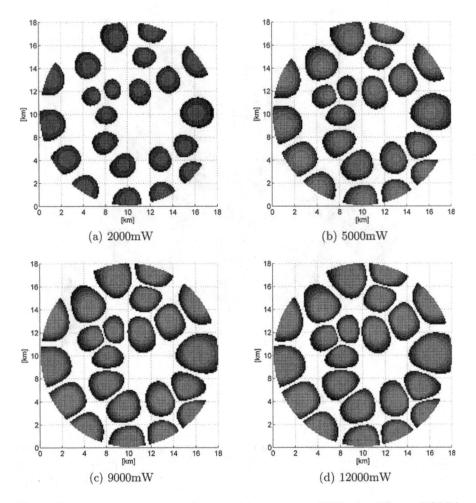

(a) 2000mW

(b) 5000mW

(c) 9000mW

(d) 12000mW

Fig. 5. Coverage areas corresponding to minimum target SNIRs for different HSDPA transmit powers

also to the cell capacity in terms of throughput. In contrast, the coverage gain is small.

This effect is also confirmed by the next two figures. The first, Fig. 6 shows the coverage area in percent for an increasing HSDPA transmit power. Figure 7 shows the corresponding mean outage probability over all NodeBs, where outage is defined as the event that the total required transmit power exceeds 20W. The percentage of coverage raises steeply for lower HSDPA transmit powers, but begins to diminish for higher transmit powers. The dashed line in Fig. 7 shows the transmit power for an outage probability of 1%, which is ca. 8W. The dashed lines in Fig. 6 show the corresponding coverage for 1% outage probability for

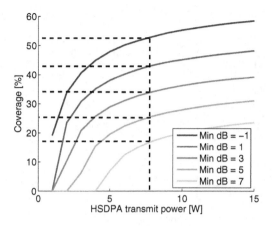

Fig. 6. Coverage for increasing HSDPA transmit power with constant mean DCH load

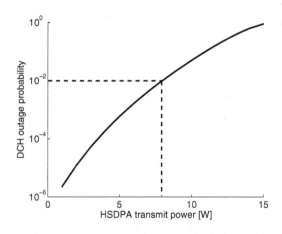

Fig. 7. Mean DCH outage probability for increasing HSPDA transmit power with constant mean DCH load

the DCH users. These figures illustrate the trade-off between coverage for the HSDPA service and DCH outage probability.

A similar effect can be observed if the mean DCH load is increased with a constant HSDPA transmit power. In Fig. 8, the coverage for the 5 target-SINRs is shown for DCH loads from 0.1 to 0.6. The HSDPA transmit power is 5W. The decrease in coverage is not so strong as the increase in case of rising HSDPA transmit powers shown in the previous tow figures. Nevertheless, the outage probabilities in Fig. 9 show that the DCH load should not increase above ca. 0.23 in this scenario, if the DCH service qualities are to be maintained.

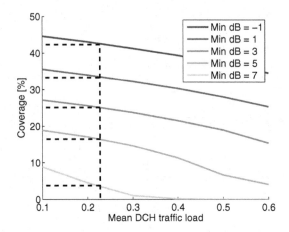

Fig. 8. Coverage for increasing mean DCH load with constant HSDPA power

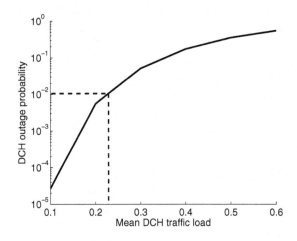

Fig. 9. Mean DCH outage probability for increasing mean DCH load with constant HSDPA power

5   Conclusion

The inclusion of the HSDPA service into the UMTS network planning process requires the estimation of the signal quality in the cell areas, which depends on the attenuation and on the interference. We have proposed a semi-analytical method for the calculation of the spatial received interference and SINR distribution which considers the variable transmit powers for the dedicated channel users. We have shown that the approximation of the SINR distribution with a lognormal distribution is of adequate accuracy for this purpose. The numerical results and examples show, that several trade-offs exist between HSDPA transmit power, coverage area, offered DCH traffic load and DCH outage probability. All these trade-offs should be considered in the planning process since a neglection could lead to insufficient service qualities for both HSDPA and DCH users.

References

1. Holma, H., Toskala, A., eds.: WCDMA for UMTS. John Wiley & Sons Ltd. (2002)
2. Berggren, F., Jäntti, R.: Asymptotically Fair Scheduling on Fading Channels. In: Proceedings of VTC '02, Vancouver, Canada (2002)
3. van den Berg, H., Litjens, R., Laverman, J.: Hsdpa flow level performance: the impact of key system and traffic aspects. In: MSWiM '04: Proceedings of the 7th ACM international symposium on Modeling, analysis and simulation of wireless and mobile systems, New York, NY, USA, ACM Press (2004) 283–292
4. Bonald, T., Proutière, A.: Wireless downlink data channels: User performance and cell dimensioning. In: MobiCom '03: Proceedings of the 9th annual international conference on Mobile computing and networking, San Diego, CA, USA, ACM Press (2003) 339–352
5. Staehle, D., Mäder, A.: An Analytic Model for Deriving the Node-B Transmit Power in Heterogeneous UMTS Networks. In: IEEE VTC Spring, Milano, Italy (2004)
6. Viterbi, A., Viterbi, A.: Erlang Capacity of a Power Controlled CDMA System. IEEE Journal on Selected Areas in Communications 11(6) (1993) 892–900
7. Muammar, R., Gupta, S.C.: Cochannel Interference in High-Capacity Mobile Radio Systems. ITC COM-30(8) (1982) 1973–1978
8. Elayoubi, S.E., Chahed, T., Hébuterne, G.: On the capacity of multi-cell UMTS. In: In Proc. of GLOBECOM 2003. Volume 22., IEEE (2003) 487–491
9. Fenton, L.F.: The Sum of Log-Normal Probability Distributions in Scatter Transmission Systems. IRE Transactions on Communication Systems 8(1) (1960) 57–67
10. 3GPP: Radio frequency (RF) system scenarios. Technical Report TR 25.942, 3GPP (2003)

Service Level Agreement Enforcement for Differentiated Services

Paulo Rogério Pereira

INESC ID, Rua Alves Redol, 9. 1000-029 Lisboa, Portugal
Tel.: +351-213100345, Fax: +351-213145843
prbp@inesc.pt

Abstract. This paper describes a hierarchical architecture of active policies that performs the management of a differentiated services (DiffServ) network. These policies monitor quality of service (QoS) parameters and dynamically optimize some aspects of the existing equipment and services to provide the best possible QoS to users. This helps the enforcement of a Service Level Agreement (SLA) between a provider and users. The results show that the use of active policies improves the service offered to users, by constantly adapting to the network state, and helping to fulfill SLAs with minimum costs to the service provider.

1 Introduction

Quality of Service (QoS) is defined as the collective effect of service performance which determines the degree of satisfaction of a user of the service [1]. Quality is measured through parameters such as service availability, delay, jitter, throughput and packet loss ratio [2].

The importance of QoS is such that many service providers offer services with a specified level of quality as defined in a Service Level Agreement (SLA) with users [2][3].

An important problem is how to evaluate and assure the QoS specified in the SLA. The QoS objectives specified in a SLA are high-level policy goals, sometimes not using the same parameters that can be measured or controlled on the network. Thus a refinement process is necessary to relate the different abstraction levels.

To address these problems, this paper introduces the concept of active policies [4] to help SLA fulfillment. Active policies are active objects which evaluate the QoS users are obtaining and dynamically optimize some aspects of the network operation at different abstraction levels, improving the QoS, whenever possible, up to the set goals.

The active policies are used in a scenario of a differentiated services (DiffServ) network [5] and the QoS improvements analyzed.

The paper is organized as follows. Section 2 describes the active policy model. Section 3 describes the scenario implemented, the active policies deployed and the simulation results. Section 4 compares our approach with related work. Finally, section 5 draws the conclusions and points further research topics.

M. Cesana, L. Fratta (Eds.): Wireless Syst./Network Architect. 2005, LNCS 3883, pp. 158–169, 2006.

2 Active Policies

Active policies are organized in a hierarchy where each active policy operates at a certain abstraction level, specialized on managing a certain problem over a subpart of the network. This division allows decomposing the SLA management problem in several simpler problems. The overall architecture of the active policies cooperates to enforce the SLA. Each active policy does a certain effort and relies on the effort of other lower-level active policies to achieve a specified QoS objective.

Figure 1 shows the internal modules of an active policy. Each active policy monitors some parameters of the managed objects under its responsibility and calculates the corresponding QoS parameters. A reactive management module provides quick responses to urgent problems. A proactive management module acts based on the history of past QoS to fine tune the operation of the reactive module and ensure a more precise SLA enforcement.

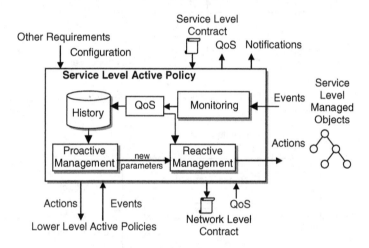

Fig. 1. Active policies internal modules

The active policies' monitoring module is shown in figure 2. For the monitoring operation, the first step is to sample the system parameters required for determining the QoS. The data is read from the managed objects or from other lower level policies. Then, it is converted to the required format and pre-processed, for instance with some low-pass function to filter peaks. Finally, the QoS parameters are calculated.

The reactive module, shown in figure 3, tries to fulfill an objective that is configured. The reactive module has a set of acting rules that fire the execution of some actions or the generation of events according to the QoS measured. The limiters verify if the actions make sense, limiting the modifications to what is allowed. The exception generation block verifies if there is a QoS degradation or if it not possible to act to fulfill the objectives. The appropriate exception actions are taken.

The proactive module, shown in figure 4, does planning tasks. Internally, it is similar to the reactive module, but acts according to the evolution of the observed QoS, instead of depending directly on the QoS. Additionally, the proactive module, instead of acting over the managed objects, can reconfigure the policies themselves. This feedback provides more precise QoS fulfillment.

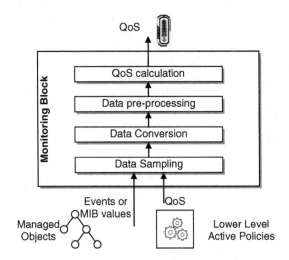

Fig. 2. Active policies' monitoring module

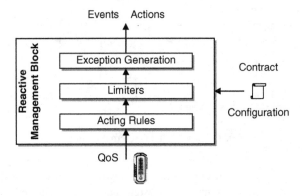

Fig. 3. Active policies' reactive module

Acting rules can have a set of thresholds, with or without hysteresis, count events, act based on time, use feedback control, or combinations of these. The rules may be used in different active policies, just by configuring the parameters they use and modify.

Basically, active policies act over the network, when certain thresholds on the QoS are crossed, to avoid SLA violation. Naturally, policies have to start acting long before the QoS limits are crossed. The actions are usually stronger as the limits are approached. On the other hand, if the QoS is better than specified in the SLA, the reverse actions are possible to reduce the service provider costs, without SLA violation. For instance, an admission control system may admit some more flows, allowing the service provider to charge more. To ensure stability, the programmer has to know if a certain action contributes to improve or worsen the QoS and the actions in the direction of improving the QoS should be more intense than the actions in the direction of degrading the QoS. If the contribution of a certain action is unknown, a perturbation method [6] may be applied to determine the contribution. The idea in this method is to force explicit system perturbations and use a statistical model to estimate dependency strengths for each one.

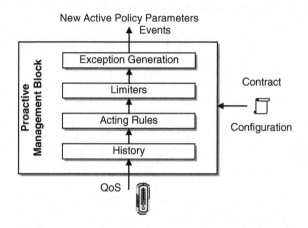

Fig. 4. Active policies' proactive module

Examples of actions the active policies might perform are: modifying Random Early Detection (RED) parameters for increasing packet discard, especially for out-of-profile packets; restricting the admission of new flows into the system; activating extra lines or increasing the bandwidth available for some paths; and selectively degrading the class of certain flows.

The active policies architecture should be deployed using a management by delegation technique [7], placing the active policies near the objects they manage. The delegation adds flexibility as it allows system modifications during operation. The higher level policies have a global vision of the network state, while the lower level policies are near the managed equipment, minimizing management and signaling traffic. This architecture adds flexibility, increases scalability and fault tolerance.

3 System Architecture

3.1 Active Policies Hierarchy

A scenario of a DiffServ network was built. The service provider wants to offer some QoS to users. The DiffServ model allows offering scalable QoS differentiation by aggregating the traffic in three traffic classes: Expedited Forwarding (EF), Assured Forwarding (AF) and Best Effort (BE). Packets are classified and marked on entering the network, being forwarded to their destination according to the per-hop behavior of their class. The EF class emulates a virtual circuit. The AF class offers some guarantees and the BE provides no guarantees at all.

Figure 5 shows the active policies deployed and how they are related to each other. The different levels in figure 5 correspond to different abstraction levels. The top-level QoS requirements are refined through each abstraction level. For each abstraction level, QoS parameters that can be measured are identified, the corresponding QoS requirements are determined and actions adequate for that abstraction level are specified. The active policies cooperate with each other to fulfill the QoS objectives for each level and consequently, the top-level QoS objectives.

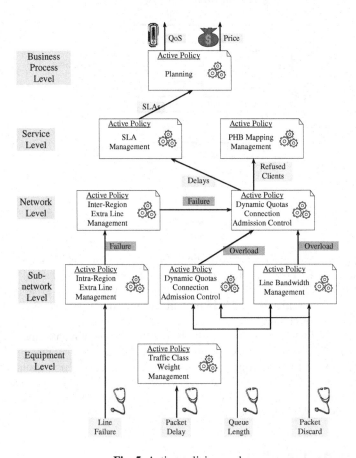

Fig. 5. Active policies used

At the Equipment level, policies are local to each device. Policies at this level monitor the delay in each traffic class and dynamically adjust the weight of the different classes and out-of-profile packet discard. In this way, the existing network resources are divided through the traffic classes to ensure the QoS relations between classes, no matter the load of the classes.

The Network level is sub-divided in two sub-levels to ease implementation and improve scalability. Sub-network level policies are responsible for a region, or a specific equipment. Network level policies are responsible for the entire network. Policies at this level perform measurement based admission control, select backup lines and dynamically adjust the bandwidth available for some paths.

The Service level is the first that sees end-to-end QoS parameters. Policies at this level monitor end-to-end QoS and try to enforce end-to-end SLAs by adjusting parameters of lower level policies that do not have this end-to-end view. Examples are: increasing out-of-profile packet discard, reducing flow admissions, modifying the bandwidth for some paths. Policies also selectively degrade the traffic class of some flows when there is overload.

A more detailed description of the operation and configuration of each active policy used is given in [4].

As is it difficult to specify the exact thresholds where the policies should operate, a planning policy, at business process level, makes long-term adjustments to ensure a more precise SLA fulfillment.

3.2 SLA Management Without Planning

First, the results without the planning policy are presented and analyzed. The results with planning will be analyzed in the next subsection.

The results presented were obtained with the NS2 network simulator [8], for a network with 15 core nodes. The simulations were made with the exact same traffic pattern in two different situations: without active policies and with the active policies operating. Several simulations were made with different random number seeds and the 95% confidence interval was plotted in all the graphs.

Figure 6 shows the average end-to-end delays obtained with the following QoS objectives: $SLA(delayEF) = 60$ ms and $SLA(delayAF) = 120$ ms, and all policies operating, except the planning policy. These results show it is possible to enforce these SLAs with some error. The error from the EF SLA objective is about 24 to 32% without the policies and about 7 to 16% with the policies. The error from the AF SLA objective is about 12 to 26% without the policies and about 13 to 24% with the policies. Although the results are better with the active policies, they show it is difficult to set the exact policies operation points to have precise SLA enforcement.

Figure 7 shows the average traffic load in each class for each border node (PoP, or Point of Presence), where traffic is generated. Without the active policies, a fixed worst case admission control is used. Under these conditions, the network is fully loaded with 15 users connected per node, starting to refuse new users above this limit. On the other hand, the active policies use a measurement based admission control that can allow more connections in the AF class. Indeed, as the traffic in many flows is bursty, the average load in the network is much lower than the worst case load for a given user connection pattern. Modifications in the bandwidth division for each class also allow a slight increase in the number of EF users. The decrease observed in the number of EF clients for a load of 20-50 connections, when the active policies are used, is due to the downgrade of the traffic class of some flows by the mapping management active policy, as the network load increases. The use of the active policy has the advantage that, instead of having an indiscriminate downgrade of the class of flows, only selected flows have their class downgraded according to the existing load. From the graph of the average BE clients, it can be seen that there are less BE users when the active policies are used. This is caused by less flows having their traffic class downgraded when the active policies are used and results in increased service availability and a profit increase for the service provider.

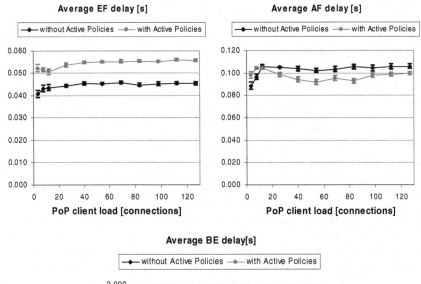

Fig. 6. Average delay per traffic class

Figure 8 shows the average throughput for the AF traffic class. The throughput decreases when the active policies are used. There was no packet loss both for EF and in-profile AF traffic. This was one of the high-level QoS objectives for these classes. Having no packet loss for the AF class means that the decrease in AF throughput is caused by less out-of-profile traffic being transported. Since more flows are transported, and the throughput specified in the contract is assured, the service provider profit increases.

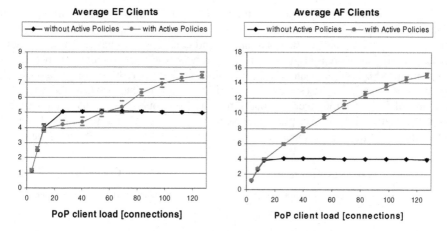

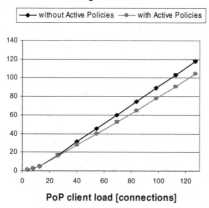

Fig. 7. Average traffic per traffic class

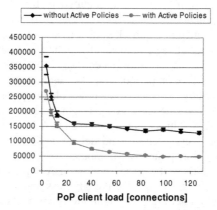

Fig. 8. Average throughput for the AF traffic class

Figure 9 shows the average jitter for the EF and AF classes. The active policies cause an increased jitter, as they reconfigure the network frequently. Each modification in the network changes the load pattern and consequently changes the end to end delay, causing an increased jitter. This is especially true when the delay is below the limit imposed by the SLA and the bandwidth for a path is reduced, or the admission of additional users increases the traffic load. However, in the EF class, there is a reduction of the jitter for a certain load range, as some bursty flows have their traffic class downgraded to a lower priority class for these loads. Globally, the disadvantage of an increased jitter is compensated by the improvement in other QoS parameters.

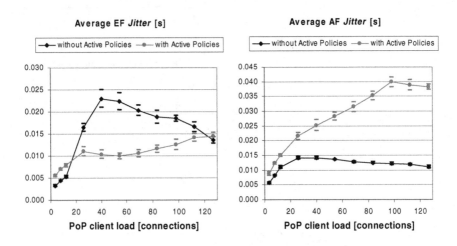

Fig. 9. Average jitter per traffic class

3.3 Planning Policy

The top level planning active policy adjusts the SLAs of the SLA management active policy to obtain better long-term results.

Now, the previous delay objectives, as required in the SLA, are used to set the *SLA(delayEF)* and *SLA(delayAF)* to be used by the SLA management active policy. Both are modified by an integral feedback system as shown in figure 10. The integrator gain is set to 0.25, for both classes, to make slight changes in the SLAs for each sampling period. The sampling period is large as compared to the network delays, but much smaller than the SLA verification period. The planning policy works at higher abstraction level than the other active policies, so its timescale of operation is much larger than the timescales of lower level policies. An anti-windup mechanism was added to the integrators to limit the SLA values to a range of 0.25 to 4 times the required SLA.

Figure 11 shows the average end-to-end delays obtained with all the active policies, including the planning policy, as compared with those without any policies. These graphics show that the static error from the SLA objective is greatly reduced by the planning policy to about 1 to 8% for the EF class and 1 to 6% for the AF class. Now the delays are about one order of magnitude nearer the specified value of 60 ms for the EF class, and 120 ms for AF.

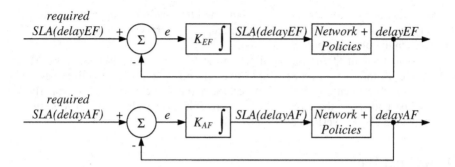

Fig. 10. SLA control system

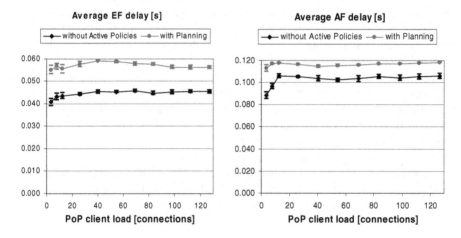

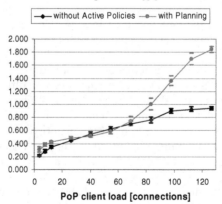

Fig. 11. Average delay per traffic class

As for the other QoS parameters, such as the jitter, the throughput, the packet loss, the service availability (number of users accepted), there were no significant differences when the planning policy was used.

The objectives of 60 ms for the delay in the EF class and 120 ms for the AF are achievable. Naturally, not all SLA objectives are possible to enforce. But even when it is not possible to enforce the objectives, the active policies still work properly and do their best to place the QoS as near as possible to the objectives. The system is stable even in traffic overload conditions.

4   Related Work

The works of [9][10] present policy hierarchies for distributed systems. However, these works do not integrate with service level management, nor refine the requirements through several policy abstraction levels that act over the network down to the equipment, nor allow easy policy reuse. The policies of [11] restrict the network behavior, instead of improving its operation as in the case of the active policies. The work in [12] focuses on the policy language and provides some examples of a differentiated services network with SLAs. However, the system lacks an automatic tuning mechanism and does not cover end-to-end QoS.

The work in [13] presents an architecture for QoS management integrated with traffic engineering. Although there are some similar aspects to our work, the active policies hierarchy has the advantage of providing several complementary mechanisms to enforce QoS and a planning policy to improve accuracy.

The work in [14] uses joint buffer management and scheduling to provide proportional and absolute QoS guarantees. However, this work does not have several abstraction levels and does not cover end-to-end QoS.

5   Conclusion

It can be concluded that the QoS specified in SLAs can be provided within certain limits by using active policies that dynamically adjust network parameters to optimize network performance.

The planning policy performs automatic threshold adjustments to provide a more precise fulfillment of QoS requirements, circumventing the difficulty in setting policy operating points. However, it is difficult to evaluate to which limits the SLAs can be assured. This is a difficult topic that may be addressed in future research.

A set of acting rules can be used to build the majority of the active policies. The acting rules can be reused for different situations, just by changing the system variables they monitor, the system variables they control and the configuration parameters of the rules.

The active policies hierarchy provides several abstraction levels, with greater flexibility, autonomy, improved scalability and fault tolerance, as compared with non-hierarchical alternatives.

The architecture presented assumed a single service provider. The expansion for multiple service providers is a possible future research direction. The use of a price model [15] is a further possible future research direction.

References

1. Terms and Definitions Related to Quality of Service and Network Performance Including Dependability. ITU-T Recommendation E.800. August 1994
2. A. Westerinen, J. Schnizlein, J. Strassner, M. Scherling, B. Quinn, S. Herzog, A. Huynh, M. Carlson, J. Perry, S. Waldbusser. Terminology for Policy-Based Management. IETF RFC 3198. November 2001.
3. Lundy Lewis. Service Level Management of Enterprise Networks. Artech House. September 1999. ISBN: 1580530168.
4. Paulo Pereira, Djamel Sadok, Paulo Pinto: Service Level Management of Differentiated Services Networks with Active Policies. Proceedings of the 3rd Conference on Telecommunications (ConfTele'2001), Figueira da Foz, Portugal, April 2001, pp. 542-546. ISBN: 972-98115-2-0.
5. S. Blake, D. Black, M. Carlson, E. Davies, Z. Wang, W. Weiss. An Architecture for Differentiated Services, IETF RFC 2475, December 1998.
6. A. Brown, G. Kar, A. Keller. An Active Approach to Characterizing Dynamic Dependencies for Problem Determination in a Distributed Application Environment. Proceedings of the 7th International IFIP/IEEE Symposium on Integrated Management (IM'2001), Seattle, EUA, 14-18 May 2001.
7. Germán Goldszmidt, Yechiam Yemini. Distributed Management by Delegation. Proceedings of the 15th International Conference on Distributed Computing Systems, June 1995.
8. UCB/LBNL/VINT Network Simulator (version 2). http://www.isi.edu/nsnam/ns/
9. René Wies. Policies in Network and Systems Management - Formal Definition and Architecture. Journal of Network and Systems Management, Plenum Publishing Corp., 2(1):63-83, March 1994.
10. Thomas Koch, Christoph Krell, Bernd Krämer. Policy Definition Language for Automated Management of Distributed Systems. Proceedings of the 2nd International Workshop on Systems Management, IEEE Computer Society, 19-21 June 1996, Canada.
11. M. Sloman, J. Magee, K. Twidle, J. Kramer. An Architecture for Managing Distributed Systems. Proceedings of the 4th IEEE Workshop on Future Trends of Distributed Computing Systems, Lisbon, Portugal, IEEE Computer Society Press, pp. 40-46, 22-24 September 1993.
12. L. Lymberopoulos, E. Lupu, M. Sloman. An Adaptive Policy Based Framework for Network Services Management. Plenum Press Journal of Network and Systems Management, Special Issue on Policy Based Management, 11(3):277-303, Sep. 2003.
13. P. Trimintzios, G. Pavlou, P. Flegkas, P. Georgatsos, A. Asgari, E. Mykoniati. Service-Driven Traffic Engineering for Intradomain Quality of Service Management. IEEE Network, 17(3):29-36, May/June 2003.
14. Nicolas Christin, Jörg Liebeherr. A QoS Architecture for Quantitative Service Differentiation. IEEE Communications Magazine, 41(6):38-45, June 2003.
15. Luiz A. DaSilva. Pricing for QoS-Enabled Networks: A Survey. IEEE Communications Surveys, 3(2):2-8, 2nd Quarter 2000.

MIPv6 Binding Authentication for B3G Networks

Domenico Celentano[1], Antonio Fresa[1], Maurizio Longo[2],
Fabio Postiglione[2], and Anton Luca Robustelli[1]

[1] Co.Ri.TeL - Via Ponte Don Melillo, I-84084 Fisciano (SA) - Italy
[2] Dipartimento di Ingegneria dell'Informazione ed Ingegneria Elettrica,
Universitá degli Studi di Salerno, Via Ponte Don Melillo, I-84084, Fisciano (SA), Italy
{celentano, fresa, robustelli}@coritel.it,
{longo, fpostiglione}@unisa.it

Abstract. In last years, the introduction of new wireless communication systems has stimulated the technical and scientific community to investigate future evolution scenarios for 3G networks, generically referred to as Beyond-3G or 4G. In order to guarantee high end-to-end quality of service and security, Beyond-3G networks will cope with some issues such as session security in wireless environments and seamless mobility among different coverage domains and, possibly, access technologies. In this paper we analyze the security threats emerging from some mechanisms for mobility management, and we propose a solution to improve the security level under the assumption that both communicating terminals are attached to a 3GPP IP Multimedia Subsystem that supports both the Session Initiation Protocol and the Mobile IP version 6 protocol.

Keywords: Beyond-3G networks, IP Multimedia Subsystem, Mobility management, Mobile IP version 6, Binding authentication, Session initiation protocol.

1   Introduction

The rapid spread of new radio access technologies, such as IEEE 802.11 and IEEE 802.16 (aka Wi-Fi and WiMAX respectively), has stimulated investigations on the evolution scenarios for third generation (3G) networks, typically referred to as Beyond-3G (B3G) or 4G [1, 2]. A B3G network is expected to be high-speed and *user-centric*, to provide seamless global roaming and integration between different IP-based services with high end-to-end *Quality of Service* (QoS) [3, 4, 5]. It will be interconnected to the existing circuit and packet switched networks, and will allow mobile users to use always the most adequate access technology for each connection and service: this approach is called Always Best Connected (ABC) [6].

In such a heterogeneous environment, key issues are certainly security provision for applications exchanging data in diverse wireless networks [7] and seamless mobility (*handoff*) between different coverage domains and, possibly, access technologies [8].

M. Cesana, L. Fratta (Eds.): Wireless Syst./Network Architect. 2005, LNCS 3883, pp. 170–183, 2006.

To cope with such issues, several solutions have been proposed where mobility is supported from different layers of the TCP/IP stack reference model. Thus, they can be classified into different categories according to the layer in which mobility management mechanisms are implemented:

- *Application layer solutions*, involving some layer 5 signalling protocols [9];
- *Transport layer solutions* [10], for instance based on the Stream Control Transmission Protocol (SCTP) [11];
- *Network layer solutions*, most of them based on the use of the Mobile Internet Protocol (IP) version 6 (MIPv6) protocol [12], an extension to IPv6 in order to meet the mobility requirements;
- *Link layer solutions*, focusing on the issues related to the roaming between networks with different radio technologies [13];
- *Cross-layer solutions*, aiming to handle the handoff procedure by means of the interworking between two different layers, such as layer 2 and layer 3 (S-MIP [14]).

Nevertheless, the available proposals present security vulnerabilities when adopted in heterogeneous wireless networks. In particular, serious threats are currently associated to the delivery of messages sent by a mobile terminal toward other corresponding users while notifying its new contact address during roaming activity.

In this paper, we focus on the B3G network defined by 3GPP, a standardization organization of 3G-and-beyond mobile networks. Its core is a network infrastructure called the *IP Multimedia Subsystem* (IMS) [15, 16], based on the Session Initiation Protocol (SIP) [17], a signalling protocol proposed by the Internet Engineering Task Force (IETF), for providing real-time multimedia services (video conferencing, presence services, multi-party gaming, content sharing etc.) to mobile subscribers.

Since recent developments seem to converge toward the general adoption of MIPv6 as the mobility layer, we analyze the security threats emerging from some MIPv6 mechanisms for mobility management, and we propose a new method to improve the security level, under the assumption that both communicating terminals are attached to an IMS network.

The paper is organized as follows. Section 2 describes the role of the IMS in B3G networks and its functionalities. Section 3 presents a brief overview of the mobility management mechanisms in a network based on the MIPv6 protocol and points out some advantages of a MIPv6-based IMS. In Section 4, our proposal is presented to improve security during handoff and the consequent binding authentication procedure. In Section 5, we provide some concluding remarks.

2 The IP Multimedia Subsystem

The IP Multimedia Subsystem (IMS) [16] represents the core of the next generation mobile networks. It is a IPv6-based architecture for providing both real-time

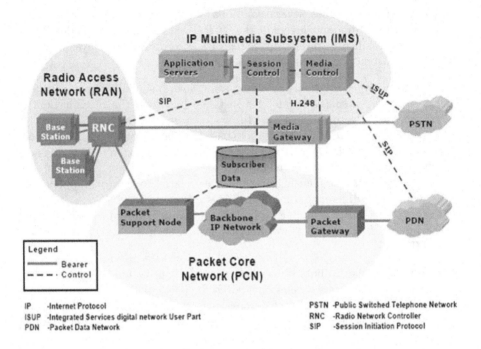

Fig. 1. The IMS architecture

multimedia communication services and data transport services and it can be connected to the Public Switched Telephone Network (PSTN) and Internet by specific gateways. It is organized in different layers: the access, transport, and control layers (the last one is further separated into media control, session control, and application control). A simplified version of the IMS is depicted in Fig. 1.

The wireless connection between a User Equipment (UE), representing the mobile subscriber, and the core network is provided by the Radio Access Network (RAN); several RANs, based on different radio technologies, can coexist. They also provide low level (layer 2) mobility management.

The Packet Core Network identifies the transport layer for signalling and media flows (*user plane*), and high-level mobility management. The 3GPP adopted SIP as the signalling protocol for managing real-time multimedia sessions. In order to achieve this, new network nodes have been added, on top of the existing General Packet Radio Service (GPRS) core network: signalling flows are managed by the Call Session Control Function (CSCF) nodes, whereas multimedia flows are managed by the Media Resource Function (MRF) elements, employing the Real-time Transport Protocol (RTP) [18].

Figure 2 reports a network scenario representing two roaming UEs, where the *Home Network* represents the network domain of the telecom operator to which the user is subscribed, while the *Visited networks* represent other service providers networks the roaming subscriber can attach to.

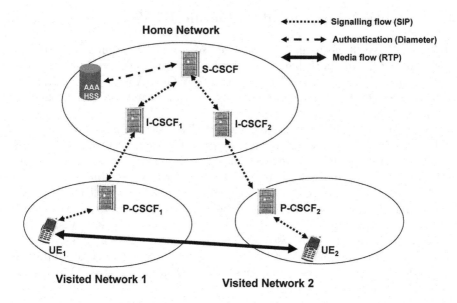

Fig. 2. A typical network scenario representing two roaming User Equipments. Both users are subscribed to the same telecom operator (Home Network). Diameter is a recently proposed authentication protocol [19].

The CSCF functionalities are distributed among three different types of servers (see Fig. 2):

- *Proxy CSCF* (P-CSCF) represents the first contact point to the IMS network for the mobile UE; it is usually located in the Visited Network, and forwards the SIP signalling to the Home Network;
- *Serving CSCF* (S-CSCF) is the main node among the CSCFs since it has to process the SIP signalling, take decisions and manage the multimedia sessions; it is located in the Home Network;
- *Interrogating CSCF* (I-CSCF) is located in the Home Network and is responsible to select the appropriate S-CSCF; it can implement topology hiding functions between operators.

The users' subscription data are stored in a database in the Home Network: the Home Subscriber Server (HSS). Every user record contains the S-CSCF assigned to the user, its present location, security information and the user profile. The interaction among the three CSCF nodes and the HSS allows the complete management of the SIP signalling for multimedia sessions.

Telecom service providers should guarantee seamless mobility among different coverage domains and access technologies for their customers, preventing session hijackings and attacks during handoff.

3   Mobility Management in Mobile IP Version 6

MIPv6 is a layer-3 mechanism to manage user terminal mobility in all-IP networks. It can handle both handoffs between different radio access technologies (*vertical handoff*), for instance between UMTS WCDMA and IEEE 802.11, and handoffs between two domains covered by the same wireless access technology (*horizontal handoff*).

MIPv6 is designed in order to allow an IPv6 user terminal to be reached and to reach other users when roaming. It provides transparent support for host mobility, including the maintenance of active Transmission Control Protocol (TCP) connections and User Datagram Protocol (UDP) port bindings.

A UE, typically referred to as Mobile Node (MN), is identified by a permanent *Home Address* (HoA) from its Home Network (HN) address space. When it roams away from its HN and detects a new access network, a Visited Network, through the *Neighbor Discovery mechanism*, it acquires a *Care-of-Address* (CoA) by means of either a stateless or a stateful address configuration process. Subsequently, it updates its current position to its Home Agent (HA) by sending a *Binding Update* (BU) message.

MIPv6 must adopt the *Routing Header Type 2* and the *Home Address Option* headers in order to be transparent to the upper layers and to allow the session to be maintained. As a consequence, every packet directed to the MN passes through the HA that forwards it to the MN (also known as *triangular routing*).

However, the MN can notify its CoA directly to the endpoints MN is communicating with, also referred to as Correspondent Nodes (CNs), by sending them a BU message, in order to request that the CNs forward further packets directly to the MN. This mechanism, called *Route Optimization*, eliminates the triangular routing toward the HA and hence reduces the end-to-end delay: this is particularly necessary for real-time communications in order to avoid QoS degradations in every B3G network.

Therefore, MIPv6 can provide, in line of principle, seamless roaming services for mobile nodes if Route Optimization is performed, but presents some security vulnerabilities when adopted in heterogeneous wireless networks. In particular, possible security threats are associated to the BU messages sent by the MN to its CN(s), as detailed in the following.

3.1   Security Issues

Security between MN and HA is guaranteed by the IPSec framework with the *Encapsulation Security Payload* (ESP) protocol [20], in conjunction with Routing Header Type 2 and Home Address Option, as IPSec security associations do not need to be re-created during handoff procedure. Then, BU mechanism between MN and HA can be considered safe.

On the other hand, BU messages between MN and CN(s) can be protected by the Return Routability Procedure (RRP), as suggested in [20] and sketched in Fig. 3. After the acquisition of a CoA and the subsequent BU with the HA, the MN sends two packets to the CN carrying two different cookies: the first

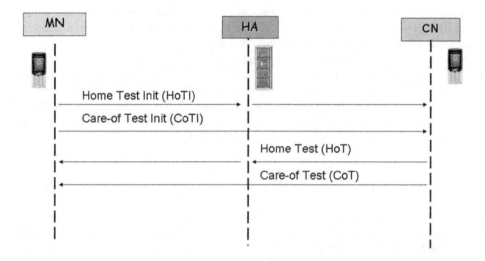

Fig. 3. The Return Routability Procedure (RRP)

packet (Home Test Init - HoTI) is addressed to the HA and then routed to the CN while the latter (Care-of Test Init - CoTI) is sent directly to the CN and, then, it can follow a different path.

After receiving both packets, the CN generates a *Home Keygen Token* and a *Care-of Keygen Token* and sends them respectively through HA, encapsulated in the Home Test (HoT) packet, and directly to the MN, in the Care-of Test (CoT) packet. These two tokens are derived from a private secret key K_{cn} and random numbers (nonces) by means of the *HMAC_SHA1* hashing function [21, 22].

The concatenation of the Home Keygen Token and the Care-of Keygen Token provides the MN with the key K_{bm} needed by the correspondent node to authenticate the subsequent binding update messages from MN directly to CN.

If the authentication data of the BU request is valid, the CN adds an entry in its *Binding Cache* for the particular MN and sends back a Binding Acknowledgment (BA) response. Upon receipt of such a message, the MN creates an entry for the CN into its *Binding Update List*.

Unfortunately, the RRP mechanism is vulnerable to attacks along the path between the HA and the CN, where a malicious node, aware of a session between MN and CN, might simulate a handoff of the MN by sending fake HoTI and CoTI messages. In such a way, it can obtain K_{bm} and send a fake BU to the CN in order to redirect the MN-CN communication to itself (*impersonation attack*) or possibly also forward the traffic to the MN, after analysing it, as in traditional *man-in-the-middle* attacks.

3.2 MIPv6 for IMS Networks

The IMS defines a security mechanism which verifies that the IPv6 packet source address of SIP messages, sent by the MN, corresponds to the IPv6 address reported in the SIP headers. Hence, this requires that the MN use the same address (either the HoA or the CoA) for both the IPv6 packet source address and the IPv6 address used within SIP headers. Therefore, several scenarios are possible for address management by the MN [9]:

i) The MN uses the CoA as source address and then provides it at SIP registration procedure and for session establishment. So, the MN needs to re-register the new CoA with the S-CSCF every time it changes its point of attachment to the network; this corresponds to using a SIP-based mobility management. In real-time communications, this could cause loss of RTP packets while the re-INVITE procedure is completed. Moreover, in this scenario, mobility is not transparent to the transport layer and causes TCP sessions interruptions [23].

ii) The MN provides both the CoA and HoA within SIP signalling. This requires some changes to the current SIP standard and therefore it is neither easily feasible nor recommended.

iii) The MN provides the HoA at SIP registration, for session establishment and as IPv6 source address. In that way the MN does not need to re-register or re-invite other nodes when it changes CoA, but it updates the new CoA through MIPv6 signalling. If we suppose that the SIP proxy P-CSCF supports the MIPv6 stack (every IPv6 node should support MIPv6), then the SIP application can be completely unaware of changes of MN's CoA.

The third scenario suggests the integration of MIPv6 in the IMS and appears as the most promising because it has a low impact on the existing protocols and nodes, and mobility management is transparent to the transport and application layers.

4   Binding Authentication in MIPv6-Based IMS Networks

As a consequence of the analysis of the previous section, we address MIPv6 security threats in an IMS network. As already mentioned, an extension to the IMS is required so as to support MIPv6 by integrating its functionalities in the P-CSCF node, the first contact point for the MN within the IMS core network.

As P-CSCF is a MIPv6 node and would also act as CN for all the MNs registered to the IMS through it, the P-CSCF would store a Binding Cache containing the associations between HoA's and CoA's for the various MNs.

MIPv6 guarantees, of course, that the HA in the Home Network is always aware of the current CoA of the MN.

At registration to IMS (by SIP REGISTER messages), a roaming MN provides its HoA and its contact entity to the P-CSCF of the *originating network* [16] (henceforth $P - CSCF_1$) and so allows the P-CSCF to be aware of the MN current address [9].

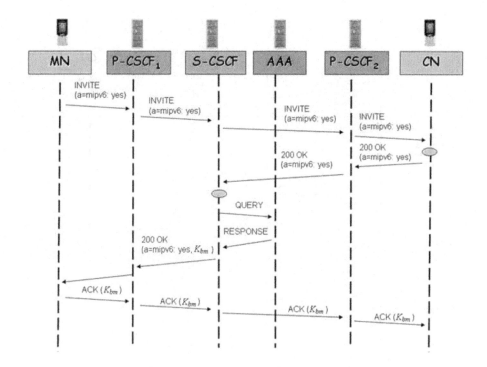

Fig. 4. Generation and distribution of the authentication key K_{bm} to MN and CN

4.1   A New Mechanism for Binding Authentication

Instead of adopting the standard MIPv6 RRP mechanism, we propose to create at call setup (SIP INVITE message) the authentication key K_{bm} for the subsequent MN-CN binding update procedures, and distribute it to the MN and CN within the body of the SIP 200 OK and ACK messages. It is important to highlight that this procedure is performed only at beginning of a communication session, while MIPv6 RRP between MN and CN should be repeated, as the binding update, after *every* terminal handoff.

Furthermore, security management is entirely delegated to the IMS infrastructure. Indeed, the K_{bm} authentication key is generated by the *Authentication, Authorization, Accounting* (AAA) *Server* and distributed by S-CSCF as pointed out in Fig. 4.

In this scenario both communicating terminals are customers of the same telecom service provider (the Home network and hence the S-CSCF are the same). Otherwise, the authentication key K_{bm} must be distributed by the S-CSCF in the Home network of the CN. As K_{bm} has a validity limited only for MN-CN BU messages in a single communication session, such a policy can be considered safe.

The INVITE message from the MN must convey an extension to the Session Description Protocol (SDP) [24], i.e. the attribute a=mipv6 yes, in order

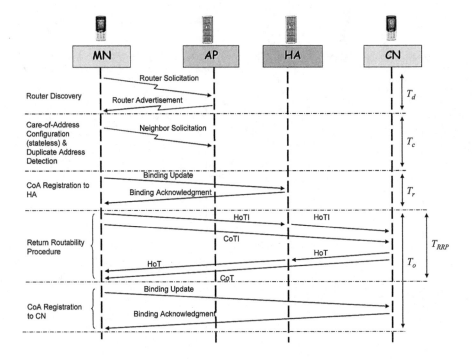

Fig. 5. Delays occurring during a mid-session handoff procedure. The first three messages (involving in the figure only the MN and the Access Point - AP) are sent *multicast*.

to inform the CN and the S-CSCF that the MN is going to use the binding authentication via IMS. If the CN supports such a feature, it responds by adding the same attribute in the SDP carried by the response 200 OK. The S-CSCF has to parse these messages and ask the AAA server a new K_{bm} if both messages convey the new SDP attribute. Such a key is then added to the 200 OK to the MN, that forwards it to the CN by adding it to the SDP body of the ACK message.

4.2   Assessment

The distribution of the key is rendered secure by employing IPSec with ESP between any SIP user (MN and CN) and its own P-CSCF. It is worth noting that, in general, mobile terminals can be located in different administrative domains served by distinct P-CSCFs, and the message flows inside the IMS, a proprietary and protected network, is intrinsically secure.

As already mentioned, since RRP must necessarily follow the BU procedure between Mobile Node and Home Agent, a further advantage offered by authentication via IMS is that BU messages from MN to HA and from MN to CN can be sent simultaneously, providing a consistent reduction of the *handoff latency*.

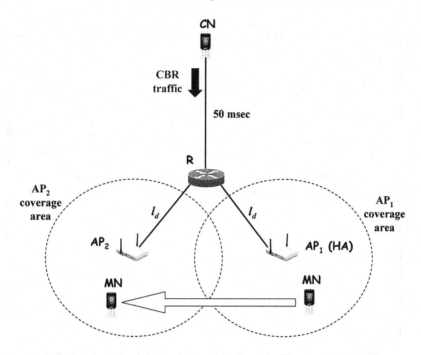

Fig. 6. Network scenario adopted in NS-2 simulations

Indeed, the handoff latency T_{ho} can be defined as the sum of many contributions [25]. The most relevant ones are represented in Fig. 5: the *movement detection time* T_d, i.e. the time elapsed between the moment in which the MN becomes aware that it has to change its current attachment point to a new one); the *CoA configuration time* T_c including Duplicate Address Detection; the *binding registration time* T_r for the BU between MN and HA; the *route optimization time* T_o that is the time to complete the route optimization procedure, including the RRP.

Thus, the handoff delay can be computed as

$$T_{ho} = T_d + T_c + T_r + T_o. \tag{1}$$

The delay T_o must be considered in T_{ho} because in real-time multimedia communications (typical in every B3G networks) packets arriving at receiver before the route optimization, can be too late and then dropped.

This value T_o can be lowered if the RRP before BU mechanism between MN and CN is eliminated and the binding authentication is performed by the IMS network as proposed. Under the assumption that the BU to CN follows the BA from the HA, the handoff latency T'_{ho} is

$$T'_{ho} = T_{ho} - T_{RRP} \tag{2}$$

and T_{RRP} is the delay introduced by the RRP,

$$T_{RRP} \cong \max\{RTT_{MN-CN}, RTT_{MN-HA-CN}\}, \tag{3}$$

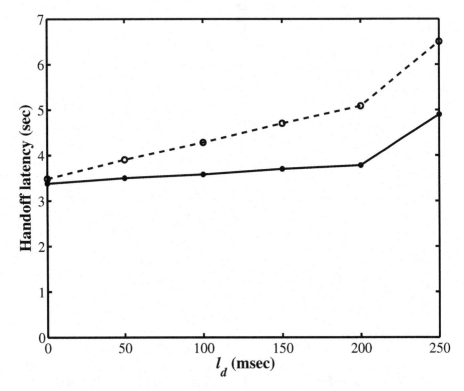

Fig. 7. A comparison between the handoff latency with different mechanisms of binding authentication: our proposal (solid line) and the mechanism including RRP (dashed line)

where RTT_{MN-CN} and $RTT_{MN-HA-CN}$ are the Round Trip Times between MN and CN in direct communications and via HA, respectively.

In order to point out the benefit of the proposed mechanism for binding authentication, a preliminary analysis has been performed by means of the NS-2 network simulator [26], extended to support MIPv6 by means of MobiWan [27].

Assuming a handoff occurring during a real-time session (mid-session handoff), the nodes involved in the procedure are the MN, the Access Points (APs), the CN and the HA. As a consequence, the network scenario adopted in NS-2 numerical experiments is displayed in Fig. 6, where the CBR traffic represents a real-time flow between CN and MN. It is composed by packets with length $L = 100$ bytes transmitted every 20 msec. The propagation delay on the link between the CN and the router R has been set to 50 msec, in order to achieve typical delays introduced by long distance links, while the HA has been colocated with the Access Point AP_1. The radio access technology has been assumed to be IEEE 802.11; MN speed has been set to 6 m/sec.

The handoff latency has been computed as the elapsed time between the last packet received by the MN from AP_1 and first one received from AP_2 after the route optimization procedure. The results have been collected for different values of l_d, as proposed in [28], and then presented in Fig. 7. They confirm the reduction of the handoff delay, i.e $T'_{ho} < T_{ho}$, and hence of the packet loss rate occurring during multimedia communications.

It is worth noting that the overall handoff delay is strongly influenced by the Router Solicitation interval (the default value in MobiWan is 2.3 sec) and the interval to start the route optimization procedure (default value 1 sec).

The penalties for the increase of the security level and the reduction of the handoff delay are:

  (i) the interaction between two different layers of the TCP/IP protocol stack (cross-layer) because authentication keys for layer 3 operations are carried by a layer 5 protocol,

 (ii) an increase of computational burden at S-CSCF (some scalability issues could arise),

(iii) some modifications in the behavior of the of terminal nodes (MN and CN) due to the SDP attribute a=mipv6 yes.

The proposed method for binding authentication regards MIPv6 mobility management. It is, in line of principle, compatible with some micro-mobility management techniques, such as Hierarchical Mobile IP version 6 [29].

5   Conclusions

In this paper, we analyse a MIPv6-based mobility mechanism within an IMS network domain so to achieve seamless mobility. In order to increase security during mobile nodes handoff procedures, IMS infrastructure (AAA and CSCFs Servers) can be involved to generate and distribute the authentication keys for MIPv6 binding update procedures. In such a scenario, the costly MIPv6 Return Routability Procedure can be avoided, so considerably increasing the overall security level as the vulnerability in the Home Agent-Correspondent Node link is drastically reduced.

Furthermore, the handoff delay T_{ho} and the consequent packet loss is markedly reduced, as preliminary NS-2 experiments confirm.

However, the use of the K_{bm} key would protect from potential attacks by third parties, but it would provide no protection in case the MN itself behaves maliciously. For instance, a MN can send malicious BUs to several CNs making believe it moved to a particular CoA actually corresponding to a particular user to attack. If a sufficient number of different CNs is involved, the resources of the victim node might be saturated, as in a typical *Distributed Denial of Service* (*DDoS*) *attack*. Mechanisms to prevent this kind of threats are the object of current investigations.

References

1. Varshney, U., Jain, R.: Issues in emerging 4G wireless networks. IEEE Computer **34**(6) (2001) 94–96
2. W.W.R.F.: Book of Visions. (2001)
3. Zahariadis, T., Kazakos, D.: (R)evolution toward 4G mobile communication systems. IEEE Wireless Communication **10**(4) (2003) 6–7
4. Hui, S.Y., Yeung, K.H.: Challenges in the migration to 4G mobile systems. IEEE Communication Magazine **41**(12) (2003) 54–59
5. Lach, H.Y., Janneteau, C., Petrescu, A.: Network mobility in beyond-3G systems. IEEE Communication Magazine **41**(7) (2003) 52–57
6. Gustafsson, E., Jonsson, A.: Always best connected. IEEE Wireless Communication **10**(1) (2003) 49–55
7. Fresa, A., Longo, M., Robustelli, A.L., Senatore, A.: A security architecture for access to the IP Multimedia Subsystem in B3G networks. In: WPMC'04. (2004)
8. Akyildiz, I.F., Xie, J., Mohanty, S.: A survey of mobility management in next-generation all-IP-based wireless systems. IEEE Wireless Communication **11**(4) (2004) 16–28
9. Faccin, S.M., Lalwaney, P., Patil, B.: IP Multimedia Services: Analysis of Mobile IP and SIP Interactions in 3G Networks. IEEE Communication Magazine **42**(1) (2004) 113–120
10. Ma, L., Yu, F., Leung, V.C.M.: A new method to support UMTS/WLAN vertical handover using SCTP. IEEE Wireless Communication **11**(4) (2004) 44–51
11. Stewart, R., et al.: Stream control transmission protocol (2000) IETF RFC 2960, http://www.ietf.org/rfc/rfc2960.txt.
12. Johnson, D., Perkins, C., Arkko, J.: Mobility Support in IPv6 (2004) IETF RFC 3775, http://www.ietf.org/rfc/rfc3775.txt.
13. Wang, W., Akyildiz, I.F.: A new signaling protocol for intersystem roaming in next-generation wireless systems. IEEE Journal on Selected Areas in Communications **19**(10) (2001) 2040–2052
14. Hsieh, R., Zhou, Z.G., Seneviratne, A.: S-MIP: A seamless handoff architecture for Mobile IP. In: IEEE INFOCOM 2003. Volume 3. (2003) 1774–1784
15. Lin, Y.B., Pang, A.C., Haung, Y.R., Chlamtac, I.: An all-IP approach for UMTS third-generation mobile networks. IEEE Network **16**(5) (2002) 8–19
16. TS 23.228: IP multimedia subsystem; Stage 2, 5.9.0, 3GPP Rel. 5 (2002)
17. Rosenberg, J.D., et al.: Session Initiation Protocol (SIP) (2002) IETF RFC 3261, http://www.ietf.org/rfc/rfc3261.txt.
18. Schulzrinne, H., et al.: RTP: A transport protocol for real-time applications (2003) IETF RFC 3550, http://www.ietf.org/rfc/rfc3550.txt.
19. Calhoun, P., Loughney, J., Guttman, E., Zorn, G., Arkko, J.: Diameter base protocol (2003) IETF RFC 3588, http://www.ietf.org/rfc/rfc3588.txt.
20. Arkko, J., Devarapalli, V., Dupont, V., Dupont, F.: Using IPsec to protect mobile IPv6 signaling between mobile node and home agents (2004) IETF RFC 3776, http://www.ietf.org/rfc/rfc3776.txt.
21. Krawczyk, H., Bellare, M., Canetti, R.: HMAC: Keyed-Hashing for Message Authentication (1997) IETF RFC 2104, http://www.ietf.org/rfc/rfc2104.txt.
22. Eastlake, D., Jones, P.: US Secure Hash Algorithm 1 (SHA1) (2001) IETF RFC 3174, http://www.ietf.org/rfc/rfc3174.txt.
23. Hsieh, P.Y., Dutta, A., Schulzrinne, H.: Application layer mobility proxy for real-time communication. In: World Wireless Congress, 3G Wireless. (2003)

24. Handley, M., Jacobson, V.: SDP: Session description protocol (1998) IETF RFC 2327, http://www.ietf.org/rfc/rfc2327.txt.
25. Nakajima, N., Dutta, A., Das, S., Schulzrinne, H.: Handoff delay analysis and measurement for SIP based mobility in IPv6. In: IEEE ICC '03. Volume 2. (2003) 1085–1089
26. NS-2, The Network Simulator ver. 2: (UCB/LBNL/VINT) http://www.isi.edu/nsnam/ns/.
27. Ernst, T.: MobiWan: NS-2 extensions to study mobility in Wide-Area IPv6 Networks (2002) http://www.inrialpes.fr/planete/pub/mobiwan/.
28. Perez-Costa, X., Hartenstein, H.: A simulation study on the performance of Mobile IPv6 in a WLAN-based cellular network. Computer Networks **40** (2002) 191–204
29. Soliman, H., Castelluccia, C., Malki, K.E., Bellier, L.: Hierarchical Mobile IPv6 Mobility Management (HMIPv6) (2005) IETF RFC 4140, http://www.ietf.org/rfc/rfc4140.txt.

Dynamic Resource Allocation in Quality of Service Networks[*]

Antonio Capone[1], Jocelyne Elias[2], Fabio Martignon[3], and Guy Pujolle[2]

[1] Department of Electronics and Information, Politecnico di Milano
capone@elet.polimi.it
[2] University of Paris 6, LIP6 Laboratory, 8 rue du Capitaine Scott,
75015, Paris, France
jocelyne.elias@lip6.fr, guy.pujolle@lip6.fr
[3] Department of Management and Information Technology,
University of Bergamo, Italy
fabio.martignon@unibg.it

Abstract. Efficient dynamic resource provisioning algorithms are necessary to the development and automation of Quality of Service (QoS) networks. The main goal of these algorithms is to offer services that satisfy the QoS requirements of individual users while guaranteeing at the same time an efficient utilization of network resources. In this paper we introduce a new service model that provides quantitative per-flow bandwidth guarantees, where users subscribe for a guaranteed rate; moreover, the network periodically individuates unused bandwidth and proposes short-term contracts where extra-bandwidth is allocated and guaranteed exclusively to users who can exploit it to transmit at a rate higher than their subscribed rate. To implement this service model we propose a dynamic provisioning architecture for intra-domain Quality of Service networks. We develop an efficient bandwidth allocation algorithm that takes explicitly into account traffic statistics to increase the users' benefit and the network revenue simultaneously. We demonstrate through simulation in realistic network scenarios that the proposed dynamic provisioning model is superior to static provisioning in providing resource allocation both in terms of total accepted load and network revenue.

1 Introduction

Efficient dynamic resource provisioning mechanisms are necessary to the development and automation of Quality of Service networks. In telecommunication networks, resource allocation is performed mainly in a static way, on time scales on the order of hours to months. However, statically provisioned network resources can become insufficient or considerably under-utilized if traffic statistics change significantly [1].

Therefore, a key challenge for the deployment of Quality of Service networks is the development of solutions that can dynamically track traffic statistics and

---

[*] This work is partially supported by the National Council for Scientific Research in Lebanon.

M. Cesana, L. Fratta (Eds.): Wireless Syst./Network Architect. 2005, LNCS 3883, pp. 184–197, 2006.

allocate network resources efficiently, satisfying the QoS requirements of users while aiming at maximizing, at the same time, resource utilization and network revenue.

Recently, dynamic bandwidth allocation has attracted research interest and many algorithms have been proposed in the literature [1, 2, 3, 4, 5, 6, 7, 8]. These approaches and related works are discussed in Section 2.

In this paper we propose a new service model that provides quantitative per-flow bandwidth guarantees, where users subscribe for a guaranteed transmission rate. Moreover, the network periodically individuates unused bandwidth and proposes short-term contracts where extra-bandwidth is allocated and guaranteed exclusively to users who can better exploit it to transmit at a rate higher than their subscribed rate.

To implement this service model we propose a distributed provisioning architecture composed by core and edge routers; core routers monitor bandwidth availability and periodically report this information to ingress routers using signalling messages like those defined in [2]. Moreover, if persistent congestion is detected, core routers notify immediately ingress routers as proposed in [5].

Ingress routers perform a dynamic tracking of the effective number of active connections, as proposed in [9, 10], as well as of their actual sending rate. Based on such information and that communicated by core routers, ingress routers allocate network resources dynamically and efficiently using a modified version of the max-min fair allocation algorithm proposed in [11]. Such allocation is performed taking into account users' profile and willingness to acquire extra-bandwidth based on their bandwidth utility function. The allocation is then enforced by traffic conditioners that perform traffic policing and shaping.

We evaluate by simulation the performance of our proposed bandwidth allocation algorithm in realistic network scenarios. Numeric results show that our architecture allows to achieve better performance than statically provisioned networks both in terms of accepted load and network revenue.

In summary, this paper makes the following contributions: the definition of a new service model and the proposition of a distributed architecture that performs dynamic bandwidth allocation to maximize users utility and network revenue.

The paper is structured as follows: Section 2 discusses related work; Section 3 presents our proposed service model and provisioning architecture; Section 4 describes the proposed dynamic bandwidth allocation algorithm; Section 5 discusses simulation results that show the efficiency of our dynamic resource allocation algorithm compared to a static allocation technique. Finally, section 6 presents some concluding remarks.

2   Related Work

The problem of bandwidth allocation in telecommunication networks has been addressed in many recent works. In [11] a max-min fair allocation algorithm is proposed to allocate bandwidth equally among all connections bottlenecked at the same link. This allocation assumes that the utility [12] or benefit to each application is the same for a given throughput. In essence, this flow control mechanism attempts to maximize the bandwidth allocated to each application, with no regard to differences in applications. An extension to the max-min fair allocation algorithm that takes into account users'bandwidth utility function has been proposed in [7], where the authors introduce a new fairness criterion, the utility max-min fairness, to perform bandwidth allocation. Mathematical models that take into account users utility functions and link capacity constraints to perform charging, routing and flow control are presented in [8, 13].

In our work we extend the max-min fair allocation algorithm proposed in [11] to perform a periodical allocation of unused bandwidth to users who expect more than their subscribed rate.

Dynamic bandwidth provisioning in Quality of Service networks has recently attracted a lot of research attention due to its potential to achieve efficient resource utilization while providing the required quality of service to network users [1, 2, 3, 4, 6].

In [1, 3], the authors propose a dynamic core and edge provisioning architecture for differentiated services IP networks. The basic role of dynamic edge provisioning is to perform dynamic ingress link sharing and dynamic egress capacity dimensioning. The core provisioning architecture consists of a set of dynamic node and core provisioning algorithms for interior nodes and core networks, respectively. The node provisioning algorithm adopts a self-adaptive mechanism to adjust service weights of weighted fair queuing schedulers at core routers while the core provisioning algorithm reduces edge bandwidth immediately after receiving a Congestion-Alarm signal from a node provisioning module and provides periodic bandwidth re-alignment to establish a modified max-min bandwidth allocation to traffic aggregates.

The work discussed in [1] has similar objectives to our dynamic bandwidth allocation algorithm. However, the service model considered in [1, 3] differs from our proposed model and traffic statistics are not taken into account in the allocation procedure. Moreover, in our work we suggest a distributed architecture implementation, while in these papers only a centralized scheme is considered.

A policy-based architecture is presented in [4], where a measurement-based approach is proposed for dynamic Quality of Service adaptation in DiffServ networks. The proposed architecture is composed of one Policy Decision Point (PDP), a set of Policy Enforcement Points that are installed in ingress routers and bandwidth monitors implemented in core routers. When monitors detect significant changes in available bandwidth they inform the PDP which changes dynamically the policies on in-profile and out-of-profile input traffics based on the current state of the network estimated using the information collected by the monitors. However, this scheme, while achieving dynamic QoS adaptation for multimedia applications, does not take into account the users utility function and their eventual willingness to be charged for transmitting out of profile traffic, thus increasing network revenue.

The authors in [5] propose a segmented QoS fault tolerance mechanism, named Segmented Adaptation of Traffic Aggregates, to enhance end-to-end QoS and to reduce the occurrences of end-to-end QoS failures. Dynamic adaptation of traffic aggregates can be performed on in-profile traffic in the case of congestion events where resource utilization levels at core routers exceed the given thresholds and explicit congestion notification signals are utilized to notify the edge routers. The relevant traffic load class is reduced, be it by dropping, reclassification or reshaping.

In [2], a generic pricing structure is presented to characterize the pricing schemes currently used in the Internet, and a dynamic, congestion-sensitive pricing algorithm is introduced to provide an incentive for multimedia applications to adapt their sending rates according to network conditions. As in [2], we take into account users bandwidth utility functions to evaluate our proposed allocation algorithm based on the increased network revenue that is achieved. However, the authors consider a different service model than that proposed in our work and focus mainly on the issue of dynamic pricing to perform rate adaptation based on network conditions.

The idea of measuring dynamically the effective number of active connections as well as their actual sending rate is a well accepted technique [6, 9, 10]. In [6], the authors propose an active resource management approach (ARM) for differentiated services environment. The basic concept behind ARM is that by effectively knowing when a client is sending packets and how much of its allocated bandwidth is being used at any given time, the unused bandwidth can be reallocated without loss of service. This concept is in line with our proposed bandwidth allocation algorithm. Differently from our work, however, ARM does not guarantee to the user a minimum subscribed bandwidth throughout the contract duration since unused bandwidth is sent to a pool of available bandwidth and it can be used to admit new connections in the network, in spite of those already admitted.

3 Service Model and Dynamic Provisioning Architecture

We first introduce our proposed service model, then we present a distributed provisioning architecture which implements such service model by performing the dynamic bandwidth allocation algorithm described in Section 4; finally, we present the signalling messages used to assure the interaction between network elements.

3.1 Service Model

We propose a service model that, first, provides a quantitative bandwidth guarantee to users and then exploits the unused bandwidth individuated periodically in the network to propose short-term guaranteed extra-bandwidth. In this process, different weights can be assigned to network users to allocate extra-bandwidth with different priorities; such weights can be set statically offline, based on the service contract proposed to the user, or can be adapted on-line based, for example, on the user bandwidth utility function.

Our proposed service model is therefore characterized by:

- a quantitative bandwidth guarantee, expressed through the specification of user's subscribed rate;
- short term guaranteed extra-bandwidth: the network is monitored on-line to individuate unused bandwidth that is allocated with guarantee, during the update interval, to users who can exploit it to transmit extra-traffic;
- a weight that expresses the user's priority in the assignment of extra-bandwidth;
- a bandwidth utility function, $U(x)$, that describes the user's preference for an allocation of x bandwidth units. In line with [3, 12] we consider the utility function as part of the service model. Without loss of generality, we do not consider the pricing component of a bandwidth utility function.

3.2   Architecture and Control Messaging

To implement our service model we assume a distributed architecture constituted by core and edge routers, as shown in Fig.1; traffic monitors are installed on ingress and core routers to perform on-line measurements on the incoming traffic flows and network capacity utilization, respectively.

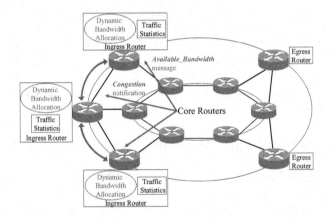

Fig. 1. The proposed distributed architecture that supports dynamic bandwidth allocation

Core routers exchange messages with ingress routers to report the link utilization or to notify a congestion situation.

Each ingress router collects the measurements performed by traffic monitors and exchanges periodically update messages with all other ingress routers to report the current incoming traffic statistics.

Moreover, a dynamic bandwidth allocation algorithm is implemented in all ingress routers: it takes into account the traffic statistics gathered at ingress routers and the network information reported by core routers to allocate network resources dynamically and efficiently.

The messages exchanged between network routers, illustrated with arrows in Fig.1, are similar to the control messages that have been proposed in [1] to report persistent congestion or resource availability. A subset of the messages defined in the RNAP protocol [14] can be used for these purposes.

4   Dynamic Bandwidth Allocation Algorithm

We propose a novel dynamic provisioning algorithm that allocates network capacity efficiently based on traffic statistics measured on-line. Bandwidth allocation is performed by ingress routers periodically and is enforced using traffic conditioners. We denote the interval between two successive allocations performed by the algorithm as the *update interval*, whose duration is T_u seconds. Moreover, core routers monitor link utilization, and if congestion on some links is detected for more than T_c seconds, bandwidth re-allocation is immediately invoked to solve this situation.

In the following we present in details the bandwidth allocation algorithm, that proceeds in two steps: in the first step, bandwidth is allocated to all active connections trying to match their near-term traffic requirements that are predicted based on statistics collected by ingress routers.

In step two, spare bandwidth as well as bandwidth left unused by idle and active connections is individuated on each link. Such available extra-bandwidth is allocated with guarantee during the current update interval exclusively to connections that can take advantage of it since they are already fully exploiting their subscribed rate.

Note that in the bandwidth allocation process, a fraction of bandwidth is reserved and left unallocated on each link to allow the accommodation of new connections. In our simulation we set this fraction equal to 5%.

To illustrate the allocation algorithm, let us model the network as a directed graph $G = (N, L)$ where nodes represent routers and directed arcs represent links. Each link $l \in L$ has associated the capacity C_l. A set of K connections is offered to the network. Each connection is represented by the notation (s_k, d_k, sr_k), for $k = 1, \ldots, K$, where s_k, d_k and sr_k represent the connections source node, destination node and the subscribed rate, respectively; furthermore, we assume that each connection has associated r_min_k, which represents the minimum bandwidth the application requires. Let a_k^l be the routing matrix: $a_k^l = 1$ if connection k is routed on link l, $a_k^l = 0$ otherwise. We assume that a communication between a user pair is established by creating a session involving a path that remains fixed throughout the user pair conversation duration. The session path choice method (i.e., the routing algorithm) is not considered in this paper.

At the beginning of the $n - th$ update interval, each ingress router computes the transmission rate, b_k^{n-1}, averaged over the last T_u seconds, for all connections $k \in K$ that access the network through it. This information is then sent to all other ingress routers using control messages as described in the previous Section, so that all ingress routers can share the same information about current traffic statistics and perform simultaneously the same allocation procedure.

The amount of bandwidth allocated to each source k during the $n - th$ update interval, r_k^n, is determined using the two-steps approach described in the following:

- First step: Connections having $b_k^{n-1} < r\_min_k$ are considered *idle*; all other active connections are further classified as *greedy* if they used a fraction greater than γ of their subscribed rate sr_k (i.e. if $b_k^{n-1} > \gamma \cdot sr_k$), otherwise they are classified as $non - greedy$. In our implementation we set $\gamma = 0.9$.

  Let us denote by K_i, K_{ng} and K_g the sets of idle, non-greedy and greedy connections, respectively.

  Idle connections are assigned their minimum required transmission rate, i.e. $r_k^n = r\_min_k, \forall k \in K_i$.

  Non-greedy connections are assigned a bandwidth that can accommodate traffic growth in the current update interval while, at the same time, save unused bandwidth that can be re-allocated to other users. Several techniques have been proposed in the literature to predict the near-term transmission rate of a connection based on past traffic measurements. In this work we only consider the last measured value, b_k^{n-1}, and we propose the following simple bandwidth allocation: $r_k^n = \min\{2 \cdot b_k^{n-1}, sr_k\}, \forall k \in K_{ng}$. In this regard we are currently studying more efficient traffic predictors that could allow improved bandwidth allocation.

  Greedy connections are assigned in this step their subscribed rate sr_k, and they also take part to the allocation of extra-bandwidth performed in step two, since they are already exploiting all their subscribed rate.

- Second step: After having performed the allocations described in step one, the algorithm individuates on each link l the residual bandwidth R_l, i.e. the spare bandwidth as well as the bandwidth left unused by idle and non-greedy connections. R_l is hence given by the following expression:

$$R_l = C_l - (\sum_{k \in K_i \cup K_{ng}} r_k^n \cdot a_k^l + \sum_{k \in K_g} sr_k \cdot a_k^l), \forall l \in L$$

where the first summation represents the total bandwidth allocated in step one to idle and non-greedy connections, while the second summation represents the bandwidth allocated to greedy connections.

Such extra-bandwidth is distributed exclusively to greedy connections using the algorithm detailed in Table 1, which is an extension of the allocation algorithm proposed in [11]. This algorithm takes as input the set K_g of greedy connections, the link set L and the residual capacity on each link R_l, and produces as output the amount of extra-bandwidth $f_k^n, k \in K_g$ that is assigned to each greedy connection during the $n - th$ update interval, so that finally $r_k^n = sr_k + f_k^n, \forall k \in K_g$.

To take into account users weights it is sufficient to substitute n_l in Table 1 with w_l, which is defined as the sum of the weights of all greedy connections that are routed on link l.

It should be clarified that our algorithm can temporarily present some limitations in bandwidth allocation, since the bandwidth allocated to a user can at

Table 1. Pseudo-code specification of the bandwidth allocation algorithm

(1) initiate all $f_k^n = 0$, $\forall\, k \in K_g$
(2) remove from the link set L all links $l \in L$ that have
    a number of connections crossing them n_l equal to 0
(3) for every link $l \in L$, calculate $F_l = R_l/n_l$
(4) identify the link α that minimizes F_α
    i.e. $\alpha \mid F_\alpha = min_k(F_k)$
(5) set $f_k^n = F_\alpha$, $\forall\, k \in K_\alpha$, where $K_\alpha \subseteq K_g$ is the set
    of greedy connections that cross link α
(6) for every link l, update the residual capacity and the
    number of crossing greedy connections as follows:

$$R_l = R_l - \sum_{k \in K_\alpha} f_k^n \cdot a_k^l$$
$$n_l = n_l - \sum_{k \in K_\alpha} a_k^l$$

(7) remove from set L link α and those that have $n_l = 0$
(8) if L is empty, then stop; else go to Step (3)

most double from an update interval to the successive one. This could affect the performance of users that experience steep increases in their transmission rate. In Section 5 we evaluate numerically this effect showing at the same time how it is counterbalanced by increased network revenue in all the considered network scenarios under several traffic load conditions.

5   Numeric Results

In this Section we compare the performance, measured by the average accepted load and network extra-revenue versus the total load offered to the network, of the proposed dynamic bandwidth allocation algorithm with a static provisioning strategy, referring to different network scenarios to cover a wide range of possible environments. The simulation tool we used was J-Sim simulator version 1.3 [15].

5.1   Performance Metrics

We are interested in measuring the following performance metrics: the average accepted load and network extra-revenue.

The average accepted load is obtained averaging the total load accepted in the network over all the bandwidth update intervals.

We define, in line with [2], the average network extra-revenue as the total charge paid to the network for all the extra-bandwidth utilization, averaged over all the bandwidth update intervals. In this computation we consider only network extra-revenue generated by greedy users that are assigned extra-bandwidth by our proposed dynamic allocation algorithm. The revenue deriving from the static subscription of guaranteed rates (sr_k) is not considered since we focus on the extra network revenue that dynamic allocation can generate.

As already stated, we do not consider the pricing component of bandwidth utility functions, and we assume that network extra-revenue can be measured as the extra-utility perceived by network users. Furthermore we assume, in line with [8], that the utilities are additive so that the aggregate utility of rate allocation is given by the sum of the utilities perceived by all network users.

Using the notation introduced in the previous section, the average network extra-revenue can be obtained averaging over all the update intervals n the quantity:

$$\sum_{k \in K_g} U(b_k^n) - U(sr_k)$$

where sr_k and b_k^n represent, respectively, the subscribed rate and the average transmission rate in the $n - th$ update interval for all connections $k \in K$.

5.2   Network Scenarios

In the first scenario we gauge the effectiveness of the proposed traffic-based bandwidth allocation algorithm. We consider, in line with [1, 2], the scenario illustrated in Figure 2, that consists of a single-bottleneck with 2 core nodes, 6 access nodes, 24 end nodes (12 source-destination pairs) and traffic conditioners at the edge. Each ingress conditioner is configured with one profile for each traffic source and drops out-of-profile packets. All links are full-duplex and have a propagation delay of 1 ms. The capacity of the links connecting the two core nodes and the access nodes to core nodes is equal to 3 Mb/s, and that of the links connecting the end nodes to access nodes is 2 Mb/s. The buffer size of each link can contain 50 packets.

We use 12 Exponential On-Off traffic sources; the average On time is set to 200 s, and the average Off time is varied in the 0 to 150 s range to simulate different traffic load conditions while at the same time varying the percentage of bandwidth left unused by every connection.

Six sources have a peak rate of 40 kb/s and a subscribed rate of 100 kb/s while the remaining sources have a peak rate of 1 Mb/s and a subscribed rate of 300 kb/s; the minimum bandwidth required by each source, r_min_k, is equal to

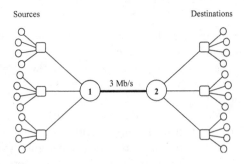

Fig. 2. Network topology with a single bottleneck

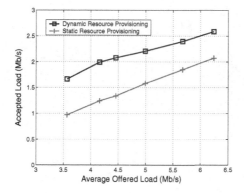

Fig. 3. Average total accepted load versus the average total load offered to the network of Fig. 2

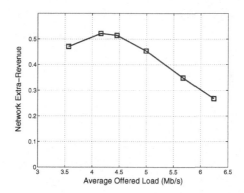

Fig. 4. Average total network extra-revenue obtained using dynamic bandwidth allocation versus the average total load offered to the network of Fig. 2

10 kb/s. The algorithm updating interval, T_u, is set to 20 s and the congestion detection interval, T_c, is set to 5 s. We assume, for simplicity, that all users have the same weight w_k and the same utility function proposed in [7,12], $U(x) = 1 - e^{\frac{x^2}{x+h}}$, that models the perceived utility of real-time elastic traffic for an allocation of x bandwidth units. The parameter h setting is the same as in [12].

Note that a realistic characterization of network applications is outside the scope of this paper. The specification of the utility function allows us exclusively to gauge the extra network revenue that can derive from the deployment of our proposed bandwidth allocation algorithm.

Figures 3 and 4 show, respectively, the average total load accepted in the network and the corresponding total extra-revenue as a function of the average total load offered to the network. It can be observed that our dynamic provisioning algorithm is very efficient in resource allocation compared to a static provisioning algorithm for all values of the offered load, providing improvements up to 60% in the total accepted traffic.

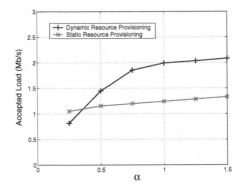

Fig. 5. Average total accepted load versus the rate scaling factor α in the Single-bottleneck topology of Fig. 2

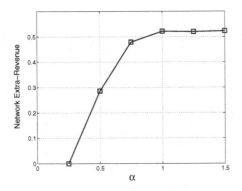

Fig. 6. Average total network extra-revenue using dynamic bandwidth allocation versus the rate scaling factor α in the Single-bottleneck topology of Fig. 2

The maximum network extra-revenue is achieved when the average Off time of exponential sources is equal to 100 s, corresponding to an offered load approximately equal to 4 Mb/s. In this situation, in fact, the average number of idle connections (i.e. 4) is sufficiently high to exalt our dynamic allocation algorithm that reallocates unused bandwidth to active users who can take advantage of it, sending extra-traffic and generating network revenue. With lower Off time values (i.e. with higher offered loads) the total extra-revenue slightly decreases as less connections are idle, in average, and consequently less bandwidth is available for re-allocation.

To investigate the impact on the performance of the update interval duration, we have considered, in the same scenario, different values for T_u, i.e. 40 s and 60 s. We found that the average increase in the total accepted load, expressed as a percentage of the traffic admitted in the static allocation case, was of 32% for $T_u = 40$ s and 21% for $T_u = 60$ s, while for $T_u = 20$ s it was 47% (see Fig. 3). These results allow to gauge the trade-off between performance improvement and overhead resulting from a more frequent execution of the allocation algorithm.

In the same scenario of Figure 2 we then fixed the average Off time of Exponential sources to 100 s while maintaining the average On time equal to 200 s, and we varied the peak rate of all sources scaling them by a factor α, with $0.25 \leq \alpha \leq 1.5$. Figures 5 and 6 show the total accepted load and the total extra-revenue in this scenario.

At very low load the static provisioning technique achieves slightly higher performance than dynamic provisioning. This is due to the fact that in this situation static provisioning is in effect sufficient to accommodate all incoming traffic; on the other hand, dynamic provisioning needs some time (in the worst case up to T_u seconds) to track the transition of sources from the idle to the active state. For all other traffic loads the advantage of the proposed dynamic bandwidth allocation algorithm is evident both in terms of accepted load and network extra-revenue.

A more realistic scenario is shown in Fig. 7. It comprises 6 nodes and 8 bidirectional links, all having a capacity equal to 2 Mb/s and propagation delay of 1 ms. In this topology, 6 Exponential On-Off traffic sources are considered, and their source and destination nodes are indicated in the Figure. Table 2 reports for all the connections the peak rate, the subscribed rate and the path of the

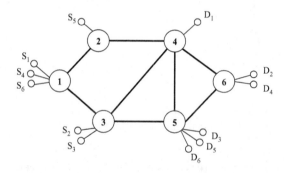

Fig. 7. Network topology with a larger number of links

Table 2. Peak rate, subscribed rate and path for the connections in the network scenario of Figure 7

Connection	Peak Rate (kb/s)	Subscribed Rate (kb/s)	Path
1	100	250	1-3-4
2	100	250	3-4-6
3	100	250	3-4-5
4	1000	500	1-2-4-6
5	1000	500	2-4-5
6	1000	1000	1-3-5

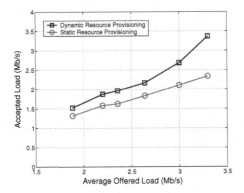

Fig. 8. Average total accepted load versus the average total load offered to the network of Figure 7

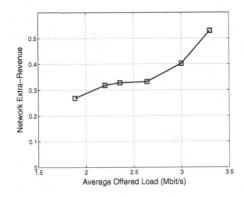

Fig. 9. Average total network extra-revenue using dynamic bandwidth allocation versus the average total load offered to the network of Figure 7

connection. All other parameters are set as in the previous scenarios. Note that, with such paths choice, various connections compete for network capacity with different connections on different links.

Also in this scenario the dynamic allocation algorithm outperforms static allocation, as shown in Figures 8 and 9, thus proving the benefit of the proposed scheme. These results verify that our allocation algorithm allows service providers to increase network capacity utilization and consequently network extra-revenue with respect to static provisioning techniques.

6   Conclusion

In this paper we proposed a novel service model where users subscribe for guaranteed transmission rates, and the network periodically individuates unused bandwidth that is re-allocated and guaranteed with short-term contracts to users who can better exploit it.

We described a distributed dynamic resource provisioning architecture for quality of service networks. We developed an efficient bandwidth allocation algorithm that takes explicitly into account traffic statistics to increase the users perceived utility and the network extra-revenue.

Simulations results measured in realistic network scenarios show that our allocation algorithm allows to increase both resource utilization and network revenue with respect to static provisioning techniques.

References

1. A. T. Campbell and R. R.-F. Liao. Dynamic Core Provisioning for Quantitative Differentiated Services. *IEEE/ACM Transactions on Networking*, pages 429–442, vol. 12, no. 3, June 2004.
2. H. Schulzrinne and X. Wang. Incentive-Compatible Adaptation of Internet Real-Time Multimedia. *IEEE Journal on Selected Areas in Communications*, pages 417–436, vol. 23, no. 2, February 2005.
3. A. T. Campbell and R. R.-F. Liao. Dynamic Edge Provisioning for Core IP Networks. In *Proc. IEEE/IFIP Int'l Workshop on Quality of Service IWQOS*, Pittsburgh, USA, June 2000.
4. T. Ahmed, R. Boutaba, and A. Mehaoua. A Measurement-Based Approach for Dynamic QoS Adaptation in DiffServ Network. *Journal of Computer Communications, Special issue on End-to-End Quality of Service Differentiation, Elsevier Science*, 2004.
5. H. de Meer and P. O'Hanlon. Segmented Adaptation of Traffic aggregates. In *Proc. 9th International Workshop on Quality of Service IWQOS*, pages 342–353, Karlsruhe, Germany, 6-8 June 2001.
6. M. Mahajan, M. Parasharand, and A. Ramanathan. Active Resource Management for the Differentiated Services Environment. *International Journal of Network Management*, pages 149–165, vol. 14, no. 3, May 2004.
7. Z. Cao and E. Zegura. Utility Max-Min: An Application-Oriented Bandwidth Allocation Scheme. In *Proc. IEEE Infocom'99*, New York, USA, March 1999.
8. F. Kelly. Charging and rate control for elastic traffic. *European Transactions on Telecommunications*, pages 33–37, vol. 8, 1997.
9. J. Aweya, M. Ouellette, and D. Y. Montuno. A simple, scalable and provably stable explicit rate computation scheme for flow control in computer networks. *Int. J. Commun. Syst.*, pages 593–618, vol. 14, no. 6, August 2001.
10. J. Aweya, M. Ouellette, and D. Y. Montuno. Design and stability analysis of a rate control algorithm using the Routh-Hurwitz stability criterion. *IEEE/ACM Transactions on Networking*, pages 719–732, vol. 12, no. 4, August 2004.
11. D. Bertsekas and R. Gallager. *Data Networks, 2nd Edition*. Prentice-Hall, 1992.
12. L. Breslau and S. Shenker. Best-Effort versus Reservations: A Simple Comparative Analysis. In *Proc. ACM SIGCOMM*, pages 3–16, September 1998.
13. J. W. Lee, R. R. Mazumdar, and N. B. Shroff. Non-Convex Optimization and Rate Control for Multi-Class Services in the Internet. *IEEE/ACM Transactions on Networking*, pages 827–840, vol. 13, no. 4, August 2005.
14. H. Schulzrinne and X. Wang. RNAP: A resource negotiation and pricing protocol. In *Int. Workshop Netw. Oper. Syst. Support Digital Audio Video*, pages 77–93, Basking Ridge, NJ, June 1999.
15. J-Sim. Available at www.j-sim.org. Ohio State University.

A P2P-Based Framework for Distributed Network Management

Andreas Binzenhöfer[1], Kurt Tutschku[1], Björn auf dem Graben[1],
Markus Fiedler[2], and Patrik Arlos[2]

[1] Department of Distributed Systems,
Institute of Computer Science, University of Würzburg,
Am Hubland, 97074 Würzburg, Germany
{binzenhoefer, tutschku, adgraben}@informatik.uni-wuerzburg.de
[2] Dept. of Telecommunication Systems, School of Engineering,
Blekinge Institute of Technology, 371 79 Karlskrona, Sweden
{markus.fiedler, patrik.arlos}@bth.se

Abstract. In this paper we present a novel framework supporting distributed network management using a self-organizing peer-to-peer overlay network. The overlay consists of several *Distributed Network Agents* which can perform distributed tests and distributed monitoring for fault and performance management. In that way, the concept is able to overcome disadvantages that come along with a central management unit, like lack of scalability and reliability.

So far, little attention has been payed to the quality of service experienced by the end user. Our self-organizing management overlay provides a reliable and scalable basis for distributed tests that incorporate the end user. The use of a distributed, self-organizing software will also reduce capital and operational expenditures of the operator since fewer entities have to be installed and operated.

1 Introduction

A peer-to-peer (P2P) system is a highly distributed application architecture. The underlying technology has so far only received a doubtful reputation due to its use in file sharing applications. P2P algorithms, however, might be highly helpful in implementing novel distributed, self-structuring network management concepts. In this work we suggest the application of a current generation, structured P2P overlay network for fault and performance management with the aim of enhancing conventional management functions.

In general the goal of Network Management is "to ensure that the users of a network receive the information technology services with the quality that they expect" [1]. However, monitoring and provisioning of that quality in an end-to-end manner as perceived by a user [2] is rarely achieved. The monitoring is usually carried out by rather centralized entities (Network Management Systems) and only in those parts of the network a provider is responsible for. Coordination of the monitoring among different administrative domains is rarely achieved, which also affects possibilities to locate faults and to evaluate end-to-end QoS.

M. Cesana, L. Fratta (Eds.): Wireless Syst./Network Architect. 2005, LNCS 3883, pp. 198–210, 2006.

A central fault testing and QoS monitoring architecture typically results in additional, complex entities at the provider. The operator has to ensure the reliability of the entities and assess their scalability. The systems have to scale with $O(N^2)$ due to the $N(N-1)$ potential relationships among N end systems. In addition, relaying monitoring data consumes bandwidth, delays its availability, and might get lost in case of a network failure. A decentralized QoS monitoring, as for example, located on the user's end system, might avoid these disadvantages. The use of a distributed, self-organizing software will reduce capital and operational expenditures (CAPEX and OPEX) of the operator since fewer entities have to be installed and operated. Scalability can be achieved by re-using resident resources in conjunction with local decisions and transmission of less data.

We propose a new, distributed, self-organizing, generic testing and QoS monitoring architecture for IP networks. The architecture will complement today's solutions for central configuration and fault management such as HP OpenView [3] and IBM Tivoli [4]. The architecture is based on equal agents, denoted as Distributed Network Agents (DNA), which form a management overlay for the service. In this context the word *agent* is not to be understood as an agent as used by the Artificial Intelligence community, but rather as a piece of software running on different peers, like, e.g., an SNMP-Agent. The self-organization of the overlay is achieved by Kademlia [5], a P2P-based Distributed Hash Table (DHT).

The suggested architecture facilitates the autonomic communication concept [6] by locally determining the perceived QoS of the user from distributed measurements and by exploiting the self-organization capabilities of the DHT for structuring the overlay. It will be able to communicate with standard-NMS via well-established interfaces. Thus, it can be seen as a QoS-enabling complement of existing Network Management solutions.

The remainder of the paper is structured as follows: Section 2 introduces the architecture of a DNA and shows how the framework can be used for local and distributed tests. In Section 3 we give an overview of the current P2P generation and motivate why we chose Kademlia as the basis of the DNA overlay. Some details about the implementation of our prototype will be given in Section 4. The functionality of the DNA is validated by simulation in Section 5. Section 6 finally concludes the paper and summarizes our future work.

2   The DNA Framework

The DNA framework represents an independent distributed application intended to support the central network monitoring station. In general a central monitoring entity has three major disadvantages:

- It is a single point of failure. Once the single central monitoring unit fails, the network will lose its control entity and will be without surveillance. The same problem could, e.g., be caused by a distributed denial of service attack. That is, the functionality of the entire network management depends on the functionality of a single central unit.

- It does not scale. On the one hand the number of hosts that can be monitored at a given time is limited by the bandwidth and the processing power of the central monitoring unit. On the other hand there is a growing number of services that has to be monitored on each host due to the diversity of services that emerge during the evolution of the Internet.
- It has a limited view of the network. While a central network manager is able to monitor, e.g., client A and Server B, it has hardly any means of knowing the current status of the connection between the two monitored devices themselves.

The DNA application is able to support the central unit in two ways. At first, the DNAs constantly monitor the network in a distributed way and send a message back to the central server in case the condition for some trigger event is met, similar to SNMP traps. Secondly the central server can query the current state of the DNA on demand. In case the central server fails, the DNAs will still be functional and can store the gathered information until the central server goes back online again. First ideas have been discussed briefly at [7]. The DNA framework can be used as a plug and play platform for overlay network monitoring approaches like [8] and [9].

2.1   The Basic Concept

The Distributed Network Agent (DNA) is based on a modular concept shown in Figure 1. The main component of the DNA, the so-called Mediator, runs as a daemon in the background and is responsible for the communication between the user and the individual test modules. A test module consist of several tests that are similar in respect of their functionality. They represent the functionality of the DNA and can be added or removed without any influence on the operability of the DNA architecture. The user is able to connect to the Mediator using the graphical user interface (GUI) or the command line. He can manually start tests or read the results of tests that have already been performed. Figure 1 summarizes the design of the DNA framework. The Mediator either receives a test request from the user or autonomically schedules a test itself. It then performs the corresponding test using the provided Interfaces and finally sends the results to the GUI upon request. Any test module that implements all features required by the Interface component can be added to the DNA framework. A description of the features required by the Interface component and their purpose is given in the following:

- *Default Tests:* Each test module has to provide a list including all tests that will be run when the module is called by the Mediator without any parameters. This list of default tests will be executed when the user did not specify any details. Advanced users, however, are able to choose another subset of tests from the module that is adapted to their specific needs. The default test sequence offers the possibility to implement a test module that, e.g., includes tests dealing with different kinds of IP configuration. In this

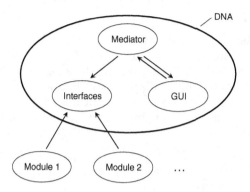

Fig. 1. The modular framework of the DNA

example the default test sequence could cover all properties of a static IP, while support for DHCP might be optional.

- *Test Dependencies:* If not specified otherwise all selected tests of a test module are performed in parallel. However, the DNA offers the possibility to use test dependencies. That is, a test module can provide a list containing the dependencies of its individual tests. The Mediator does not start a test until all its dependencies were performed successfully. The following two tests provide a simple example for test dependencies: A test that checks the state of a network interface card (NIC) and a second test that pings a predefined host using the same NIC. Obviously the second test is dependent on the first one, since it can only succeed if the NIC is up and running. The Mediator would therefore only execute the second test if the first test already finished successfully.

Since a great fraction of network problems is actually caused by local errors like misconfiguration and software failures, we outline a test module containing local tests in the following section. Before a DNA takes part in the DNA overlay, it can run the local test module to eliminate any possibility of local errors.

2.2 Local Tests

In this section we briefly describe a test module containing local tests, which is an inherent part of our prototype discussed in Section 4. First, we summarize the set of default tests and give a brief description of the remaining tests in the module afterwards. All local tests are bound to a specific network interface card, which can be selected by the user.

Default Test Sequence. The default test sequence contains eight tests, which can be divided into "Hardware and TCP/IP" and "Local configuration and network connectivity". The five tests in the latter category all depend on the three tests dealing with hardware and TCP/IP.

Hardware and TCP/IP

- *NICStatus:* This test returns information about the network interface card and its current state, including a driver check and the like. It is mainly used to eliminate the possibility of hardware failures or problems with the driver.
- *NetConnectionStatus:* This test is used to check the current connection status of the NIC. Causes for an error include a cable that is not plugged in, or a network interface card still running an authentication process.
- *PingLocalHost:* The functionality of the TCP/IP stack is validated by sending a ping request to the loopback address (127.0.0.1).

In case all three tests finish successfully, the Mediator will call the remaining five tests of the default test sequence.

Local configuration and network connectivity

- *IPConfiguration:* This test verifies that a valid IP address is assigned to the NIC. It also checks if the associated gateway is on the same subnet as the IP address.
- *DNSConfiguration:* The test verifies that at least one DNS server is assigned and can be reached by a ping request. Furthermore, the functionality of the DNS server is tested performing a predefined DNS lookup and optionally a reverse lookup. If the ping message failed whereas the lookup was successful, no warning message is reported.
- *DHCPLease:* In case of using DHCP on a machine running Windows, the IP address is checked to ensure that the network interface card is not set up to use a so called Automatic Private IP Address (APIPA). This might occur, if the server has no more capacities to provide a new IP address or if the user participates in an encrypted wireless LAN (e.g. WEP) using an invalid key.
- *PingOwnIP:* To exclude a communication problem between the operating system and the NIC, the IP address assigned to the adapter is pinged.
- *PingWellKnownHosts:* This tests sends a ping request to a list of predefined well known hosts. If a specified number of hosts in this list does not respond in time, the test returns an error.

Additional Local Tests. The following three tests belong to our local test module but are not part of the default test sequence, since they are specific to the Windows OS. Advanced users can include the tests in case the DNA is running on a Windows based platform.

- *EventViewer:* The test searches in the "Event Viewer Log" for error events caused by TCP/IP or DHCP. If the Windows event viewer has recorded problems with respect to TCP/IP or DHCP those errors will be forwarded to the GUI of the DNA.
- *HostsAndLmHosts:* Before Windows uses DNS or WINS it tries to resolve a domain name using the HOSTS or LMHOSTS file. If one of these files contains a wrong entry the resolution of the corresponding name fails. The test searches for syntax errors in both files and sends ping requests to valid entries.

– *RoutingTable:* The Windows routing table is divided into a dynamic and a persistent part. This test pings the gateways of both tables and reports an error message, if one of them is not reachable.

2.3 Distributed Tests

In this section we describe how to use the DNA framework to implement distributed test modules. A distributed test is a test that is performed in conjunction with at least one other DNA. To be able to communicate with each other the DNAs build an overlay network on top of the monitored network. To perform a distributed test a DNA can then either connect to a randomly chosen DNA or to a specific DNA chosen by the user. Section 3 describes the P2P based DNA overlay in detail.

The following two distributed tests point out the possibilities of the distributed DNA framework that arise by extending a simple local test to a distributed test:

– *PingWellKnownHosts:* If a single DNA or a central network manager does not receive a ping reply from a well known host, either the host or any link on the path to this host could be down. Using the DNA framework, however, a DNA can ask another DNA to ping the same host and evaluate the returned result. In case another DNA is able to ping this host, the possibility that this host is down can be ruled out and the cause of the error can be narrowed down to a network problem between the DNA and the well known host. If the DNA has knowledge about the network topology, which could, e.g., be gained using network tomography, the distributed ping test can also be used to pinpoint the broken link or to locate a bottleneck by comparing the delay of the ping messages.

– *DNSProxy:* In general a DNA can use another DNA as a temporary proxy or relay host. In case a DNA loses the connection to its DNS server and can thus no longer resolve domain names, it can use another DNA as a DNS proxy. That is, the DNA forwards the DNS query to another DNA that in turn tries to resolve the domain name using its own DNS server. This way the DNA is able to bridge the time its DNS server does not respond to DNS queries. In a similar way two DNAs with a broken direct connection could use a third DNA that still has a connection to both DNAs, as a temporary relay host.

As stated above the DNAs build an overlay network to be able to communicate with each other. They are able to communicate with a random DNA in the overlay or to search for a specific DNA. The following two tests provide examples of how to build distributed applications based on this aspects of the DNA framework:

– *PortScan:* If a DNA peer is running a webserver or offers some other service that requires an open port it usually is probed by a central network manager to ensure a continuous service. On the one hand this method does not scale with the number of services the central network manager has to monitor, on the other hand the peer running the service has no influence on the time of the next check. Using the DNA framework, however, the peer is able to ask a random DNA to see if it can reach the offered services. This is also a scalable way to monitor a large number of services. The DNAs monitor the services running on their peers in a distributed way and only send a message back to the central network manager in case of an error.

- *Throughput:* Usually it is not easy for a user to verify a service level agreement or to measure the bandwidth to another point in the network. The possibility to search for a specific DNA enables a peer taking part in the DNA overlay network to search for a specific communication partner and ask for a throughput test. A very simple way to do so is to constantly send traffic to the other DNA for a certain period of time and simply measure the average throughput. However, there are more sophisticated ways, which we intend to integrate in future work.

The above tests are just some examples of how to use the DNA framework. A future possibility consists in passive monitoring of data streams between the peers at both peers and exchanging the measurement results in order to determine potential bottlenecks as described in [10]. In Section 6 we summarize our ideas for a new, distributed passive QoS monitoring concept. The next section discusses general security issues and a way of how to deploy new test modules to the DNA overlay network.

2.4   Deployment of New Tests

Considering a running DNA overlay network, one can not assume that all DNAs are always having the same test modules. An obvious way to deploy new test modules is to send the modules on demand. That is, if A asks B to perform a distributed test but B does not have this specific test, A simply sends the test module to B. However, this implies that B implicitly trusts A. This is a security risk that is obviously not negligible. In fact a framework that allows other machines to run arbitrary code would be the perfect tool for distributed denial of service attacks.

One way to solve this problem is to only download new test modules from a central trust server. That is, all DNAs trust a central entity and only run code that is signed by this central authority. While this solution is sufficient for small networks it does not scale to larger networks. A scalable implementation of the DNA framework therefore needs a distributed trust model. Since there is an independent research area dealing with security and this paper is mainly intended to be a proof-of-concept for a P2P based framework for network monitoring, we will refrain from addressing security issues. There exist, however, different approaches to build distributed trust models for P2P systems. In [11], e.g., Josephson proposes a scalable method for P2P authentication with a distributed single sign-on service, that could be used as the trust model for our DNA.

3 The P2P-Based DNA Overlay

To be able to search for other peers, the individual DNAs build an overlay network. The main purpose of this overlay is to keep the DNAs connected in one logical network and to enable a single DNA to find another DNA in reasonable time. The current generation of structured P2P networks is able to locate other peers using only $O(\log(n))$ messages while keeping connections to only $O(\log(n))$ other peers in an overlay network of size n [12]. We chose the Kademlia algorithm [5] as the basis of the DNA overlay. Kademlia offers a set of features that are certainly not unique to it, but that are so far not offered by another single algorithm all at once. In detail those features are:

1. *Symmetry:* Due to the symmetry of the XOR metric $d(x, y) = d(y, x)$, the DNA overlay network is symmetric as well.
2. *Unidirectionality:* For any identifier x and an arbitrary distance $s > 0$ there is exactly one point y such that $d(x, y) = s$. Thus, independent of the originating peer, lookups for the same peer will all converge along the same path.
3. *Parallel queries:* One of the most advantageous features is the possibility to send out parallel queries for the same key to different peers. This way, time-outs on one path do not necessarily delay the search process, guaranteeing faster and more reliable searches under high churn[1] rates.
4. *Arbitrary Neighbors*: In [5] neighbors in the overlay were chosen by the time of last contact to obtain more reliable connections. Neighbors, however, can be chosen by any criterion like trustability or reliability. The best known approach is to chose peers according to their ping times to guarantee low latency paths when searching.
5. *Low periodic traffic:* In contrast to most other algorithms Kademlia uses almost no periodic overhead traffic but exploits the search traffic to stabilize the overlay network connections. Configuration information spreads automatically as a side-effect of key lookups.
6. *Security:* As a result of its decentralized nature Kademlia is resistant against denial of service attacks. The security against attackers can even be improved by banning misbehaving peers from the peers buckets.

The DNA overlay enables fast searches for random and specific communication partners. In Section 5 we discuss results obtained from our simulator in detail.

4 The DNA Prototype

As a proof of concept and practicability of our work, we implemented a prototype of the DNA. While the general concept is platform independent, the implementation was done in *.NET*, as the WMI Interface offers the opportunity to access all kind of information about the local system state as well as the state of the

---

[1] The rate at which peers join and leave the overlay network.

network in very few lines of code. The DNA prototype was implemented within the scope of an industrial cooperation with Datev, one of the largest information service providers and software firms in Germany as well as Europe. This provided us with the opportunity to prove the functionality of the concept by successfully running the DNA in a realistic testbed with over 50 machines. One of the main advantages besides those mentioned in the previous sections turned out to be the plug and play character of the DNA framework. Due to the Kademlia based overlay network, the DNA framework is self-configuring. To include a new DNA into the existing overlay, the user just has to start the client and it will automatically find its position in the overlay network. On the other hand, if a client fails, the overlay network proved to be self-healing by automatically updating the neighbor-pointers needed to keep the overlay network stable. The next section contains a simulative evaluation of the stability of the proposed solution.

5   Simulation Results

In this section we prove the functionality and the scalability of our DNA prototype by simulation. The simulator is written in *.NET*, based on the code used for the prototype. The network transmission time for one hop was chosen according to an exponential distribution with a mean of 50 ms. If not stated otherwise, we let a number of nodes join the overlay network and begin a churn phase once the overlay has initially stabilized. To generate churn we model the online time of a peer by means of an exponentially distributed random variable. The longer a peer stays online on average, the less churn there is in the overlay network. To provide credible simulation results, we produced several simulation runs and calculated the mean as well as the corresponding confidence intervals.

To show the scalability of the DNA we regard the time needed to complete a search for other peers in dependence of the overlay size. First, we regard a system without any churn, i.e. we let n DNAs join the system, wait until the overlay

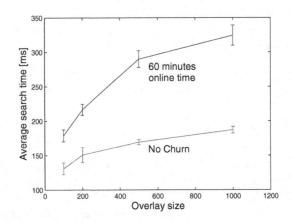

Fig. 2. Duration of a search as a function of the overlay size

network stabilizes and then let a number of random DNAs search for other peers. The concave curves in Figure 2 show that the search in our prototype does indeed scale. In a network of 1000 peers a search for another DNA takes less than 200 ms. To see the influence of churn on the search time, we repeated the same simulations and set the average online time of a peer to 60 minutes. To keep the size of the overlay constant on average, we chose a corresponding Poisson arrival process to let new DNAs join the network. The results are also shown in Figure 2. Due to timeouts caused by the churn in the system, searches take longer than in the scenario without churn. However, as seen from the concave curves, the search algorithm scales when the system becomes larger and enables fast searches for other peers.

In previous studies [13, 14] we showed that the size of the network itself is not the crucial factor in terms of scalability and overlay stability. In fact the robustness of the overlay is mainly influenced by the current churn rate. A good way to prove the stability of the overlay network is therefore to look at the correctness of the neighbors of a peer under churn. In general the functionality of a structured P2P-overlay can be guaranteed, as long as the information about a peers neighborhood is not lost. In case the information about more distant peers is lost, the performance of the overlay might get slightly worse, but the underlying algorithms will still be functional. We study the correctness of the direct neighbors to evaluate the stability of the DNA overlay. We generate a churn phase and create a snapshot within this phase. The real neighbors of a peer (as obtained form the global view offered by the simulation) are compared to the neighbors currently seen by the peer. In Figure 3 we show how many of its five direct neighbors a peer actually knows in dependence of the churn rate in the system. On average a peer knows more than 4.5 of its 5 direct neighbors even if the average peer stays online for only 30 minutes. Note that the correctness of a peer's neighbors does not depend on the size of the network at all. The curve progression is almost identical for 500 and 100 peers. That is, the degree

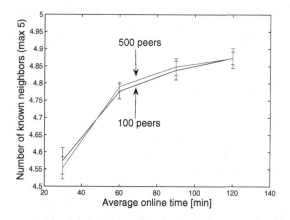

Fig. 3. Average number of known direct neighbors

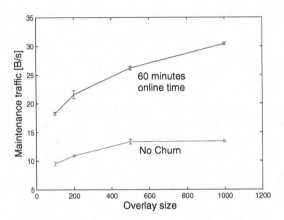

Fig. 4. Average maintenance traffic in dependence of the system size

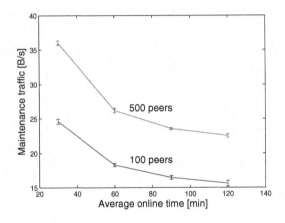

Fig. 5. Average maintenance traffic in dependence of the churn rate

of stability of the overlay network does not depend on the size but on the current churn rate of the system.

The above results show that the DNA overlay offers scalable search times and is robust against churn. The remaining question is how much bandwidth the DNAs need to maintain the overlay network. Figure 4 plots the average maintenance traffic of a single peer against the total number of peers in the overlay network. Again the lower curve represents a system without any churn. The larger the overlay network gets, the more neighbors are maintained and the more traffic is needed to keep these neighbors up-to-date. As can be seen in the figure the consumed bandwidth scales very well to the size of the system. The upper curve summarizes the same results for an average online time of

60 minutes. It has a similar progression, but illustrates that a peer uses more maintenance traffic during a churn phase.

To study the influence of churn on the bandwidth needed for maintenance in more detail, we did a parameter study for the churn rate in Figure 5. The average online time of a peer varies between 30 and 120 minutes. The shorter a peer stays online on average, i.e. the more churn there is in the system, the more maintenance traffic is produced by the DNA client. That is, the DNA adapts automatically to the current churn rate. As stated above, the DNA needs more maintenance traffic in a larger network, as there are more neighbors that have to be kept up-to-date.

6   Conclusions and Future Work

In this paper we presented a novel technique for distributed fault and performance management. The proposed DNA framework is based on a self-organizing P2P overlay network (Kademlia) and offers plug and play functionality when integrating new DNA clients. The system is able to perform local tests on the client and distributed network tests in conjunction with other DNA clients. As a proof-of-concept, we built a running prototype and in addition proved its scalability by simulation. We investigated the robustness and reliability of the DNA in terms of churn behavior, i.e. the fluctuation of the size of the overlay network. A local test module, as well as examples for distributed tests were described in detail. The proposed distributed end-to-end architecture facilitates the provisioning and monitoring of new services offered by service providers.

Future work will be devoted to the integration of a new passive end-to-end QoS monitoring concept featuring performance management from the user point of view. The results of such test will be available to standard-network management systems via well-established interfaces, like SNMP traps or MIB variables. Thus, it can be seen as a QoS-enabling complement of existing network performance management solutions.

Acknowledgments

The authors would like to thank Phuoc Tran-Gia and Stefan Chevul for the helps and discussions during the course of this work. Additional thanks go to the EuroNGI FP6 Network of Excellence for supporting this work.

References

1. Subramanian, M.: Network Management – Principles and Practice. Addison-Wesley (2000)
2. M. Fiedler (ed.): EuroNGI Deliverable D.JRA.6.1.1 – State-of-the-art with regards to user-perceived Quality of Service and quality feedback (2004) URL: http://www.eurongi.org/, http://www.ats.tek.bth.se/eurongi/dwpjra611.pdf.

3. (HP OpenView Management Software)
   URL: http://www.openview.hp.com/.
4. (IBM Tivoli Software)
   URL: http://www.ibm.com/tivoli/.
5. Maymounkov, P., Mazieres, D.: Kademlia: A peer-to-peer information system based on the xor metric. In: IPTPS 2002, MIT Faculty Club, Cambridge, MA, USA (2002)
6. (Autonomic Communication (IST FP6 Project))
   URL: http://www.autonomic-communication.org/.
7. Binzenhöfer, A., Tutschku, K., auf dem Graben, B.: DNA – A P2P-based Framework for Distributed Network Management. In: Peer-to-Peer-Systeme und - Anwendungen, GI/ITG Work-In-Progress Workshop in Cooperation with KiVS 2005, Kaiserslautern (2005)
8. Wawrzoniak, M., Peterson, L., Roscoe, T.: Sophia: an information plane for networked systems. In: SIGCOMM Comput. Commun. Rev. Volume 34., ACM Press (2004) 15–20
9. Chen, Y., Bindel, D., Song, H., Katz, R.H.: An algebraic approach to practical and scalable overlay network monitoring. In: SIGCOMM Comput. Commun. Rev. Volume 34., ACM Press (2004) 55–66
10. Fiedler, M., Tutschku, K., Carlsson, P., Nilsson, A.: Identification of performance degradation in IP networks using throughput statistics. In Charzinski, J., Lehnert, R., Tran Gia, P., eds.: Providing Quality of Service in Heterogeneous Environments. Proceedings of the 18th International Teletraffic Congress (ITC-18), Berlin, Germany (2003) 399–407
11. Josephson, W.K., Sirer, E.G., Schneider, F.B.: Peer-to-peer authentication with a distributed single sign-on service. In: The 3rd International Workshop on Peer-to-Peer Systems IPTPS'04, San Diego, USA (2004)
12. Xu, J., Kumar, A., Yu, X.: On the fundamental tradeoffs between routing table size and network diameter in peer-to-peer networks. In: IEEE Journal on Selected Areas in Communications. Volume 22. (2004)
13. Binzenhöfer, A., Tran-Gia, P.: Delay Analysis of a Chord-based Peer-to-Peer File-Sharing System. In: ATNAC 2004, Sydney, Australia (2004)
14. Binzenhöfer, A., Staehle, D., Henjes, R.: On the Stability of Chord-based P2P Systems. University of Würzburg, Technical Report No. 347 (2004)

Time-Discrete Analysis of the Crawling Strategy in an Optimized Mobile P2P Architecture

Tobias Hoßfeld[1], Andreas Mäder[1], Kurt Tutschku[1], and Frank-Uwe Andersen[2]

[1] Department of Distributed Systems, Institute of Computer Science,
University of Würzburg,
Am Hubland, 97074 Würzburg, Germany
{hossfeld, maeder, tutschku}@informatik.uni-wuerzburg.de
[2] SIEMENS AG Communications,
Siemensdamm 62, 13623 Berlin, Germany
frank-uwe.andersen@siemens.com

Abstract. Mobile networks differ from their wireline counterparts mainly by the high costs for air transmissions and by the mobility of the users. A new entity, denoted as the *crawling peer*, is suggested in order to optimize the resource mediation mechanism for a mobile P2P file sharing application. In [1], we have investigated the performance of a crawling peer by means of simulations. Now, we show a time-discrete analysis of the crawling peer's performance in order to investigate different scenarios and to enable parameter-sensitivity studies for further improvements of the crawling peer's strategy.

Keywords: Crawling peer, mobile P2P architecture, file-sharing, queueing theory.

1 Introduction

Currently, UMTS network operators are looking for applications which *a)* exploit, qualitatively and quantitatively, the potential of the UMTS technology and *b)* motivate the user to adopt the new technology. In that way, *mobile P2P file-sharing* is an interesting candidate for such an application.

Mobile networks differ from wireline networks mainly by the limited capacity of radio channels and by the mobility of the users. The high costs of air transmission ask for a minimization of any signalling. The user mobility results in rapidly varying on-line states of users and leads to the discontinued relaying and buffering of signalling information. This can be accomplished for example by entities which on behalf of others store content, i.e. *caches*, or entities which locate information, i.e. *crawlers*.

P2P is a highly distributed application architecture where equal entities, denoted as *peers*, voluntarily share resources, e.g. files or CPU cycles, via direct exchange. The advantages of P2P services are the autonomous, load-adaptive, and resilient operation of these services. In order to share resources, the peers have to coordinate among each other which causes significant amount of signalling traffic [2, 3]. P2P applications support two fundamental coordination functions: *a) resource mediation* mechanisms, i.e. functions to search and locate resources or entities, and *b) resource access control*

M. Cesana, L. Fratta (Eds.): Wireless Syst./Network Architect. 2005, LNCS 3883, pp. 211–225, 2006.

mechanisms, i.e. functions to permit, schedule, and transfer resources. In particular, mediation functions are responsible for the high amount of signalling traffic of P2P services. The *overall performance* of P2P applications is determined by the individual performance of the basic P2P control functions.

A P2P file swapping user is mainly interested in a short exchange time for files. Therefore the mediation time, i.e. the time to locate a file, and the time to exchange the file has to be minimized. Furthermore, the P2P user does not want to pay for a large amount of mediation traffic on the air interface. The reduced mediation traffic, the discontinued signalling, and the short mediation times needed for mobile P2P file sharing networks ask for new architecture solutions for these kinds of services.

An efficient solution might state the use of new entities, in particular of the so-called *crawling peer*. Our architecture concept is presented in [4] and additionally comprises a cache peer and a modified index server. The crawling peer (CP) is placed in the wired part of the mobile network and locates files on behalf of mobile peers. The crawling peer can locate files even when a mobile peer is not online. As a result, the search traffic is shifted to the wireline part of the network and the radio links are relieved from signalling traffic.

Research on the mediation performance in P2P systems is fundamental. The crawling peer might be an alternative to highly distributed concepts such as *Distributed Hash Tables*, as used in Chord [5], or *flooding concepts*, as used in Gnutella.

In [1], we have investigated the performance of a crawling peer by means of simulations. Now, we present an analytical performance evaluation based on time-discrete analysis in order to investigate different scenarios and to enable parameter-sensitivity studies for further improvements of the strategy of the crawling peer.

This paper is organized as follows. Section 2 describes the mobile P2P architecture. In Section 3 we discuss at which index servers mobile specific contents may be located. The considered network and the crawling peer are modeled in Section 4. The analytical approach is explained in Section 5. Some numerical results are given in Section 6 and Section 7 concludes this work.

2   Mobile P2P Architecture

The suggested mobile P2P architecture for third generation mobile networks first introduced in [4] is depicted in Figure 1. The suggested concept is based on the architecture of the popular eDonkey P2P file sharing application and was enhanced by three specific entities: the *cache peer*, the *mobile P2P index server*, and the *crawling peer*.

The *cache peer* is a modified eDonkey peer located in the wireline part of the mobile P2P architecture that can be triggered to download often requested files and then offers these files to the community. It is located in the wireline and operator controlled part of the mobile network. The cache peer is assumed to have a high-speed Internet connection and sufficient large storage capacity. The application of the cache peer reduces the traffic caused by popular content on the radio interface [6]. The *mobile P2P index server* is a modified eDonkey index server. It tracks the frequently requested content, triggers the cache peer to fetch it, and forces the mobile peers to download the file from the cache peer, if available.

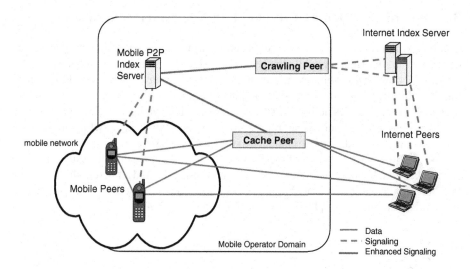

Fig. 1. Architecture concept for a P2P file-sharing service optimized to mobile networks

The *crawling peer* is also located in the wireline part of the suggested mobile P2P architecture and searches content on behalf of other mobile peers. The crawling peer can locate files even when a mobile peer is not online. As a result, the search traffic is shifted to the wireline part of the network and the radio links are relieved from signalling traffic. It has to be noted that a mobile peer should not be allowed to contact external eDonkey servers. If a mobile peer would contact external index servers directly then the mobile P2P index server can not track the files requested by mobile peers, that would result in less effective caching. Hence, the crawling peer is not queried directly by mobile peers. The mobile P2P index server triggers the crawling peer to search for content if it does not know the location of a file.

In general, an eDonkey peer, either a wireline peer or a mobile peer, can send search queries in a *local* or a *global* way. Local queries are restricted to the index server only to which the requesting peer is connected to. Global queries are sent by the peer to multiple index server sequentially until sufficient sources of the requested content are found. If a peer starts a global query, it causes additional signalling traffic proportional to the number of index servers visited. The order of contacting index server is arbitrary and does not consider any properties of the servers, e.g. number of files currently indexed. A more intelligent search strategy leads to significant improvements. The crawling peer might gather statistics about the index servers and preferably contact the servers that offer the most files first. This gives a better chance to find any results faster. In addition, a fast locating of files would also lead to reduced signalling traffic for global queries.

When executing an intelligent search strategy, the crawling peer has also to consider the *credit point system* in the eDonkey network [7], which prevents a peer of issuing too many search queries to an index server. The crawling peer should query only index servers for which it has enough credit points.

3   Content Location in a Hybrid P2P File-Sharing Network

In a hybrid P2P network, index servers keep information on peers and respond to requests for that information, while the peers are responsible for hosting the information, since the index servers only operate as index database of the contents and do not store the files. In the proposed mobile P2P architecture, the crawling peer locates contents on behalf of the mobiles and sends search queries to the available index servers in the network. If an index server has not registered the file for which the crawling peer asked, the crawling peer sends the search query to the next index server.

The performance evaluation of the crawling strategy requires the file request success probability which models whether an index server has registered a file for which a query is sent or not. The success probability f_i on an individual index server i may be derived from the measurements in [1]. There, it is defined as

$$f_i = \frac{\mu(\tilde{F}_i)}{\sum_{i \in \mathcal{I}} \mu(\tilde{F}_i)}, \tag{1}$$

i.e. according to the distribution of the file registrations at the index servers. The measured number of registered files at index server i is denoted by $\tilde{F}_i$ and the mean number of registered files at server i by $\mu(\tilde{F}_i)$.

In this case the success probability f_i on an individual index server simply depends on the ratio of registered files at this server to the total number of available files in the network. However, in P2P file-sharing networks, like the eDonkey network, the creation of *user groups* can be seen at the different index servers. Users which have the same or similar interests are also connected to the same server. This allows short lookup times when searching for contents which can be classified to this area of interest. User groups may be communities which are interested for example in movies in French language or in the latest computer games for PSP.

The mobile P2P file sharing application is supported additionally by the mobile network operator. As a result a mobile subscriber using that service achieves the best performance if it connects to the operator's index server within the mobile P2P architecture. But this means that is very likely that the mobile P2P users will also create a user group at this index server, the *mobile P2P community*.

We assume that there are mobile specific content types like ring tones (midi files or mp3 files), digital images, small videos, or games, which are shared and of interest for the mobile P2P users. This means that the mobile users will search for and download mobile specific content, whereby most of the files will be registered at the operator's index server. Thus, the success probability to find a mobile specific content at another index server may be assumed to be equal for all other index servers. This results is the following file request success probability p_s at an arbitrary index server when the crawling peer searches on behalf of the mobiles at all index servers $\mathcal{I}$ in the network:

$$p_s = \sum_{i \in \mathcal{I}} \frac{f_i}{|\mathcal{I}|}. \tag{2}$$

According to our measurements in [1] it holds $p_s = 0.7246\%$ and the number $|\mathcal{I}|$ of index servers was $|\mathcal{I}| = 138$. If the crawling peer asks every index server, the

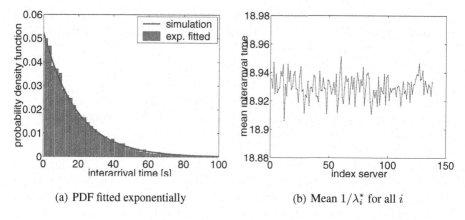

(a) PDF fitted exponentially

(b) Mean $1/\lambda_i^*$ for all i

Fig. 2. Observed interarrival times by simulations

probability that the file is available in the network and registered at any index server, i.e. the probability to successfully locate a file, is given by

$$1 - \prod_{i=1}^{|\mathcal{I}|} (1 - p_s),\qquad(3)$$

which is about 63.35% for the measured values p_s and $|\mathcal{I}|$.

In [1] we have implemented a simulation to evaluate the performance of the crawling peer and its strategy. In the mobile network the users generate a Poisson arrival process with rate λ of requests for files which cannot be found in the mobile domain. Now, the crawling peer comes into play and starts to query the index servers in the file-sharing network. As parameter for the success probability of the crawling peer at an arbitrary index server we used p_s as defined in (2) and performed some simulation runs.

Figure 2 shows the results of the simulation runs. We take a look on the observed search queries of an arbitrary index server. In Figure 2(a) the probability density function (PDF) of the observed file request interarrival time at a single, arbitrary index server is plotted. The simulated curve is fitted with the PDF of an exponential distribution and a very good match is obtained. Thus, the file request arrival process still follows a Poisson process, however with a different rate $\lambda_i^* < \lambda$. Due to the same success probability for all index servers, all index servers behave equal. This can also be noticed when comparing the mean interarrival times $\frac{1}{\lambda_i^*}$ of all index servers $i \in \mathcal{I}$ which show only slightly differences. This observation, that the file request queries sent to individual index server still follow a Poisson process and that all index servers experience the same file request rate, was the starting point of the analytical approach.

4   Network and Crawling Peer Model

We consider a mobile P2P-network as proposed in [4] and as introduced in Section 2. In the mobile network, the users generate a Poisson arrival process of requests for files which cannot be found in the mobile domain. Therefore the requests are delegated to the crawling peer (CP). The request arrival rate is denoted with λ. The CP then asks for the file at the known index servers in

$$\mathcal{I} = \{1, \cdots, N\} \tag{4}$$

according to a specific request strategy, the NoBan-strategy [1]. The search stops if either at least one request was successful, since we assume that additional sources – if available – can be found by eDonkey's source exchange mechanism, or, if no source has been found.

The banning of clients has been introduced lately by the creators of the "lugdunum index server", which is the software platform of choice for the majority of the index servers in the public eDonkey network. The index server has for each requesting client a number of credit points. For each file request, the credit is decreased by normally 16 points, while in turn in each second one point is added. A more detailed description of the banning mechanism can be found on the web [7].

The banning mechanism is modelled as following. An index server i has for each requesting peer, i.e. also for the crawling peer, a number of credit points c_i. Initially, the credits are set to a value of c_{init}, which is around 1000 credits according to the references we found on the web. On each request at i, the credits are reduced by Δc points, while in turn in each second one point is added. So, a client is banned from a server if the request would cause a negative amount of credit points. Once the crawling peer is banned at an index server, it stays banned forever. This is a worst case assumption since we have no information about the ban time as it is implemented in the public eDonkey network.

Our *NoBan strategy* [1] avoids banning and achieves a small response time and a high probability to locate a file which is close to the maximal value (3). For each file request x a list $\mathcal{L}_x$ of all index servers exists which denotes if server $y \in \mathcal{L}_x$ was already requested for request x:

$$\mathcal{L}_x(y) = \begin{cases} 0, & \text{if server } y \text{ not yet requested,} \\ 1, & \text{if server } y \text{ already requested.} \end{cases} \tag{5}$$

The set S_x of not yet requested index servers for request x is therefore

$$S_x = \{i \in \mathcal{I} : L_x(i) = 0\}. \tag{6}$$

If the crawling peer has low credits c_i at an index server i, the search request is blocked at server i. This probability is denoted as $p_{b,i}$. A file request x is always forwarded to the next available, not yet requested index server. This means that the next server i to be contacted for file request x is $i = \min\{j \in S_x : c_j \geq \Delta c\}$ which has sufficient credit points, $c_i \geq \Delta c$.

A request x is blocked completely if no more server $y \in S_x$ can be contacted due to available credits:

$$\forall y \in S_x : c_y < \Delta c. \tag{7}$$

We denote this blocking probability with p_b. In the case of a blocked request it is $S \neq \emptyset$. Otherwise ($S = \emptyset$), each server was contacted, i.e. the search request was answered successfully or unsuccessfully.

5   Analytical Approach

In this section, we investigate the NoBan strategy under the assumption that the file request success probabilities f_i on each index server are equal, as motivated in Section 3,

$$\forall i, j \in \mathcal{I} : f_i = f_j =_{def} p_s. \tag{8}$$

As a consequence, all servers are equal and are therefore asked randomly for a file request x. In particular, the next index server is in this case randomly chosen from the set S_x of remaining, not yet asked servers. Since the file request arrivals follow a Poisson process with rate λ, the observed arrivals at each individual server i still follow a Poisson process, demonstrated in Figure 2. We denote the obtained rate at an individual index server with λ_i^*. Because of this notice, we can describe the analysis model as depicted in Figure 3.

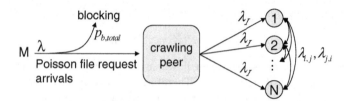

Fig. 3. Illustration of the analysis model

The Poisson file requests arrivals are split equally among the N index servers:

$$\lambda_{\mathcal{I}} = \lambda N (1 - p_{p,i}). \tag{9}$$

If a search request is unsuccessfully answered at server i, the request is forwarded to a not yet requested server $j \in S$. The corresponding rate is

$$\lambda_{i,j} = \lambda_{\mathcal{I}} (1 - p_s) \tag{10}$$

which holds for all $i \neq j$. The observed rate at an index server i follows as

$$\lambda_i^* = \lambda_{\mathcal{I}} + \sum_{j \neq i} \lambda_{j,i} = \lambda_{\mathcal{I}} (N(1 - p_s) + p_s). \tag{11}$$

The probability $p_{b,total}$ that a search request is totally blocked, i.e. at all index servers, is

$$p_{b,total} = \prod_{i=1}^{N} p_{b,i}. \tag{12}$$

However, the derivation of the probabilities p_b and $p_{b,i}$ is more complex due to interaction with the search query rate λ, the number of index servers N, and the number of credit points c_i at index server i. In the following we use a numerical approach to retrieve the blocking probabilities $p_{b,i}$ and the observed search query rate λ_i^* at an in-dex server i. The distribution of the number c_i of credit points at each server i can be calculated by using time-discrete analysis. In order to get $p_{b,i}$ an equation system is then numerically solved using again iteration. We start with the description of the compuation of the steady state distribution of the credit points c_i for a given rate λ_i^*.

Let $X = c_i$ be a random variable which desribes the number of credit points of the CP at an arbitrary index server i and T describes a point in time. The time is discretized in intervals of length $\Delta T = 1\text{second}$. Then, $P(X = j|T = n)$ denotes the state proba-bility that the CP has j credit points at time $n\Delta T = n$ seconds. The state probabilities form the components of the vector

$$\mathbb{X}_n = \begin{pmatrix} P(X = 0|T = n) \\ P(X = 1|T = n) \\ \vdots \\ P(X = c_{max}|T = n) \end{pmatrix}. \tag{13}$$

The expression $\mathbb{X}_n(j)$ returns the j-th element of the vector $\mathbb{X}_n$, i.e.

$$\mathbb{X}_n(j) = P(X = j|T = n). \tag{14}$$

In this time-discrete analysis, we use the power method to compute numerically the dis-tribution of the number of credit points. Therefore, the state space has to be finite. This condition is fulfilled for eDonkey index servers and we consider a maximum number c_{max} of credit points.

The start vector $\mathbb{X}_0$ is defined as follows and initializes the iterative computation of the state probabilities $\mathbb{X}_n$:

$$\mathbb{X}_0(j) = \begin{cases} 0 & ,0 \le j < c_{max}, \\ 1 & ,j = c_{max}. \end{cases} \tag{15}$$

The probability $\mathbb{P}_n(j, k)$ denotes the conditional probability that the amount of credit points is j at time $n\Delta T$ under the condition that the CP issued $K_n = k$ search queries within the last time interval ΔT:

$$\mathbb{P}_n(j, k) = P(X = j|K_n = k). \tag{16}$$

The random variable K_n denotes the number of search queries from $(n - 1)$ seconds until n seconds. Since the arrivals of search queries at an index server follow a Poisson process with rate λ_i^* (search requests per time unit ΔT), the number of search queries is Poisson distributed:

$$P(K_n = k) = \frac{(\lambda_i^* \Delta T)^k}{k!} e^{-\lambda_i^* \Delta t}, \quad k = 0, 1, 2, \dots. \tag{17}$$

The power method requires again a finite number of states in order to describe the conditional probabilities $\mathbb{P}_n(j, k)$. Thus, the α-quantile of the distribution of K_n is used to assume the maximal number k_{max} of search queries:

$$P(K_n \le k_{max}) = \alpha. \tag{18}$$

The conditional probability $\mathbb{P}_{n+1}$ can now be computed iteratively. First, we consider the case that $K_n = 0$ search queries were issued by the CP to the index server during the last second. After each second, the amount of credit points is increased by one. Since no search query was issued, at least one credit point is availabe, i.e., $\mathbb{P}_{n+1}(0,0) = 0$. In order to truncate again the state space, $\mathbb{P}_{n+1}(c_{max}, 0)$ sums up the remaining probabilites.

$$\mathbb{P}_{n+1}(j,0) = \begin{cases} 0 & ,j = 0, \\ \mathbb{X}_n(j-1) & ,0 < j < c_{max}, \\ \mathbb{X}_n(c_{max}-1) + \mathbb{X}_n(c_{max}) & ,j = c_{max}. \end{cases} \tag{19}$$

Next, we consider $K_n = k$ search queries for $k = 1, 2, \cdots, k_{max}$. A single search request costs Δc credit points. The probability $\mathbb{P}_{n+1}(j,k)$ that the transition to a number of credit points j that is larger than $k\Delta c$ is $\mathbb{X}_n(j + k\Delta c - 1)$. The transition to $j > c'_{max} = c_{max} - k\Delta c + 1$ is not possible as $k\Delta c$ credit points are consumed. To achieve less than $k\Delta c$ credit points either not enough credit points were available or the required credit points were assumed for the k queries. We obtain the following equation:

$$\mathbb{P}_{n+1}(j,k) = \begin{cases} \mathbb{X}_n(j-1) + \mathbb{X}_n(j+k\Delta c - 1) & ,0 \leq j < k\Delta c, \\ \mathbb{X}_n(j+k\Delta c - 1) & ,k\Delta c \leq j < c'_{max}, \\ \mathbb{X}_n(c_{max}-1) + \mathbb{X}_n(c_{max}) & ,j = c'_{max}, \\ 0 & ,j > c'_{max}. \end{cases} \tag{20}$$

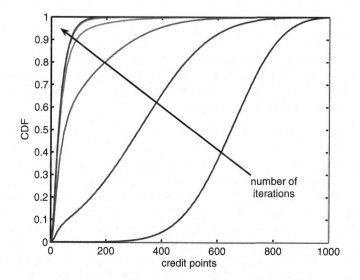

Fig. 4. Number of iterations to get credit point distribution

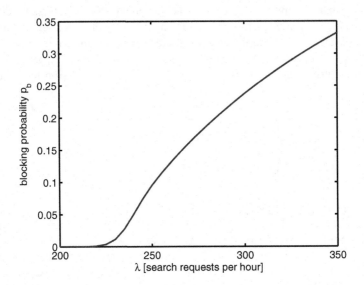

Fig. 5. Blocking probability for a single server system, $N = 1$, for different rates λ

In order to compute the state probability $\mathbb{X}_{n+1}(j)$, Bayes theorem is applied using (17), (19), and (20):

$$\mathbb{X}_{n+1}(j) = \sum_{k=0}^{k_{max}} \mathbb{P}_{n+1}(j,k) \cdot P(K_n = k). \tag{21}$$

The computation of $\mathbb{X}_{n+1}$ is now iterated until the steady state $\mathbb{X}$ is reached, i.e.

$$\mathbb{X}_n = \mathbb{X}_{n+1} = \mathbb{X}. \tag{22}$$

In practice, the condition whether the steady state is reached or not is realized by checking the absolute difference of the mean number of credit points for two consecutive iteration steps. If the difference is smaller than a given threshold ϵ, the terminating condition is fulfilled and the iteration is stopped:

$$|\mathrm{E}\left[\mathbb{X}_{n+1}\right] - \mathrm{E}\left[\mathbb{X}_n\right]| < \epsilon. \tag{23}$$

This numerical method is a very robust and efficient approach. Figure 4 shows the cumulative distribution function of the credit points for the different iteration steps $\mathbb{X}_n$. The arrow indicates the number of iterations which were executed. Only a few iterations are required until the terminating condition (23) is fulfilled.

Figure 5 shows the computed blocking probabilities for different search request arrival rates λ. In this case, we only consider a single server, i.e. $N = 1$, which is contacted for each file query. It can be seen that for file request rates smaller than 350 requests/hour the blocking probability p_b is vanishing. But the blocking probability significantly increases for larger rates resulting in inacceptable blocking probabilities, e.g. for $\lambda = 300$ requests/hour the blocking probability is already $p_b = 0.23$. However, in real eDonkey networks, there exist several index servers, thus a server does not see all of the requests. In our measurements, we investigated $N = 139$ servers.

With the knowledge of the distribution of the number of credit points $X = c_i$ at an index server i for a given rate λ_i^*, the occuring blocking probability $p_{b,i}$ can be computed that a search request is blocked at the server due to not enough credit points. However, the rate λ_i^* depends on the blocking probabilities $p_{b,j}$ of the other index servers $j \neq i$. Since we already know from Section 3 that we may consider all N index servers to be equal with respect to blocking probabilities $p_{b,i}$ and observed search query rates λ_j^*, it holds the following equation system for the steady state:

$$p_{b,i} = \sum_{j=0}^{\Delta c-1} \mathbb{X}(j) = \sum_{j=0}^{\Delta c-1} P(X = j),$$

$$\lambda_i^* = \frac{\lambda}{N} + \sum_{y=1}^{N-1} \lambda \cdot P(B = 1|Y = y) \cdot P(Y = y). \tag{24}$$

Hereby, Y is a random variable which describes the number of already contacted index servers. B is a random variable that the considered index server i is chosen. This means that B follows a Bernoulli distribution.

The conditional probability $P(B = 1|Y = y)$ denotes the probability that the index server i is contacted after y other index servers were contacted. $P(Y = y)$ is the probability that all y servers have not successfully answered a search query or that these servers were blocked. This means

$$P(Y = y) = \binom{N}{y} \left((1 - p_{b,i}) \cdot (1 - p_s) + p_{b,i} \right)^y. \tag{25}$$

According to the NoBan strategy a server is not contacted twice for the same search query. Thus, if already y servers were contacted, the probability that index server i is chosen follows as

$$P(B = 1|Y = y) = \frac{1}{N - y}. \tag{26}$$

Inserting (25) and (26) in (24) leads to

$$p_{b,i} = \sum_{j=0}^{\Delta c-1} \mathbb{X}(j) = \sum_{j=0}^{\Delta c-1} P(X = j),$$

$$\lambda_i^* = \frac{\lambda}{N} + \sum_{y=1}^{N-1} \binom{N}{y} \cdot \lambda \cdot \frac{1}{N - y} \cdot \left((1 - p_{b,i}) \cdot (1 - p_s) + p_{b,i} \right)^y. \tag{27}$$

The equation system (27) can now be solved numerically by iterating again until the steady state is reached, i.e., until the blocking probability $p_{b,i}$ and the observerd search query rate λ_i^* at server i only changes slightly by a threshold ϵ in succeeding iteration steps. The success probability p_s that an index server has registered the searched file is given as input parameter. The iteration is initialized with $p_{b,i} = 1$.

6   Numerical Results

In this section, we present some numerical results for different parameters. We vary over a large range of realizations for the parameters. This is made possible by the time-discrete analysis and can be very efficiently numerically computed outperforming more time-consuming simulations.

First we take a look on the observed interarrival time of search queries which are forwarded to an individual index server i by the crawling peer. The total search queries in the system being issued to the crawling peer is described with the file request arrival rate λ. Figure 6 shows on the x-axis the file request arrival rate λ and on the y-axis the observed mean interarrival times $\frac{1}{\lambda_i^*}$ at an arbitrary index server i. The higher the load in the system, i.e. the higher the file request rate, the higher is also the load for individual index servers, which is expressed by smaller mean query interarrival times $\frac{1}{\lambda_i^*}$. From the convex shape of the curve, it can be seen that the crawling peer is a very efficient solution to realize resource mediation in P2P file-sharing networks and that the CP distributes the load in the network among the different index servers. Thus, it is possible to accomplish flash crowd arrivals of search requests without loosing the quality of the service.

It can be expected that a higher rate λ also leads to higher blocking probabilities $p_{b,i}$ which is investigated next. Again, we vary over the total file request rate λ in the network which is given on the x-axis in Figure 7. The resulting blocking probability $p_{b,i}$ that the crawling peer cannot forward a search request to an individual index server i is plotted versus λ. It can be seen that the crawling peer supports up to a mean number of 440 search requests per hour while achieving a blocking probability $p_{b,i}$ close to zero.

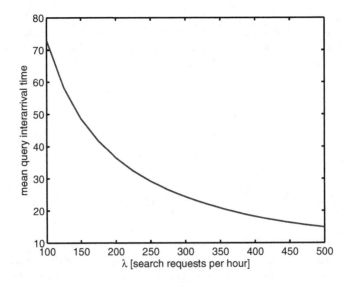

Fig. 6. Observed mean interarrival times $\frac{1}{\lambda_i^*}$ at an arbitrary index server i

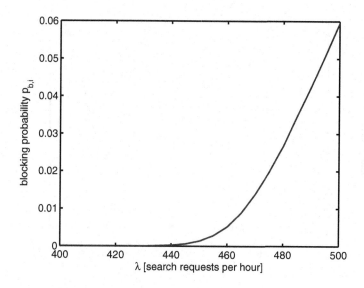

Fig. 7. Blocking probability for different search arrival rates λ

If the total load in the system is permanently higher over time, e.g. about 500 requests per hour, the crawling peer has to block some search requests to the index server i due to not enough credit points and to avoid therefore to be banned at server i. Nevertheless, the total blocking probability $p_{b,total}$ is still for this rate close to zero, cf. Eq. (12).

The mobile network operator which supports the P2P file-sharing service can dimension the network in such a way that the experienced quality of the file-sharing service satisfies the user and the blocking probability falls below a given threshold. If the service provider operates k crawling peers in the mobile domain, the load can be distributed among the k CPs. This means that each of the k CPs only sees $\frac{1}{k}$ of the total load λ, i.e. each CP has then only to accomplish a file request rate $\frac{\lambda}{k}$. Now, the operator can choose k such that $p_{b,i}$ is vanishing. According to Figure 7 this means to find the minimal k such that $\frac{\lambda}{k} < 440$ requests per hour.

Another parameter that is of interest is the maximal number c_{max} of credit points which a peer can gather at an index server. c_{max} influences how strong a peer is rewarded if it does not contact the index server for longer periods of time. The maximal number of credit points help to accomplish bursts in the arrival of search requests. If the file request arrival process shows a higher variance, a smaller number of maximal credit points will lead to higher blocking probabilities.

Figure 8 shows the blocking probability $p_{b,i}$ in dependence of the maximal number c_{max} of available credit points. The blue curve indicates the numerical solution of the time-discrete analysis which explains the small zigzag of the solution curve due to numerical inaccuracies. We only have fitted the numerical solution polynomial for visualization purposes to obtain a smoother curve without zigzag. From Figure 8, it can be seen that the blocking probabilities $p_{b,i}$ at individual index server stay constant if the maximal possible number of credit points exceeds a value of about 500 credit points. In

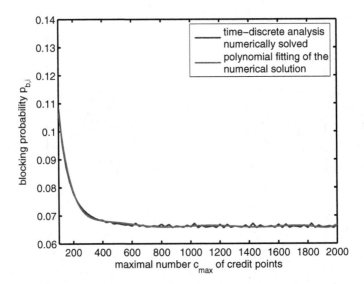

Fig. 8. Blocking probability in dependence of the maximal number of available credit points

that case, this results in a much more user-friendly (in terms of blocking probabilities), but still effective prevention of hammering the index server.

7   Conclusion and Outlook

Mobile networks differ from their wireline counterparts mainly by the high costs for air transmissions and by the mobility of the users. The crawling peer is suggested in order to optimize the resource mediation mechanism for a mobile P2P file-sharing application. The objective of this work was to investigate the crawling peer component, which optimizes the resource mediation mechanism in a mobile P2P architecture. We presented a time-discrete analysis for describing interactions between performance factors, like the observed arrival rate and the blocking probability. The computation of the performance factors was done using the power method and numerical iteration techniques. This approach enables parameter sensitivity studies and might lead to optimal value for tradeoff parameters. It helps to dimension the mobile P2P network in such a way that the experienced quality of the file-sharing service, e.g. in terms of successfully answered search requests, satisfies the user and that the blocking probability is below a given threshold.

In particular, we investigated the observed search queries at an arbitrary server and the resulting blocking probabilities for different arrival rates of search queries. As a result of the analysis, we found out that the crawling peer is a very efficient solution to realize resource mediation in P2P file-sharing networks and that the CP distributes the load in the network among the different index servers. Thus, it is possible to accomplish flash crowd arrivals of search requests without loosing the quality of the service.

Furthermore, the analysis makes the dimensioning of the mobile P2P file-sharing architecture possible. The mobile network operator which supports the P2P file-sharing service can dimension the network in such a way that the experienced quality of the file-sharing service satisfies the user and the blocking probability falls below a given threshold. Next we investigated the influence of the maximal number of credit points on the blocking probabilities. The time-discrete analysis shows that the blocking probabilities at an individual index server stay constant if the maximal possible number of credit points exceeds a certain value. In that case, a much more user-friendly (in terms of blocking probabilities), but still effective prevention of hammering the index servers is realized.

Acknowledgement

The authors would like to thank Dirk Staehle and Marie-Ange Remiche for the fruitful discussions during the course of this work.

References

1. Hoßfeld, T., Mäder, A., Tutschku, K., Tran-Gia, P., Andersen, F.U., de Meer, H., Dedinski, I.: Comparison of crawling strategies for an optimized mobile p2p architecture. In: 19th International Teletraffic Congress (ITC19), Beijing, China (2005)
2. Tutschku, K., deMeer, H.: A measurement study on signaling on gnutella overlay networks. In: Fachtagung - Kommunikation in Verteilten Systemen (KiVS) 2003, Leipzig, Germany (2003) 295–306
3. K. Tutschku: A Measurement-based Traffic Profile of the eDonkey Filesharing Service. In: 5th Passive and Active Measurement Workshop (PAM2004), Antibes Juan-les-Pins, France (2004)
4. Oberender, J., Andersen, F.U., de Meer, H., Dedinski, I., Hoßfeld, T., Kappler, C., Mäder, A., Tutschku, K.: Enabling mobile peer-to-peer networking. In: Mobile and Wireless Systems, LNCS 3427, Dagstuhl, Germany (2005)
5. Balakrishnan, H., Kaashoek, M.F., Karger, D., Morris, R., Stoica, I.: Looking up data in p2p systems. Communications of the ACM **43**(2) (2003)
6. Hoßfeld, T., Tutschku, K., Andersen, F.U., de Meer, H., Oberender, J.: Simulative performance evaluation of a mobile peer-to-peer file-sharing system. In: NGI2005, Rome, Italy (2005)
7. Newsgroup: alt.pl.edonkey2000: Explanation on blacklisting by servers.
   http://groups.google.de/groups?selm=
   79enjv06ablmsk5rmovd7nrckrhiiorj1s%404ax.com&output=gplain

P2P-Based Mobility Management for Heterogeneous Wireless Networks and Mesh Networks*

Amine M. Houyou, Hermann De Meer, and Moritz Esterhazy

University of Passau, Faculty for Mathematics and Computer Science,
Chair of Computer Networks and Communication,
Innstr. 33, 94032 Passau, Germany
{houyou, demeer, esterhaz}@fmi.uni-passau.de

Abstract. The recent emergence of a whole plethora of new wireless technologies, such as IEEE802.15, IEEE802.11, and UMTS, etc, has exposed the limitations of mobility solutions in the next generation Internet. Current mobility management systems are operator specific, centralized, and focused on single link technology. A rethink of how to exploit context awareness, lead by the emergence of sensor networks and pervasive computing, is explored. This paper suggests a roaming technique taking pervasiveness and self-awareness into consideration, by first, moving the intelligence to the mobile terminals. The mobile devices should look themselves for the most suitable wireless network. We also propose to organize the wireless mesh networks in a context-aware peer-to-peer network.

Keywords: Mobility management, heterogeneous wireless networks, context-awareness, peer-to-peer.

1 Introduction

Wireless Networks took the world by storm during the last two decades thanks to their universal coverage and the possibilities of roaming they offer. The success of GSM technology led the way to introducing UMTS standard, which promises more bandwidth for Internet applications. This evolution will continue towards the vision of *wireless mesh networks* (WMN) [1], where wireless networks could be categorized according to their coverage into: large area networks (e.g. Satellite), cellular macro-technologies (e.g. GSM, UMTS), and small area broadband (e.g. WLAN, WiMax). A variety of wireless mesh routers, running independently, are assumed to coexist in a dense urban environment. They connect mesh-clients, i.e. mobile nodes supporting those wireless technologies, to a backbone network. Already mobile devices are able to connect through several of these technologies; either simultaneously (using multi-homing), by selecting an alternative wireless radio or possibly dynamically following the promises of cognitive radios[15], or agile radios[16], and software radios [18].

---

* This work has been supported by the EuroNGI network of excellence (EU-IST -507613), with special funding for the project "A Contribution Towards Always Best Connected (ACT-ABC)".

M. Cesana, L. Fratta (Eds.): Wireless Syst./Network Architect. 2005, LNCS 3883, pp. 226–241, 2006.
© Springer-Verlag Berlin Heidelberg 2006

Separately to how the mobile terminal is capable to support this heterogeneity, the assumption is that the mesh-client should be allowed to connect to the most suitable wireless mesh infrastructure. This choice of connectivity has brought up the term an Always-Best-Connected network [12], which is our ultimate goal in this study.

In this paper this problem is approached from the following viewpoints: The wireless infrastructure so far has been laid out by operators attempting to reach their customers through investing into well-organized and hierarchically structured cellular networks. The idea of random mesh networks might sound, at first glance, far-off and unmotivated economically. Nevertheless, similar trends are already happening with home users adopting WiFi in large scale. The end result is the emergence of hot-spots around our urban surroundings, which individuals are willing to pay for. In a way, operators reach their users through a new generation of wireless access islands that would well be used to allow a value return investment to home users. This would be possible if users were willing to offer parts of their wireless resources in a controlled manner to the outside world in return of a reduced rate for their subscriptions. Similar sharing examples could be found in other domains such as power grids, where individuals can feed their excess solar electric energy back into the power Grid. This idea of sharing would be an alternative to such uncontrolled pirating phenomena, namely war-driving [21]. Another point is the organization of WMN infrastructure, which cannot be envisaged through the existing 3G mobile systems location management[1] techniques [23]. The latter relies on pre-defined cell IDs stored in a database system. A mobile node only needs to report its current cell ID, for incoming calls to be directed to it. Some predictive measures could be also taken knowing the topology and direction of the movement of a mobile node [33]. A home location registry (HLR) can also store the location updates (LUs), sent from a communicating terminal, or use paging to indicate to dormant devices their current cell IDs [5].

In the mesh environment infrastructure has to be organized beyond a single technology or a single operator; it has to be light-weight compared to using the 2G/3G roaming agreements between network operators. It also has to cater for small providers offering much smaller networks of different technologies.

Using peer-to-peer (P2P) for location-aware queries has recently attracted increasing interest. Scholl et al. [26] suggest a P2P framework that locates geographically close peers and requests location-based information, such as local bookshops, etc. Their search takes into account the spacio-temporal movement and velocity of the mobile peer to indicate the validity of a response. Another promising approach using P2P for location management is named Palma (a P2P Architecture for Location Management) [27]. Palma concentrates on managing the mobile's current location or point of attachment similarly to virtual location registry (VLR) or HLR in GSM. The architecture uses the properties of Tapestry distributed hash tables protocol (DHT) to organize location servers (LS), which store the terminal's ID. Palma allows correspondent nodes (CNs) to efficiently retrieve the mobile node's current LS of attachment. It does not, however, aim at terminal mobility neither does it offer any handover management mechanism. It also does not support existing communication between a CN and a MN.

---

[1] Location management consists of procedures that allow the network to identify the point of attachment of a mobile node.

In this paper, a P2P distributed and decentralized architecture is shown to organize wireless mesh networks in a location-based service[2] [25]. It is used to allow mobile terminals to stay always best connected, beyond a single technology or operator. This paper is a step forward towards our ultimate target of a full context-aware service [6]. In fact, the framework proposed here can easily be extended to integrate other contextual information along side the location of a mobile agent.

Our paper differs from [26] in that we do not need to consider spacio-temporal validity of queries neither do we care of the geographic closeness of a given peer. Our main aim consists in organizing the objects stored by the peers in a geographic-aware manner rather than trying to locate the peers themselves. Compared to Palma [27], our paper utilizes location-awareness to minimize interruption times of existing communication, reaching real-time demands. The work presented in this paper does not aim at redeveloping micro-mobility solutions at the link or network layer, like this is the case with hierarchical mobile IP, HAWAII, etc [2].

The proposed P2P architecture is described in Section 2. The design decisions are motivated, in that section too, while defining the object space. The architecture, designed in Section 2, makes use of DHTs. The choice and modifications to two candidate protocols are explained. Also the way they deal with the system requirements such as, mobility of peers, load-balancing, and flexible/rich querying, is discussed under the same section. The proposed architecture could be used depending on the location awareness capabilities at the end-device. It is assumed, in Section 3, that the end-device knows its movement pattern via an integrated navigation system (similar to [10]). The terminal should be able to detect its capabilities and location, and to query the P2P architecture. It also triggers its own handover process at both link and network layers, based on its location-awareness. A simulation comparison for the terminal handover is made in Section 4 between the location-aware triggers and the "blind" discovery mechanisms traditionally used in an IEEE 802.11b and IPv6 environment. Section 5 concludes the paper.

2   P2P Management of Location-Based Topology Organization

In this section, two different P2P protocols are presented, namely Chord [28] and CAN [22], to meet some design decisions. The aspects of organization, mobility, load-balancing, and querying are discussed. P2P technology has evolved, since the days of Napster as a file sharing technique between equal entities named peers, to become one of the fastest growing Internet technologies. The key aspect of interest in P2P is the decentralized location of objects queried through different types of P2P protocols. The latter protocols have evolved from an early server-based indexing of all existing file entries and their location, to the extremes of the chaotic Gnutella, and reaching the organized distributed hash tables (DHTs). Here, we concentrate on the potentials of DHTs, only, as a variation of the more general term of P2P paradigm.

The main advantage of using DHTs in P2P applications was to provide a scalable system capable of storing large numbers of items while minimizing the routing cost and offering a load-balanced indexing of entries among peers. Chord [28], for instance, requires each peer node to store routing information for $O(logN)$ other peers,

---

[2] Schiller defines Location-based services (LBS) as the recent concept that integrates the geographic location, i.e. special coordinates, with the general notion of a service [25].

where N is the total number of participating peers. Similarly, it takes a maximum $O(logN)$ routing messages to find any content in a Chord ring. Content addressable networks (CAN) [22], on the other hand, uses d-dimensional virtual address space for locating data. Each peer owns a given zone of the virtual space, and needs to store routing information to about $O(d)$ other peers. The routing cost however is on average $O(dN^{1/d})$, which then depends on N, the number of peers in the system.

The main argument for using DHTs is that they provide a highly scalable, but self-organized distributed system. This section first motivates the use of DHTs and explains the exact design decisions taken to select the DHT protocol. An implementation with Chord is thoroughly explained, while listing the different design decisions that enable location based queries in Chord. For richer range type of queries an implementation of the proposed architecture is given with CAN. The two techniques rely, however, on similar roles for the participating nodes in the P2P system.

2.1 A Wireless Resource as a Shared Object in a DHT

In comparison with a P2P file-sharing application, the content shared in this DHT system are objects representing wireless resources accessible in a transparent way, and assigned a unique ID. The objects are described on two levels. First, an object description gathers a list of diverse attributes of a given wireless infrastructure. In Figure 1, a single "wireless resource" is identified as being geographically collocated access points (WLAN) or node Bs (UMTS) belonging to the same operator, while in the same IP-subnet. In other words, the mesh-routers in this case could be said to be the IP-gateways or GGSN nodes used to identify a single IP sub-domain.

To search for a given wireless resource, it is sufficient to look up access points that the mobile terminal is allowed to access in its vicinity. The attribute, out of this list of properties of the "wireless resource", used to address each single instance or object in the P2P object space is the location attribute. Global positioning system (GPS) coordinates are used to create a multi-dimensional space of keys representing a single object. Based on their latitude and longitude coordinates, the objects are distributed in a geographic manner among the peers.

In a file-sharing P2P application, a hash function such as SHA-1 is applied to the string representing the name of given file (e.g. SHA-1 [Mobi-play-track1] = key). The DHT protocol first indicates which peer should store the tuple (key,value) (where the value is the file itself) and the way to get to it. The application uses a get(key), at the DHT interface, to search for the file/resource.

In Figure 1, the peers are some entities connected through existing network topology in the form of an overlay formed of fixed AccessPeers and some mobile Search-Peers.

The objects stored and shared on this overlay of peers can vary from a single AP to possibly a larger wireless domain as a single instance. An example would be to list network type roughly as either: a broadband micro-cell, a wide-area cell as in UMTS, or a macro-cell as in satellite (Figure 1 shows the two latter categories) [1]. Then for each cell an XML description template is filled up with as many attributes as possible (e.g. location, radio frequency/modulation scheme, network control information, router advertisement (look at Section 4), access restrictions, etc.). In our architecture we suggest to use geographic proximity combined to whether the access points/base-stations belong to the same IP-domain as way to aggregate a group of APs represented as a single object in our DHT object-space. The hash function in this case needs to represent the GPS latitude and longitude values of a single wireless resource as a unique ID that is storable and retrievable via an overlay. The DHT interface is then used to access those XML files describing the access network on demand. It is up to the query generating node to define priorities on the preferred technology to reduce the level of response. The found resources could also be aggregated per peer in a single response message to reduce the amount of generated messages. This kind of querying demands more than just a "get" function normally used by a file sharing application. Complex queries could include "if...then" requests. In addition, the load balancing also plays an important role in choosing the right DHT implementation. We need a system that takes into account the immensely different capabilities of the peers. A peer could be hosted on a user machine in a home network, while others could be larger servers used by cellular network operators. These server machines should store considerably more information.

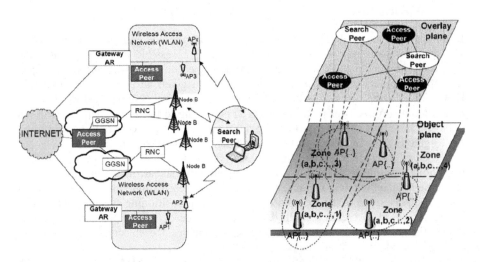

Fig. 1. WMN Topology Organization Using a Peer-to-Peer System (e.g. UMTS-IEEE802.11)

Fig. 2. Roaming on Overlays: Zone Separation for a Chrord-based Organization of the WMN

Furthermore, the mobility of the peer entity has to be taken into account. The mobile peer should not be burdened with managing shared resources in order to reduce the costly communication overhead. The mobility entities in a mobile peer use the DHT search to locate wireless resources. A clear separation is made between this role and that of what the processing of the obtained information.

2.2 Modifying Chord to Implement Location Aware Architecture

In this section we deal with the organization of the wireless mesh networks. For this purpose, we propose the following distinction in the roles taken by the different peers according to the Chord protocol [28]:

SearchPeer: is a member of the Chord ring as a leach node. It represents a moving node that both identifies the context of the mobile node and is meant to search and retrieve "nearby" wireless network resources. It translates the location-based query to a search to the DHT to retrieve all matching values.

This SearchPeer is hosted by a computer on board of the moving vehicle (in our studied scenario) and is connected via any active wireless interface providing connectivity to the large Internet. Since this peer is meant to change its point of attachment on micro-level, i.e. changing constantly its context, it is not required to store any context related information neither is it meant to take the role of a full Chord peer. The searchPeer ID is its hashed home IP address which should be within the IP subdomain of a router that can act as a home agent [20]. The hash function is applied to the global home IP address of the mobile node. Relying on the DHT routing mechanism all DHT-related messages from and to the SearchPeer will reach the home agent first. When using MIPv6 [20], the messages are then further forwarded to the care-of-address (CoA) identifying the position of the mobile node. The SearchPeer, despite its dynamic care-of-address, keeps a fixed ID. In the case of a micro-mobility scenario the mobile node may often change its IP address while attached to several IP domains. A further binding effect of the IP address adds to the DHT routing cost. However, the advantage of this added cost is keeping the consistency of the DHT finger tables and reducing the churn rate. This is the rate at which new peers usually join or leave the system.

Furthermore, the DHT needs to stay consistent keeping in mind the stochastic behaviour of "mobile peers" in the system. Once the mobile has left a given foreign network, in general, the home agent is informed. The home agent can be, first, explicitly informed by the old foreign network that the node has left the network. It could also be implicitly informed when receiving an association message carrying the new care-of-address [20]. In the case where the node leaves the network for good, the foreign network updates the reachability status [19] of the mobile node (to unreachable) and informs the home agent to stop forwarding incoming packets to the old CoA. If the home agent removes the home IP address from its known active addresses that would cause all routing messages sent to that address on the Chord ring getting dropped too. The SearchPeer node is eventually removed from the Chord ring.

AccessPeer: is a full peer node capable of storing and managing content values and can be reached by other peers based on the Chord protocol. In other words, any peer can forward searches and requests for specific keys. It represents dedicated servers running the DHT roaming application. The AccessPeer also plays the role of forwarding search requests as well as filtering out the information sent back as a response.

The Object Space: the object space under Chord consists of an XML description file, retrievable by the roaming application. The content or object space is no longer randomized through the use of a hash function such as SHA-1, distributing the keys among the peers in load-balanced way [28]. In contrast, we rely for our system on Geocoding [25] to represent a geographic-aware distribution of (key,value) pairs among peers. This could be compared to an online map service that can generate a zip code from entered GPS coordinates. The problem with Chord is that its query language requires a precise known object ID that can generate a precise key value, making range queries difficult. For that reason we partition the ID of our wireless objects and use part of that ID to search for resources within a larger geographic area. Taking the zip example, one could imagine a global zip code dividing the earth in a grid of squares or zones, the size of Texas, with incrementing the integer ID per geographic square. Knowing the maximum number of squares, enough to cover the earth area, we form the first part of a given object with the ID of the square where it is located. This square is further divided into smaller zones, while giving a unique ID to each part of that square. This could be repeated depending on the area searched until reaching the size of a micro-cell, shown as a concatenation of IDs (a,b,d, ..,3) on Figure 2. The search needs only to look up all resources whose IDs lie in the range of a macro-cell. The search matching the most significant part of the macro-cell is processed further at the concerned peers. The search message will take the form of an XML file with different list of wishes that need to be matched at the AccessPeer (Figure 2) before a response is processed. This includes some attributes such as: the preferred wireless technologies at the mobile terminal, user credentials stating which services the user is allowed to access, etc. Another filter used is the rest of the location attribute, which could specify a "nearest neighbour query" [26], i.e. the shortest distanced resources from a given path or a given position point. These types of geographic queries assume a processing of the query request beyond a simple key matching as it is the case for file sharing applications. The wireless resource XML description could aggregate a list of APs depending on the priorities indicated by the user. More complex query processing could provide a kind of P2P data-base [13].

Load Balancing: For load-balancing purposes, we use the "virtual servers" extension to Chord, where a SearchPeer is clearly distinguished as being represented with a null number of virtual servers. The AccessPeer on the other hand depending on its storage and processing capabilities could be modelled as a number of virtual servers. Managing wireless resources includes deciding which resource should be managed by which group of virtual servers. This could take some attributes into account such as whether the AccessPeer has the right security attribute to find out about a given resource. The results to these changes of Chord are rather extensive and out of the scope of this paper.

2.3 Improved Range Querying Under a CAN-Based Implementation

The more appropriate DHT protocol that best solves the aspects of range queries [24] is CAN. Next, a CAN-based solution is presented. To address content, a four-dimensional object space is chosen, which allows geographic range queries. Assuming R the set of objects representing instances of wireless resources with a geographic ID (x,y), where x is the longitude coordinate, and y latitude one. Each wireless resource can be assumed to cover at least a rectangular radio area. The object space, then, represents "geographic ranges", whose keys are distributed in a four dimensional Cartesian system. The first two dimensions represents the (low,high) range of the range x values, the two other dimensions represent the (low,high) range of y values. Now to generate a search, our roaming application defines a series of squares concatenated to cover a given path (i.e. a street and its surroundings). To define a search range is to first choose the path, draw squares along it, and find out the coordinate range of each square. Let us assume the first square on the path has x_1, x_2, y_1, y_2 coordinates, where $x_1 < x_2$ and $y_1 < y_2$. Looking closer at the DHT object space, but taking just the longitude coordinates, Figure 3 shows the range (x_1, x_2) indicating a single object (or point) on the two dimensions needed to describe longitudes. If we query that range then it is up to the peer owning the zone 1, to generate a response.

Similar filtering capabilities at the AccessPeer are assumed in the CAN system as those in Chord. For load balancing, however, the zones are sized depending on the number of objects in it to match the peers' heterogeneous capabilities.

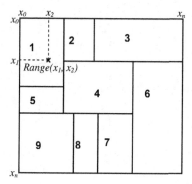

Fig. 3. Location Range Queries Based on CAN: A Single Dimension for Longitude Ranges

3 Location Aware Terminal Handover

Having explained the P2P architecture for storing location-based wireless resources, we move on to the mobile terminal side, where location awareness is first used to define the queries, but also to select technology for a handover. The actual way the handover occurs still relies on the mechanisms used for each technology, but we aim at dealing at least with an all-IP-world relying, here, on Mobile IPv6 [20]. A thorough analysis of mobile IP variations has been carried out recently [2], [29], and [14]. In our studied scenario we use a small mobile network[3], which should be distinguished from using a mobile router that supports the network mobility protocol (NEMO) [8]. Furthermore, any of the IP micro-mobility protocols could apply in this case.

A movement-aware handover application is implemented. The application is able to track the movement of a vehicle, generates a search for appropriate resources, and manages the handover based on the approaching access point. Figure 4 depicts how the application modules are designed to interact with each other and with the underlying protocols. Due to lack of space, a summarized implementation of the proposed architecture is presented. A proof of concept is aimed here via the development of a prototype system that uses a navigation-based system to generate both search requests and also to decide on the terminal handover procedure.

The simulation model generates some simple searches and retrievals, while focusing on implementing in details the handover procedure adapted to the chosen link and network layers. After the driver of the vehicle entered the desired destination into the navigation system it will start calculating a route accordingly. Then, the navigation tracks the movement of the vehicle and correlates it with the calculated route. The MN can foresee the future movement making it possible to choose the next AP.

---

[3] We define a small mobile network to be a network of mobile terminal sharing the same mobility context, e.g. a group of portable devices (phone, PDA, laptops, a vehicle's computer system) attempting to access the Internet during a Bus ride.

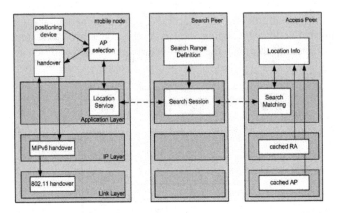

Fig. 4. Terminal Handover Management

The positioning module resembles that of a navigation system, the movement is tracked along a path on a map (e.g. a unidirectional movement along a concatenation of few streets) based on a current location, speed and direction of the MN. This module also detects path changes. The search is emulated using a ***Search Peer*** module. Matching our range query with its multiple attributes, a list of APs is returned with two key pieces of information: AP related location and technology (frequency used at the AP), and IP-layer related information based on a router advertisement (RA) of the access router (AR) to which the AP is attached to. This RA is cached automatically as part of the stored description of a given AP. Further processing at the peers could reduce the number of possible answers by only providing aggregated APs matching more complex preferences or priorities. This is however out of the scope of this work. The current implementation in the simulation model places the returned APs on a map and makes a location-only based handover, since the APs are of the same technology. A sequence of neighboring APs are selected using Voronoi graphs.This decision is being extended to take into account the application class and its requirements. Based on this information, a handover decision among heterogeneous WMN is made depending on several objectives that need to be optimized [4], including the minimum interruption time, QoS utility function, price, etc.

4   Simulation Results

To analyze how a location aided handover performs under OMNeT++ [30] in comparison to standard MIPv6, different test-beds have been setup implementing the application interactions discussed in Section 3. This implemented model demonstrates the effect of improved movement detection on the overall terminal delay handover. Some simplifications are made to extract that specific effect from the whole handover procedure at both the link and network layers.

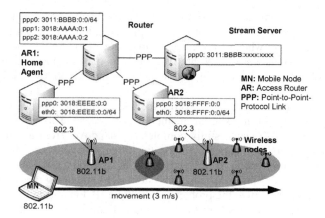

Fig. 5. Simulation Topology Layout

4.1 Simulation Assumptions

In order to isolate the effect of movement detection, the simulation model is based on a simple topology - shown in Figure 5-. This simple topology should optimize the triangulation effects and routing of mobile IPv6. It also minimizes the binding phase of MIPv6. Terminal mobility is of most interest here rather than route switching. IPv6 modifications that focused on improving binding updates delays, concentrated mostly on reducing the number of hops to the home agent. Some approaches introduced hierarchical proxies to the home agent closer to the access networks. These proxies only update the remote corresponding nodes and home agent once the MN changes such an attachment point. This is in fact a summary of how HMIPv6 presents a solution to micro-mobility at the IP layer [2].

In this simulation model, OMNeT++ implementation of MIPv6 is first used unchanged [30]. Although the authors of IPv6Suite [31] claim to have a complete implementation of the MIPv6 RFC, it turned out that layer2 triggers, defined theoretically to trigger movement, were not running well enough to conduct constructive measurements, under OMNeT++. The other way to detect movement defined by MIPv6 [20] is a special router interval option (RIO) that is part of every RA. With the RIO the MN awaits the next RA and detects movement through the missing of an expected RA. Each IPv6 neighbors (nodes and routers) keep a reachability state of each other. Once movement is detected, this state is turned to zero, removing nodes from the routing tables for instance.

Also part of the simulation model [31] is a rather realistic implementation of the IEEE802.11b standard, except its theoretical association phase (or AAA). This is kept very simple. However one could argue that this can easily be handled by the DHT framework [9]. The users of the framework would have priorly signed in to the wireless management services in order to search for wireless resources, therefore obtaining the ESS ID and AAA details in advance.

In fact, the theoretical analysis of handover delay in 802.11 is carried out to a certain extent in several other papers [17],[7],[3],[29],[32]. It is well-known result that the movement detection and the search phases at the link layer take up to 90 % of the handover delay [7], compared to a short AAA phase. The movement detection delays, however, vary depending on the hardware implementation. In the simulation model movement is detected whenever the signal to noise ratio (SNR), measured at the physical layer of the MN's WLAN interface card, decreases below a given threshold. Right then, a long probing phase of each of the 13 channels follows, searching for a new AP.

New proposals such as IEEE 802.11i use the historic build-up of neighbor cells and caching that information in a similar manner to ARP cache. This information is first gathered from MNs that successfully completed a handover from a cell to the next, building a map of neighboring cells. A MN attaching to the network could receive this cell map and therefore restrict the probing to those expected cells. This approach may work perfectly within a single distribution system (DS) managing an extended service set (ESS), but it cannot solve the problem of multiple IP domains or frequent network changes. In this paper, the used approach aims at a more heterogeneous environment, where the mobile node could select one of many "access points" that belong to different technologies. The movement detection is done independently of the underlying technology, making the choice of the next AP a matter of application and movement context.

In the simulation model, the movement-aware trigger at the link layer specifies the frequency channel which the expected AP uses. This information is entered in the XML template describing the AP. Movement awareness is also used to indicate when to start the probing phase. On the routing side, the movement aware software entities, at the terminal, gather enough information about their "expected network" during the querying of the DHT framework. The handover trigger takes the form of a router advertisement fed directly into the neighbor reachability state machine. This avoids a normally lengthy movement detection mechanism, while reducing the complexity of the neighbor reachibility state machine. The terminal sends a RA of the old AR with a lifetime set to zero to its own Neighbor Discovery (ND) module [19] to clear the entry in the neighbor cache. Right after, the MN sends the new AR's cached advertisement to its own ND module to complete handover.

4.2 Chosen Scenario Description

As shown in Figure 5, three Ethernet-based subnets are connected using three routers. One access router is assumed to be the home agent (AR1), while the second is a visited one (AR2). The two subnets include, each, an IEEE 802.11b access point. The third router connects the two access routers and a server via point-to-point protocol links (PPP). The PPP links offer a data rate of 10 MBits/sec, Ethernet 100 MBits/sec, and 802.11b with 11 MBits/sec. The MN, initially attached to AP1, is assigned an IP address (by AR1) using Automatic IP; the server on the other hand has a static address assigned. The average RA interval of all routers is set to 1.25sec (MinRAIntervall = 1sec, MaxRAIntervall = 1.5sec).

The server has two applications running: a ping6 and a UDP server. The ping6 application is configured to auto reply to any incoming ping requests. On the other hand the UDP server is streaming one 600bytes UDP datagram every 0.005sec up to 0.01sec. This results into an average data rate of 640kBits/sec, which could be a comparable rate to receiving a live video on a PDA screen for instance.

The experiment is conducted with a mobile node (MN) traveling at a speed of 3m/sec (about 10 km/hr for longer measurement time)[4] starting from an initial position with coordinates [88,247]. The two APs were positioned at [147,247][5] and [194,247], respectively. Both APs have a radio propagation radius of about 85m. The MN, at the start-up conditions, is connected exclusively to the first AP. Every setup was simulated 200 times with different random seeds to gather statistically significant data. In the Location-aided case, the MN triggers handover based on its movement and position knowledge at the position [150,247], whereas in the standard handover the MN would loose connectivity to the old AP at a position near [234,247].

In order to allow fine grained measurements of delays while handing over some measurement points (shown in Table 1) are used.

Table 1. Overview of the measuring points

Threshold too low	**802.11:** time of loss of connection to old AP
Restart active scan	**802.11:** time of restarting scan
Probe channel	**802.11:** time to probe one channel
Star of Authentication	**802.11:** start of AAA
Layer2 Trigger	**802.11:** end of 802.11 handover
New RA	**MIPv6:** time to receive new RA from new AR
movement detected	**MIPv6:** time of movement detection
start BU	**MIPv6:** beginning of binding update
handover complete	**MIPv6:** first ping after handover completion

The simulation returns the instance in time at which each event occurred during each run.

4.3 Obtained Simulation Results

Figure 6 records the sequence of the measured event instances for the two types of handover as they both progress in time (from Table 1). The graphs in Figure 6 is taken from one of the simulation runs plotting on two parallel lines the event instance for the two scenarios, i.e., location-aided (shown as *"improved"* on the upper timeline), and standard IEEE 802.11 handover followed by MIPv6 handover according [31] (shown as *"standard"* on the lower timeline).

It can clearly be seen in Figure 6 that the handover latency is brought down from 1850msec to only 125msec using the location triggers at both layers. In the standard case, probing all 802.11 channels, then inserting a new router advertisement, and detecting movement engulf a considerable portion of the overall delay, as expected. Another important result is considerably reduced number of handshakes and probing events, in the improved handover case.

The next graphics looks closer again into the standard handovers to evaluate the level of accuracy of the chosen model. Taking the results of the 200 simulation runs, distributions of the separate event relating to movement detection are given in Figure 7. These events are given in Table 1.

---

[4] The topology was too small for standard triggers to deal with speeds higher than 100km/hr.

[5] OMNET++ coordinates are in meters. The movement coordinates and speed are defined in the model.

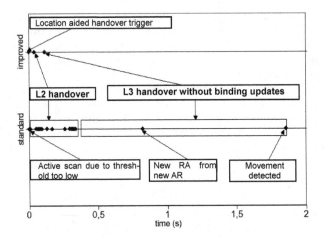

Fig. 6. Time line of events for standard MIPv6 and location aided handover - L2 stands for handover event sequence at the link layer. L3 handover refers to the measured MIPv6 events required during the handover procedure.

As expected, the search phase for a new AP based on the blind triggers used in the model lead to the largest part of delay with an average 350msec required for that phase. The Authentication, Authorization and Accounting (AAA) delay is far below the real values [7]. This can be traced back to the rather rudimentary AAA implementation in the IPv6Suite [31]. Assuming the AAA was still needed, it could be shown through practical measurements [7] that the dominant factor during the handover procedure would still be the search for a new AP.

Now taking a look at the MIPv6 delays, the first thing that comes to one's eye is a rather large delay to detect movement and receiving a new RA from the new AR and a rather small delay for completing binding update (remembering the simple topology chosen for this purpose). This confirms our expectations, but it is worth noting that having used the model's 1.25sec RA interval, the movement is detected quite slowly. If the MN receives a RA right after completing the handover at the link layer, the IPv6 could complete right away. This effect is seen in scenario 3 in Figure 8.

This figure shows the impact of 802.11 location-aided handover and the improvements of MIPv6 handover separately. It compares four scenarios, where each of the link and network layer triggers are switched "on" and "off" interchangeably.

The final delay distribution plotted in Figure 8, adds up all intermediate latencies. It is taken to be the moment at which the communication with the CN is resumed. This moment occurs at the "handover complete" event given in Table 1. For this purpose frequent Ping messages were sent from the MN to the CN (server) to simulate a highly interactive application.

Analyzing the obtained delay distributions, first, it can be seen that only the combination of both location-aware triggers can improve the handover significantly. The second observable deficiency of the chosen model is shown when *"MIPv6 off"*. The delay and variance increase dramatically. This could be all attributed to the rather infrequent router advertisements applied for those scenarios (a RA every 1.25 sec as specified in [31]). This effect is nonetheless totally removed once looking at scenarios (1) and (2), where the *"MIPv6 on"* trigger is used. A more detailed analysis of the different effects such as increasing the RA frequency to 0.05sec is given in [11]. It is however worth noting that the power cost of receiving very frequent RAs at the MN is quite high. Some other aspects of the scenarios are further discussed in [11] such as the effect of using multiple mobile nodes in the visited network, or the final effect of speed of the mobile nodes. This is done with speeds reaching more than 100Km/hr, where the movement-aware triggers immensely improved the connectivity and interruption delays.

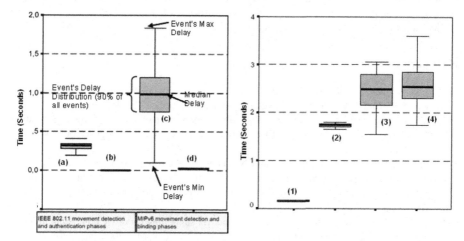

Fig. 7. Delay distributions of major handover events at link and network layer with no location-aware triggers: (**a**): Access point (AP) search phase, (**b**): AAA phase at link layer, (**c**): MIPv6 movement detection phase from reception of new RA till terminal mobility completion, (**d**): Routing update and mobility binding phase

Fig. 8. Comparison of the cumulative handover latencies for the different scenarios: "*on*" refers to the enabled location aware triggers at the Link or Network layers: "*off*" refers to disabling the triggers: (**1**) 802.11 *on* – MIPv6 *on*: (**2**) 802.11 *off* – MIPv6 *on*: (**3**) 802.11 *on* – MIPv6 *off*: (**4**) 802.11 *off* – MIPv6 *off*

5   Conclusions and Future Work

This paper advocates using a novel P2P location-based service to organize heterogeneous wireless mesh networks topology organization and discovery. The decision to use DHTs, however, requires that the object space identification and distribution be fitted, accordingly, to the DHT interface used. The design decision was made to organize objects as geographically collocated access networks of the same technology and belonging to the same operator. In Chord some extensive modifications are needed to cater for location-centric storage of resources. A less randomizing "hash" function is used, while the object space is organized geographically. Mobility of part of the peers and the disparity of the peers' storage capabilities have also been catered for by the modified Chord implementation. CAN, on the other hand, requires less efforts or modifications, while being more suitable, in its original version, than Chord to deal with range queries. Furthermore it was seen that the way to make use of the location-based stored resources, depends greatly on the terminal's pervasive capabilities. A scenario demonstrating the feasibility of such a system has been presented. It allows mobile devices to use navigation facilities on board of a transportation vehicle to learn about their location-context. An application running on the mobile terminals accesses the P2P system, locates the wireless resources along a planned itinerary, and triggers handover at the lower layers. The simulated improvements in an IPv6 and IEEE 802.11b environment have cut the interruption time of communication, due to handover, by more than 10 times to a mere 170msec (suitable for real-time applications). Using other methods to learn about the location of a terminal is planned for further research. Currently adding other context information, besides location, is seen as an essential extension to the system. A multitude of goals need to be optimized while deciding on the next wireless access point in heterogeneous conditions.

References

[1] I. F. Akyildiz, X. Wang, W. Wang. Wireless mesh networks: a survey. Computer Networks Journal, Elsevier, Vol.47. No. 4. March 2005, pages: 445 - 487.

[2] I. F. Akyldiz, J. Xie, S. Mohanty. A survey of mobility management in next generation all-IP based wireless systems. IEEE Wireless Communications, august 2004, Vol. 11, No. 4, pages 16- 28.

[3] F. K. Al-Bin-Ali, P. Boddupalli, and N. Davies. An inter-access point handoff mechanism for wireless network management: The sabino system, Proc. of the International Conference on Wireless Networks, ICWN '03, June 23 - 26, 2003, Las Vegas, Nevada, USA, pages: 225-230

[4] S. Balasubramaniam, J. Indulska. Vertical handover supporting pervasive computing in future wireless networks. Computer Communications, Vol. 27, No. 8, May 2004, pages 708-719.

[5] A. Bar-Noy et al. Mobile users: To update or not to update?. Wireless Networks, Vol. 1, No 2, July 1995, pages 175-186.

[6] G. Chen and D. Kotz. A Survey of Context-Aware Mobile Computing Research, Dartmouth Computer Science Technical Report TR2000-831, Dartmouth College US. 2000.

[7] T. Cornall, B. Pentland, and P. Khee. Improved handover performance in wireless Mobile IPv6. The 8th International Conference on Communication Systems, Vol. 2, 25-28 November 2002, pages 857–861.

[8] V. Devarapalli, R. Wakikawa, A. Petrescu and P. Thubert. Network Mobility (NEMO) Basic Support Protocol, RFC3963. IETF. January 2005.

[9] E. C. Efstathiou and G. C. Polyzos. A Peer-to-Peer Approach to Wireless LAN Roaming. Proc. of the 1st ACM International Workshop on Wireless Mobile Applications and Services on WLAN Hotspots, WMASH 2003, San Diego, CA, USA, September 19, 2003. ACM 2003, pages:10-18

[10] M. Egen, S. Coleri, B. Dundar, J. Rahul, A. Puri, P. Varaiya. Application of GPS to mobile IP and routing in wireless networks. Vehicular Technology Conference, Vancouver, Canada, 24-28 September 2002, Proc. IEEE 56th, Vol. 2 , pages 1115-1119.

[11] M. Graf Esterhazy. Location Aided Handover in MIPv6. Diploma Thesis (Equivalent to Masters) at University of Passau, May 23, 2005.

[12] E. Gustafsson, A. Johnson. Always Best Connected. IEEE Wireless Communications, Vol. 10, No.1. February 2003, pages 49-55.

[13] M. Harren, J. M. Hellerstein, R. Huebsch, B. T. Loo, S. Shenker, I. Stoica. Complex Queries in DHT-based Peer-to-Peer Networks. Peer-to-Peer Systems: First International Workshop. Cambridge, MA, USA, IPTPS March 2002, Springer-Verlag, Vol. 2429 / 2002, pages 242 – 250.

[14] R. Hsieh, Z.-G. Zhou, and A. Seneviratne. S-MIP: A seamless handoff architecture for Mobile IP. IEEE INFOCOM 2003 - The Conference on Computer Communications, March, 7-8, 2003, Vol. 22, No. 1, Pages 1774 - 1784.

[15] B. Lane. Cognitive radio technologies in the commercial arena. FCC Workshop on Cognitive Radios, 19 May 2003.

[16] M. McHenry. Frequency Agile Spectrum Access Technologies. FCC Workshop on Cognitive Radios, 19 May 2003.

[17] A. Mishra, M. Shin, and W. Arbaugh. An empirical analysis of the IEEE 802.11 MAC layer handoff process, April 2003.

[18] J. Mitola III. Software Radio Architecture: Object- Oriented Approaches to Wireless System Engineering. Wiley Inter-Science, New York, 2000.

[19] T. Narten, E. Nordmark, W. Simpson. Neighbor Discovery for IP Version 6. RFC2461, IETF (1998).

[20] C. Perkins, D. Johnson, J. Arkko. Mobility support in IPv6. IETF Internet Draft. (2003).

[21] J. Powers. Configuring Wireless LANs to Meet DOD Security Requirements. Capstone paper part of a Masters Thesis at University of Colorado (2003).

[22] S. Ratnasamy, P. Francis, M. Handley, R. Karp, and S. Shenker. A scalable content addressable network. In Proc. 2001 ACM SIGCOMM Conference, Berkeley, USA, August 2001.

[23] A. Roos, M. Hartman, and M. S. Lee. "Critical issues for roaming in 3G", IEEE Wireless Communications, Vol. 10, No.1, pages 29-35. February 2003.

[24] O. D. Sahin, A. Gupta, D. Agrawal, A. El Abbadi. Query Processing Over Peer-to-Peer Data Sharing Systems. Technical Report UCSB/CSD-2002-28, University of California at Santa Barbara, 2002.

[25] J. Schiller and A. Voisard. Location-Based Services. Morgen Kaufmann/Elsevier, San Fransisco, CA, USA, 2004, ISBN: 1-55869-929-6.

[26] M. Scholl, M. Thielliez, A. Voisard. Location-based Mobile Querying in Peer-to-Peer Networks. In OTM 2005 Workshop on Context-Aware Mobile Systems, Springer Verlag, November 2005

[27] K. Sethom, H. Afifi, G. Pujolle. Palma: A P2P based Architecture for Location Management. The 7th IFIP International Conference on Mobile and Wireless Communications Networks (MWCN 2005), Marrakech, Morocco, 2005, September 19-21.

[28] I. Stoica, R.Morris, D.Karger, M.Kaashoek, and H. Balakrishnan. Chord: A scalable peer-to-peer lookup service for Internet applications. In Proc. 2001 ACM SIGCOMM Conference, August 27-31, 2001, San Diego, CA, USA, pages 149-160.

[29] N. Van den Wijngaert, C. Blondia. A Location Augmented Low Latency Handoff Scheme for Mobile IP. Proc. of the 1st Conference on Mobile Computing and Ubiquitous Networking (ICMU04), Yokosuka, Japan, January 2004, pages 180-185.

[30] A. Varga. The OMNeT++ discrete event simulation system. Proc. of theEuropean Simulation Multiconference (ESM'2001), Prague, Czech Republic, June 6-9, 2001

[31] A. Varga, A. Sekercioglu, J. Lai, E. Wu and G. Egan. A simulation suite for accurate modeling of IPv6 protocols. Proceedings of the 2nd international OMNeT++ Workshop, Vol. 2, pages 2–12, 2002.

[32] H. Velayos and G. Karlsson. Techniques to reduce IEEE 802.11b MAC layer handover time. 2003.

[33] F. Yu and V. Leung. Mobility-based predictive call admission control and bandwidth reservation in wireless cellular networks. Comp. Networks, Vol. 38, No. 5, 2002, pages 577-589.

The Throughput Utility Function: Assessing Network Impact on Mobile Services

Markus Fiedler[1], Kurt Tutschku[2], Stefan Chevul[1],
Lennart Isaksson[1], and Andreas Binzenhöfer[2]

[1] Dept. of Telecommunication Systems,
School of Engineering, Blekinge Institute of Technology,
371 79 Karlskrona, Sweden
{markus.fiedler, stefan.chevul, lennart.isaksson}@bth.se
[2] Dept. of Distributed Systems, Institute of Computer Science,
University of Würzburg, Am Hubland, 97074 Würzburg, Germany
{tutschku, binzenhoefer}@informatik.uni-wuerzburg.de

Abstract. Based on the need for distributed end-to-end quality management for next-generation mobile Internet services, this paper presents a ready-to-deploy quality assessment concept for the impact of the network on the performance of mobile services. We consider the Throughput Utility Function (TUF) as a special case of the Network Utility Function (NUF). These functions combine the observed network utility at the inlet and the outlet of a mobile network. NUF and TUF capture the damping effect of the network onto user-perceived quality from an end-to-end perspective. As opposed to sometimes hard-to-evaluate QoS parameters such as delay and loss, the NUF is highly intuitive due to its mapping to a simple value between 0 and 100 %, which reflects user perception. We demonstrate the capabilities of the proposed TUF by measurements of application-perceived throughput conducted in a mobile, i.e. GPRS and UMTS network.

1 Introduction

The success of Internet results largely from the *end-to-end (E2E) concept* [1]. Among other benefits, the E2E concept empowers the end-hosts to adapt their data flow autonomously to varying load conditions. By the concept, however, the adaptation is decoupled from the network control. Hence, the network and in particular the network operator is not anymore aware about the requirements of the end-hosts, e.g. their desired throughput. As a result, network management can not address the specific application needs and might disappoint the user.

IP-based *mobile services*, such as mobile streaming, mobile gaming, or mobile file sharing, emerge rapidly due to the advent of highly capable user equipment and increased wireless link capacities. As well as in wireline networks, mobile services need sufficient end-to-end network performance in order to met the users' *Quality of Service (QoS)* needs. In mobile networks, however, QoS is typically achieved by network-centric mechanisms, such as *Radio Access Bearer Service*

M. Cesana, L. Fratta (Eds.): Wireless Syst./Network Architect. 2005, LNCS 3883, pp. 242–254, 2006.

or *CN Bearer Service* in UMTS, [2], or highly influenced by the interconnecting networks. In this way, a gap arises for arbitrary applications between the *user-perceived QoS* and the *network-provided QoS*. In particular, applications which are not designed for signaling their QoS needs or applications which are relayed via non-QoS capable interconnection networks are disadvantaged in obtaining QoS. Unfortunately, this is true for the majority of today's IP-based applications.

As a result, mechanisms are needed which assess the user-perceived QoS between two end hosts for arbitrary application and networks. The concept of a *Network Utility Function (NUF)* [3] constitutes such an approach. Originally, *utility functions* [4] relate the state of applications and networks with the user satisfaction. They are used for rate control and resource allocation [5, 6]. The NUF, used in this work, complements the original concept. It characterizes the change of the utility of the network for a single flow caused by the network behavior, e.g. introduction of (varying) delay and loss or reduction of throughput between two end-hosts. Such a degradation, which may for instance be due to volatile radio conditions, limited capacities or congestion, will be denoted as *damping* in this work. The utility is measured between two end-hosts. It characterizes the quality of a network connectivity with a mapping onto a scale from 0 to 100 %. Thus, the network performance is easy to understand and valuate even for an unexperienced user, which is not necessarily the case for traditional QoS parameters such as delay, delay jitter or loss.

A key characteristic for the utility of a connection is the *perceived E2E throughput*. The perceived throughput is a speed-related parameter [7] and is important both for streaming applications as well as for elastic applications [8]. Throughput difference measurements have turned out to be easy to implement and highly robust since they are based on passive measurements and do not need synchronized clocks [9]. They can easily characterize the change of the perceived throughput between end-hosts. The *Throughput Utility Function (TUF)* makes use of the advantages of throughput difference measurements. It is investigated in this work for mobile services in GPRS and UMTS networks. In [10], we describe a *decentralized QoS monitoring* approach in which the TUF will be embedded.

The remainder of this paper is organized as follows. Section 2 presents the utility-function-based NUF/TUF concept. Section 3 discusses the environment in which the TUF will be investigated. Section 4 develops the TUF for user-perceived throughput in mobile networks, and Section 5 presents a measurement-based case study for UMTS and GPRS. Finally, Section 6 provides conclusions and outlook.

2   The Concept of the Network Utility Function (NUF)

Utility functions are a mathematical tool that is typically used to model the relative preferences of players or bidders in games or auctions. Utility functions reflect the ordering of user preferences regarding the various outcomes of the game by assigning a simple numerical value to each outcome [11]. Utility

functions are efficiently applied in network optimization, e.g. [4, 5, 6], where individual improvements for users on the throughput and the costs are indented.
The NUF concept extends the utility concept by characterizing the damping of
the quality and the usefulness of a service caused by the behavior of the network, including network stacks. The network utility is considered between two
end-hosts, e.g. a server and a service-consuming client.

Let U_{in} denote the value of the utility function at the sender, e.g. at a server
located at the inlet of the network, and let U_{out} describe the utility at the
receiver, i.e. at a client located at the outlet. The performance damping of the
network due to delay, delay jitter, loss or throughput changes is captured by the
network utility function U_{Netw} in an E2E view. U_{Netw} defines the relationship
between the utilities at the inlet and the outlet as:

$$U_{out} = U_{Netw} \cdot U_{in} . \tag{1}$$

The value range of U_{in}, U_{out} and U_{Netw} varies between 0 % in the worst case to
100 % in the best case. Compared to technical QoS parameters such as delay,
delay variation and loss, the network utility function is rather intuitive for users,
providers and operators [11]. In general, non-specialists cannot necessarily state
whether a one-way delay of, let's say, 200 ms represents a problem for a certain
application. However, using the NUF, they can rate the perceived service quality
on an easy-to-understand scale between 0 and 100 and define thresholds for
unacceptability [12].

Service providers and operators can use the utility values to take measures
against the network quality problems. For example, they can search for network
segments reporting bad conditions. In addition, they can reconfigure the service
or the network; or they can compensate affected users; or they can shut down
the service for maintenance. Percentage values are also highly appreciated as key
performance indicators in business processes, e.g. for demonstrating successful
of quality assurance in service provisioning [13].

The network utility function U_{Netw} reaches its best value of 100 % if no
network is present or if the network behaves perfectly. The later means that
the sent data streams are received instantaneously with no loss and unchanged
inter-packet times. In this case, the perception of the quality by the user is that
of the application alone, that means for Eqn. 1 that $U_{out} = U_{in}$. A lower value
of U_{Netw} indicates a disadvantageous change of traffic properties between the
corresponding endpoints. In the worst case, the perceived utility U_{out} reaches
zero, which can be related either to a very badly behaving network, i.e. $U_{Netw} \rightarrow$
0, or a very bad service quality already on the sender side, i.e. $U_{in} \rightarrow 0$, or a
combination of both.

The network utility function U_{Netw} should capture the network impact on
a service in such a way that it matches the changes in the user perception and
that the same rating applies for the sender and the receiver side. Moreover, the
network utility function can capture multiple effects which impact the service
quality. In case the influences are rather independent of each other, one can
define the network utility function U_{Netw} as a product of specific utility functions
$U_{Netw,i} \in [0, 1]$:

$$U_{\text{Netw}} = \prod_i U_{\text{Netw},i}.$$ (2)

For example, if the E2E throughput was considered as the utility of a connection, the U_{Netw} is denoted as *throughput utility function (TUF)*, which is the focus of this paper. In the case of a TUF, the specific utility functions $U_{\text{Netw},i}$ in Eqn. 2 can characterize the change of the throughput, introduced as *m-utility function* in Section 4, or the fluctuation of the throughput, i.e. the coefficient of throughput variation, denoted as *c-utility function*. The m-utility function captures the effect of loss and the c-utility function the effect of delay jitter. A NUF reflecting the impact of one-way delays could be defined as well, but this is a matter of future work.

3   Investigation of the Throughput Utility Function Concept in a Mobile Environment

The applicability of the TUF concept for IP data connections in mobile networks is evaluated by measurements of the perceived end-to-end throughput using a mobile link. Therefore, User Datagram Protocol (UDP) test traffic is sent with constant bit rate (CBR) from a server to a client process, cf. Fig. 1. In the measurements of the *downlink scenario*, cf. part (a) of Figure 1, the client is connected via a mobile link to a base station (BS) and the server is attached to the IP backbone via 100 Mbps Ethernet. In the *uplink scenario*, cf. part (b) of Figure 1, it is vice versa, i.e. the server is connected by a mobile link and the client is attached to the IP backbone with a 100 Mbps Ethernet line.

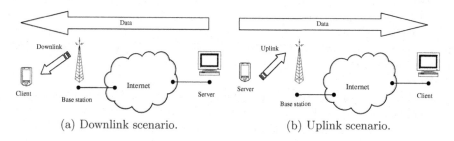

(a) Downlink scenario.   (b) Uplink scenario.

Fig. 1. Mobile scenarios

During the measurements, the server is trying to send UDP datagrams of constant length L_A as regularly as possible. Each datagram contains a sequence number for packet loss detection. In general, the datagrams are sent with a *inter-packet delay* $T_{I,A} > 0$, i.e. they are not sent back-to-back.[1] Hence, the *offered traffic on application level* is

$$o_A = \frac{L_A}{T_{I,A}}.$$ (3)

---

[1] A detailed description of the UDP traffic generator is provided in [14].

Considering UDP and IP overhead, the *offered traffic on link level* computes as

$$o_L = \frac{L_A + 28 \text{ Bytes}}{T_{I,A}} \tag{4}$$

and the *offered link load* to

$$A_L = \frac{o_L}{C_L}, \tag{5}$$

where C_L denotes the link capacity.

In GPRS networks, the link capacities amount $n \times 9.05$ kbps for Coding Scheme (CS) 1 and $n \times 13.4$ kbps for CS2, where n denotes the number of time slots allocated in up- or downstream direction. The number of allocated slots is typically different for up- and downlink and is upper-bounded by terminal limitations and operator settings. Moreover, the number of available slots can vary significantly in a cell depending on the number and priority of other ongoing telephone calls or data transmissions. Hence, the actual capacity of a GPRS link might deviate largely on short time scales and can not easily be predicted. A similar variability for the actual available throughput can be observed in UMTS networks. Nominally, the UMTS link capacities are determined by the codes used for channel discrimination in CDMA and have typical values of 64, 128 or 384 kbps. The available bandwidth, however, might change due to varying cell load and changing inter- and intra-cell interference.

As a result of the varying link capacity in GPRS and UMTS networks, the sender application does not know about the currently available capacity, i.e. the available bandwidth on a small time scale. Hence, if a sender application generates a packet stream with constant bit rate, the packets might temporally be blocked, the sender might pile up a backlog of datagrams. These are either sent with varying inter-packet time, introducing jitter, or they are dropped if a buffer overflow occurs, introducing packet loss. The "blocked sender" approach helps to discover the network behavior by simply looking at the traffic variations at the sender.

In case of the above mentioned *uplink scenario*, i.e. the server is connected by a mobile link, the UDP traffic generator tries to overcome a possible "blocked sender" state by transmitting packets with shorter inter-packet delay until the cumulative backlog is gone. However, if the offered traffic on link level exceeds the capacity of the uplink, i.e. $A_L > 100$ %, then the backlog becomes permanent. At first, the effective inter-packet delay exceeds the nominal value $T_{I,A}$, and the average throughput at the server side drops below the (nominally) offered traffic.

In the *downlink scenario*, where the server is connected by a 100 Mbps Ethernet link, a bottleneck at the inlet does not exist and the nominal inter-packet time $T_{I,A}$ can be maintained. A fraction of

$$\ell \simeq A_L - 1 \tag{6}$$

of the traffic will be lost inside the mobile network if the bit rate generated at the sender exceeds the capacity of the mobile link.

4   The Throughput Utility Function for Mobile Services

The adaptation of the NUF concept for the throughput in mobile networks will be described next. First, the parameters for characterizing the throughput utility will be introduced. After that, the components of throughput utility function in mobile environments will be outlined.

4.1   Parameters for Characterizing the Throughput Utility

The characterization of the throughput utility of an E2E connection is based on the concept of the *Throughput histogram Difference Plots (TDP)*, denoted the *bottleneck indicator* introduced in [9]. This concept builds upon the comparison of summary statistics of perceived throughput during an *observation interval* ΔW. Each throughput value denotes the average bit rate perceived during a small *averaging interval* ΔT, typically between 100 ms and 1 s.

In order to apply the concept, the packet streams for an E2E connection are transformed into *throughput time series* $\{R_{A,q}\}_{q=1}^{n}$ at the sender and at the receiver. Each time series contains $n = \Delta W / \Delta T$ throughput values:

$$R_{A,q} = \frac{\sum_{\forall p: T_p \in]T_0+(q-1)\Delta T, T_0+q\Delta T]} L_A}{\Delta T} \quad \text{for} \quad q \in \{1, \ldots, n\} \qquad (7)$$

T_p denotes the timestamp of a packet p obtained on application level. For the sender, this timestamp is the instant just before sending the packet. For the receiver, the timestamp is obtained at the instant just after receiving the packet. In this way, the time series capture the whole E2E behavior, in particular they include the behavior of the IP stacks of the sender and the receiver. T_0 is the start time of the time series at the sender respectively at the receiver. The start time is defined by the first packet in a stream both at sender and at receiver, i.e. the first packet triggers the start of the time series. This assumption is motivated by the fact that the receiving application begins to act upon reception of the first packet. The *average throughput* for the whole E2E connection is obtained as

$$m = \frac{1}{n} \sum_{q=1}^{n} R_{A,q}, \qquad (8)$$

and the *coefficient of throughput variation* for the E2E connection is

$$c = \sqrt{\frac{1}{n-1} \sum_{q=1}^{n} \left(\frac{R_{A,q}}{m} - 1 \right)^2} = \frac{s}{m}, \qquad (9)$$

where s denotes the *standard deviation* of the throughput. Eqn. 9 focuses on the relative variation as compared to the average throughput. The parameters m, s and c are obtained from the observed time series. All three parameters depend on the selection of the observation window ΔW. However, only c and s depend also on the averaging interval ΔT. The values of c and s become smaller as ΔT grows [14].

A condensed form of the *bottleneck indicator* consists of two parameters: the *average throughput* and the *coefficient of throughput variation*. Each of them are observed at the sender and at the receiver:

- sender parameters:
    1. the average throughput at the sender, i.e. the inlet to the network: m^{in};
    2. the coefficient of throughput variation at the sender: c^{in};
- receiver parameters:
    1. the average throughput at the receiver, i.e. the outlet of the network: m^{out};
    2. the coefficient of throughput variation at the receiver: c^{out}.

4.2 Components of the Throughput Utility Function in Mobile Environments

The aim of the throughput utility function is to capture the main influences of mobile networks and to map these influences to a single utility value, cf. Eqn. 1. The mapping is achieved by selecting an appropriate product of specific utility functions, cf. Eqn. 2. The specific utility functions have to be selected such that their parameters describe the change of utility due to problems encountered in mobile networks as accurately as possible. Typically, the following effects can be observed in mobile networks [14, 15, 16]:

1. Considerable data loss ($m^{out} < m^{in}$) either in the wireless or in the wireline part of the mobile network;
2. Exploding burstiness
    (a) at the receiver ($c^{out} \gg c^{in}$) especially when the offered traffic approaches the capacity of the mobile link ($A_L \to 1^-$). Such additional burstiness should reflect in reduced TUF values;
    (b) at the sender ($c^{in} \gg c^{out}$) in uplink scenarios when the mobile link is overloaded ($A_{Link} > 1$), which is followed by a strong shaping due to the limited capacity of the channel. As overload implies a mismatch between transportation needs and facilities, the TUF should signal this by displaying very small values.

On this background, we introduce the following utility functions:

1. The *m-utility function*

$$U_m = (1 - \ell)^{k_m},\tag{10}$$

where

$$\ell = \max\left\{1 - \frac{m^{out}}{m^{in}}, 0\right\}\tag{11}$$

denotes *loss* during observation interval ΔW, and k_m is a parameter governing the slope of utility reduction as ℓ increases. The shape of Eqn. 10 has been chosen such as to cushion considerably large loss if $k_m \gg 1$, which was not possible with the initial linear approach discussed in [3].

2. The *c-utility function*

$$U_c = \begin{cases} (\max\{1 - |\gamma|, 0\})^{k_c^-} & \text{for } \gamma < 0 \\ (\max\{1 - \gamma, 0\})^{k_c^+} & \text{for } \gamma \geq 0 \end{cases}, \tag{12}$$

where

$$\gamma = c^{\text{out}} - c^{\text{in}} \tag{13}$$

denotes the absolute change of the coefficient of variation seen from the viewpoint of the receiver. Depending on the sign of that change, we use different parameters to control the slope of U_c, which has the same basic shape as U_m:

(a) For $\gamma \geq 0$, i.e. $c^{\text{out}} \geq c^{\text{in}}$ equivalent to growing throughput variations, we apply the parameter k_c^+;

(b) For $\gamma < 0$, i.e. $c^{\text{out}} < c^{\text{in}}$ equivalent to sinking throughput variations, we apply the parameter k_c^-.

The next section will exemplify the impact of these functions on the TUF $U_{\text{Netw}} = U_m \cdot U_c$.

5 Case Study

We present the results of a measurement study carried out in a real UMTS/ GPRS network using the same hardware and software in both cases. We apply one observation interval of $\Delta W = 1$ min and an averaging interval of $\Delta T = 1$ s.[2] The packet length in the UMTS case was $L_{A,\text{UMTS}} = 480$ Bytes and in the GPRS case $L_{A,\text{GPRS}} = 128$ Bytes. We chose the following TUF parameters:

1. For the m-tuility function, $k_m = 10$ in order to make the m-utility function decrease very rapidly as a function of rising loss;
2. For the c-utility function,
   (a) $k_c^+ = 1$ in order to capture additional throughput variations introduced by the mobile network;
   (b) $k_c^- = 2$ in order to capture the overload case implying heavy throughput variations at the sender. As overload reduces the perceived utility dramatically, the decrease of the c-utility function needs to be amplified as compared to case (a), and therefore, $k_c^- > k_c^+$.

We start our investigations by looking at the downlink case.

5.1 UMTS Downlink

Fig. 2 displays measured values of utility functions in a UMTS downlink scenario. As there is hardly any traffic lost, the m-utility function U_m is close to the

---

[2] Beyond these "snapshots", investigations of the dynamics of the throughput process and thus of the TUF values, by considering different observation intervals are matters of future work. A temporal variation of TUF values might for instance be caused by volatile radio conditions – temporarily bad signal-to-noise ratios are most likely to tear down TUF values due to loss and increased throughput variations – or by resource competition between different traffic streams in a bottleneck [9].

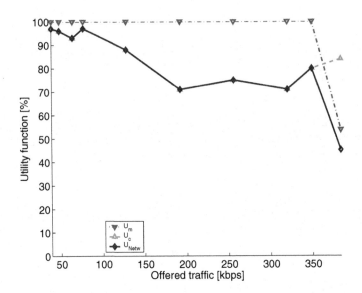

Fig. 2. Utility functions U_{Netw}, U_m and U_c versus offered traffic o_A in the UMTS downlink case

optimal value of 100 %. Thus, the TUF U_{Netw} is mainly governed by the c-utility function U_c. We furthermore observe a trend that the traffic variations at the receiver grow as the offered traffic o_A increases, which is reflected in decreasing values of U_c.

One particular case deserves some extra attention. Offered traffic on application level $o_A = 384$ kbps implies offered traffic on link level $o_L = 407$ kbps, which exceeds the link capacity $C_L = 384$ kbps. The offered link load (5) amounts to 106 %, implying 6 % loss (6). This damps U_m and thus U_{Netw} in a considerable way.

5.2   GPRS Downlink

Fig. 3 shows measured values of utility functions in a GPRS downlink scenario. We observe that in come cases, both m- and c-utility functions are low, which indicates considerable loss and growth in variations. As compared to the offered traffic, no real trend can be seen, which is due to extremely volatile conditions in the GPRS network. Detailed studies of the throughput process reveal periods of complete data loss during the observation window ΔW [14]. Consequently, the TUF values are low to very low.

5.3   UMTS Uplink

We now turn our focus to the UMTS uplink case, for which the results are displayed in Fig. 4. As long as the offered traffic is below the critical level of 59 kbps

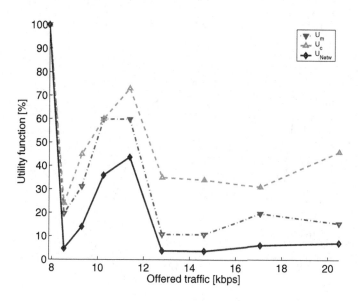

Fig. 3. Utility functions U_{Netw}, U_m and U_c versus offered traffic o_A in the GPRS downlink case

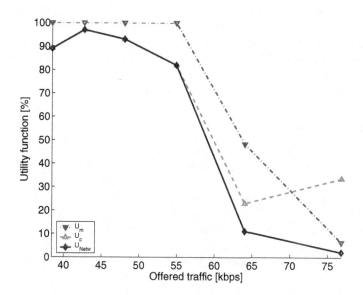

Fig. 4. Utility functions versus U_{Netw}, U_m and U_c versus offered traffic o_A in the UMTS uplink case

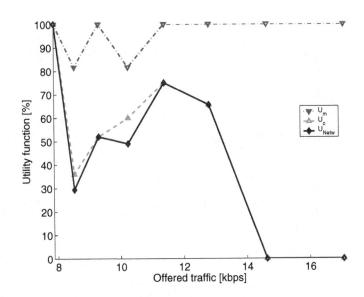

Fig. 5. Utility functions versus U_{Netw}, U_m and U_c versus offered traffic o_A in the GPRS uplink case

for which the link load reaches 100 %, the m-utility function signals no loss. Thus, the TUF is governed by the c-utility function. The later signals rather small problems due to variations with a rising tendency as the critial load is approached.

However, for offered traffic $o_A > 59$ kbps, we face overload of the mobile link. We observe heavy throughput variations at the sender and considerable E2E data loss, reflected in low values of the corresponding utility functions.

5.4   GPRS Uplink

Our final investigation deals with the GPRS uplink, cf. Fig. 5. As the m-utility function is close to one despite in some cases with rather little loss, the c-utility function dominates the TUF. However, no real trend can be seen as again, we face quite volatile conditions in the GPRS channel (cf. Sect. 5.2). Interestingly enough, we observe perfect behavior ($U_{\text{Netw}} = U_m = U_c = 1$) in one of the measurements ($o_A \simeq 7.8$ kbps). Here, the GPRS network was able to deliver all packets in a regular fashion. On the other hand, we reach some kind of break-point for offered traffic of about 13 kbps. Here, the sender starts to jitter, which indicates overload. For $o_A > 13$ kbps, the corresponding throughput variations are so intense that the c-utility function and thus the TUF are torn down to zero.

6   Conclusions and Outlook

We have described and demonstrated a practicable concept for distributed end-to-end QoS monitoring and assessment on service level, the Network Utility

Function (NUF). The NUF relates utility functions at network inlet and outlet and thus captures the damping effect of the network onto user-perceived quality. We investigated a special NUF related to throughput changes imposed by mobile links, the Throughput Utility Function (TUF). The TUF captures changes of throughput averages due to lost traffic, and variations on rather short time scales caused by delay jitter and shaping. Based on measurements of application-perceived throughput via mobile networks (GPRS, UMTS), it was demonstrated that the utility functions proposed in this work are capable of valuating the utility impacts of typical performance problems in mobile networks. In general, this valuation behaves as expected. For instance, UMTS displays a better throughput performance in terms of less loss and variations as as compared to GPRS, which is known from practice. Also, overload is detected correctly in all cases.

Future work will address the adaptation of the TUF, its sub-functions and the corresponding parameters to the needs of specific services and related quantitative ratings by real users. A particularly interesting option is the possibility to determine threshold values regarding user acceptance of particular services. In case the value of the TUF drops below such a threshold, a QoS alarm should be issued. This can happen by sending notifications (e.g. SNMP traps) towards a Service or Network Management System. These notifications may then trigger countermeasures such as adapting the service or the allocation of network resources in order to improve the user perception. Further, the dynamic behaviour of the TUF e.g. due to volatile radio conditions such as hand-overs or traffic conditions such as cross traffic, and the impact of other traffic generation patterns or transport protocols (e.g. TCP) might be studied. And last but not least, the NUF concept might be studied for non-throughput-related parameters as well.

Acknowledgements

The authors would like to thank the Network of Excellence *EuroNGI* for sponsoring this work through the *AutoMon* project and the colleagues from the EuroNGI work package WP.JRA.6.1 *Quality of Service from the user's perspective and feed-back mechanisms for quality control* for valuable input and discussions.

References

1. Jerome H. Saltzer, David P. Reed, and David D. Clark. End-to-end arguments in system design. *ACM Transactions on Computer Systems*, 2(4):277–288, November 1984.
2. 3rd Generation Partnership Project. Technical Specification Group Services and System Aspects; Quality of Service (QoS) concept and architecture - TS 23.107 (Release 5). URL: ftp://ftp.3gpp.org/specs/latest/Rel-5/23_series/23107-5d0.zip.
3. M. Fiedler, S. Chevul, O. Radtke, K. Tutschku, and A. Binzenhöfer. The Network Utility Function: A practicable concept for assessing network impact on distributed systems. In *19th International Teletraffic Congress (ITC19)*, pages 1465–1474, Beijing, China, September 2005.

4. F. P . Kelly. Charging and rate control for elastic traffic (corrected version). *European Transactions on Telecommunications*, 8(1):33–37, Jan. 1997.

5. R. J. La and V. Anantharam. Utility-based rate control in the Internet for elastic traffic. *IEEE Transactions on Networking*, 10(2):272–285, April 2002.

6. M. Dramitinos, G. D. Stamoulis, and C. Courcoubetis. Auction-based resource allocation in UMTS High Speed Downlink Packet Access (HSDPA). In *Proceedings of the First EuroNGI Conference on Traffic Engineering (NGI 2005)*, Rome, Italy, April 2005.

7. ITU-T. Recommendation I.350: General aspects of quality of service and network performance in digital networks, including ISDNs. URL: http://www.itu.ch/.

8. J. Charzinski. Fun Factor Dimensioning for Elastic Traffic. In *Proceedings of the ITC Specialist Seminar on Internet Traffic Measurement, Modeling and Management, Sept. 18–20, Monterey, USA*, 2000.

9. M. Fiedler, K. Tutschku, P. Carlsson, and A.A. Nilsson. Identification of performance degradation in IP networks using throughput statistics. In J. Charzinski, R. Lehnert, and P. Tran Gia, editors, *Providing Quality of Service in Heterogeneous Environments. Proceedings of the 18th International Teletraffic Congress (ITC-18)*, pages 399–407, Berlin, Germany, September 2003.

10. A. Binzenhöfer, K. Tutschku, B. auf dem Graben, M. Fiedler, and P. Carlsson. A P2P-based framework for distributed network management. In *Proceedings of the Second EuroNGI Workshop on New Trends in Network Architectures and Services (WP IA 8.2)*, Loveno di Menaggio, Como, Italy, July 2005. Springer (LNCS).

11. M. Fiedler (ed.). EuroNGI Deliverable D.WP.JRA.6.1.1 – State-of-the-art with regards to user-perceived Quality of Service and quality feedback, May 2004. URL: http://www.eurongi.org/, http://www.ats.tek.bth.se/eurongi/dwpjra611.pdf.

12. H. Hlavacs, J. Lauterjung, G. Aschenbrenner, E. Hotop, and C. Trauner. QoS measurement. Deliverable D-3400, CODIS, November 2003. URL: http://www.ani.univie.ac.at/~hlavacs/.

13. T. Ingvaldsen, T. Jensen, H. Kjønsberg, H. Abrahamsen, and E. Smørdal. On key performance indicators for end-to-end performance in cellular networks. In *Proceedings of the Seventeenth Nordic Teletraffic Seminar (NTS 17)*, pages 37–48, Fornebu, Norway, August 2004.

14. M. Fiedler, L. Isaksson, S. Chevul, J. Karlsson, and P. Lindberg. Measurement and analysis of application-perceived throughput via mobile links. The Olga Casals Lecture at HET-NETs 05. In *Proceedings of HET-NETs'05*, Ilkley, UK, July 2005.

15. S. Chevul, J. Karlsson, L. Isaksson, M. Fiedler, P. Lindberg, and L. Strandén. Measurements of application-perceived throughput in DAB, GPRS, UMTS and WLAN environments. In *Proceedings of RVK'05*, Linköping, Sweden, June 2005.

16. L. Isaksson, S. Chevul, M. Fiedler, J. Karlsson, and P. Lindberg. Application-perceived throughput process in wireless systems. In *Proceedings of ICMCS'05*, Montreal, Canada, August 2005.

Measurement of Application-Perceived Throughput of an E2E VPN Connection Using a GPRS Network

Stefan Chevul[1], Lennart Isaksson[1], Markus Fiedler[1], and Peter Lindberg[2]

[1] Department of Telecommunication Systems, Blekinge Institute of Technology,
371 79 Karlskrona, Sweden
{stefan.chevul, lennart.isaksson, markus.fiedler}@bth.se
[2] AerotechTelub AB, 351 80 Växjö, Sweden
peter.lindberg@aerotechtelub.se

Abstract. Based on the need for secure and reliable mobile communication, this paper investigates the application-perceived throughput of an end-to-end (E2E) VPN connection using IPSec over GPRS. GPRS is of particular interest regarding performance issues due to its wide deployment but limited capacity. To this end, different encryption and authentication algorithms are considered. The throughput is measured on small time scales and interpreted with aid of summary statistics, histograms and autocorrelation coefficients. The results reveal a clear influence of the network and the chosen security solution, seen from variations of application-perceived throughput on the one-second time scale, which has to be considered when assessing the appropriateness of network for a specific task. The different statistical metrics considered will later be used in our research to maintain the security and Quality of Service (QoS) of the service decided by the user.

1 Introduction

Internet has changed the way people and businesses operate. Communication from any Internet access point, including mobile networks such as General Packet Radio Service (GPRS) or Universal Mobile Telecommunications System (UMTS) has enabled organizations to have a mobile workforce. Ideally, employees on the move can access company resources just as easily as if they were sitting in the companies' office. However, mobile access services are using radio waves, thus they are considered to be subjected to a very hostile environment where security attacks such as masquerade, replay, modification of message contents *etc.* might occur even though precautions have been taken to encrypt the GPRS channel. Many organizations provide security for their mobile workforce, also known as road warriors, using Virtual Private Network (VPN) [4]. One of the major advantages of VPN is being a cost effective mechanism to secure communication between two endpoints. Multiple communication streams through a VPN connection are achievable. Web, email, file transfers, videoconferencing, streaming multimedia and any other traffic that uses TCP/IP for transport are secured by encryption.

M. Cesana, L. Fratta (Eds.): Wireless Syst./Network Architect. 2005, LNCS 3883, pp. 255–268, 2006.

Networked applications such as web, email, streaming multimedia *etc.* rely upon the ability of timely data delivery. The achievable throughput is a quality measure for the very task of a communication system, which is to transport data in time. Throughput is thus one of the most essential enablers for networked applications, if not the most important one. While in general, throughput is defined on network or transport level (*e.g.* for TCP), the *application-perceived throughput* that is investigated in this paper reflects the perspective of the application, *i.e.*, captures the behavior of all communication stacks in-between the endpoints. Streaming multimedia applications require some amount of throughput on a regular basis, for elastic applications or traffic such as file transfer, the achieved throughput determines download time. For situation-dependent services, *e.g.* for Intelligent Transport Systems and services (ITS), short response times are of outmost importance [2].

Looking at the Open System Interconnection (OSI) model, the conditions on layer n affect layer $n + 1$, $n + 2$ (*etc.*). In the end, the application (and thus the user) is affected by any kind of problem in the lower layers. For instance, traffic disturbances on network level are packet reordering, delays and loss. The latter can be compensated *e.g.* by retransmissions, which on the other hand increases the delay. Non-interactive applications usually cope well with (approximately) constant delays, even if those are comparably large. This is however not the case for interactive applications, where long delays disturb the interaction of both communication partners. End-to-end throughput variations reveal loss and delay variations, but not one-way delays [2, 3]; the latter can be measured on the network level as described in [1]. On the other hand, comparative throughput measurements on small time scales are capable of revealing existence, nature and severeness of a bottleneck [3]. Thus, the consideration of E2E delays is left for further study. Reference [2] discusses the concept of application-perceived throughput in detail.

In this paper, we advocate the mobile user's and its applications' view on throughput. As described in [2], security affects the user-perceived QoS through increased processing times and additional overhead. A VPN connection based on IP Security (IPSec) [5] in tunnelling mode adds at least 22 Bytes to each packet, which can be a considerable amount of overhead considering that GPRS has limited capacity. Also when short packets are used the overhead could become lager than the actual application payload. Our active measurements of application-perceived throughput values averaged over some short time interval (currently $\Delta T = 1$ s) during an observation window of duration $\Delta W = 60$ s reflect impairments that happen on OSI layers 1 to 7. We chose to avoid interfering traffic as far as possible in order to get a clear picture of the best-case throughput properties of the VPN enhanced GPRS mobile channel.

The remainder of the paper is organized as follows. The statistical parameters used to summarize and compare the perceived throughput processes at server (= sender) and client (= receiver) are presented in Section 2, and the measurement setup is described in Section 3. We then investigate the selected summary statistics of active measurements of application-perceived throughput for GPRS in Section 4, and Section 5 presents conclusions and outlook.

2   Application-Perceived Throughput Statistics

First, we take a look at how to construct the *throughput time series* or *throughput process* containing $n = \Delta W / \Delta T$ values. Let $\{T_p, L_p\}_{p=1}^k$ be a set of packets as sent by a server application or received by a client application (*cf.* Section 4). From this, we obtain the values of the throughput time series as

$$R_{A,s} = \frac{\sum_{\forall p : T_p \in](s-1)\Delta T, s\Delta T]} L_p}{\Delta T}. \tag{1}$$

The impact of the network is captured by the following summary statistics:

1. *Average application-perceived throughput:*

$$\bar{R}_A = \frac{1}{n} \sum_{s=1}^{n} R_{A,s}. \tag{2}$$

A change of this parameter between server and client reflects missing traffic at the end of the observation interval. That share of traffic might have been lost.

2. *Standard deviation of the application-perceived throughput:*

$$\sigma_{R_A} = \sqrt{\frac{1}{n-1} \sum_{s=1}^{n} \left(R_{A,s} - \bar{R}_A\right)^2}. \tag{3}$$

A rising (sinking) standard deviation reflects a growing (reduced) burstiness of the traffic between sender and receiver, while a sinking standard deviation means a reduction of burstiness. In the latter case, the throughput histogram becomes more narrow, which means that the traffic has been shaped.

3. *Application-perceived throughput histogram:*

$$h_{R_A}(i) = \frac{\text{number of } R_{A,s} \in](i-1)\Delta R, i\Delta R]}{n}. \tag{4}$$

If the throughput histogram at the receiver is broader than that at the sender, the burstiness has increased; otherwise, the traffic has been shaped [3]. Compared to standard deviation values, the throughput histograms contain more detailed information.

4. *Lag-j autocorrelation coefficient of the application-perceived throughput:*

$$\hat{\rho}_{R_A}(j) = \frac{\sum_{s=1}^{n-j}(R_{A,s} - \bar{R}_A)(R_{A,s+j} - \bar{R}_A)}{(n-j)\,\sigma_{R_A}^2}. \tag{5}$$

Changes of the autocorrelation coefficients reflect changes of the after-effect within the throughput process imposed by the network. Moreover, the autocorrelation coefficients allow to detect and compare periodicities within the throughput processes at the server's and client's side.

As GPRS allows only for a couple of packets to be sent or received per second, an averaging interval of $\Delta T = 1$ s was chosen. With an observation window of duration $\Delta W = 1$ min, the throughput time series to be analysed consist of $n = 60$ values.

3   Measurement Setup

For the measurements of application-perceived throughput, two scenarios were considered: the first is called the *downlink scenario* (*cf.* Fig. 1), in which the client is connected to a base station (BS) and the server to the Internet via 100 Mbps Ethernet. The second one is called the *uplink scenario* (Fig. 1), in which the server is connected to a BS and the client to the Internet via 100 Mbps Ethernet. These names are based on the way the data traffic is directed regarding BS. A Virtual Private Network connection based on IPSec in tunnel mode was configured between the server and the client. IPSec in tunnel mode is implemented by the Encapsulated Security Payload (ESP) header. The ESP provides confidentiality for the message content by encrypting and authenticating the entire original IP packet.

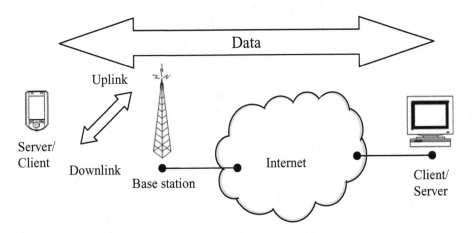

Fig. 1. Uplink and downlink scenario

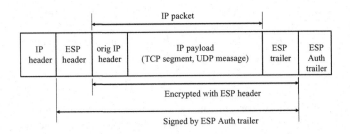

Fig. 2. IPSec ESP header

Fig. 2 shows an ESP packet and how the original IP packet size increased with at least 22 Bytes. In our measurements several encryption (3DES and DES) and authentication (SHA-1 and MD5) algorithms were tested. Microsoft Windows XP Professional Edition, which was used in our measurement, unfortunately did not support the Advanced Encryption Standard (AES) [8] algorithm.

The measurements are produced by using a User Datagram Protocol (UDP) generator. The generator is trying to send UDP datagrams of constant length as regularly as possible with a sequence number inside each datagram. The datagrams are not sent *back-to-back*, but spaced in order to yield a certain load. The minimal time the packets are spaced is hereafter called *inter-packet delay*. The software tries to keep this value as closely as possible. It was developed in *C#* running on both server and client, and these are producing and monitoring the datagram stream. The original *C#* time stamp resolution is limited to 10 milliseconds, which is not good enough for our purposes. Thus, specific coding was necessary to improve the time stamp resolution to one thousand of a millisecond. This was achieved by using *performance counters* in conjunction with the system time to provide smaller time increments. To this aim the `kernel32.dll` functions `QueryPerformanceCounter` and `QueryPerformanceFrequency` were used.

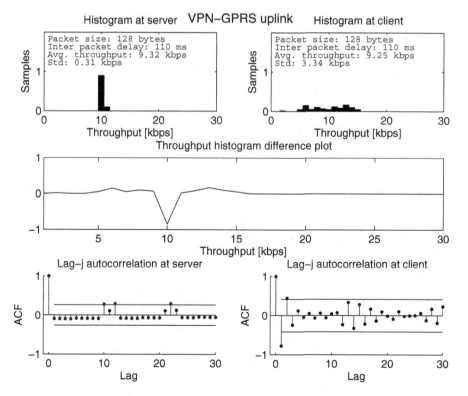

Fig. 3. VPN 3DES-SHA-1 GPRS uplink scenario, with 110 ms inter-packet delay

4   Measurements and Results

In the following, we present measurement results including throughput averages measured during $\Delta W = 60$ s on small time scales ($\Delta T = 1$ s)and interpreted with aid of summary statistics, histograms and autocorrelation coefficients. All autocorrelation plots include a confidence interval of approximately 95 % and present the throughput histograms with $\Delta R = 1$ kbps.

4.1   Uplink

The first case presented is an application-perceived throughput measurement of a VPN connection with Triple DES (3DES) [7] encryption and Secure Hash Algorithm 1 (SHA-1) [6] authentication algorithm on the uplink scenario. By choosing an *inter-packet delay* of 110 ms, the server transmission rate was set to 9.32 kbps, *cf.* Fig. 3 (top-left), which is matched by the measured averaged throughput. The client received the datagrams in a scattered stream with throughputs of 1 to 15 kbps. The average throughput measured at the client amounts to 9.25 kbps. The standard deviation grew from 0.31 kbps to 3.34 kbps. We observe a shared bottleneck in the throughput histogram difference plot, *cf.* Fig. 3 (middle). The

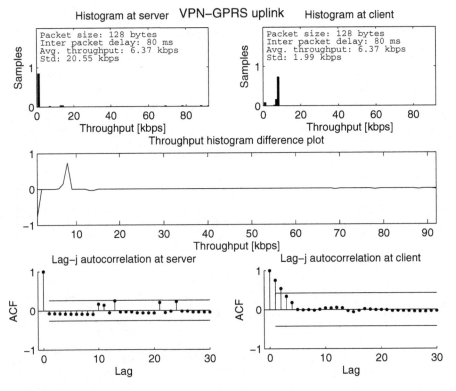

Fig. 4. VPN 3DES-SHA-1 GPRS uplink scenario, with 80 ms inter-packet delay

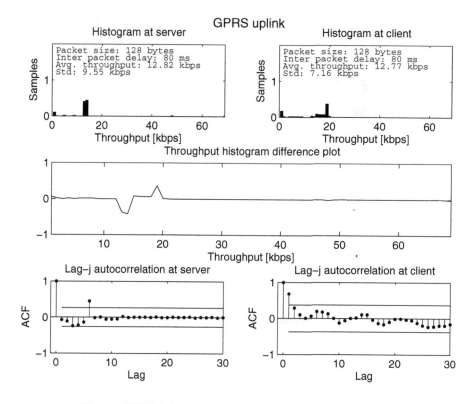

Fig. 5. GPRS uplink scenario, with 80 ms inter-packet delay

autocorrelation, *cf.* Fig. 3 (bottom) is quite small, while the throughput correlation pattern is changed significantly by the network.

In the second case, the offered throughput is increased to 12.8 kbps by reducing the *inter-packet delay* to 80 ms. However, the average throughput at the server's side only reaches 6.37 kbps. By looking at Fig. 4 (top-left) we observe a strange peak at 1 kbps in the throughput histogram at the server's side. The server is sending at 1 to 85 kbps; the standard deviation exceeds the average throughput. At the client side, the throughput histogram is more compact with throughput between 1 to 10 kbps; the standard deviation is reduced by about factor ten. No traffic is lost, indicating that datagrams were buffered and sending was delayed until there was available capacity on the GPRS link. A shaping bottleneck can be seen in the throughput histogram difference plot, *cf.* Fig. 4 (middle). The correlation at the server side indicates low correlations, *cf.* Fig. 4 (bottom-left). At the client side the autocorrelation reaches high positive values for small lags of some seconds, *cf.* Fig. 4 (bottom-right).

Fig. 5 depicts a generic GPRS uplink scenario without any encryption or authentication. The *inter-packet delay* still amounts to 80 ms, similar to the previous VPN 3DES-SHA1 scenario shown in Fig. 4. The server transmission

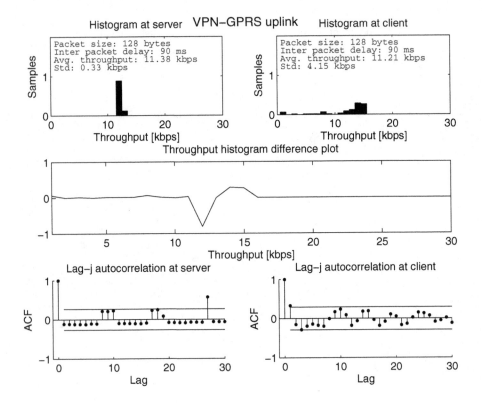

Fig. 6. VPN 3DES-MD5 GPRS uplink scenario, with 90 ms inter-packet delay

rate became 12.8 kbps, which is matched by the measured average throughput
cf. Fig. 5 (top-left). The strange peak seen at 1 kbps in Fig. 4 (top-left) is less
intense in Fig. 5 (top-left) which indicates that the overload in the former VPN
case (cf. Fig. 4 (top-left)) was introduced by VPN overhead. At the server and
client side datagrams appeared as scattered streams with throughputs of 1 to 15
kbps at the server and 1 to 20 kbps at the client. We observe a shared bottleneck
in the histogram difference plot, cf. Fig. 5 (middle). The network destroys the
4 s throughput periodicity, but introduces some extra long-term correlation, cf.
Fig. 5 (bottom).

In the next case presented in this section, the SHA-1 authentication algorithm
has been replaced with the Message-Digest algorithm 5 (MD5) [9] algorithm. By
choosing an inter-packet delay of 90 ms the server transmission rate was set and
measured to 11.38 kbps, cf. Fig. 6 (top-left). Thus, the bottleneck that showed up
in case of an inter-packet delay of 80 ms for VPN is avoided. The client received
the datagrams in very scattered stream with throughputs of 1 to 15 kbps. The
standard deviation grew from 0.33 kbps to 4.15 kbps. The throughput histogram
difference plot, cf. Fig. 6 (middle), reveals a shared bottleneck. The channel
introduces some extra correlation, cf. Fig. 6(bottom).

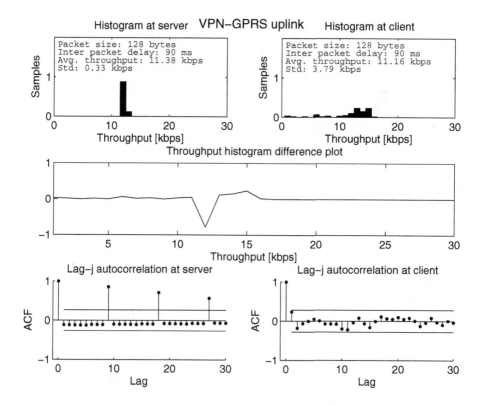

Fig. 7. VPN SHA1 GPRS uplink scenario, with 90 ms inter-packet delay

In the next measurement the ESP protocol is configured to only use the SHA-1 authentication algorithm and no encryption algorithm. The server transmission rate was set to 11.38 kbps by choosing an inter-packet delay of 90 ms, *cf.* Fig. 7 (top-left). The client received the datagrams in a very scattered stream with throughputs of 1 to 15 kbps. The standard deviation grew from 0.33 kbps to 3.79 kbps. The throughput histogram difference plot, *cf.* Fig. 7 (middle) reveals a shared bottleneck. At the server side the autocorrelation displays a periodic behavior of 9 s, while the client the periodicity is less pronounced, *cf.* Fig. 7 (bottom).

Summarizing the results, we cannot see any major difference in performance depending on which VPN solution was chosen. However, the additional VPN overhead reflects in the fact that the GPRS channel becomes overloaded at a smaller level of offered load.

4.2   Downlink

Turning our attention to the downlink scenario, we consider a VPN connection with 3DES encryption and SHA-1 authentication algorithm. The server transmission rate was set to 8.53 kbps, *cf.* Fig. 8 (top-left), which is matched

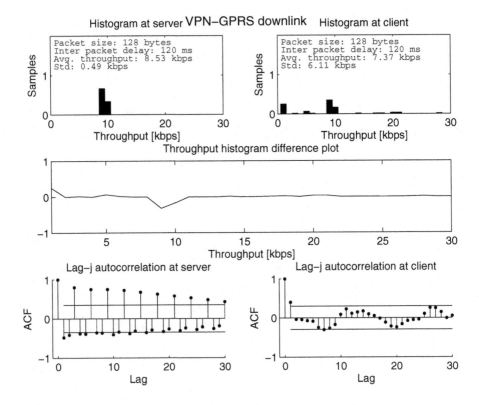

Fig. 8. VPN 3DES-SHA-1 GPRS downlink scenario, with 120 ms inter-packet delay

by the measured averaged throughput. The client received the datagrams in a highly scattered stream with throughputs of 1 to 28 kbps. The measured average throughput amounts to 7.37 kbps. From Fig. 8 we can see that the standard deviation grows roughly by factor 12. We observe a shared bottleneck in the throughput histogram difference plot, *cf.* Fig. 8 (middle). At the server side the autocorrelation displays a periodic behavior of 3.5 s. At the client, that periodicity is replaced by another less pronounced one with a period of about 12 s, *cf.* Fig. 8 (bottom), stemming from GPRS packet loss process.

In Fig. 9 no encryption or authentication is used, thus the figure depicts a general GPRS downlink scenario. The inter-packet delay still amounts to 120 ms, similar to the previous VPN 3DES-SHA-1 scenario shown in Fig. 8. The server transmission rate became 8.53 kbps, which is matched by the measured average throughput and similar to the scenario shown in Fig. 8. The client received the datagrams in a highly scattered stream with throughputs varying from 1 to 28 kbps. The measured average throughput amounts to 7.22 kbps, which is slightly less compared to VPN 3DES-SHA-1 scenario shown in Fig. 8 (right). The standard deviation grows roughly by factor 12 *cf.* Fig. 9, similar to the

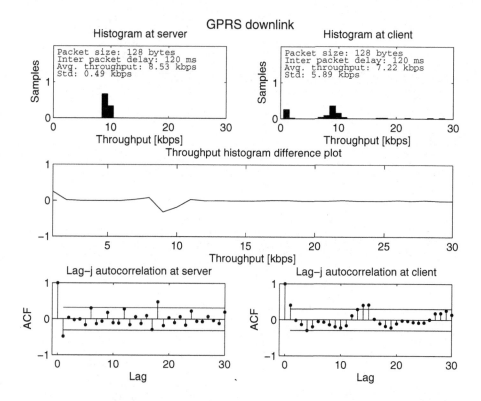

Fig. 9. GPRS downlink scenario, with 120 ms inter-packet delay

previous VPN 3DES-SHA-1 scenario. We observe a shared bottleneck in the throughput histogram difference plot, *cf.* Fig. 9 (middle). The channel introduces extra correlation, *cf.* Fig. 9 (bottom).

From the comparison of the cases VPN 3DES-SHA-1 and generic GPRS shown in Fig. 8 and Fig. 9 and the related statistical data, it becomes obvious that VPN did not change the performance in any perceptible way. Thus, obviously, the perceived quality problems when using a VPN connection over GPRS are stemming from the very GPRS connectivity.

4.3 Loss Ratios

Figures 10 and 11 show the loss ratios on GPRS uplink and GPRS downlink, respectively. In both figures different VPN connection configurations, such as 3DES-SHA-1, 3DES-MD5 and SHA-1, are shown together with a general GPRS connection without the use of VPN. In the downlink scenarios, *cf.* Fig. 11, high losses occur rather frequently. However, no real trend can be seen. The different encryption and authentication algorithms used by the VPN do not seem to increase the measured loss. In the uplink scenarios, *cf.* Fig. 10, the loss is

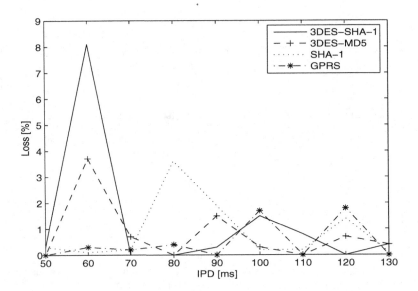

Fig. 10. Loss ratios on uplink

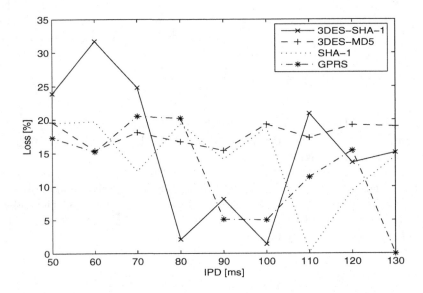

Fig. 11. Loss ratios on downlink

rather small compared to the downlink scenarios. From the rise of the standard deviation at the sender, we can deduct that an overload situation occurs given a nominal inter-packet delay between 50 and 80 ms. This seems to have some negative effect on the loss ratios of the different VPN configurations, *cf.* Fig. 10.

5   Conclusions and Outlook

This paper focuses on measurements of application-perceived throughput on rather short averaging intervals. The influence of an end-to-end IPSec VPN connection over, the widely deployed, GPRS network in both uplink and downlink direction on relevant summary statistics is illustrated and discussed. Several different encryption and authentication algorithms, such as 3DES-SHA-1, 3DES-MD5, and SHA-1, were used in the IPSec VPN configuration.

The measurement show that GPRS networks introduces large amounts of jitter and loss in the downlink, which can be seen from throughput deviations based on one-second averages. This impact on throughput histograms and auto-correlation functions are clearly visible. The different VPN tunnel configurations did not have any major affect on the throughput characteristics at the sender, besides the additional overhead introduced by the ESP. High data loss in the downlink direction was observed; no major contribution of the ESP overhead can be seen, although loss might occur sooner. In the uplink direction, shared bottlenecks have been identified when nominal capacity is surpassed. The sender seems to act as a shaper by buffering packets until they can be sent thus avoiding data loss.

Based on the presented analysis, an end-to-end VPN connection through GPRS mainly experiences problem typical to the GPRS network itself such as considerable jitter, high data loss in the downlink direction and volatile conditions. The application programmer considering the use of GPRS networks should be conscious of these issues.

These results are aimed at optimizing network selection based on requirements provided by users and applications with regard to security and QoS [2].

Future work will address the impact of VPN connection over GPRS on Transmission Control Protocol (TCP) performance. The interaction between GPRS and applications is of particular interest. Also, measurements of E2E delays and corresponding statistics with synchronized measurement points will be considered.

References

1. P. Carlsson, D. Constantinescu, A. Popescu, M. Fiedler, and A. Nilsson. Delay performance in IP routers. In *Proceedings of HET-NETs '04 Performance Modelling and Evaluation of Heterogeneous Networks*, Ilkley, UK, July 2004.
2. M. Fiedler, S. Chevul, L. Isaksson, P. Lindberg, and J. Karlsson. Generic Communication Requirements of ITS-Related Mobile Services as Basis for Seamless Communications. In *Proceedings of the First EuroNGI Conference on Traffic Engineering (NGI 2005)*, Rome, Italy, April 2005.
3. M. Fiedler, K. Tutschku, P. Carlsson, and A.A. Nilsson. Identification of performance degradation in IP networks using throughput statistics. In J. Charzinski, R. Lehnert, and P. Tran Gia, editors, *Providing Quality of Service in Heterogeneous Environments. Proceedings of the 18th International Teletraffic Congress (ITC-18)*, pages 399–407, Berlin, Germany, September 2003.

4. B. Gleeson, A. Lin, J. Heinanen, G. Armitage, and A. Malis. A Framework for IP Based Virtual Private Networks. In *RFC 2764*, February 2000.

5. S. Kent and R. Atkinson. Security Architecture for the Internet Protocol. In *RFC 2401*, November 1998.

6. National Institute of Standards and Technology. Secure Hash Standard. In *Federal Information Processing Standards Publications (FIPS) PUB 180*, May 1993.

7. National Institute of Standards and Technology. Data Encryption Standard. In *Federal Information Processing Standards Publications (FIPS) PUB 46-3*, January 1999.

8. National Institute of Standards and Technology. Advanced Encryption Standard. In *Federal Information Processing Standards Publications (FIPS) PUB 197*, November 2001.

9. R. Rivest. The MD5 Message Digest Algorithm. In *RFC 1321*, May 1998.

Scenarios for Mobile Community Support

Bernhard Klein and Helmut Hlavacs

Institute for Distributed and Multimedia Systems, University or Vienna,
Lenaugasse 2/8, 1080 Vienna, Austria
{bernhard.klein, helmut.hlavacs}@univie.ac.at

Abstract. Ubiquitous community support systems have the potential
to ease daily life through delivering valuable interactive information and
member contacts right in the place where they are needed. Since in real
life humans move permanently between communities, we aim in our position paper at building an inter-operable community infrastructure based
on the mobile JXME open source peer-to-peer system which focuses on
seamless switching between different community types. On top of the
JXME based file sharing service we currently implement a situation
aware search layer to compensate the limited interaction possibilities
of small screens. We show that raw context data can be gathered directly from the smart phone. To avoid cumbersome retrieval times we
apply sociological and personal behaviour models to predict information
requests.

1   Introduction

Most people use their phones to maintain relationships. However, spontaneously
accessing remote data at any time using a mobile devices is becoming increasingly popular. Unfortunately, typical usage patterns of mobile devices differ from
their stationary counterparts, e.g., in terms of access time and content granu-
larity, resulting in the fact that existing mobile content in many cases is not
situation specific enough. *Communities* offer this type of personalized information and additionally give access to *other community members* in case the offered
static content within the community is not sufficient. Mobile community support systems like SMS based communities [2], Instant Messaging solutions and
Mobile Blogs initially caught high interest. However, the broad usage of mobile
community support systems today is still an exception.

A major reason may be given by the fact that existing mobile community systems have been simply ported from desktop systems to mobile devices. However,
the porting of desktop systems to mobile devices can only be successful if the
offered mobile community services take into account the specific features of the
device. Small screen size, memory limitations, reduced processing power, limited
battery life time and low bandwidth connections have to be considered for the
design of mobile community services. Another important aspect is the consideration of mobility and how it can be actively supported. Community infrastructures have to offer a seamless and real time access to all communities available

M. Cesana, L. Fratta (Eds.): Wireless Syst./Network Architect. 2005, LNCS 3883, pp. 269–280, 2006.
© Springer-Verlag Berlin Heidelberg 2006

at the user locations. Unfortunately, usually community hosts create their own infrastructure, here duplicating effort and creating proprietary software. Telecom providers and phone companies aiming at offering the same service to two different communities have to develop a bridge between the communities and incorporate smart overlay services to guarantee short retrieval times. Also, communities offer many opportunities for content misuse like spamming, publishing of illegal content, alteration and deletion of content, or metadata manipulations. Considering that today's mobile devices advance to real mobile computers hosting extremely private data for personal information management, the infection of mobile phones with malicious codes such as viruses, worms, and spyware is just a matter of time. Unfortunately the security infrastructure has just begun to evolve. Nonetheless community owners cannot expect users to create value for sites where security is not guaranteed.

The main contribution of this paper is a methodology to seamlessly construct a personal community environment around a moving person, based on mobile phone technology. The flexibility of such a community support system is granted through a mobile peer-to-peer network. To provide convenient access to the community we make use of a situation-aware retrieval system which utilizes individual behaviour patterns for timely information delivery.

The organization of the paper is as follows. In Section 2 we define requirements for mobile community support. Section 3 outlines the specific role of smart phones as mobile clients. In Section 4 we introduce a community roaming framework. In Sections 5 and 6 a specific mechanism is illustrated to enhance community service discovery from simple file mapping to a more advanced rich metadata query mechanism. Related work and a summary are given in the final sections.

2   Scenarios and Concept Overview

The idea of our proposed community service is to enhance the standard communication functionality of mobile phones with a *permanent community environment*. Therefore we foresee a scenario where different community types augment the real world such that the user feels always embedded in his personal community sphere (Figure 1). Acceptance of mobile applications depend heavily on user convenience. Therefore, in our research on mobile community infrastructure we especially focus on adequate mobility support, situation aware information access and timely information delivery.

To make the usage of mobile community support systems simple, the underlying infrastructure must explicitly support *seamless* community roaming. In other words the community support infrastructure must free the community member from complicated interactions which occur during joining or leaving digital communities. To overcome the restrictions imposed by small screens of mobile devices, it is essential to support *environmental awareness*. Therefore the underlying infrastructure must be able to map situations to the right community content. In our case, content discovery relays on present *user context*, i.e., measurement values and predefined profiles. However, the *history* of contexts might

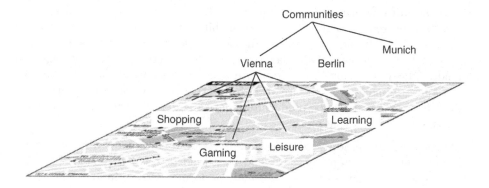

Fig. 1. Hierarchical seamless community concept

provide far more information about the user and might be extremely valuable for finding content in the future. By recognizing patterns from the context history (including the user's behaviour) a system could exhibit repetitive behaviour patterns and act in a proactive manner.

As an illustrative example for the connection between *global* and *local* interest groups consider the following scenario. A person interested into sports may register to a global interest group *sports*, which represents a *class* of communities rather than a community itself. Instances of the class *sports* may then be created, for example, for a shopping mall where sports equipment is offered in various shops. Additionally, a sports community may be created for each individual sports shop of the mall. When entering the mall the person then automatically becomes member of the mall's sporting community, and additionally becomes member of the community of each sports shop he passes by or enters.

3   Smart Phones as Access Clients

Smart phones have evolved from pure voice telephony to sophisticated hand held computers, thus coupling phone capabilities with the additional functionalities of a PDA. In this scenario the smart phone becomes a personal repository of digital information, and together with the Internet connection may perfectly be suited as a ubiquitous access client for mobile community support systems [4].

Personal Organizer: Smart phones have the ability to handle a number of applications to support personal information management, for example, calendar entries, contacts, and tasks. These applications should not be seen as isolated applications, but rather be integrated into the community environment.

User Generated Media: Many mobile devices include hardware that let users generate their personal media, like taking photos and video. With the growing memory space we can assume that people will also use mobile phones to store their favorite music.

Sensors and Metadata Management: Different kinds of contextual data can be captured through sensors on a mobile phone. The Symbian operating system offers interfaces to capture the active user profile, active applications, contact lists, call logs, SMS mailbox statistics, Bluetooth discovery logs and finally GPS positioning information. Ad-hoc network connections may be used to request missing sensor information from other nearby community members. Such metadata can also be used to automatically describe the generated media as part of the authoring process.

Privacy Management: Often users apply ring-tone profiles to manage their privacy. These ring-tone profiles could be extended to community profiles. We thereby assume that activities are usually performed at certain locations with a certain group of people (Figure 2). In our scenario users would specify different community profiles for different activities like work, home and leisure. With the definition of community profiles users may specify their community interests and situation specific access rules to avoid unnecessary interruptions of the daily life. GPS-notifications may be used to automatically determine situation relevant community profiles.

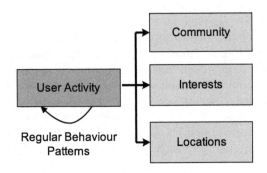

Fig. 2. Community Profile

Mobile Internet: Modern Smart phones are equipped with short range personal area networks like Bluetooth or have direct access to the internet through the wireless telecom network. These new networking capabilities support a rich multimedia interaction model that enables users to share digital content directly through their mobile phones.

4   Seamless Community Roaming

Our definition of seamless communities indicates that the end-user is member of certain global interest communities, but has no perception of local community boundaries being crossed while moving around. The idea of seamless community mobility is desirable in many aspects, especially with respect to (i) wide area community membership, and (ii) access to valuable situation specific community knowledge during the entire day. This means that the end-user is not interrupted during his daily life, but may benefit from community support when needed. In the following we define major components of our seamless community framework.

Global Interest Communities: In our approach, global communities representing specific themes are realized by mapping them to existing local communities as illustrated by the above described sporting community scenario.

Location Awareness: Local communities are always bound to a specific area on the earth surface, i.e., there may be a community for the city of Vienna (defined for the area of Vienna), one for the districts of Vienna, or one for a shopping mall within a certain district (Figure 1). Location technology is then used to *manage community membership*, for example by using the Global Positioning System (GPS). Thus, if the current GPS coordinates are within the boundaries of existing communities, then the user automatically joins them, or leaves them once the area is left. We propose to describe the boundaries of a community with a circle, which is completely defined using a center with (x, y)-coordinates and a radius r.

Peer-to-Peer Infrastructure: Communities in peer networks are groups of peers with common interests, exchanging information with other group members or performing some collaborative work together. Barriers like connection establishment and managing community services must be hidden from the user. The peer network infrastructure [8] is highly flexible and therefore best suited to handle the dynamics of mobile community access and ad-hoc community management. To realize the seamless community support system we choose JXTA [6] for J2ME devices (JXME) as peer-to-peer (P2P) network. JXTA is an open source project initiated from SUN Microsystems that defines a set of protocols for ad-hoc P2P computing. At the core, JXTA supports peer and member administration, group management, and messaging. JXME in specific is a stripped down version of JXTA to support small mobile devices with small memories and restricted processing power.

Shared Taxonomy: Our community services must allow for the semantic matchmaking of interests in community activities. In order to avoid data heterogeneity in the community domain we follow an taxonomy-based approach. A taxonomy is similar to a dictionary or glossary, but with greater detail and structure and expressed in a formal language (e.g., RDF) that enables computers to match content. A single taxonomy can be applied to solve the integration problem and to conceptualize community activities and interests [14]. Each layer specifies a special category of terms together with a describing set of metadata attributes and values. The resulting domain model can be formatted as machine readable RDF graph and stored on globally available domain provider peers. During the profile specification the user can view the entire community taxonomy and personalize it through selection of interesting categories. Since mobile devices have restricted processing power and small memories, the taxonomies used to describe shared community structures have to be lightweight. We therefore propose a flat hierarchical structure with no more than 3-5 layers (Figure 3).

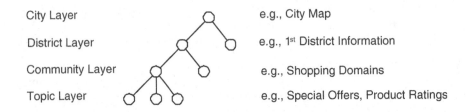

City Layer   e.g., City Map

District Layer   e.g., 1st District Information

Community Layer   e.g., Shopping Domains

Topic Layer   e.g., Special Offers, Product Ratings

Fig. 3. Domain model and metadata structure

Trust Based Authentication: Two major concerns are of importance when trying to achieve seamless communities: transparent end-user *authentication* and *security* across different local community support systems. To enable automatic entering and leaving of communities the community support system must offer a single sign-on authentication system similar to the Liberty Alliance [12]. In our security scenario, we foresee three different parties, each of them with certain duties. The *telecom provider* is responsible for maintaining user authentication information. *Community owners* manage role models for community participation and grant access rights. *Mobile users* manage their profile information and store it on the mobile phone. Since mobile devices cannot store large user registries for community authentication, a public key based security system is essential. Decryption of digital certificates does not consume too many resources and revocation of privileges is achievable through limiting the lifetime of certificates. The authentication process itself is separated into two major steps (Figure 4). First the user issues a request to the telecom provider to get a time limited anonymized digital certificate, which is stored on the mobile phone and updated periodically. With this certificate users can specify their community profile by selecting certain domains which raise their interest. During runtime, the mobile peer detects appropriate communities and automatically joins the community support system by sending the certificate to the community provider, who in return offers community services. In case users misuse the community infrastructure, e.g., by introducing viruses, the community owner can immediately block this specific user through a local blacklist and send a revocation request to the telecom provider. If this initial suspicion is confirmed through further revocation

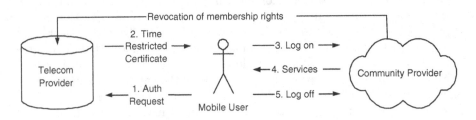

Fig. 4. Authentication, single sign-on and revocation of certificates

requests from other community owners, the telecom provider consequently may stop the renewal of digital certificates and the user is not able to use the seamless community infrastructure any more.

5   Context Based Service Discovery

If a user joins a peer group, the community management system should immediately start querying for relevant content as it was specified by the user in the community profile. We are currently implementing such a ubiquitous content management service (UCMS) on top of the JXME peer-to-peer network. The core capabilities include functionality for sharing, indexing, searching, and file exchange.

Overlay Network: When a user starts sharing file content stored on the local file system of the mobile phone, the UCMS will create a content advertisement. Content advertisements provide meta-information describing the content, including the content name, length, and MIME type. The internal mechanism of the JXME platform ensures that once an advertisement is published in the JXME virtual network, the advertisement will be captured by its *rendezvous* peers. A rendezvous is a specialised peer that keeps information about currently joined community peers. Within JXME every peer can become a rendezvous peer. The decision on who becomes a rendezvous peer usually depends on the resource capabilities, e.g., memory size or battery life of the mobile devices. If a search query is initiated, JXME will generate a search object in form of an XML document and send it to the closest rendezvous peer. The rendezvous peer will query collected advertisements and either return results, or in case of a failure, forward the query to other rendezvous peers within the global interest group.

Query Routing: To avoid scalability problems within the JXME network [13], it is advisable to use distributed hash tables (DHTs) [15]. This design retains many advantages of a central index, such as completeness and speed of queries, while providing the scalability and robustness of full decentralisation. For example, assume that people share their favorite music files within a pedestrian area with possibly hundreds of participants. Maintaining an index might get quite complex since people permanently would join and leave the community, and the playlist might get quite large. To assure efficient index maintenance we suggest to separate the search process into two major steps (Figure 5). We propose to create distributed hash tables on all available rendezvous nodes within an existing community. The DHTs would index available *community topics* and point to member peers who currently share community content of this same topic. After a rendezvous receives such a query, it will query his index for suitable content provider peers and forward the query to edge peers. On the side of the edge peers additional filtering could be applied which would allow for more complex searches. For instance the search could be further filtered by *location, time* or *originator relevance*. We believe that this metadata should not be encoded into the DHT, since *community topics* are the main glue binding communities to-

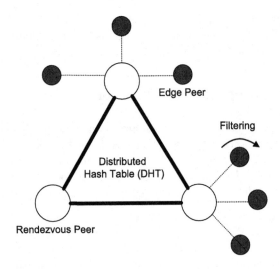

Fig. 5. Service Discovery based on Rendezvous Peers

gether, and location, time and author relevance are not as important. Instead, local query engines should filter by such criteria.

6 Behaviour Based Precaching

People usually move around because they want to accomplish certain tasks in a certain location and within a certain community of people. Since mobile devices are used by human beings, the resulting network structure and traffic is influenced by individual and social behaviour. We therefore propose a system that is able to capture mobile device usage and monitors social interactions between mobile ad-hoc users.

Social Network Analysis: To visualize a network of personal relationships, sociograms, represented by weighted graphs, are typically used [5]. This graph consists of attributed nodes defining the buddies and edges connecting other buddies whenever communication was established in the past. The weights associated with each edge represent the intensity of the direct interactions between individuals. The intensity of relationships is defined by the frequency and/or duration of the contact, stability over time [11] and pursued interaction types (face-to-face, (a)synchronous communication, resource exchange). In Figure 6 a visualization of such personal network can be seen, where communication partners closer to the focus maintain strong relationships to the person under consideration, and others far away weak relationships. One may even distinguish between different partner types, in this case between friends/relatives and colleagues at work, if further defining attributes like time and locations are applied to the social network analysis. We assume that people who have often met in

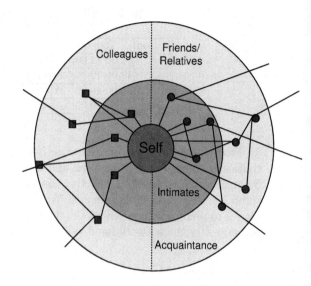

Fig. 6. Visualization of personal networks using sociogram

the past will continue to do this in the future. Thus, social tie
understood as probability of spatial collocation and vice versa.
the probability for a meeting depends on equivalence of interests
activity, relationship intensity and effort to reach this meeting.

Mobility and Activity Pattern Analysis: To capture user acti
the history of selected community profiles as an approximation.
earlier, Symbian offers the possibility to detect currently used a
the currently active user profile. Unfortunately, capturing the b
nificant user locations is more complicated. Therefore we have to
information from the GPS receiver in certain time intervals. The
time interval is important to determine the importance of the loc
user [1]. Longer stay times indicate higher significance for the user.
then be recorded in an *activity transition matrix*. An activity trar
stores transitions between activities for each person depending on
A sample matrix for consequent activities and a matrix for depend
activity and locations describing parts of the daily life of a student
in Table 1 and Table 2.

Table 1. Activity Transition Matrix

Person	Time	Activity	Next Activity	Probability
A	07:00-12:00	Work	Food	0.7
A	12:00-12:30	Food	Work	0.5
A	13:00-14:00	Work	Leisure	0.3
A	16:00-20:00	Work	Home	0.7

Table 2. Activity-Location Transition Matrix

Person	Time	Activity	Location	Probability
A	07:00-12:00	Work	University	0.7
A	12:00-12:30	Food	Cafeteria	0.4
A	13:00-18:00	Work	University	0.7
A	18:00-20:00	Leisure	Theater	0.3

From these datasets contextual activity graphs may be constructed [9]. Activities are represented by vertices, and transitions between them are represented by arcs, weighted by the respective conditional transition probabilities as measured for the given time intervals. We believe that by applying learning techniques to predict future behaviour, the number of necessary query requests, and consequently the network bandwidth, may be decreased dramatically.

7   Related Work

The success of virtual communities encouraged researchers from the early beginning to look for ways how to extend communities for their users.

Since humans as social beings are naturally members of several communities it is not surprising that community interoperability was a major subject for many publications. One method uses community ontologies to integrate heterogeneous community content from different communities. Koch [10] for instance used community and profile ontologies to map equivalent subjects or user interest between two separated communities, such that an exchange between several communities could be established. A major disadvantage of this approach was that community interactions were still separately managed and community exchange needed to be separately executed.

Since virtual communities seemed to restrict the access to stationary usage scenarios, several attempts have been made to develop ubiquitous access by using mobile devices. Brown et al. [3] developed mobile access clients and used a global positioning system to map community content to specific locations in the real world. Unfortunately users reflect mobile devices as highly personal and are very careful with their privacy. Unwanted messages sent out from the community could easily be regarded as SPAM and would lead to switch of any location based community clients.

Since virtual communities tend to span global societies, and mobile communities in contrast are much smaller and usually span personal networks, researches tried to find new ways to establish short range adhoc communities, where people could exchange their interests. The Iclouds system from Heinemann [7] demonstrates an approach to exchange different community interests on a basis of a trading model. This adhoc community support system uses the Bluetooth network to scan for Bluetooth devices in its proximity. After identification, both community parties automatically exchange their have- and wish-lists and execute matchmaking services to identify a match of interests. This approach works fine as long as the user is able to formulate his interests. However, we argue that people most of the time have problems in expressing their informational needs and a more open community discovery mechanism is needed.

8 Summary

In this paper we outlined a smart phone based seamless community infrastructure for supporting user communication, collaboration and item exchange in real mobile environments.

Seamless community roaming is achieved through detecting group formations through location technology, peer-to-peer communication between mobile devices and a certificate based authentication system, which allows a feasible authentication between community members even in varying communication conditions. On top of this infrastructure we proposed a content management system to publish and exchange context based content between the community members. Rendezvous peers form an overlay structure indexing community topics which are shared on edge peers to avoid bandwidth consuming network flooding. Additional filtering is delegated to edge peers to keep the overlay maintenance costs small. Thereby we can compensate the restructuring of the peer-to-peer network caused through the mobility of the peers. Since retrieval times of peer-to-peer networks increase with the amount of participating community members we apply the knowledge of routine behaviour to pro-actively query for relevant community content.

As part of our future work, we will evaluate the efficiency of community formations and the efficiency of content discovery in our community management system according to individual and collective behaviour patterns.

References

1. D. Ashbrook, T. Starner: Learning Significant Locations and Predicting User Movement with GPS, Proceedings of International Semantic Web Conference (ISWC), Sardinia, Italy, 2002, pp. 101-108.
2. D. Bell, B. Hooker and F. Raby: FLIRT: Social services for the urban context, Conference on Human - Computer Interaction (HCI), Greek, 2003.
3. B. Brown, M. Chalmers, M. Bell, I. MacColl, M. Hall and P. Rudman: Sharing the square: collaborative visiting in the city streets, Conference on Human Factors in Computing Systems (CHI), Portland, USA, 2005.
4. F. De Rosa and M. Mecella: Peer-to-Peer Applications on Mobile Devices: A Case Study with .NET on smartphone, .NET Technologies 2004, Workshop Proceedings, 2004.
5. L. C. Freeman: Visualizing Social Groups, American Statistical Association, Proceedings of the Section on Statistical Graphics, 2000, pp. 47-54.
6. J. Gradecki: Mastering JXTA: Building Java Peer-to-Peer Applications. John Wiley & Sons, 2002.
7. A. Heinemann, J. Kangasharju, F. Lyardet, and M. Mühlhäuser: iClouds - Peer-to-Peer Information Sharing in Mobile Environments, Euro-Par 2003, pp. 1038-1045.

8. L. Iftode, C. Borcea, N. Ravi, P. Kang and P. Zhou: Smart Phone: An Embedded System for Universal Interactions, Workshop on Future Trends of Distributed Computing Systems (FTDCS), Suzhou, China, May, 2004.

9. A. Jardosh, E. M. Belding-Royer, K. C. Almeroth and S. Suri: Towards Realistic Mobility Models for Mobile Ad hoc Networks, in proceedings of ACM MobiCom, September 2003, pp. 217-229.

10. M. Koch: Community-Unterstützungssysteme–Architektur und Interoperabilität, Habilitation, Technische Universität München, Fakultät für Informatik, Dezember 2003.

11. J.A. Schellenberg: An Introduction to Social Psychology, Random House, New York, 1999.

12. Sun Nokia Whitepaper: Identity Federation and Web services–technical use cases for mobile operators, Dezember 2004, https://www.projectliberty.org/resources/whitepapers/Nokia_Sun_US_2812.pdf, 15.3.2005.

13. N. Theodoloz: DHT-based Routing and Discovery in JXTA, University of Lausanne, Thesis.

14. H. Wache, T. Vögele, U. Visser, H. Stuckenschmidt, G. Schuster, H. Neumann and S. Hübner: Ontology-Based Integration of Information–A Survey of Existing Approaches, Proceedings of IJCAI-01, Seattle, WA, 2001, pp. 108-117.

15. K. Wehrle, S. Götz and S. Rieche: Distributed Hash Tables, P2P Systems and Applications, LNCS 3485, Springer-Verlag Berlin Heidelberg, pp. 79-93.

Author Index

Lecture Notes in Computer Science

For information about Vols. 1–3880

please contact your bookseller or Springer